THE COMPANION GUIDE TO

KENT AND SUSSEX

THE COMPANION GUIDES

GENERAL EDITOR: VINCENT CRONIN

*It is the aim of these Guides to provide a Companion,
in the person of the author, who knows intimately
the places and people of whom he writes, and is able to
communicate this knowledge and affection to his readers.
It is hoped that the text and pictures will aid them
in their preparations and in their travels, and will
help them to remember on their return*

THE GREEK ISLANDS · SOUTHERN GREECE
PARIS · THE SOUTH OF FRANCE
ROME · VENICE · LONDON
FLORENCE · JUGOSLAVIA
THE WEST HIGHLANDS OF SCOTLAND · UMBRIA
SOUTHERN ITALY · TUSCANY · EAST ANGLIA
SOUTHERN SPAIN · IRELAND

In Preparation

CONTINENTAL GREECE · MADRID & CENTRAL SPAIN
EDINBURGH & THE BORDER COUNTRY · NORTHUMBRIA
WALES · DEVON & CORNWALL · SOUTH-WEST FRANCE
BURGUNDY · THE ILE DE FRANCE

The Guides to Rome, Venice, Florence and London are
available in paperback in the *Fontana* edition

THE COMPANION GUIDE TO

Kent and Sussex

KEITH SPENCE

COLLINS
ST JAMES'S PLACE, LONDON
1973

William Collins Sons & Co Ltd
London · Glasgow · Sydney · Auckland
Toronto · Johannesburg

TO PENNY

First published 1973
© Keith Spence 1973
ISBN 0 00 211190 x
Set in Monotype Times
Made and printed in Great Britain by
William Collins Sons & Co Ltd Glasgow

Contents

꒜

Illustrations

❧

Maps

❦

'Whereof some part is drawn out of credible records, part is spoken of mine own knowledge, and part is fetched from other men by information.'

William Lambarde, *A Perambulation of Kent*, 1570

Preface

❧

THE counties of Kent and Sussex seem at first sight to have everything in common. As a matter of simple geography, each has a coastal strip, backed by rolling chalk downs, which form a giant encircling horseshoe round a rich central agricultural plain shared by both counties. Each has a superb cathedral city, crowded seaside holiday resorts, splendid country houses and castles, small ports now remote from the sea and safe from the destruction of the waves, tidal estuaries where sea-birds gather, villages lost deep in the hills. Each is now to a large extent a dormitory for London, with new houses for commuters springing up as far afield as Margate and Chichester. Each has felt the impact of industry, Kent very obviously in the factories along the Thames and Medway and the coalfields east of Canterbury, Sussex to a lesser extent, though perhaps as insidiously in the long run, in the rapid growth of light industry.

Yet these similarities mask very real differences. The farm-lands of the Weald were within historical times the impenetrable woodland of the Andredsweald, the Forest of Anderida, useful for fattening pigs in the clearings or supplying wood to power the forges, but at the same time cutting Sussex off from the civilising influences of London and the rest of the country. Kent, on the other hand, was on the main road to everywhere. In prehistoric times the trackway along the North Downs had brought traders right across Kent to Hampshire and beyond. The Romans landed in Kent, coming to reconnoitre in the first century BC and to conquer a hundred years later. Hengist and Horsa chose Kent as the jumping-off point for their physical invasion, as did St Augustine for his work of spiritual conversion. Admittedly, William the Conqueror landed at Pevensey Bay, but as soon as his way to London was clear he left Sussex behind and turned to Kent, as more worthy of his attention. The Dutch sailed up the Medway to humiliate Charles II's navy, and Kent has been in the firing line in both World Wars. On more peaceful occasions, the most famous of all pilgrimages led to Canterbury; and the cliffs of Dover rather than Beachy Head have been the traveller's traditional first sight of England.

All this coming and going left Kent very much aware of its importance and identity. There was a definite Kentish temper when Sussex was little more than an amorphous grouping of South Saxons. When Wordsworth addressed the men of Kent as the 'vanguard of liberty' he was uttering sentiments that had been put in similar terms for hundreds of years.

The character of Kent is expressed in terms of its towns, oasthouses and orchards, rather than its natural features. Here Sussex has the advantage. The North Downs have never had a Kipling or a Belloc to sing their praises; they are less spectacular and more lived-in than the South Downs, which loom up at you as you approach them from the north with the impact of the Alps in miniature, and where you can lose yourself within twenty minutes of Brighton or Worthing. Kent has nothing to compare with the exquisite string of tiny Saxon churches stretched out below the downs, with Chanctonbury or Cissbury Ring, or with the trio of Arundel, Petworth and Midhurst, where the feudal past seems more alive than the tourist present. Brighton remains the paragon of seaside towns; and Sussex has the strange antiquity of Ashdown Forest, untamed by the armies of summer picnickers.

I have lived in both counties – though never far from the boundary between them – and have no conflict of local patriotism to incline me to one or the other. Between them they have an incomparable wealth of places to see: Sandwich, Rye and Winchelsea; Cranbrook, Tenterden and Goudhurst; the uplands of Sheppey and the lowlands of Romney Marsh; the wooded heights of Blackdown; the quiet waters of the two Rothers, of the Teise, Beult, Eden, Adur and Arun; the aloof and awe-inspiring nobility of Canterbury Cathedral, and the homelier, friendlier appeal of Chichester. Kent and Sussex may lack the high drama of wilder regions, but they are unique in their concentration of beauty, accumulated through centuries of creation and renewal.

Acknowledgments

❧

This book would have been impossible to write without the help of the anonymous host of passers-by who directed me across unexplored towns and through labyrinths of country lanes; vicars and churchwardens who trustingly lent me keys to their locked churches, and gave me access to vestries and belfries; and owners of country houses, who almost without exception allowed me to look over their homes unannounced and at the most unofficial of times. I would also like to thank the numerous librarians, archivists, owners of houses and experts who checked relevant sections in proof, and saved me from countless errors and omissions. There is no space to give them all by name, but special thanks are due to the following for their assistance: Lt.-Cdr. J. P. Angell (Clerk to the Conservators of Ashdown Forest), Lord Astor of Hever (Hever Castle), Stanley Atkin (Borough Librarian, Dartford), Geoffrey S. Bagley (Hon. Curator, Rye Museum Association), R. G. Bird (Borough Librarian, Tunbridge Wells) and Miss J. Mauldon (Reference Librarian), Denys E. Bower (Chiddingstone Castle), P. G. Burton (Agent, Chevening), Mrs S. J. Corall (Reference Librarian, Dover), Viscount De L'Isle (Penshurst Place), A. G. S. Enser (Borough Librarian, Eastbourne), Robert H. Goodsall (historian of Kent), Mrs P. Haines (Reference Librarian, Hastings), H. R. H. Harmer (Reference Librarian, Chichester), Eileen A. Hollingdale (Local History Librarian, Brighton), R. J. Marsh (City Librarian, Rochester), W. S. Mitchell, Anne M. Oakley (Archivist, Canterbury Cathedral Library), Arthur Percival (Hon. Sec. the Faversham Society), R. W. Puttock (Castle Manager, Arundel), Mrs B. A. Sutherland (Administrator, Bateman's), and P. A. Tritton (Parham). The task of checking through the entire first draft was undertaken by Marcus Crouch (Deputy County Librarian, Kent), to whom I owe an immense debt; and the bulk of the book was admirably typed by Daphne Owen Jones. My final thanks go to an unknown trudger along the Pilgrims' Way, who told me that I was following the route of the Pilgrim Fathers to America, and thus lightened a dismal November morning.

CHAPTER ONE

The Darent Valley, Dartford and Gravesend

❧

DURING the last decade Kent has lost more ground to the planners than has been taken by the sea in a thousand years. In 1965 the north-west corner of the county was bitten off and given to London; thus Erith and Bromley, Bexley, Chislehurst and Orpington joined the ranks of the Greater London suburbs, and semi-countrified places like Biggin Hill lost whatever rural status they might have retained. To put it in terms of a distinction whose origin has long been forgotten: while the Men of Kent east of the Medway have had nothing to worry about, the Kentish Men on the London side of the river have given up a good quarter of their territory. So the entrance into Kent is no longer from Deptford, as it was when William Lambarde wrote his *Perambulation of Kent* in 1570, or from Bexley, as it was until recently, but from Dartford, fifteen miles outside London.

The main road through **Dartford** is Watling Street, the Roman highway from London to Canterbury, which runs straight as the surveyor's art could make it down a hill to the River Darent and up the other side. This was the start of the Roman Derenti Vadum and the Saxon Derentford. What is left of the old town, among the chemical, engineering and papermaking works, clusters down by the river – the parish church, a few timbered buildings, the High Street with its coaching inns. The Darent seems a small stream to have given rise to so much growth. Edmund Spenser wrote of 'the silver Darent, in whose waters clean Ten thousand fishes play and deck his pleasant stream'; but if you lean over the bridge now you are more likely to see old car tyres and tin cans. You can follow its course southwards through the park behind the public library; to the north it flows past Dartford's industries and across the salt marshes to the Thames.

The library, or rather the museum which forms part of it,

is a good place to start from, as it takes the story of the Thames Valley back a quarter of a million years ago, when Swanscombe Man chipped his flints and hunted elephant among the marshes. The museum has a sequence of exhibits beginning in prehistoric times – Stone Age tools and weapons, an Iron Age Belgic cremation, swords and ornaments from a Saxon burial of about AD 700. The library, largely of sandstone with plenty of cupolas and carved swags, was given to the town in 1916 by the Scottish-born tycoon Andrew Carnegie (of the Carnegie Trust). Behind it in the park are some paving stones from the Roman Watling Street, and a reconstruction of a few feet of masonry which formed the entrance to the Roman villa at Farningham, five miles up the Darent valley.

The church is a massive flint and stone building, rather grimy externally, with a square tower jammed in the corner between north aisle and chancel. There was probably a Saxon church on the site; the lower sections of the tower were built about 1080, perhaps by Bishop Gundulf of Rochester. The Norman church was added to in later centuries, including a chapel to St Thomas à Becket (the North Chapel), and in the fourteenth century the nave and aisles were rebuilt in their present form. The most drastic modern alteration was the building of a new chancel arch in 1862 to replace an unusually low medieval arch. The church suffered severely in the great flood of September, 1968. The highwater mark is carved on the pillar by the pulpit steps, level with the tops of the choir stalls, and a good eighteen inches above the previous record flood in 1866.

The most impressive monument is to Sir John Spilman and his wife, below the arch between north chapel and chancel. Spilman, who was a goldsmith and jeweller to Queen Elizabeth I, came from Lindau in Germany. Apart from his other skills, he was a papermaker, and in 1586 started a papermill in Dartford, presumably about where the vast Wiggins Teape mill now stands. It is said to have been the first commercially successful papermill in the country. Sir John, with twirled black moustache and gilded armour, looks well satisfied with life; his German wife in black dress and ruff kneels facing him. Sir John, who died in 1626, is also said to have introduced lime trees to this country. The arms of his wife, incorporating a man in a jester's cap, appear on the tomb; the use of this device as a watermark may be the origin of the term 'foolscap'. Few of the medieval and Tudor brasses are on view, but there are rubbings of all of them in the little room under the tower.

By the church, on the corner of Bullace Lane, is the Wat Tyler, a half-timbered pub where Tyler and his men are reputed to have stopped for a drink on their way to London during the rebellion of 1381. The revolt was part of the general unrest felt throughout the country after the Black Death, aggravated by the dislike felt for new taxes. Tyler's followers released prisoners and destroyed manorial records; the meeting at Mile End between 100,000 rebels and the young King Richard II, who promised to honour their grievances but went back on his word, is one of the most dramatic episodes of English history. As to the connection with Dartford, it is known that a John Tyler of Dartford killed a government tax collector during the rebellion, and that Dartford was a rallying point for the rebels; but apart from that, as the town guide-book puts it, the connection 'hangs on the flimsy thread of unverified legend.'

Dartford's industries lie to the north towards the Thames. Behind the station is the Burroughs Wellcome works, a head-quarters of insulin production, with the Darent widened out into a lagoon in front of it; and down Priory Road are the Dartford Paper Mills (Wiggins Teape), giant successor to Spilman's Elizabethan enterprise. Westwards Kent becomes Greater London half way across **Crayford Marshes,** which still have cattle grazing on them in a quite unindustrial way. Though Dartford is now chiefly known to road-users for its tunnel under the Thames, the approach road to the tunnel lies well east of the town.

Heading south up the Darent valley along the Sevenoaks road (A 225), the first village of any distinct character you come to is **Sutton-at-Hone,** with the country just about holding its own against the town. The church lies down a lane west of the main road. In Victorian times it was ruthlessly altered by Ewan Christian, architect to the Ecclesiastical Commissioners. The entrance was cut downwards about three feet, so that the door handle in the south porch is now nearly six feet off the ground.

Inside Christian inserted an arcade of dumpy grey marble

columns, topped with yellowish curlicued capitals – things to
wonder at in a simple medieval church. Against the south wall
stands the noble tomb of Sir Thomas Smith (or Smythe), who
died in 1625. An inscription gives the career of a true merchant
adventurer, who was among other things 'late Governour of
ye East-Indian, Moscovia, French and Sommer-Iland Com-
panies: Treasurer for the Virginian Plantation: Prime Under-
taker (in the year 1612) for that noble Designe, the Discoverie
of the North-West Passage.' Smith was knighted by James I
in 1603, and sent as ambassador to Russia the following year.
He retired to Sutton in 1620, after accusations that he had
enriched himself from the funds of the Virginia Company.
Sutton Place, where he lived, has been pulled down; but its
brick Tudor wall, with saplings growing out of it, survives
across the main road from the church.

   St John's Jerusalem (National Trust) at Sutton is one of the
gems of this valley (chapel and garden open Wednesday afternoons). It was a Commandery of the Knights Hospitallers, a
half-military, half-religious order founded after the first
Crusade. Henry VIII dissolved the Order in 1540; now all that
remains of the Commandery is the east end of the chapel,
with its three lancet windows, and the massive flint walls,
hidden by later brickwork. Abraham Hill, who was one of the
founders of the Royal Society, and introduced cider-making
from Devon to Kent, bought St John's in 1665; and a century
later Edward Hasted, whose monumental history of Kent has
never been superseded, lived there for twenty years and broke
himself with the money he spent on improvements. The garden
is as perfect in its way as the house, with a moat all round it
fed by and forming part of the Darent, a formal flower garden,
and magnificent trees – copper beech, cedar, horse chestnut
and weeping willow. The whole place has an astonishing
serenity within a stone's throw of a busy main road and only
a couple of miles from Dartford's swarming industries.

   Across the river from Sutton are the villages of **Darenth** and
South Darenth, linked by a narrow road with open views along
the valley. Between road and river a small square of tangled
woodland marks the site of a Roman villa, which was excavated at the end of the last century; bricks from the villa can
be seen embedded in the masonry of St Margaret's Church,
Darenth. This church is built on three different levels, rising

towards the altar; the east end gives a curious grotto-like effect, with crude vaulting and deeply cut window splays. Norman wall paintings round the windows were renewed in the 1930s, but have since largely faded again. The tub-shaped stone font dates from the first half of the twelfth century, and has a frieze of animal and human figures in an arcade; one panel shows a baby being completely immersed in a font.

The main landmark of this stretch of the valley is industrial – the enormous Victorian brick chimney of the **Horton Kirby** Paper Mills, square at the base and round for the top sixty or so feet. In 1972 the foundations of a large Roman villa were uncovered near the village, including a vast granary 130 feet long.

Though **Farningham** stands at the junction of two trunk roads, it manages to avoid them both, thanks to a loop in the A 20; it was one of the first villages to be bypassed. The wide main street crosses the Darent by an eighteenth-century bridge, and downstream is a weird brick and flint folly, a kind of two-dimensional bridge which could never carry anything. The gardens of the grand eighteenth-century Lion Hotel run down to the river, across the road from the tall white weatherboarded Mill House. In the centre of the village an enormous barn, with roof tiles laid in patterns, stands end on to the road. Opposite is the church, mainly thirteenth and fourteenth century, with a square battlemented tower slightly later, and a Victorian Gothic vestry tacked on behind. There is a splendid fifteenth-century font, illustrating a different sacrament (ordination, baptism, confirmation, etc.) on each of the eight sides. The figures are carved with tremendous vigour. A stylishly dressed bride and groom clasp hands, a demon grabs a penitent by the shoulder, a priest anoints the breast of a dying man. In the churchyard at the back is a square-domed mausoleum to Thomas Nash, who died in 1778 and was the uncle of John Nash, the architect of Brighton's Royal Pavilion. In the old days the girls of the village used to try and throw a pin through the hole in the wall above the inscription, hoping (or fearing) that the devil would peer out if they succeeded.

West of Farningham the A 20 brings you up Farningham Hill (a notorious stretch of road for fatal crashes) to the sprawl of **Swanley**, which nevertheless has its rustic side. This is **Swanley Village**, a mile to the north, which consists of a

narrow street of old houses and an odd little Victorian church
down a byroad. On the other side of Farningham the A 20
swings south-east across the Downs, past the giant transmitter
mast at the top of **Wrotham Hill** (for Wrotham, see p. 206).
The chief lure hereabouts is the **Brands Hatch** motor racing
circuit; avoid both the main road and the lanes behind the
circuit when a race meeting is on.

Continuing along the A 225, a mile south of Farningham is
Eynsford, a picture-postcard village, with timbered houses, a
narrow stone bridge with a ford beside it across the Darent,
and the stone walls of a ruined Norman castle. As the centre
of Eynsford lies off the main road, the banks of the Darent can
be used for general relaxation, and on a fine summer afternoon
the whole village seems to be paddling, fishing, or lazing about
by the stream. The church has a spindly wood-shingled spire,
with a brightly painted clock face on the tower dated 1904
and surrounded with the encouraging opening lines of Brown-
ing's *Rabbi Ben Ezra*,

> Grow old along with me,
> The best is yet to be.

The way in leads under the tower, past the bellringers' ropes
and through a fine Norman doorway. The inside is lopsided,
as in Tudor times a chapel replaced the north transept, and
the north wall was rebuilt to give the whole place an asymmetrical effect. The east end is a rounded Norman apse. For so
prosperous a village, there are few monuments, apart from a
moving seventeenth-century memorial slab on the floor of the
south transept. 'In this silent dormitorie' lies Mary Bosvile,
who died in 1659 aged seventeen, and who 'like a jewell taken
out of a box was shewen to the world and put up againe.' Her
mother, Lady Sarah Bosvile, died the following year: 'thus in
a short space death tooke away root & branch, mother &
daughter.'

When its high flint wall was unbroken, **Eynsford Castle**
must have brought a harsh military note into the peaceful
valley. It was built about 1100, by a Norman family who called
themselves de Eynsford after the place where they settled. A
good deal of the curtain wall still stands, some of it to its full
height of nearly thirty feet. In the fourteenth century the castle
seems to have become largely derelict, though it was later

patched up from time to time. In the eighteenth century it was used as kennels for hunting dogs by the Hart-Dykes of Lullingstone. Now the austere walls are lightened by plants which have colonised the flint. One rarity from Nepal (*Leycesteria formosa*), with brilliant green leaves, white spring flowers and mauve autumn berries, finds it a perfect substitute for a Himalayan cliff.

The road to **Lullingstone** runs from Eynsford for about a mile beside the quiet meanderings of the Darent, passing under a handsome striding brick viaduct of the Swanley–Sevenoaks branch line. The magnificent **Roman villa** lies about half a mile north of Lullingstone Castle, and is protected now against the weather by a large wooden hangar, with glass cases displaying small objects found on the site. The villa was first discovered in the mid-eighteenth century, when workmen digging post holes for a park fence brought up fragments of mosaic. Systematic excavation, begun after the Second World War, has resulted in an amazingly complete picture of life in the Romano-British countryside.

The site is a natural one for a farm, with the Darent supplying water transport and grazing, and the hills on either side providing both ploughland for corn and timber for building and fuel. The land was farmed in pre-Roman times; the first flint and mortar house was built by a native farmer eager to become Romanised, and adopting the ideas of comfort brought north by the new masters of Britain. Towards the end of the second century the house was occupied by a Roman, possibly an important government official who used it as a country retreat. It was probably this magnate who brought with him the two bearded ancestral busts, now in the British Museum, of which casts are shown at Lullingstone. For most of the third century the house was abandoned, and the next occupant found these busts and set them up as cult objects. They are certainly austere and dignified enough to make suitable objects of veneration.

The two sophisticated mosaic floors were added about the middle of the fourth century. In the Reception Room, Bellerophon riding the winged horse Pegasus spears a diminutive Chimaera, the whole thing looking like a prototype for a medieval St George and the Dragon. Four cheerful dolphins surround the figures, and in the four corners of the design are the four seasons, one of them (Summer) completely obliterated by the eighteenth-century posthole. On the floor of the apsidal dining-room leading off the reception room Europa rides unconcernedly to her fate on the back of Jupiter disguised as a bull.

While plenty of other villas have baths and mosaics, one feature is unique to Lullingstone. This is the Christian chapel, founded about 385 when the owner was converted. Its plaster walls were painted with the Christian Chi-Rho monogram, and six half-life-size figures standing with arms outstretched in the early Christian attitude of prayer. Towards the end of the fourth century the farm was abandoned, and only the chapel remained in use. Then early in the fifth century a fire burnt the whole thing to the ground; soil washed down from the hills above covered the ruins; and they remained hidden for 1,500 years.

Like the villa, **Lullingstone Castle** is a product of centuries of change, though it does not need the expertise of an archaeologist to decipher it. You approach the house (not really a castle at all) through a massive brick-built gatehouse, built about 1497. In front of you, across an enormous lawn, stands what appears to be a wide three-storey eighteenth-century house, with lakes formed by damming the Darent stretching away to the south; and on the north side of the lawn a small church, with flint walls, miniature cupola, classical porch, and medieval windows. It is largely the glorified mausoleum of generations of owners of the Castle, with the whole east end occupied by magnificent tombs and monuments. And the inscriptions do much to elucidate the story of Lullingstone.

In the middle of the fourteenth century the Manor of Lullingstone passed to the Peche family. A descendant, Sir John Peche, was responsible for much of what we see today – the gatehouse, and the Tudor mansion behind the Georgian façade. He must have been something of a prodigy. In 1494, aged twenty-one, he won the prize in the Royal Jousts before King Henry VII. The following year he was Sheriff of Kent and brought Perkin Warbeck, the pretender to the throne, prisoner to London. He was knighted in 1497, and was later Lord Deputy of Calais. After the death of Henry VII in 1509, he became a trusted adviser of the young Henry VIII, and accompanied him to the Field of the Cloth of Gold in 1520. He died in 1522, and his youthful-looking effigy lies beneath a sumptuously carved stone canopy, with peach stones (a rebus or visual pun on the name Peche) among the foliage. He set up the carved oak rood screen which divides the church in two.

Sir John left no direct descendants, and Lullingstone passed to his nephew, Sir Percyvall Hart, whose vast painted tomb, with effigies of him and his wife, is on the south side of the chancel. The inscription above gives a flattering portrait of the old man, who died in 1580 aged eighty-four, and managed to hold on to his court offices through the reigns of Henry VIII, Edward VI, Mary and Elizabeth. As 'Chief Sewer' he supervised the arrangements of the royal table, the seating of guests, and the tasting and serving of dishes, and as 'Knight Harbinger' he was responsible for arranging lodgings when the king was on tour with his retinue.

The whole west wall of the north chapel is filled by an elaborate monument to the last of the Lullingstone Harts, another Percyvall, who died in 1738. It takes the form of pseudo-Gothic plaster arcading, inset with a great number of little armorial shields and a long inscription describing how since the days of Queen Anne 'Mr. Hart's steady Attachment to the Old English Constitution Disqualified him from sitting any more in Parliament.' Politics apart, he built the present front to the house, and made considerable internal alterations. He added the fine plaster ceiling to the church, and also the little marble font, in a wooden case to the left as you enter the door. With Percyvall the male Hart line died out. His daughter, Anne, married Sir Thomas Dyke, descended from a family of Wealden ironmasters, and from then on successive Hart Dykes have inherited Lullingstone.

In spite of its Queen Anne façade, much of the interior of Lullingstone Castle is little altered since Tudor times. The Great Hall is still a Tudor hall though with Queen Anne panelling. One wall of the hall is dominated by a triptych of old Sir Percyvall, painted in 1575, and his two sons. He looks much as Henry VIII might have been expected to look had he reached white-haired and healthy old age. In his waistband is the silver-hilted knife which went with the office of Chief Sewer; it is now kept in the dining-room.

A wide staircase leads up to the apartments prepared by Mr Percyvall Hart for Queen Anne's visits. The treads were made deliberately shallow to help the overweight queen, who had great difficulty in climbing stairs. The staircase is lit by a ten-candle lantern, reputedly the only lantern to survive from Whitehall Palace, which was burnt down in Anne's reign. At the foot of the stairs hangs a portrait of Sir William Hart Dyke, who was a friend of Disraeli, and who when young worked out with his friends the rules of lawn tennis on the Lullingstone grass.

Upstairs, Queen Anne's state drawing-room has a remarkable barrel-vaulted plaster ceiling, decorated with pendants, and medallions of Romulus, Tarquin and other illustrious or notorious Romans. The walls are oak-panelled over Tudor brickwork. At one end is a portrait of Queen Anne; at the other her nail-studded travelling chest, with her favourite doll inside it, strikes an oddly pathetic note. Downstairs the dining-room used to house a display of silver, but £10,000 worth was stolen recently, though luckily the Chief Sewer's knife was not taken. Above the fireplace is the jousting helmet of Sir John Peche, still with its orange and yellow plumes (perhaps a rebus on the colours of a peach). The library, lined with calf-bound tomes, is now used as a private sitting-room; and from here a vestibule leads under a great Tudor arch back to the garden, with its giant cedars, lawns and lake.

Until a few years ago the Hart Dykes ran a silkworm factory at Lullingstone, but this has now been moved to Ayot St Lawrence, in Hertfordshire. The house is full of hangings, curtains and coverings made by the present Lady Hart Dyke.

Though it is only a few miles from Bromley and Orpington, **Shoreham**, two miles south of Lullingstone, remains astonishingly remote. No main roads pass through it, and it is still very much the quiet riverside village where Samuel Palmer painted his visionary pictures of the Kentish countryside. The focal point of Shoreham is the little bridge over the Darent, with a watersplash ford beside it; the river runs beside the road for a short way. Near the bridge is Palmer's white Water House. He lived here with his father and old nurse from 1827 to 1833, fired by William Blake's mystical fervour and visited by a group of young fellow-disciples. Blake himself came down to

Shoreham at least once before his death in 1827. Palmer described 'all the village appurtenances' as he had known them – 'the wise-woman behind the age, still resorted to; the shoemaker always before it, such virtue is in the smell of leather; the rumbling mill, and haunted mansion in a shadowy paddock.'

The church (usually locked because of vandalism) is at the eastern entrance to the village, with a long avenue of trimmed yews running parallel to it. It is built of flint, with a tiled roof, and has a brick and flint eighteenth-century tower, with a brick pinnacle at each corner. The massive entrance to the south porch is said to be carved from a single piece of oak. Inside the most magnificent feature is the fifteenth-century carved oak rood screen right across the nave, with a door behind the pulpit for access. The organ was originally erected in Westminster Abbey in 1730.

Inside the door is a brilliantly coloured Victorian painting by Charles West Cope, showing one of the highlights of nineteenth-century Shoreham history. This was the homecoming in 1875 of Verney Cameron, son of the vicar of Shoreham and a naval lieutenant, who led the second Livingstone relief expedition, sent out to Africa by the Royal Geographical Society. When Cameron met Livingstone's men at Tabora, in what is now Tanzania, the great explorer was already dead; but members of the expedition pushed on and were the first Europeans to cross Africa from one side to the other. In the picture the venerable vicar stands by the church porch, awaiting his black-bearded son, who is being welcomed in triumph by the villagers of Shoreham, from cartwheeling boys to the oldest inhabitant in a Bath chair.

In the King's Arms, across the river from the church is an 'ostler's box', a kind of sentry box where the ostler would wait to look after customers' horses. On the inside of the box a window opens directly into the bar, and through it can be seen a waxwork ostler ready for action.

A mile and a half farther along the Darent valley is Otford, almost on the outskirts of Sevenoaks (see p. 221).

Returning to Dartford, and heading east along the Gravesend road, you come to a landscape of giant cement-works' chimneys and huge areas gouged out of the ground by chalk quarries and stone and gravel workings. One of the most spectacular of these is the Atlas Stone Co.'s workings at the suitably named village of **Stone**, north of the A 226. A chalk outcrop has been left sticking up from the quarry, with grass and trees on the top, marking the former land level and rising at a rough estimate about eighty feet above the quarry floor; and much of Stone is perched above a man-made cliff. Stone church lies down a little side road, with views over the chimneys of Greenhithe to the Thames and across to the Essex shore. An old drawing shows it with a shingled spire, but it now has a low tower. Inside much of the stone tracery is so fine that it is believed to have been carved about 1260 by the masons responsible for Westminster Abbey; the overall effect of the soaring arches is somewhat spoilt by organ pipes poking up where the north window in the chancel should be. At the bottom of Stone Hill is a pub with a nostalgically rural name, The Lads of the Village.

It is worth making a detour round **Greenhithe**, with glimpses of the Thames, deepwater jetties, and a narrow street of houses and pubs typical of all old sailing towns.

Huge quarries form the background to **Swanscombe**, which lies half a mile south of the main road. The blackened, flint-built church had a spire on its squat tower until 1902, when lightning destroyed the tower and did much internal damage. The lower part of the tower is Saxon. In Palaeolithic times Swanscombe Man (see Dartford, p. 17) lived and hunted on the gravel levels to the north; and it was at Swanscombe in 1066 that the people of Kent defied William the Conqueror and won the right to continue their ancient privileges. Chief of this was the custom of gavelkind, whereby land was divided equally among all the sons of the family instead of going to the eldest. According to a picturesque legend, each man carried a green branch over his head, and Duke William, like Macbeth, found a forest marching towards him. When he came within earshot, the Kentish army threw away their branches and revealed themselves as fully armed and ready to fight if their demands were not met. William prudently granted their terms, and received Dover Castle in return.

You know you are in **Northfleet** by the looming brick tower of Sir Gilbert Scott's Roman Catholic church, built in 1914. Northfleet has the remnants of a green, now covered by tarmac, south of the road, with the parish church behind it.

The church is basically fourteenth-century, though the floor was raised in the nineteenth century and the roof is modern. The fourteenth-century carved oak screen is said to be the oldest in Kent. In the churchyard are tombs to local worthies, including the Rosher family, one of whom (Jeremiah) tried to turn Northfleet into a resort in the 1830s. Hidden away in a quarry north of the road are the enormous Bowater paper works, worth looking at over the fence.

Southfleet, a couple of miles inland across the A 2 from Northfleet, is an old village in orchard country, built round a crossroads, with a big stone and flint church. Roman tiles used here and there in the walls came from the Roman settlement at Springhead (Vagniacae) on Watling Street near by. Unusually, the church has never had any major structural alterations since it was built in the fourteenth century. Inside it is spacious, with enormous chancel and wide aisles. The octagonal font is carved on all sides; among the carvings are St Michael, winged and in armour, weighing souls, and a yale – a goatlike heraldic beast, with grinning mouth and serrated horns.

Inland again from Southfleet are two villages which must be among the most straggling in the whole country: Longfield, about three miles end to end, and Meopham (pronounced Meppam) about four. The centre of Meopham is the green, with a wide triangle of turf complete with neat cricket pavilion on one side of the road, and the suitably named Cricketers pub on the other. Back from the road is a well preserved black-painted smock windmill. The church is nearly a mile north of the green, a bulky building, mainly flint with brick here and there.

Only two miles from Meopham, yet in utter remoteness, is Luddesdown – a manor house, church and a few houses sheltered and hidden by enveloping folds of the downs. Luddesdown Court is said to be the oldest house in continuous occupation in England, if not in the world; the occupants certainly go back to Odo, Bishop of Bayeux, one of the great warrior-prelates who came over with the Conqueror. Odo's manor, perhaps an adaptation of an earlier Saxon house, is L-shaped, with the main rooms (great hall, solar and ladies' bower) on the first floor, and rooms for stores or cattle beneath. The walls are of solid flint, nearly three feet thick, and none of the later alterations or additions have lessened the simple strength of the building. Early this century the roof of the great hall fell in – strangely enough, through the contraction of beams in a hot summer – but it was replaced before the internal damage became too serious. In the hall, which was reached by an outside stair, the stone medieval fireplace is still as it was. On the walls are the remains of a painted frieze, probably thirteenth-century if not earlier. Patches of the medieval plasterwork survive. In one place a ship has been scratched in the plaster, with the date 1340, similar to the ships used at the siege of Calais in 1347; another inscription refers to a payment of 3½d. at the Feast of Epiphany, and is dated 1321. The solar has been much divided by Elizabethan screening, but here again there is wall decoration, of cloaked knights and painted curtains. Tacked on at the north end is a small flint bearpit, with ledges for doves above. The church next door is mainly a Victorian rebuilding of a medieval structure, mentioned in Domesday; there is plenty of Victorian painted decoration on walls and roof. Court and church can be visited by prior arrangement.

Two miles south along the narrowest of lanes is **Dode** church, all that remains of a village decimated by the Black Death in 1349. The little flint-walled Norman church, with slit windows, was re-roofed and restored early this century. It is extremely hard to find, as most of the signposts in the area have been smashed off by lorries or vandals (this goes for much of the North Downs).

Though it is so near Rochester, **Cobham** is remarkably self-contained and unspoilt, with its church and almshouses, and the wings and courtyards of **Cobham Hall,** set in a landscaped park. Medieval manor house, Tudor mansion, altered by successive owners and finally sold because of upkeep costs, Cobham was restored by the Ministry of Works in the early 1960s and is now a girls' public school.

The Cobhams first came here at the beginning of the thirteenth century, building themselves a manor house surrounded by a park, but nothing of this survives. The framework of the house as we see it today dates from the time of William Brooke, tenth Lord Cobham, a notable figure at Queen Elizabeth's court. He built the long Tudor wings north and south of the old manor house, each wing with a cupolaed tower at either end, the resulting house forming an E shape without the central bar of the E. His son, Henry Brooke, the eleventh Baron, was the last of the Cobham line. In 1603 he joined Sir Walter Raleigh in the abortive attempt to place Lady Arabella Stuart on the throne instead of James I, and was tried and sentenced to death. Luckier than Raleigh, his sentence was commuted to life imprisonment, but Cobham Hall was forfeited to the Crown.

Ten years later James gave Cobham to his second cousin Ludovic Stuart, the Duke of Lennox (later Lennox and Richmond). The Stuarts were fervent royalists; two of the third Duke's sons were killed in the Civil War (their double portrait hangs in the Gilt Hall); and the fourth Duke took charge of burying the body of Charles I at Windsor after his execution. Charles Stuart, the sixth and final Duke, was responsible for the next important stage in the building of Cobham. In the 1660s he built the present central block on the side of the old medieval house which had lingered on between the Tudor wings. He was more famous for his marriage than his building activities. In 1667 he married Frances Stuart, one of the greatest beauties of Charles II's court, and known as 'La Belle Stuart'. Unlike many of her friends, she was unwilling to become yet another royal mistress; though Charles insisted that she sat to the engraver Roettier for the figure of Britannia, and she has appeared on the coinage ever since (see Goodwood, p. 428). In a splendidly novellettish scene, one stormy night La Belle Stuart crept from Whitehall wrapped in a dark cloak, met the Duke of Richmond at Southwark, drove down with him to Cobham, and lived happily as Duchess until he died five years later. As in all good romances, the king finally forgave her, and she returned to court (perhaps ironically) as Lady of the Bedchamber.

Cobham passed by devious processes of inheritance to the Earls of Darnley, and it was the third and fourth Earls at the end of the eighteenth and beginning of the nineteenth centuries who added the finishing touches. First of all James Wyatt, and subsequently George and John Repton, adorned, altered, enlarged and rebuilt Cobham inside and out. The Reptons' landscaping father, Humphry, laid out the garden and park, planting the giant cedars which still shade the lawns, and the lime avenue which once stretched away to

Cobham village. In Tudor times Cobham had been famous for its garden; the chronicler Holinshed wrote of 'a rare garden there, in which no varietie of strange flowers and trees do want, which praise or price maie obtaine from the furthest part of Europe or from other strange countries.'

A tour round the house is chiefly memorable for the contrast between massive stone Tudor fireplaces and delicate eighteenth-century plasterwork ceilings. The wide granite staircase up to the gallery was built in 1602, as the final feature of the Tudor house. At the top of the stairs is the picture gallery, now hung with rubbings of the brasses in Cobham church. The Darnley state coach (kept on the upper floor) was built about 1715 and is a great showpiece. Glorious in gilding and scarlet, it still rocks gently on strong leather springs. The present Lord Darnley wanted to use it at the 1953 coronation, but it was not considered roadworthy by the police.

Downstairs is the Repton library, now the school library, with a curious doorway of fake books. On the mantelpiece is a small photograph of an urn, which links Cobham with the history of English cricket. After the Australians defeated England at the Oval in 1882, a mock obituary appeared in the *Sporting Times* lamenting the death of English cricket, and ending up: 'The body will be cremated and the ashes taken to Australia.' Hence the term 'the Ashes' for a test series between England and Australia. As a sequel, an English team left for Australia 'to recover the Ashes' with Ivo Bligh, later Lord Darnley, as Captain. Bligh's team won two out of three matches. After the second Australian defeat, some of Melbourne's young ladies burnt a bail, put the ashes in an urn and gave it to Bligh. He was so taken with one of the girls, Miss Murphy, that he married her; and she is the Edwardian Countess whose portrait hangs in the long gallery. The urn was kept at Cobham for many years, and is now at Lord's.

The Gilt Hall is the most sumptuous room in Cobham. It rises two storeys high to an elaborate gilded plasterwork ceiling, and was the banqueting hall in the seventeenth-century central block. Wyatt or, more probably, Sir William Chambers, converted it into a music room by adding the musicians' gallery and organ gallery. The dining-room, where you can have a cup of tea after going round Cobham, has marble recesses for hot and cold food at either end, a large wine cooler in the outer wall, and a fine Tudor chimney-piece. The chapel was gothicised by Wyatt, and has Victorian stained glass windows.

Wyatt's most extraordinary work at Cobham lies away in the woods to the east of the house, but is well worth a tramp of a mile or so to get there (if wet, wear boots). This is the **Mausoleum**, begun in 1783 as the burial place for the Darnleys but never consecrated, because, so the story goes, the Bishop of Rochester refused to have anything to do with a building ill-omened enough to have its foundation stone laid in a thunderstorm. You get there from Cobham down a tunnel of trees, then across a field track marked by a line of gigantic oaks, some of them suitably blasted, then into the thickets and bracken of the Great Wood. Suddenly, at the top of a rise, you see a pyramid of stone above the trees – the roof of the mausoleum. Magnificent in its crumbling desolation, the mausoleum exudes a brooding melancholy. Young saplings sprout from the roof; the niches in the round chapel are defaced with charcoal scrawls; and below ground rows of recesses wait vainly for generations of dead Darnleys. It cries out to be restored; yet restoration might take away more than was gained by it.

The dead lords of Cobham lie more fittingly in and around the village church. **Cobham church** is famous for its memorial brasses. The chancel is paved with them – fifteen altogether, from 1299 to 1529, with a few others elsewhere in the church. They lie there in two rows with their feet pointing towards the east, the lords in armour and the ladies in high head-dresses with pet dogs at their feet: John, Margaret and Maud de Cobham, and the Lady Joan, five times married, beside her third husband, Sir Nicholas Hawberk. Most notable in the story of Cobham was the fourteenth-century Sir John, who in 1367 restored and beautified the church (on his brass he holds a model of it in his hands). He was a companion of the Black Prince in the wars against France, built Cooling Castle (see p. 40) a few miles to the north in the Hoo peninsula, and together with Sir Robert Knollys rebuilt Rochester bridge. He was tried and condemned to death by Richard II (commuted to banishment), was restored to favour by Edward IV and died in 1407. The brasses are worth looking at closely for their tiny figures of saints, or kneeling children.

The watersplash and bridge at Eynsford, in the Darent valley.

Fourth-century mosaic floor from the Roman villa at Lullingstone. In the foreground Jupiter, transformed into a bull, carries off Europa.

Rochester Cathedral, with the Medway behind.

A few yards south of the church, across a strip of grass, is the College, built and endowed by Sir John de Cobham in 1362 for five priests, converted into almshouses in Elizabethan times, and modernised in 1956. The College is a little quadrangle of flint and stonework, with doors leading off to the pensioners' rooms, each with the name of his or her village – Hoo, Halling, Shorne. On the south side is the medieval hall, now a common room, and in the garden at the back are the ruins of the medieval kitchen. Modern planners could learn something from this idyllic Elizabethan old people's home.

Also open to visitors in Cobham is **Owletts**, at the western end of the village. It was built in Charles II's time by a prosperous farmer, Bonham Hayes, and has an ornate plaster ceiling, dated 1684, above the staircase well, incorporating cherries, hops and other sources of Kentish farming wealth. Sir Herbert Baker, the architect with Lutyens of Imperial New Delhi, lived here from 1917 until his death in 1946.

Across the road from the church is the timbered Leather Bottle pub, mentioned in *Pickwick* and full of Dickensiana; and near by is a gigantic iron village pump, set up in 1848 to mark a Darnley coming-of-age. For those who collect unlikely names, the Cobham general store is run by Mr Gander, while Mr Goosey is landlord of the pub next door.

In **Sole Street**, round the corner from Cobham, is Yeoman's House, with a fourteenth-century great hall which may be seen by appointment (it is leased by the National Trust). The great main beam and kingpost are very fine. The house was bought and restored by Sir Herbert Baker.

Back on the A 227, you have a straight run down to **Gravesend**. The first thing you notice about the town is the unmistakable smell of the sea, mixed with a whiff of Thames mudflats, but there none the less. In past centuries whole fleets used to anchor off Gravesend, and the river is still full of shipping of all shapes and sizes, from tankers and dredgers to sailing dinghies. Down near the foreshore are two customs buildings – an eighteenth-century brick structure, and a modern successor with huge windows overlooking the Thames and a roof sprouting aerials and radar. Gravesend still calls itself the 'gateway to the Port of London'. In earlier times, before the railway took over the traffic, Gravesend owed its importance to its monopoly of passenger traffic by water to

London – the so-called 'long ferry'. In 1380 Gravesend was sacked by the French, and the ferry privilege was granted to the town as a means of raising money to repair the damage. Once their right was established, the Gravesend men stuck to it for over four hundred years. On the whole they seem to have given good value for money: the fare remained at two-pence from 1515 until 1737, when it was raised to sixpence. The long ferry evolved its own special transport, the tilt-boat, so named not because it was liable to turn over (though that was known to happen) but because the forty or so passengers were covered with a 'tilt' or awning. (The 'short ferry' still carries foot passengers to Tilbury.)

Old Gravesend is a small rectangle bounded on the south by the main road and on the north by the Thames. Much of this area is now a huge car park, with derelict buildings all around. The parish church (St George's) was built after a disastrous fire in 1727 which destroyed most of the town; it is a brick barn, with a tower topped by a white pinnacle, and was rebuilt largely by a grant from George II. The internal symmetry is destroyed by the huge granite columns of a Victorian north aisle. St George's is a place of pilgrimage to Americans, as Princess Pocahontas was buried in the chancel of the old church in 1617; there is a bronze statue of her in the churchyard. Pocahontas, daughter of a powerful Red Indian chief, was only thirteen in 1608 when she saved Captain John Smith, one of the early Virginia colonists, from execution at her father's hands. The story goes that she fell in love with Smith, but on hearing that he was dead eventually married another settler, John Rolfe, after being baptised under the name Rebecca. Rolfe brought her to England in 1616, where she was fêted at the court of James I; but the following year she died of fever on her way down the Thames back to Virginia. A more romantic version of the story makes her die of a broken heart after finding out that Smith was still alive and meeting him face to face.

Though much of Pocahontas's story is disputed, there is no doubt at all about the contribution of another epic figure to Gravesend – General Gordon. Gordon was in command of the Royal Engineers there from 1865 to 1871, and was respon-sible for the reconstruction of the Thames fortifications; in addition he did a lot of work for the Ragged School and other institutions. Both Gravesend and Tilbury were fortified in Tudor times, and Gordon brought the defences up to date. The Tilbury fort can still be seen straight across the Thames; the Gravesend earthworks have now been made a public garden, with the Gordon Promenade along the river, and a statue of the general among the paths and flower beds.

The High Street leads straight down the hill to the Town Pier, and still has some weatherboarded houses left. Half way down are the massive Doric columns of the Town Hall, with a way through them to the Borough Market, looking like a miniature Covent Garden; 'Chartered 1263' is inscribed over the entrance. At the end of the eighteenth century, Hasted tells us, Gravesend was famous for its market gardens, and especially its asparagus, which was known as 'Gravesend grass'.

CHAPTER TWO

Rochester and the Medway

✣

MODERN Gravesend is spreading steadily eastwards, but there are still a few miles of countryside separating it from the suburbs of Rochester. In the middle lies **Shorne**, built on the steep side of the downs. The church contains everything from Saxon to Perpendicular, plus a bit of nineteenth-century. The fifteenth-century octagonal font, like the one at Southfleet (see p. 27) has a carving on each side; the Agnus Dei, shown as a 'shorn' lamb, may be a medieval pun on the name of the village.

At **Gads Hill**, on the A 226 a couple of miles away, Shakespeare and Dickens confront each other. On the north side of the road is the Sir John Falstaff, near the spot where the sack-swilling knight lay in wait with Prince Hal to rob the 'pilgrims going to Canterbury with rich offerings, and traders riding to London with fat purses.' Shakespeare made his travellers dismount at the top of the hill, preparing to walk down the other side to stretch their legs, and in the old days it must have been quite a tiring pull up from the end of Rochester Bridge. Almost opposite the Falstaff is Gads Hill Place, where Dickens lived for the last fifteen years of his life. This is Dickens country, the area where he spent much of his life and the setting for several of his novels. He lived as a boy in Chatham, and would go for long walks with his father, often passing Gads Hill. He coveted the house, and was told by his father 'if you were to be persevering and were to work hard you might some day come to live in it.' By 1856 Dickens had worked hard enough, and bought this not particularly distinguished red brick house, with its bay windows and little white cupola on top. It is now a school, with small brown-uniformed girls running in and out. Directly opposite is a garden with lawn and tall trees, where Dickens worked in a chalet during his last years; the day before he died, in June 1870, Dickens

had been working there on *Edwin Drood*. It is now in the
grounds of the Eastgate Museum, Rochester (see p. 47).

The centre of **Higham** village has been drawn southwards
by the magnetism of Rochester, but the old nucleus lies two
miles away on the edge of the marshes down the dead end of
Church Street. The medieval church and hamlet are set in a
strange combination of orchards, pylons and industrial
chimneys. The church is built in alternating bands of flint and
stone, with a little shingled bellcote at the back. The great old
door is superbly carved with roses and is said to be fourteenth-
century, and there is a traceried rood screen of the same date.

The only thing worth looking at in **Strood**, across the
Medway from Rochester, is **Temple Manor**, hidden away
among a depressing area of riverside industry. The house,
basically a thirteenth-century inner and outer chamber on the
first floor, with an undercroft below, was built for the Knights
Templars, probably about 1240. When the order was abolished
in 1312 Temple Manor became a prosperous farmhouse. In
the seventeenth century it was extended to the east and west,
and an old engraving shows it with outbuildings and a grassy
field sloping down to the Medway, where today there are
factories and the railway. The undercroft has some fine
vaulting, and the main floor still has well-carved surrounds to
some of the lancet windows.

On the north side of the London road, the corresponding
suburb to Strood is **Frindsbury**. Frindsbury church is like an
echo of Rochester cathedral, with its square flint tower and
shingled spire standing commandingly on a bluff above the
Medway. The church was reconstructed in 1075 by a certain
Paulinus, who appears along with Bishop Gundulf of Rochester in two of the lancet windows in the chancel; and it
was much altered by the Victorians. Behind the font, in the
gloom of the south aisle, is an enormous monument, like a
huge fireplace, to Thomas Butler, who died in 1621. The
spelling of the inscription has a surrealist wildness:

> Here Doth Thomas Butler remaine
> That Sarved Queene Elyzabethe, all heer Raine
> In Ingland, Franse, and Spane.
> In Irland, Scotland, with the Best,
> And Heare-in-Grave, his Corps dooth Reste.

North of Frindsbury a side road leads down to **Upnor**, a quiet little backwater consisting of a single street of narrow weather-boarded houses sloping down to a slipway, and a splendid but seemingly little visited Elizabethan **Castle**. For over a century Upnor was a key point in the Medway defences. As the navy grew under Henry VIII and his successors, the upper reaches of the Medway below Rochester bridge were used for laying up the fleet. In 1559, the year after she came to the throne, Queen Elizabeth gave orders for a fort to be built at Upnor, well downstream from the embryo dockyards at Chatham. This original fort consisted of the large square stone building overlooking the river, and a wedge-shaped gun bastion built out into the water. Forty years later the castle was enlarged with a gatehouse and outer retaining wall, and this is more or less the form it has kept ever since. The only time Upnor was put to the test was an ignominious disaster for the navy. In 1667 the Dutch fleet under de Ruyter sailed up the Medway, broke the chain boom stretched across the river below Upnor, defied the castle guns and attacked the British fleet anchored off Chatham. Several ships were burnt, and the *Royal Charles* was captured and sailed back in triumph to Holland. The diarist John Evelyn called it 'a Dreadfull Spectacle as ever any English men saw and a dishonour never to be wiped off.' Thereafter Upnor declined into a powder magazine, a general storehouse, and a museum.

The way into the castle leads past an eighteenth-century barracks, now derelict. The outer wall, stone with brick trimmings on top, still looks good and solid; much of the stone was taken from Rochester castle. The gatehouse leads into a long courtyard, planted with a pair of Turkey oaks said to have been grown from acorns brought back from the Crimean War. The museum exhibits are in the magazine across the courtyard: guns, a collection of Romano-British pottery, and display cases with diagrams, plans and engravings of the Medway defences down the years, including some triumphal Dutch engravings of the sacking of Sheerness Fort by de Ruyter. An unusually wide spiral staircase links the magazine to the bastion below; it has a wide central well for hauling up powder, and a lead-cased handrail to lessen the risk of fire. From the bastion there are wide views up and down the Medway, and across to the cranes, stores, funnels and masts of Chatham Docks (see p. 49).

Less than a mile downstream is the sail training ship *Arethusa*, in a country setting with a few cottages and wooded hills behind. A century and a half ago more sinister super-annuated ships were anchored off Upnor – the prison hulks where convicts rotted away their lives, unless they were lucky enough to escape, like Magwitch in *Great Expectations*. Dickens, with a novelist's licence, shifted the hulks round to the north side of the Hoo peninsula, beyond the Cliffe marshes – 'the dark flat wilderness . . . intersected with dykes and mounds and gates.'

Returning to the main Hoo road (A 228) at Frindsbury, you can make a devious circuit of the peninsula, branching off down a byroad to **Hoo** (in full, Hoo St Werburgh). This consists largely of modern housing estates, though there are relics of a Georgian village at its centre. The church, on the edge of the marshes, has a tall spire which makes a graceful contrast with the giant chimney of the Kingsnorth power station. At the hamlet of **Stoke,** with a small church built on a low mound, you meet the main road again, which leads to the **Isle of Grain** at the eastern end of the peninsula and runs right through the middle of the B.P. oil refinery. Unlike Fawley on Southampton Water, which you can only admire from afar, you drive among the shining globular storage tanks and the slender chimneys with their plumes of flame. The one disadvantage if you live in **Grain** village, at the end of the road, is a permanent smell of petrol, wafted in on the prevalent south-west wind. Grain has a small esplanade, with marvellous views of the Thames and Medway shipping, and across the river to the new skyscrapers of Southend. An imaginary line from London Stone, on the north side of Grain, to Southend Pier marks the limit of the jurisdiction of the Port of London Authority.

To continue the circuit, you can double back along the main road and turn north at Lower Stoke for **Allhallows,** which like Stoke has a small church on a mound. **Allhallows on Sea** is becoming something of a resort, with a caravan park, and a wide grass expanse behind the shingle foreshore. **St Mary's Hoo,** the most remote of these remote places, is just a small cluster of windswept houses and a bare church high above the marshes. **High Halstow,** seven miles from Lower Halstow (see p. 52) as the seagull flies across the Medway, and double the distance by road, is expanding fast along its hilltop. **Northward Hill,** towards the Thames, has one of the largest heronries in Britain, looked after by the Nature Conservancy and the Royal Society for the Protection of Birds.

Like Gadshill, the village of **Cooling** links Shakespeare and Dickens. In the churchyard at Cooling is a grave with thirteen small lozenge-like stones round it, which Dickens made the family grave of Pip's relations (though he only allowed them five lozenges), where Pip met the terrifying Magwitch with irons on his leg. A little way west is **Cooling Castle,** built by the Cobhams and the home of Sir John Oldcastle, the model for Falstaff. It is now privately owned, but the turreted gatehouse and a good deal of walling can be seen from the road. The fortifications were built in the 1380s, to defend the port of Cliffe from French raiders. On one of the towers John de Cobham prominently fixed an inscription in the form of a copper legal document and seal, congratulating himself in rhyme for his patriotism in fortifying Cooling.

At some time in his life Oldcastle came under the influence of Wyclif's teachings, chief of which was the need to spread the English translation of the Bible and to fight the corruption of the established church. Of all Wyclif's followers (contemptuously called Lollards) Oldcastle was the most formidable, entrusted with military command by Henry IV and the confidant of his son Prince Hal; in this at least Shakespeare was correct. When Oldcastle encouraged the spread of Lollard opinions in Kent, and even tried to convert the prince, he was accused of heresy; and after some years in hiding on the Welsh Marshes, and in spite of the friendship of Prince Hal (by now Henry V), he was captured, tried, condemned and burnt as a heretic in 1417. He was the very opposite of the fat coward portrayed by Shakespeare. In the play *Henry IV* Falstaff was originally called Oldcastle, but Shakespeare is thought to have changed the name in deference to the wishes of the Cobham family. Indeed, in the epilogue to the second part of the play he went so far as to say 'for Oldcastle died a martyr, and this is not the man'.

Cooling was finally put out of action as a castle in the abortive rebellion against Queen Mary in 1554, led by Sir Thomas Wyatt (see Allington, p. 197). After defeating the royal forces at Strood, the rebels bombarded Cooling and destroyed much of the fortifications. Though the Lord Cobham of the time remained loyal, Wyatt was his nephew, and his two sons fought with the rebels. Wyatt was captured and beheaded, and Cobham and his sons were imprisoned in the Tower of London.

Cliffe-at-Hoo once had an importance far greater than its present remoteness would suggest. Its accessibility – near Watling Street, on the Thames and across the river from the kingdom of Essex – caused it to be chosen for a synod of the church summoned in 673 by Archbishop Theodore of Tarsus. In 774 Offa, King of Mercia, built a rough wooden church at Cliffe and dedicated it to St Helen, a favourite saint of the Mercians, and according to British legend the daughter of Coel ('Old King Cole') of Colchester. No other church in Kent is dedicated to her. The present church is a massive building, begun in 1260, with much of the walls in alternating bands of dressed stone and flints. Inside an unusual amount of wall painting still survives: wide red chevrons on the pillars, Christ in glory judging souls (south transept), and the martyrdom of St Edmund (north transept). In the later Middle Ages Cliffe became an important port, but after a disastrous fire in 1520 it faded away, until the rise of the Kentish cement industry in Victorian times brought new prosperity. It now has an important riverside petrol storage depot.

From Cliffe the B 2000 brings you straight back again to Strood and Frindsbury, across the Medway from Rochester.

Rochester has the advantage of compactness, forced on it by the course of the river, which doubles back on itself to form a promontory on which the old town stands. As you approach Rochester across the bridge, you are faced by the twin medieval grandeurs of castle and cathedral, standing side by side as reminders of secular and ecclesiastical power. Mr Jingle's Rochester is still very much the same: 'Ah! fine place – glorious pile – frowning walls – tottering arches – dark nooks – crumbling staircases – Old Cathedral too.' To Dickens Rochester was also Dullborough and Cloisterham; and especially the scene of Pip's pursuit of his great expectations, from Mr Pumblechook's gabled shop in the High Street to the crumbling red brick of Restoration House, the Satis House where Miss Havisham lived in candlelight among her rotting bridal finery. Mr Pickwick's Bull Hotel (now the Royal Victoria and Bull) is naturally thoroughly Dickensified; upstairs the ballroom, with its twin fireplaces and musicians' gallery, can hardly have been altered since the Pickwick Club assembled there.

Rochester's history began before the Romans. Their name for it, Durobrivae, is derived from the Celtic *dwr* (water) and *briva* (ferry), and there must have been a Belgic stronghold guarding so important a crossing. Watling Street crosses the Medway here; in places the walls of the medieval castle follow the walls of the Roman camp; and the Roman bridge, continuing the High Street, was roughly on the line of the modern bridge. Christianity came to Rochester in AD 604, when St Augustine ordained Justus, a missionary monk sent from Rome, as the first Bishop of Rochester; and King Ethelbert built a small stone church there. The modern name for the city derives from 'Hrofe-Caestre', the camp of Hrof or

Roffa, a pre-Christian Saxon warlord. During the Dark Ages Rochester was periodically attacked by marauding Danes, and even as late as 1075 the Saxon church was 'utterly forsaken, miserable and waste, from lack of all things within and without'. Two years later the situation was taken in hand with the consecration of Gundulf, a Norman monk, as bishop. This energetic prelate-architect immediately began work at Rochester, building the castle (though not the massive keep), a monastery, and the **Cathedral**. He was also the builder of the White Tower in the Tower of London (see also Dartford, p. 17).

Gundulf's Tower, embedded in the masonry of the cathedral's north side like a buttressed sentry box, is a good place to begin an exploration. About fifty feet of the tower still stands; it was used by Gundulf as headquarters to supervise the works, as treasury, and no doubt as possible fortress in case anything went wrong with the Normans' hold upon the restive Saxons of Kent. Its stark foursquare militarism has little in common with the rest of the cathedral's carved and fretted stonework. The spectacular **West Front** with its great Norman door is the result of centuries of tinkering and restoration. The two inner and two outer pinnacles, with their octagonal roofs and blind arcading, did not reach their present state of satisfactory medieval symmetry until J. L. Pearson restored them in 1888. Most of the front is taken up with a huge Perpendicular window, inserted in 1470 and renewed in the early nineteenth century, dwarfing the richly-carved Norman door below it. This door, with its row of diminishing arches one inside the other, surrounding a tympanum of the seated Christ in majesty with the symbols of the evangelists, is no doubt the original entrance used when the cathedral was consecrated in 1130, in the presence of King Henry I. The tall mutilated statues on either side of the door are thought to be Henry and Queen Matilda; an alternative suggestion is Solomon and the Queen of Sheba.

Inside the cathedral we are back with Mr Jingle. 'Pilgrim's feet worn away the old steps – little Saxon doors – confessionals like money-takers' boxes at theatres – queer customers those monks – Popes, and Lord Treasurers, and all sorts of fellows, with great red faces, and broken noses, turning up every day – buff jerkins too – match-locks – Sarcophagus –

fine place.' It is small as cathedrals go, but so full of architectural variety, tombs, screens and odd corners that you
could spend days there and still find something new. Much of it
is massively Norman, like Gundulf's unembellished south aisle
arcade, and the later elaborately moulded arches of the north
arcade. Gundulf's work can best be seen in the **Crypt**, where
his austere round arches give place to springing Early English
vaulting. This must have been where Mr Jingle saw the
muskets and jerkins said to have been left behind by Cromwell's men, and still there in glass cases. It is worth looking
for the medieval graffiti scratched on the crypt piers. The
cathedral has some striking examples of architectural ingenuity, like the curious arches below the vaulting in the
north transept, with one asymmetrical opening uncomfortably
squeezed against the next.

Between the north transept and the choir transept are the
worn steps where the pilgrims climbed on their way to the
shrine of St William of Perth. In 1201 William, a charitable
Scottish baker who used to give every tenth loaf he baked to
the poor, was murdered just after he had spent the night
in Rochester at the start of a pilgrimage to the Holy Land.
The monks of Rochester seized eagerly on this possible rival
to Canterbury's St Thomas, buried him in style, set up a
shrine to him, and with the money that poured in from pilgrims
repaired the damage caused by disastrous fires and set about
new building, notably the choir of 1227. It seems to have been
their intention to reconstruct the whole nave, but money ran
out before they could do more than nibble at the Norman
work.

St William has disappeared, but near where his shrine once
stood is the tomb of Bishop Walter of Merton, with his mitred
effigy lying at rest. He founded Merton College, Oxford, was
Chancellor of England, and is said to have been drowned in the
Medway in 1277. Farther east is the tomb of John de North-
woode of Sheppey, bishop from 1353 to 1360, with an effigy
richly painted in red and green. Most of the other memorials of
interest are concentrated in the south transept. Largest is the
chest tomb with its sleeping effigy of Dean Hole, who died in
1904 aged eighty-five. Samuel Reynolds Hole was the epitome
of the Victorian sporting parson – an enthusiastic fox-hunter,
a friend of John Leech the cartoonist, a writer on gardening.

He was a great organiser of rose shows (Tennyson called him 'the rose king') and grew 135 varieties in the Deanery garden at Rochester. The west front of the cathedral was restored under the supervision of this tireless man, who at the age of seventy-five went on a lecture tour of the United States and raised £500 for the work. On the wall behind this monument is a tablet to Dickens. Richard Watts, the sixteenth-century Rochester philanthropist, peers down from the wall like a bearded prophet out of William Blake.

Rochester Cathedral contains a social history of the Middle Ages in the two-hundred-odd heads carved as corbels or ceiling bosses, from dignified monks to grimacing wild men. On one of the choir pillars a fair amount remains of a painting of one of the favourite medieval cautionary tales – the Wheel of Fortune, seen as a treadmill, with the ambitious rising to the top and the man who has made good looking anxiously down the far side of the wheel. The choir walls are bright with golden lions and fleur-de-lys on a red and blue background, painted during Sir Gilbert Scott's restorations of the 1870s, and based on fragments of fourteenth-century painting found behind some old woodwork. Typical of the cathedral, in that you may miss it if you do not look for it, is the elaborately carved fourteenth-century chapterhouse door. On the left side is the Church, a female figure holding a staff surmounted by a cross; on the right the Synagogue, a blindfolded figure with a broken staff. Above them, sloping inwards towards the point of the arch, are four scholars reading books or scrolls in their studies, the contemplatives of Rochester, letting the world go by.

Though the outer bailey of **Rochester Castle** is now domesticated, with lawns, benches and a putting course, it would be impossible to tame the majestic harshness of its keep. The line of the outer walls is due to Gundulf; the keep, seventy feet square and towering to well over a hundred feet, was built by William de Corbeuil, Archbishop of Canterbury, at the end of the 1120s. In 1215 the rebel barons held the castle for nearly two months against King John's siege weapons, only surrendering when sappers undermined one of the corner towers. A tunnel was dug under the tower, shored up with pit-props. The besiegers then brought 'forty of the fattest pigs of the sort least good for eating', placed them round the pit props and set fire to them – the method used before the days of gunpowder. As the props burnt through, the tower collapsed. After this, wrote a contemporary chronicler, 'few cared to put their trust in castles'; though it was repaired and again besieged, unsuccessfully, by Simon de Montfort in 1264.

As you climb the Keep, its structure is very clear, with grand entrance on the first floor, on the second floor a galleried great hall divided down the middle by a tall arcade, and on the top floor living quarters and chapel. From the battlements there is a tremendous view in all directions: up the Medway beyond the leaping ribbon of the M 2 motorway, across the river to the unlovely sprawl of Strood, and down river over the cathedral roof, past the zigzag cladding of its spire, to the ships and mudflats of Chatham Reach.

Behind the keep is Boley Hill, with two houses worth looking at. **Satis House** has a bust of Richard Watts over the door, a twin to the monument in the cathedral. The name is said to have arisen after Queen Elizabeth spent the night there. In the morning Watts asked her if she had been comfortable, to which she replied 'Satis', the royal equivalent of 'Not bad'. (Dickens transferred the name Satis House to Restoration House, a few minutes' walk away in Maidstone Road.) Next door is the gabled and timbered **Old Hall**, where Henry VIII is said to have met Anne of Cleves, his 'Flanders mare', when she arrived in England. One of Henry's victims, Bishop John Fisher, lived in the former **Bishops' Palace** south of the cathedral. The friend of Erasmus and Sir Thomas More, he defended Catherine of Aragon against the king and refused to countenance the divorce. In 1535 the Pope made him a cardinal, at which Henry burst out: 'Well, let the Pope send him a hat when he will; but I will so provide that whensoever it cometh, he shall wear it on his shoulders, for head he shall have none to set it on.' Fisher was executed on Tower Green in 1535, and canonised four hundred years later. Also in the Close is **Minor Canon Row**, seven red-brick Georgian houses with neat white-painted windows. The fourteenth-century **Prior's Gate** spans the road just behind.

Behind the cathedral close is one of Rochester's most friendly open spaces, **The Vines**, where the monks had a vineyard, and where now there are lawns and giant plane trees. Down one of the avenues and across the Maidstone Road is **Restoration**

House, from the outside still recognisably Miss Havisham's (open occasionally in the summer). Red-brick and E-shaped, it was built in 1587, and got its name from the tradition that Charles II stayed there on his return to England in 1660. Inside there is plenty of dark panelling, taken from Frindsbury church. A broad oak second staircase is said to have been built for the king's benefit; though one wonders how the owners of the day had the time to knock it up ready for his arrival. Miss Havisham's room is a large and dignified panelled drawing-room, which it needs a strong effort of the imagination to envisage as Dickens's candlelit abode of scuttling spiders and shattered bridal dreams.

As well as the Dickensian buildings already mentioned, most of old Rochester lies in the High Street. The clock that juts over the street Dickens unflatteringly called 'inexpressive, moonfaced and weak'; but he was writing before the days of hideous Victorian public horology, and it does its job well enough. The clock juts from the front of the **Corn Exchange,** given to the town in 1706 by Sir Cloudesley Shovell, that admiral with the unforgettable name. His portrait hangs below the elaborate plaster ceiling in the council chamber of the seventeenth-century **Guildhall,** down the road. Farther up the High Street are the three gables of Richard Watts's hospital, put up in 1579 to accommodate six poor travellers, 'not being rogues or proctors' (an abbreviation for 'procurator', a religious vagrant of the day). The present building dates from 1771. Set back a few yards away is **La Providence,** a little precinct of early Victorian houses, the descendants of alms-houses founded here in 1718 by Huguenot refugees from France. The Rochester city museum is in the Tudor brick **Eastgate House,** which stands end-on to the road. It has displays of arms and armour, models of old Rochester – always much more evocative than two-dimensional reconstructions – and a Dickens Room, full of letters, pictures, books and other Dickensiana. In the garden is the chalet from Gad's Hill (see p. 37); you can go up the outside stair to the first-floor room where Dickens worked.

In spite of the M 2 near by, Rochester has to cope with the traffic going to Chatham and Gillingham, and the road bridge has been doubled in width to make it a dual carriageway. It is still administered by the Bridge Wardens, who operate from the **Bridge Chamber** near the castle. A trust for its upkeep was founded in 1391. The Cobhams and other local magnates were often the trustees, and the bridge was considered so important that in 1489 the Archbishop of Canterbury 'remitted from purgatory all manner of sins for forty days' for anyone who contributed to its upkeep. Nowadays driving over it in the rush hour is purgatory enough. The Bridge Chapel next door can be visited (by request to the Bridge Clerk, Bridge Chamber). It stood at one end of the medieval bridge, slightly upstream from the modern bridge, and was used by travellers wishing to give thanks for a safe arrival in Rochester. Round the walls are plans and paintings of the bridge at various times from the Romans on. The old bridge was demolished in 1856; its stonework went as filling for the Esplanade, and its balustrade now runs along the river bank opposite the Bridge Chamber. Little more than a mile upstream the M 2 strides across the Medway on enormous concrete stilts. Then, in a grand sweep, it makes a wide dogleg along the foot of the downs, limiting (so far, at least) the southern sprawl of Gillingham and Chatham, and running close to villages which had previously known no intrusions of railway or trunk roads.

Rochester has a flourishing dockyard, not easy to see without going down one of the side turnings off Corporation Street. Between the Maidstone Road and the river is the original **Borstal,** well barricaded, which takes it name from a village, now a Rochester suburb.

It is said that even the locals are not quite sure where Rochester ends and **Chatham** begins. The imperceptible boundary comes somewhere along Chatham High Street, but it does not really matter, as the importance of Chatham lies in its acres of dockyard and barracks both naval and military. As was mentioned earlier, the Medway's importance to the navy began in the mid sixteenth century. The peninsula now covered by the dockyards was found to be ideal for the winter jobs of refitting, caulking and scraping the ships, as there was shelter, a good rise and fall of tide, and soft rock-free mud for the vessels to rest on. Even in those early days the Medway covered in shipping must have been an awe-inspiring sight. Lambarde wrote lyrically of the Elizabethan 'Navie Royall'. 'No Towne, no Citie, is there (I dare say) in this whole Shire,

The Greyfriars, Canterbury, built over a branch of the River Stour.

Canterbury Cathedral, from the south-east. Soaring above the centre of the building is the fifteenth-century Bell Harry Tower; below it, from left to right, are the pinnacles of one of the twin west towers, the south and south-east transepts, and the Norman arcading of St Anselm's Chapel.

St Augustine's Abbey, Canterbury, founded soon after Augustine's arrival in Kent in 597AD comparable in right value with this one Fleete: nor shipping any where else in the whole world to be founde, either more artificially moalded under the water, or more gorgeously decked above.' He goes on to list 'these most stately and valiant vessels', of which just a few read like a litany of Elizabethan enterprise: 'Elizabeth Ionas, Tryumph, Whyte Beare, Merhonora, The Victorie, Arke Rawleigh, Dew Repulse, The Garlande.'

The navy's fifth and most famous *Victory* was launched at Chatham in 1765, so she was already elderly by the time of Trafalgar. Her keel was laid in 1759 during the Seven Years' War – one of twelve ships of the line laid down at the urging of William Pitt the Elder, who later chose Chatham as the title of his earldom. Building her was slow and expensive: in the 1759 naval estimates £3,500 was allocated for her hull, and subsequent costs ran to about £8,000 a year. The war was over by the time she was launched, and she was laid up at anchor – 'in ordinary', as the eighteenth century called mothballing. By 1771 she was leaking so badly that £4,000 had to be spent on repairs. Part of the **Dockyard** where the shipwrights, quarterboys, caulkers, oakumboys, joiners and sailmen sweated on the *Victory* can be visited (visits start from the Pembroke Gate, at the end of Dock Road). The tour only takes in the comparatively modern sections of the yard, round the docks which run from east to west across the Chatham promontory. Most of the ships built recently at Chatham have been submarines (the area devoted to nuclear submarines naturally cannot be visited). Workshops like the boiler-making and pattern shops are open for inspection.

The fortress-like brick **Main Gate** with twin brown towers and a large gilded royal coat-of-arms over the entrance, lies back towards the town. It leads to the old part of the dockyard, which cannot normally be visited, though the plain square dockyard church, built in 1811, can just be seen. Many of the buildings, though utilitarian, are of great elegance, like the sail and colour loft, built in 1734 by French prisoners-of-war. This huge workshop is nearly a hundred yards long; the sails for the *Victory* were made there, and you can still see rows of sewing-machines through the windows, though presumably they are no longer used for stitching mainsails for men-of-war. Even longer – nearly a quarter of a mile – is the old

C.G.K.S. D

ropery, now powered by electricity instead of capstan and muscle but still used for making rope. Oldest and most stylish is Medway House, built in 1703 and now the residence of the Flag Officer, Medway. In front of it is a wide square with a splendid collection of gaudily painted figureheads.

For centuries Chatham has had barracks as well as a dockyard. The most important of these, **Brompton Barracks**, is now the home of the Royal School of Military Engineering, with a comprehensive **Museum** (open to the public) on this particular branch of war. The main entrance to the barracks lies a short way west of the roundabout on Dock Road. The original barracks, where the museum is, consists of a continuous range of two-storey buildings built round three sides of an enormous square, with a columned portico at the centre of each side – the kind of barrack square it would almost be a pleasure to parade on. It was built in 1804–6 for the artillery; in 1812, after the experiences of the Peninsular War, Wellington set up a school there for training engineer officers and soldiers in the arts of sapping, mining, bridging and other military field works. Since then it has branched out into every aspect of the Royal Engineers' work, from military photography to chemical warfare. The museum is housed in a large elegant room, originally the barracks chapel, all pink and white paint, with a curving staircase leading to a wide gallery. A huge statue of Field Marshal Burgoyne, seventy years a soldier in the nineteenth century, dominates the room. There are special exhibits devoted to the most famous R.E.s of all time, Gordon and Kitchener. Through the Crimean arch which forms the gateway to the barrack square, and the Boer War arch on the other side of the road, you will find General Gordon again, mounted in full uniform on a supercilious Sudanese camel.

A statue of Kitchener, mounted more conventionally on a horse (now going rusty) stands half way down Dock Road, opposite Chatham's parish church. The best thing about the church is its situation, overlooking the Medway with spacious views towards the shipping moored at Rochester. It dates mainly from the nineteenth century, though a medieval church stood on the site, and there are plenty of old tombstones in the graveyard. Sadly, its use as a church is being abandoned.

Chatham's **Town Hall**, at the bottom of the hill, has some things worth looking at. Upstairs in the council chamber is an intricately detailed scale model of the *Victory*, and a sedan chair in which the commandants of the Chatham garrison used to be carried about before the days of official cars. The mayor's chain can be seen on request: it is a double chain, of which the inner band, gold decorated with coloured Venetian glass, was worn by the Doges of Venice and is said to be over a thousand years old – a not unsuitable translation from one dockyard centre to another.

Behind the town hall rises a scrub-covered hill known as the **Great Lines** after the eighteenth-century earthworks which formed part of the land defences of Chatham. In subsequent years they were a centre for military manoeuvres, and are now the site of a huge naval war memorial, consisting of a tall white column supporting a green globe, decorated with figureheads and medieval prows, with pavilions at its foot. From this point the whole Medway panorama can be seen: the slopes of the Isle of Grain, the Kingsnorth power station, clusters of barges and the occasional red-sailed yacht and an odd coalescing of Rochester cathedral and castle into a single square-towered building. Also in Chatham is Dickens's childhood home, south of the station at 11 Ordnance Terrace. Dickens's father, John Dickens, moved to the Navy Pay Office at Chatham dockyard in 1816, and spent six years at Chatham, five of them in this three-storey yellow brick house.

Gillingham is a sprawl of barracks, hospitals and nondescript houses, with nothing much to stop it as it spreads along the dead straight line of the A 2. It continues uninterrupted to **Rainham**, where suddenly a monumental church tower juts up south of the main road, like an old oak among a mass of scrub. The fifteenth-century tower, with battlements and corner turret, is built of dressed stone; the rest of the church, mainly thirteenth- and fourteenth-century, is flint, with tiled roof. Inside it is spacious, with a wide nave and north aisle, and a strange 'false' south aisle, without any arcading. The whole thing has a lopsided ruggedness, emphasised by the ancient roof timbers and kingposts, roughly adzed into shape. The church's greatest treasure is a fourteenth-century oak chest in the chapel north of the chancel; it is carved with a double row of window tracery, most of which still survives in sharp-edged detail. East of the church is a reminder of the open country beyond in a string of oasthouses, end on to the road.

Gillingham has its own quiet pleasure beach, The Strand, at the west end of the Lower Rainham Road. This runs parallel to the main road along the edge of the estuary, with orchards on either side, and little side roads leading down to mudflats with beached boats, and derelict quays. Back roads carry on to **Upchurch**, a crossroads village at the heart of a small peninsula. The medieval church has a singled spire of 'candle-snuffer' type, consisting of a pyramid base and octagonal top. From the outside the building has a curious threefold effect, as the main chancel is paralleled by additional chancels on the north and south. Another curiosity is a painting, thought to be thirteenth-century, on the wall of the south aisle. Below a red zigzag are scenes from the life of a saint, identified as Spiridon of Cyprus, a fourth-century bishop famous for a miracle in which he turned a serpent into gold to help a poor farmer. No one knows why so obscure a Near Eastern saint should have had a shrine in a Kentish church. Perhaps a soldier back from the Crusades brought stories of Spiridon's powers home with him. In 1560 a certain 'Edmund Drakes' became vicar of Upchurch. This was almost certainly Edmund Drake, the father of Sir Francis, who as a Protestant lay-preacher had fled from his native Devon about 1549 to escape persecution. Before coming to Upchurch Drake had been prayer-reader to the fleet in the Medway, and had himself lived on one of the hulks; no doubt his son learnt much of his sailing skill pottering about the tidal waters of the estuary. As an agricultural footnote to Upchurch, I saw strawberries and maize growing together in a field there.

For a riverscape of saltings, beached barges, high winds and hulks, **Lower Halstow** is the place. The Romans gathered oysters and made bricks here, and in the Middle Ages the monks farmed the low-lying fields, building earth walls to keep out the sea. The sheep they bred were the ancestors of the Romney Marsh sheep of today. The church, standing on a low mound above flood level, goes back to early Norman or even Saxon times, and is a jumble both inside and out, with Roman tiles among the stonework, and decaying medieval wall paintings inside. There is a twelfth-century lead font, moulded with kings and angels, which was plastered over at some time in the past, and only revealed after gunfire in the First World War had split the plaster.

Newington, inland among the orchards, is a biggish village stretching along the A 2. Its church, isolated a little to the north, is a magnificent building, dating mainly from the late thirteenth or early fourteenth century, with a soaring Perpendicular tower built in alternate stripes of flint and ragstone, and a long tiled roof. Inside, the tall arcades and enormously wide aisles give a feeling of tremendous spaciousness, enhanced by a lack of clutter. In the south chancel is an arcaded tomb, known as the shrine of St Robert of Newington; Robert is otherwise unknown, but may have been a pilgrim murdered while on his way to Canterbury. In the Middle Ages cripples used to thrust their legs into the recesses of the shrine, in the hope of a miraculous cure. The north aisle is covered in mural painting of about 1340: saints, among whom St Andrew with his cross is easily identifiable; a nativity scene; and above the altar a Last Judgment, with the dead pushing back their tombstones below a majestic figure of Christ. A builder carrying out renovation work on the church commented to me on the quality of the paint – simple vegetable dyes which had lasted for centuries, whereas the paints he has to use today need renewing after five years, in spite of all the scientific research that goes into them.

At the entrance to the churchyard is the 'Devil's Stone', one of two sarsens which presumably go back to pre-Christian times. According to one legend, the Devil was so annoyed with the ringing of Newington church bells that he decided to remove them. After collecting them one night in a sack he jumped down from the tower but landed on the stones and fell over. The bells rolled out of the sack and down the lane leading to Halstow, where they ended up at the bottom of a stream which has bubbled melodiously ever since.

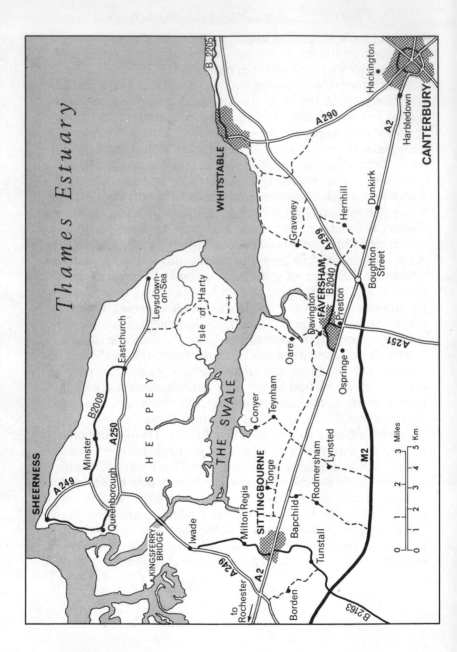

CHAPTER THREE

Along the Canterbury Road

✤

THERE are now, of course, two Canterbury roads: Watling Street, still as serviceable as ever after nineteen centuries; and the great sinuous sweep of the M 2, cutting across the countryside in lordly disdain, and so remote from the villages it passes that you cannot leave it between Sittingbourne and Faversham. Nevertheless, the M 2 is, paradoxically, the best way to get a first impression of this stretch of country, as you can enjoy it like some magnificent landscape film, with only minimal worries about the traffic – the endless pattern of apple and cherry orchards, village churches so close it seems as though you could touch them, and in the distance the industrial blur of Sittingbourne, the green slopes of Sheppey, and a glimpse of the muddy waters of the Swale.

A mile or so east of Newington the main road from Maidstone to Sheppey (A 249) crosses Watling Street. It is worth making a short southward detour here to **Borden**, not yet swallowed up by Sittingbourne near by. The church, with its low, wide tower, makes a satisfying close to the main street. Beyond the churchyard is a large thatched barn right in the village, and a good half-timbered house beside it. The church tower is late Norman, built about 1160, with a vast round-headed arch into the nave. Inside there is a striking and well preserved mural painting above the arcade showing a bearded St Christopher with staff and Christ-child. Two memorials are worth looking at. In the north aisle is a tablet to Dr Robert Plot (died 1696), scientist, naturalist and antiquarian, who in the versatile manner of the day was the first curator of the Ashmolean Museum at Oxford, and also the university's Professor of Chemistry. In the south chapel is a monument put up by Dr Plot to his father; it shows St Michael trampling on the devil, and has cannon along the top to commemorate the old man's service in the militia.

You get from Borden to **Tunstall** along Heart's Delight
Road, as pretty as the name. Tunstall is chiefly remarkable for
a huge cedar which arches across the steep village street
opposite the church. The church tower was Victorianised by
the addition of a strange saddle-backed roof (there is another
at Ospringe, see p. 68). Inside there are simple, regular
fourteenth-century arcades, and a pompous seventeenth-
century effigy of Sir Edward Hales, reclining ponderously in
full armour, and so dignified that no one has ever dared to
scratch initials on him.

Sittingbourne has had a bad press. The latest town guide
opens plaintively with the remark that 'too many authors of
books on Kent have been unfair to Sittingbourne by basing
their opinions on the things they saw in the time that it took to
travel from one end to the other'; and it is true that if you stay
in your car Sittingbourne can be just a series of traffic hold-
ups on the A 2. Yet the initial dreary impression is soon dis-
pelled once you start to explore the town. The A 2 cuts it
neatly into two halves. To the north are the factories and
paper mills built round the deep inlet of Milton Creek, and to
the south the houses, schools and administrative buildings.

The High Street, with its two extensions West Street and
East Street, still has the vestiges of a Georgian thoroughfare
about it. There are plans to shift the traffic down towards the
railway and make the High Street into a pedestrian precinct,
which would be a tremendous improvement. The big flint-
built parish church (normally locked because of vandalism)
is on the north side of the street, next door to a cinema cum
bingo hall; its fine traceried windows are set back only a few
feet from the pavement. There was an early Norman church
on the site, but most of the present building dates from the
thirteenth and fourteenth centuries. The massive west tower
was completed in the fifteenth century. In 1762 the church
roof was destroyed after workmen repairing the leads left a
fire burning during their lunch hour; and the nineteenth
century brought the usual crop of pious 'restorations'. As it
now stands, the wide nave and narrow aisles make it a most
graceful building.

South of the High Street, Central Avenue forms the axis of a
complex of administrative buildings, all kept low and in-
formal, and a refreshing contrast to the usual pompous

monuments to municipal pride. Built in the 1960s, they do their job with the minimum of fuss. At the back is the Avenue of Remembrance, lined on either side with lime trees, each with a plaque commemorating a Sittingbourne man killed in the First World War; an extension planted with copper beeches leads off the main avenue. Few war memorials anywhere show such a blend of practicality and imagination. North of the High Street you are plunged almost at once into industry, with the vast paper mills in New Road. You can get the best idea of this side of the town by going down Crown Quay Lane, which fades away into the wharves of Milton Creek amid an oddly romantic landscape of salt flats, streams and inlets, dotted with factories and timber yards, and the occasional grazing horse or cow. At the end of a track off Crown Quay Lane the **Dolphin Sailing Barge Museum** has been opened in an old tarred wooden building (open weekends). Photographs, models, charts and drawings revive the great days of the red-sailed barges, while in the creek outside dismasted hulls settle gently into the mud.

Far older than Sittingbourne is **Milton Regis**, now relegated to the status of a suburb. The 'Rex' of the name was reputedly King Alfred. Its steep High Street, lined with decrepit timber-framed and Georgian houses, is a bedlam of lorries carrying gigantic rolls of paper; at its summit is a little green, with a splendidly preserved fifteenth-century court hall at one side of it. The courtroom is on the first floor; on the ground level is the lock-up, with low barred doors. Milton's centre would make an ideal candidate for preservation, as it is not yet too far gone. The magnificent church (usually locked, key at children's home next door) is north of the town, on the edge of the marshes. Its huge black flint tower dominates a bleak outlook of saltings, power lines and a gull-covered rubbish tip. It was probably built in the early fourteenth century, but incorporates much earlier work, including Roman tiles from settlements near by. Inside it consists of nave, chancel, and south aisle, flooded with light from the big windows; strangely, there is no chancel arch. Along the nave are well preserved text boards, gilt-painted on black.

Half a mile to the north is **Kemsley Village**, built in the 1920s to house the workers at the enormous paper mills (now Bowaters) near by. The village is more like a forces' married quarters than anything else, consisting of pseudo-Georgian houses, and a social centre with a wooden cupola perched on top.

The road to Sheppey runs through **Iwade**, an unpretentious village which could be pleasant enough if the traffic gave it a chance. The church is a rustic, rough-hewn place, with a north wall that leans outwards at such an angle it seems incredible it still stands up.

The gateway to **Sheppey** is through the monumental twin archway of **Kingsferry Bridge**, 'like some great megalith', says John Newman, in his book *West Kent and the Weald*. The central section of the bridge lifts vertically for boats passing up or down the Swale; sail has right of way over road traffic, and the mightiest of diesel juggernauts have to wait while yachts pass underneath. Once over the bridge, you see why the island got its name: Sheppey means 'sheep island', and the low-lying marsh grasslands are still dotted with sheep. However, in much of Sheppey this is changing, and over on the other side of the island, near Harty, the land is being deep drained and ploughed into enormous prairie-like fields.

In the Middle Ages ships to and from London tended to avoid the north coast of Sheppey and used the Swale instead; and so in the 1360s Edward III built a castle at the northern end of the Swale to guard this important sea passage, naming it **Queenborough** in honour of Queen Philippa. The castle has vanished, but Queenborough still has vestiges of its history as a busy harbour town, notably in the High Street, which looks like a poor relation of old Portsmouth. Though it is ramshackle and run-down, Queenborough has plenty of assets which deserve to be salvaged. The view of the Medway estuary from the quay at the end of the High Street is superb: a wide seascape of boats from Thames barges to tankers, with the gleaming spheres of the Grain refinery in the background, and the inescapable giant chimney of the Kingsnorth power station. South of the High Street a narrow creek brings small boats right into the heart of the town. The eighteenth-century Guildhall, with a fine light council chamber built above an arcade, makes a dignified centrepiece to the battered buildings known to Hogarth and Nelson. The church, built about 1350, is an unassuming place, without aisles or separate chancel. The roof is completely boarded in; towards the end of the seventeenth century it was painted all over to look like blue sky, with clouds, stars, and angels in medallions. New life for Queenborough might start with the restoration of this almost-vanished decoration. **Deadmans Island**, a muddy flat across the Swale, was the burial ground of sailors and passengers who died while in quarantine, and also of prisoners in the Medway hulks.

Sheppey's prosperity is concentrated in **Sheerness**, where the Medway joins the Thames. Sheerness is an extraordinary jumble of a place, a mixture of funfair switchbacks, classical harbour buildings, factories and caravans. Though it is not obvious, Sheerness is an island beyond an island, as at the southern end of the town an artificial waterway cuts off the triangular tip of Sheppey. As early as 1547 a gun battery was set up on Garrison Point to guard the Medway, but nothing much was done about Sheerness until the defences were destroyed by the Dutch fleet under De Ruyter in 1667 (see Upnor, p. 38). Two years later a strong fortress was built at Garrison Point, and a naval dockyard, surveyed before the Dutch attack by Samuel Pepys, was laid out on the sheltered side of the point.

In 1797 Sheerness and its offshore waters were the scene of the great Nore mutiny. The sailors of the Nore Command presented a list of grievances to the commander in chief, were rejected, and took the law into their own hands, hoisting the red flag of mutiny and compelling other crews to join them. At the outset the inhabitants of Sheerness were sympathetic and supported the mutineers ('carnival with a grim undercurrent' is T. J. Woodthorpe's phrase in his history of Sheppey); but they eventually swung round to the Government, and supplies to the mutineers were cut off. The outcome was inevitable: the mutineers surrendered, four hundred sailors were arrested, and the ringleader was courtmartialled and executed.

As you come into Sheerness from Queenborough, you drive below the high frowning brick walls of the dockyard, which take up the whole of one side of West Street and continue round the corner into the High Street. The dockyard's administrative buildings, dating from the early nineteenth century, consist of a large classical compound brightened by garish figureheads; unfortunately the public can get no farther than the security guard at the main entrance. However, you can get a good idea of the rest of the scheme from Naval Terrace, now private houses, outside the main enclosure, and the large brick dockyard church, complete with portico, which has been turned into a youth centre. In 1960 the Admiralty sold the dockyard, and since 1969 it has been run as an up-to-date commercial harbour by the Medway Ports Authority.

The High Street still consists mainly of little two-storey early nineteenth-century houses; it peters out before crossing the zigzag moat that formed part of the old fortifications, and then begins again at the comical blue clock tower which is the nearest approach Sheerness has to a town centre. The main public buildings are in Broadway, which begins at the tower; the parish church, built of yellow brick, pinnacles and all, in the 1830s, has little of interest except a strange bronze memorial plaque, covered with Masonic symbols, on the outside of the west wall.

There is no coast road on Sheppey; to get from Sheerness to the island's villages you have to go inland, as far as the aptly named Halfway Houses.

East of Sheerness is the high ground that forms the spine of Sheppey and was the first part of the island to be settled. The beginnings of **Minster**, now a nondescript seaside town, go back to the seventh century, when a nunnery was founded there by St Sexburga. About 670 Sexburga, the widow of Ercombert, a Saxon king of Kent, established a nunnery (*monasterium*, hence Minster) on Sheppey. Destroyed by the Danes in 855 and attacked two hundred years later by Earl Godwin, it was re-established and rebuilt on a grand scale about 1130. The abbey church, which incorporates some of the earlier Saxon building, stands on the crest of a hill above what remains of Minster's old village centre. It is in effect a complete double church. On the north side is the monastic church or 'Nun's Chapel', and on the south the parish church, added in the thirteenth century when the arcade was pierced through the original south wall. The west tower is oddly truncated, topped by a low timber belfry; it was left unfinished when the Dissolution finally put a stop to building.

Inside the impression is one of peaceful spaciousness, with the light interior of the parochial church in contrast to the comparative gloom of the Nun's Chapel. There are some magnificent monuments, forming a textbook of medieval clothes and armour. On the south wall is the canopied tomb of Sir Robert de Shurland, who was Baron of Sheppey and Lord Warden of the Cinque Ports, and died about 1310. Behind the armoured effigy is carved a horse's head rising from the waves. According to one of R. H. Barham's *Ingoldsby Legends*, this is de Shurland's horse, Grey Dolphin. After killing a priest, the baron had been banished from the court, but hearing that the king was at anchor off Sheppey, he mounted Grey Dolphin, swam out to the ship, was pardoned, and swam back to shore. When he landed, a local witch prophesied that the horse would be his death, whereupon he drew his sword and cut off the noble animal's head. Months later, walking along the shore, he kicked the skeleton, injured his toe and died as a result, fulfilling the prophecy. An alternative explanation for the horse's head is that it was placed on the tomb to show that de Shurland, as Lord Warden, had the privilege of 'wreck of sea' – the right to ride into water at low tide and claim possession of anything washed up on shore by touching it with the tip of his lance. Across the church, in the north-east corner of the Nun's Chapel, is a fifteenth-century effigy, possibly of the unfortunate George Plantagenet, Duke of Clarence, whom Richard III murdered by drowning in a butt of malmsey wine. In the south chancel are two splendid brasses to Sir John de Northwode, in meticulously detailed armour, and his wife Lady Joan, wearing kirtle and wimple; they date from about 1330.

West of the church is the abbey gatehouse, a squat fifteenth-century building, still in good repair. The entrance arch is exceptionally wide.

Eastchurch is still a small country village, with a Perpendicular church hardly altered since it was built in the 1430s. On the south side of the chancel is a sumptuous effigied tomb to Gabriel Livesey (died 1622) and his wife Anne, with an inscription that makes no concessions to the passer-by:

> Thou that dost read these lines shall lye among
> Wormes bones and rotten carkesses er long.

Two lurid windows in the south aisle commemorate the flying pioneers Charles Stewart Rolls (partner of the Rolls-

Royce team) and Cecil Grace, both killed in flying accidents in 1910. Across the road is what looks at first glance like a typical inscribed war memorial wall behind a small garden, but in fact commemorates the founders of British aviation. All the great names – Moore-Brabazon, Rolls, Sopwith – are there, and on either side the stone is carved with small replicas of the primitive biplanes and triplanes in which they made those early lurching flights. Many of the flyers operated from East-church aerodrome, down the road that leads south from the village; the buildings are now a prison. In 1909, at Shell Beach, near Leysdown, Moore-Brabazon became the first British pilot to carry out a circular flight of one mile, and Charles Rolls at much the same time made a two-mile flight from Eastchurch aerodrome round the church tower and back.

Leysdown-on-Sea is a wilderness of holiday camps, chalets and caravan sites, with the consolation of vast views across the Thames estuary. On one side the dark brown landslides of **Warden Point** show where Sheppey is constantly losing its high ground to the sea, and on the other the marshes join the mudflats, the happy hunting-grounds of bait-diggers and bird-watchers.

A narrow road half way between Leysdown and Eastchurch zigzags down to **Harty**, a forgotten land which is the epitome of Sheppey. It has its own medieval church (at Sayes Court on the one-inch map), a neglected gem of a building along a farm track. Inside the lighting is still by paraffin lamps and candles; at the west end a rough timber framework supports the bellcote, and in the south chapel is a unique fourteenth-century chest, carved on the front panel with a pair of jousting knights and their squires. At the end of the road a long, low-built pub called the Ferry House looks across the Swale to the steeple of Faversham church. When Harty Ferry was open it was less than a mile by water, but it is now twenty-seven miles by road. The pub's landlord hopes eventually to reopen a passenger service from one bank to the other. At the moment all you can do is gaze across at the promised land, before the long trek back to the Kingsferry Bridge and Sittingbourne.

East of Sittingbourne, the fruit-growing farmlands are dotted with little villages on either side of the A 2. Nearest is **Bapchild**, whose delightful name has nothing to do with baptism, but comes from the Saxon Beccancelde, meaning either 'unhealthy chill water', or 'spring of the brook'. The church is a pretty little building, just off the main road, with a tall broach spire and a cool, white-painted interior. It is mainly Norman and Transitional; the capitals of the chalk pillars are carved with a different design on each. Behind the altar in the Lady Chapel is a long, low mural of the crucifixion, painted about 1300 and much faded. An unusual object to find in a church is a mammoth's tooth, kept in a glass case.

Rodmersham, half a mile south of Bapchild, consists mainly of prosperous Georgian farmhouses. The flint church (kept locked) has a startlingly red roof and a good Perpendicular battlemented west tower; inside there is a fifteenth-century wooden screen between chancel and side chapel, incorporating three wooden sedilia. **Tonge**, north of the main road, is hardly a village at all — just a small barn-like church in an overgrown churchyard, and a watermill which was once powered by water from the dammed-up moat of Tonge Castle. Lambarde quotes a rhyme, old in his day, perhaps deriving from the low-lying nature of the country:

> He that will not live long,
> Let him dwell at Muston, Tenham, or Tong.

Murston is a suburb of Sittingbourne; **Teynham** is a scattered village down the A 2, built partly along the main road, and partly round the station half a mile away. In Lambarde's time Teynham was the centre of fruitgrowing in Kent, where in the reign of King Henry VIII a certain Richard Harris 'planted by his great coste and rare industrie, the sweet Cherry, the temperate Pipyn, and the golden Renate', making Teynham 'the most dainty piece of all our Shyre'. The remote church is north of the railway, hidden behind farm buildings and fruit trees, and overlooking a large hop garden. You get to it down a track and through a thatched lychgate. The cruciform interior, thirteenth-century with fifteenth-century arcades, is brilliantly lit through the huge east window. At **Conyer** the road ends beside a muddy creek crammed with small boats.

Lynsted, due south across the A 2, has the perfect village centre, consisting of a church, pub and a few houses on top of a hill, with a cluster of half-timbered houses below. In 1967 it won the award for the best-kept village in East Kent. The church (kept locked) has a tower at the north-west corner with shingled broach spire and boarded belfry; the three gables of the eastern end dominate the village.

It is hard to imagine anyone not liking **Faversham**. It has streets of fine old houses, a creek that brings the sea right into the heart of the town, and enough industry to keep it from becoming just another stagnant beauty-spot. In many ways it is like Sittingbourne, but fortunately for Faversham the main road runs a little to the south, and it has never been torn apart by modern traffic – at least until the recent establishment of lorry depots there. **Faversham Creek** was in use at least as early as Roman times, and the Romans had a settlement called Durolevum in the vicinity. The name first appears in a charter of the Saxon king Coenwulf as 'the King's little town of Fafresham'; and early in the Middle Ages it was important enough to be given status as a 'limb' of the Cinque Port of Dover. As the importance of its port declined, new industries, notably gunpowder manufacture and brewing, kept Faversham prosperous; and it gives the impression of a town that has kept on a thoroughly even keel. The port still carries on a modest trade, and small coasting vessels are built here.

In its general layout, it has not altered substantially since Edward Jacob, a local historian, described it two centuries ago. 'It principally consists of four long spacious and well paved streets, forming a somewhat irregular cross, in the center whereof stands a convenient market-place, over which is the guildhall'. Jacob's own solid Georgian-fronted house is in Preston Street, the southern arm of the cross, opposite the large redbrick council offices; it is worth going into the council building for the cases of ancient Faversham documents on view inside. The old Fleur-de-Lis inn nearby is being converted into a local museum. West Street and East Street, at right-angles to Preston Street, run from one side of the town to the other, centring on the big white-painted Ship Hotel, a coaching inn built over an alley. The smartly-painted Guildhall is an early-nineteenth-century rebuilding of an Elizabethan market hall; the original sturdy wooden pillars of the arcade seem to bulge from the weight of masonry above them. Behind the hall is a fancifully ornate cast-iron Victorian pump, picked out in red, white and black.

The northern arm of the 'irregular cross' begins here, and consists of Court Street and its continuation Abbey Street. Court Street is wide and dignified, a good mixture of timbered gables and overhangs, Georgian brickwork and Victorian frontages, all harmonising together. The street is full of the smell of brewing from the huge Whitbread-Fremlin brewery on its eastern side. Faversham's own brewery, Shepherd Neame, is directly opposite; it has been there since 1698, and keeps its workings discreetly hidden away between Court Street and the creek.

At the top of Court Street, between the cottages of Church Street, you get a sudden close-up view of the most astonishing sight in Faversham – the tall west tower of the Parish Church, surmounted by a delicately fretted pinnacle of stone. This soaring steeple, like a spire with its insides cut away, was put up at the end of the eighteenth century, and is a copy of Wren's steeple on the City church of St Dunstan's-in-the-East. You can see it from all directions: in the distance from the M 2, from the shore of Sheppey, or closer at hand across the saltings towards Oare. Inside, the church is just as extraordinary. The nave was completely rebuilt in 1755 by George Dance, at a time when the central tower was found to be unsafe and taken down; Dance's arcades of elephantine Tuscan columns make a grotesque contrast with the chancel and transepts built four and a half centuries earlier. In the north transept one of the octagonal pillars still has some of its original painted decoration, done at the time of the building about 1305. Near by the vast effigy of Edward Fagg (died 1618) reclines on his tomb, while his wife, reduced to midget size, kneels beside him. The choir misericords are well worth looking at; they include a flute player, and various other human, demonic or animal figures. In the south chapel is a Decorated stone tomb canopy, with a plaque that suggests it may be the resting place of King Stephen. He was buried in Faversham Abbey church; at the Dissolution, so the story goes, his bones were dug up and thrown into Faversham Creek, but subsequently salvaged and reburied in the parish church.

Faversham's great abbey, founded by King Stephen in 1147, stood a little way north of the church, on a site now occupied by school playing fields. Excavations in the 1960s showed that the abbey church was enormous, nearly three hundred feet long. The abbey was approached along Abbey Street, the northern continuation of Court Street and one of the showplaces of Faversham, now that many of the buildings have been rescued from near-dereliction and impeccably restored, under the auspices of the Borough Council and the Historic Buildings Council. All that is left of the abbey is the guesthouse, now called **Arden's House,** a large half-timbered house with jutting first and second storeys; the stone-built walls incorporated part of the outer gateway. Its name perpetuates Faversham's most notorious scandal – the murder of Thomas Arden, by his wife and her lover. After the abbey was dissolved in 1538, Arden (or Arderne, as the name was often spelt) got possession of some of the abbey lands and set himself up in the guesthouse, eventually becoming mayor of the town. His wife Alice took a lover, Thomas Mosby, and the two of them decided to murder Arden. In collusion with two sinister accomplices called Loosebagg and Black Will, they made a number of unsuccessful attempts on his life. On the night of February 15, 1551, as Arden was playing a game of 'tables' (draughts or backgammon) with Mosby in the parlour, he was finally done away with. In the words of the Faversham Wardmote Book: 'Black Will . . . came with a napkyn in his hand, and sodenlye came behind the said Ardern's back, threw the said napkyn over his hedd and face, and strangled him, and forthwith the said Mosby stept to him, and strake him with a taylor's great pressing Iron upon the scull to the braine, and immediately drew out his dagger, which was great and broad, and therewith cut the said Ardern's throat.' After this butchery the accomplices dragged the body to a field at the back of the house and left it there. They were nearly all arrested and executed. Alice was burned to death at Canterbury, Mosby was hanged at Smithfield and Black Will was caught and burned at Flushing; only Loosebagg seems to have escaped.

The grim story, told by Holinshed in his *Chronicles*, was taken up by an unknown playwright, who wrote *The Lamentable and True Tragedie of Master Arden of Feversham in Kent*, first published in 1592. This sulphurously lurid melodrama broke right away from the tradition that only great rulers were suitable subjects for tragedy; at one time it was suggested that Shakespeare was the author, as in the play the name of Loosebag is changed to Shakebagg. Not only are the characters drawn from life, but the settings are realistic as well: the playwright brings in Rainham, Sittingbourne and Sheppey, and the streets and inns of Faversham.

Behind Arden's House a treelined footpath leads down to the church past the original grammar school, an arcaded and weatherboarded building of 1587 now used as a masonic hall. Looking across Abbey Street from the house you have a good view over the waters of the creek; and at the end of Abbey Street is the quay where Arden carried on a lucrative business as commissioner of customs, with a long Tudor brick-and-timber warehouse which he might have known. In Conduit Street, behind the Shepherd Neame brewery, the fifteenth-century timbered town storehouse on the quay has a new lease of life as the headquarters of the local sea cadets, rechristened Training Ship 'Hasarde'.

As was said earlier, until recently Faversham's main industry, apart from beer, was the making of gunpowder, which began there at least as early as Queen Elizabeth's reign. At the **Chart Gunpowder Mills** (off South Road and buried among the new houses of Nobel Court) you can get some idea of the manufacturing process; the mills, powered by a large waterwheel, are being restored by the Faversham Society, and eventually a powder-substitute will be mixed and passed through the mechanism. They date from the late eighteenth century, and are the oldest of their kind in the world to survive intact. Explosions were an ever-present risk. A particularly bad one took place in 1847 with the advent of guncotton (cotton steeped in nitric acid and sulphuric acid), when a new factory out on the marshes to the north blew up. Twenty people were killed, trees within fifty yards were uprooted, and the explosion was heard nearly as far as Maidstone. Even worse was a TNT explosion in 1916, when more than a hundred employees lost their lives. The last works were closed in 1934. Near the Gunpowder Mills, in South Road, is a monumental range of gabled almshouses; built in the 1860s, they are a fine example of Victorian philanthropy on the largest scale.

The gunpowder industry features prominently among the historical exhibits in the **Maison Dieu, Ospringe**, back on the

A 2, on the corner of Ospringe Street and Water Lane. This building consists of a timber-framed hall and stone undercroft, which formed part of a thirteenth-century hospital outside the bounds of Faversham; like all medieval hospitals, it was used by travellers as well as the sick and the infirm. The building on the other side of Water Lane has a similar undercroft. The hospital's chief buildings were on the north side of the main road and have vanished. Upstairs in the Maison Dieu are cases containing dozens of funeral urns from Roman burial sites round Ospringe. The Victorian saddle-backed tower of Ospringe church, a landmark as you drive along the M 2, lies below the road embankment, half a mile south of the Maison Dieu. The church is worth going into for the splendid reclining alabaster figure of James Master (died 1631) in his shroud. Across the road is the half-timbered Queen Court, on the site of a medieval manor house granted by Henry III to Queen Eleanor.

Faversham's southern suburb, **Preston**, has a nice medieval church among the modern housing estates. Inside there are exceptional fourteenth-century sedilia, with carved faces peering through the holes in the canopy above. There is also a grandiose tomb to Roger and Joan Boyle, grandparents of Robert Boyle, the philosopher and scientist who propounded Boyle's Law. On the western side of the town is **Davington**, again mainly modern housing. The pyramid-capped tower of the Norman church stands prominently on a hill; it forms part of **Davington Priory**, founded in 1153, which looks like a gabled manor house but in fact incorporates part of the monastic buildings.

Beyond Davington is **Oare**, a trim yachting village on a branch of Faversham Creek. Past Oare church the road ends on the south side of Harty Ferry, with a causeway leading down to the soft mud of the Swale.

Graveney, above the marshes east of Faversham, is hardly more than a hamlet but has a superb church, mainly fourteenth-century, with a low battlemented tower and startlingly red tiled roof. Inside it has the light-flooded look of a Romney Marsh church. In the north aisle is a magnificent fifteenth-century canopied brass to John Martyn and his wife Anne; he is shown in the robes of a High Court judge and holds a heart inscribed 'Jhu mcy' (Jhesu Mercy). At the feet of the figures is an inscription in Latin couplets. The church still has its old box pews.

Hernhill, on the other side of the Whitstable road, is a complete contrast. The village is enclosed by orchards; in front of the tree-filled churchyard is a small green, with neat white houses behind. The church is a Perpendicular building, with battlemented west tower.

The woods between Hernhill and **Dunkirk** saw the last of the Kentish risings against authority. In the 1830s a Cornishman called John Nichols Thom settled in the area, took the name of Sir William Percy Honeywood Courtenay, and in 1832 stood as parliamentary candidate for Canterbury, dressed as a 'Knight of Malta', as he styled himself. He spent some years in a lunatic asylum, and on his release at the end of 1837 proclaimed himself the Messiah and gathered a band of about a hundred disciples, mainly downtrodden farm labourers. In May 1838 a warrant was issued for his arrest, but he shot the constable's brother and retreated into the woods, taking his followers with him. Troops were sent in; Thom shot the officer who called on him to surrender, and was then killed himself, with several of his followers. One reason for the dissatisfaction of the locals was said to be the lack of a church, and so in 1840 **Dunkirk** church was built. The pub opposite is fittingly called the Sir William Courtenay.

Boughton Street, back towards Faversham, is a long straight village sundered by the A2 traffic, with an impressive number of half-timbered and Georgian houses; fortunately a bypass is planned. Boughton (or Boughton under Blean) church is down back roads to the south, at the top of a hill behind a large farm. It has good Early English lancets in the nave, and in the north aisle a magnificent monument to Sir Thomas Hawkins and his wife Ann, by the seventeenth-century sculptor Epiphanius Evesham. Husband and wife recline above the tomb, and their mourning sons and daughters are carved on alabaster panels at the side.

The last village on the pilgrim's journey to Canterbury was **Harbledown**, and Chaucer put it near the end of his tales:

> Woot ye nat where ther stant a litel toun,
> Which that y-cleped is Bobbe-up-and-doun,
> Under the Blee in Caunterbury weye?

Nothing could better describe the switchback of Harbledown; though 'Roar-up-and-down' would be a better description of the traffic that tears it in half. Over the brow of the hill past the parish church the pilgrims would have seen the cathedral (though trees now hide it), and would no doubt have speeded up from an amble to a canter, as the gait of horses on the road to Canterbury was called, in abbreviation for 'Canterbury gallop'. A disapproving Lollard, William Thorpe, gave a typically killjoy view of the pilgrims: 'They will ordaine to have with them both men and women that can well sing wanton songs; and some other pilgrimes will have with them bagpipes; so that in everie town that they come through, what with the noise of their singing, and with the sound of their piping, and with the jangling of their Canterburie bels, and with the barking out of dogs after them, they make more noise than if the king came there away.'

St Nicholas's Hospital for lepers at Harbledown was one of the minor attractions of the journey, as it had a relic of Becket – one of his shoes, which the pilgrims kissed as they passed by. Early in the sixteenth century the shoe was still being offered, as it was to Erasmus and Colet, two men of the new age. Erasmus was not openly hostile; but Colet was self-righteously offensive, asking the company, in Lambarde's account of the occasion, 'What mean these beasts, that we should kiss the shoes of all good men? why doe they not by the same reason offer us their spittle, and other excrements of the body to be kissed?' The hospital was founded by Archbishop Lanfranc in 1084. When leprosy died out in the next couple of centuries it became a general hospital, and is now almshouses. The small Norman church is a bare simple building, with hardly any decoration except for one capital carved with a head sprouting wings.

Down the hills below the almshouses is a spring called the **Black Prince's Well**; the three feathers of the Prince of Wales's arms are carved over the arch of the well. The water is said to be medicinal, which may account for the fact that the hospital was built near by.

CHAPTER FOUR

Canterbury

✤

FOR over eight hundred years **Canterbury** has been a place of pilgrimage; yet Becket's murder is only the half way point in the immense span of centuries that separates us from the establishment of Canterbury as a Christian centre. The ruins of St Augustine's Abbey, outside the town walls, are a good place to sense this continuity. You can stand by a ruined wall of Roman brick built by Augustine's followers at the end of the sixth century, and look across the playing fields to the chapel of a new teachers' training college shaped in the most up-to-the-minute way in the form of two soaring glass and concrete wings. Between these two visible manifestations comes the whole history of English Christendom: the conversion of Kent, the procession of archbishops who constantly tore down and rebuilt as their architects and masons explored the technology of stone, the martyrdom of Becket and the explosive prosperity his shrine brought to cathedral and city, the desecration and plunder of the Dissolution, the moulder-ing but picturesque decrepitude of the eighteenth century, the Victorian upsurge of interest in all things ecclesiastical, our own desire to conserve and embellish what is already there. Running parallel is the secular story of Canterbury as a prosperous town, living its own life and more concerned with the state of the hopfields than with the soaring grandeur of the cathedral's Bell Harry Tower.

Most visitors to Canterbury, like Chaucer's pilgrims, make straight for the cathedral, though unlike the pilgrims they can no longer see Becket's jewel-encrusted tomb, destroyed long ago by Thomas Cromwell's men, who took twenty-six cartloads of booty away with them. But in many ways it is best to leave the cathedral until last, though any exploration of Canterbury will take you past it continually, and you are never out of sight of it for long. Canterbury is not a city to be

rushed through. It is a place of sudden surprises, of little gardens opening up between buildings, of medieval stonework glimpsed across the river, of plaques on the wall and stones set in the pavement as reminders of things vanished.

Looked at on the map, Canterbury is like a crossbow, with the town walls forming the sharply reflexed arms of the bow and the Stour like a slack bowstring at the walls' two ends. The main street forms the stock of the bow, running north-west to Whitstable and south-east to Dover. For the purpose of exploration, the city falls neatly into three parts: St Peter's Street, the Westgate and all the area north-west of the Stour; the cathedral and the streets immediately round it; and the remaining quadrant, largely blitzed in 1942 and the scene of Canterbury's major rebuilding scheme, on the other side of the High Street. The area beyond the walls is not so easily defined; but apart from the university nothing worth looking at is more than twenty minutes' walk from the town centre.

When you walk round the city walls of Canterbury, you are following the original outline of the Roman town. But though the gates still correspond to the Roman gateways, nothing survives of the original Roman grid plan of streets. In Roman times Canterbury was not a garrison town but an administrative and residential centre, an embodiment of the benefits brought by the *pax Romana* to an already civilised part of England. When the Romans came for good in the middle of the first century they are unlikely to have found much of a settlement; the Belgic tribes probably had their stronghold at Bigbury, on the hills near Harbledown. But after pacification it was natural that an important town should grow where Watling Street (the London–Dover road) crossed the Stour (here divided into two arms), with other arteries of the road system radiating to Richborough and Lympne. Kent was so peaceful that walls were not needed until the end of the third century, when Saxon pirates were becoming a serious menace. Roman Canterbury had the usual baths and forum, an amphitheatre, and large villas. Part of the mosaic pavement of one of them, well below ground level, can be seen off Butchery Lane. The Roman name for the town, Durovernum Cantiacorum (Durovernum of the Kent men) probably perpetuates the original name, as the Celtic prefix *dwr-* is found where there is water to be crossed (compare Durobrivae for

Rochester). The modern name comes straight from the Anglo-Saxon Cantwarabyrig, the burgh or stronghold of the men of Kent.

So the popular picture of Augustine landing in Kent in 597 to convert a mob of savages is grotesquely inaccurate. It is true that for nearly two centuries since the withdrawal of Roman troops England had split into petty kingdoms; but a civilisation as all-embracing as the Roman does not vanish overnight. The king of Kent, Ethelbert, was a pagan, but his wife Bertha, daughter of the Frankish king, was a Christian, and on her marriage had brought Bishop Liudhard with her as her private chaplain. Liudhard had already been in England about twenty years when he asked Pope Gregory for help in the work of conversion, so that Augustine found his work well begun, and Ethelbert no doubt already half-convinced. In his brief seven years as archbishop, Augustine established Christianity as the official religion, set up an efficient church administration, and – most important of all from the point of view of Canterbury – built a priory in the present cathedral precincts, and the abbey that bears his name outside the walls. I have already mentioned the contrast between old and new that you can see from the Abbey grounds. Even more evocative is the tall stone pillar that stands in a corner of the ruins. Perhaps it was the phallic pagan monolith worshipped by King Ethelbert in his chapel, while Queen Bertha made her way through the Quenin (or Queen-in) Gate, past the future site of the abbey, to St Martin's church on the side of the hill near by.

The site of **St Augustine's Abbey** was chosen for two reasons: first, it was more suitable for the life of contemplation outside the bustle of the city; and second, the early church did not permit burial within a town's walls. This was the burial place of the early archbishops – St Augustine himself, and his successors Sts Lawrence, Mellitus and Justus (the empty tombs are now under a protecting roof); of Ethelbert, Bertha and Liudhard; and of later kings. The Saxon complex of abbey church, side chapels and ancillary buildings was swept away at the end of the eleventh century, when the great twin-towered abbey church was built almost as large as the cathedral itself. This church was torn down in its turn, along with the cloister and other monastic buildings, at the Dissolu-

tion, and the stone was shipped across the Channel for the
fortifications of Calais, or sold to local builders. What was
left was turned into a royal staging-post on the journey from
London to Dover; hence the Tudor brickwork above the
blocked up Norman arcading of the north aisle. Much of the
north-west tower, known as Ethelbert's Tower, stood until
1822. A drawing made shortly before it finally fell shows
wonderfully rich and complex interlaced arcading, rising
above a peaceful pastoral scene.

The various levels of abbey ruins make them hard to un-
ravel; the little **Church of St Pancras** to the east is simplicity
itself by comparison. Built of Roman brick, almost certainly
by Augustine, it was at one time thought to have been Ethelbert's idol-chapel before his conversion. The surviving brick
window arch at the east end is from a fourteenth-century rebuilding, using Roman bricks.

West of the abbey is **St Augustine's College** (open Wed. and
Thurs.), built in the 1840s to train missionaries for Australia,
and still a missionary college. It incorporates the abbey gatehouse, built about 1300 by Abbot Fyndon and known as the
Fyndon Gate. Charles I and Queen Henrietta Maria spent
their wedding night in the chamber over the gate in 1625, but
with the abbey's decline as a staging-post it fell on hard times,
ending up as brewery and beer-garden before being salvaged
for the missionaries. William Butterfield's flint-built quadrangle is far more austere than the fanciful turrets and decorated stonework of the Fyndon Gate. The medieval refectory,
much restored, is still used as the college dining hall; and
below the chapel is a vaulted undercroft, with panels recording
the generations of missionaries who trained at St Augustine's
before going out to Pretoria or Jamaica, Quebec or Zanzibar.

St Martin's Church, where Queen Bertha worshipped, is the
oldest church in continuous use in this country. It was founded
well before 597, and the chancel certainly goes back to this
time. In all probability this was the original Christian church
of Roman Durovernum, built in the third or fourth century
and surviving the pagan interregnum. The Venerable Bede
describes how Queen Bertha began attending services there
as soon as she arrived in England in 562, thirty-five years
before Augustine's arrival. Until Ethelbert's conversion,
Augustine used St Martin's as his base; and it seems likely

that the font inside the church was the one used to baptise Ethelbert and his courtiers. The western end of the chancel, built largely of Roman brick, was no doubt Bertha's original chapel. The western wall of the church is even older, and is thought to have been the wall of the original Roman church, restored and reused when a larger building was needed by Augustine. Though the view from the churchyard is largely blocked by the high walls of the prison, you can get magnificent end-on glimpses of the cathedral away in the distance.

This excursion outside the walls sets the scene for the Canterbury we all know, or feel we know – the Canterbury of narrow crooked streets and timber-framed houses projecting over the pavements, not all that different (if you disregard the shopfronts and close your ears to the traffic) from the town familiar to the Knight and the Pardoner, the Miller, the Reeve and the Wife of Bath. Starting at St George's Gate and walking straight through the town to Westgate, you pass many of the most interesting buildings, besides getting an idea of the small scale of the town (the main street is hardly half a mile from end to end). First, on the right, is the tower of **St George's** – all that was left after the blitz of the church where Christopher Marlowe was baptised in 1564. On the same side is a new shopping precinct, the Longmarket, with the **Roman mosaic** already mentioned in an alley off Butchery Lane. The pavement is shown in a large vaulted room, along with brooches and pottery, and the remains of a hypocaust. The medieval trading tradition of Butchery Lane is carried on by a butcher with a large blood-red bullock's head over his shop window.

Here St George's Street becomes the **High Street**. On the corner of Mercery Lane are the mighty overhanging beams of a pilgrims' inn, the Chequer of the Hope (now a tobacconist's), which once stretched right back to the Buttermarket. A little farther on the left is the half-timbered house known as Queen Elizabeth's Guest Chamber, dated 1573, with a cheerful frieze of painted and moulded cupids, grapes and barrels at second-floor level. Then comes White Horse Lane, and across it the County Hotel, built on the site of the twelfth-century house of Jacob the Jew. Opposite is an incongruous piece of redbrick Victorianism, the **Beaney Institute**, now the museum and public library. James George Beaney was one of the most colourful characters produced by nineteenth-century Canterbury. Born in 1826, he trained as a doctor, and as a young man went out to Australia. He returned to take part in the Crimean War, and then settled for good in Melbourne, where he had a profitable but chequered medical practice; he was tried twice for manslaughter and once for murder after unsuccessful operations. He never forgot his birthplace, and when he died in 1891 he left Canterbury £11,000 to found the Institute. The museum is small and well laid out, with cases among other things of fine Roman glassware, coins minted at Canterbury, and Anglo-Saxon jewellery, including the exquisite little cruciform brooch whose shape forms the 'Canterbury cross' used as the symbol of the town.

A few yards farther on the road rises to King's Bridge over the Stour. On the left is **Eastbridge Hospital**, founded soon after Becket's death as a hostel for poor pilgrims. They paid fourpence a night for the use of the lofty refectory hall, the chapel and the chill vaults below. When a fireplace was removed in the hall a magnificent tempera painting was uncovered, thought to be contemporary with the building, showing Christ giving his blessing in a gesture of Byzantine remoteness. The hospital is still used as an almshouse, one of its original functions. Across the river, on the right-hand side, are the timbered gables of the **Canterbury Weavers** house – one of the many houses taken over by Protestant weavers from the Continent towards the end of the sixteenth century, after the Massacre of St Bartholomew in France and the Spanish persecution in the Low Countries Beyond the Weavers you can see the town ducking-stool, a joke nowadays but in reality a homely and effective instrument of torture, as anyone who has struggled for breath under water will know. Over the river the High Street becomes St Peter's Street, taking its name from a medieval church set back behind a small garden, a building thought to be on the site of a Roman church, with Saxon work and Roman tiles in the bell tower.

The splendid **Westgate** loses much of its impressiveness by being isolated as a traffic island and by having buses continually scraping under its arches. In its day it must have been an effective part of the fortifications. For a long time it was used as the town prison. The Rev. William Gostling, a canon of the cathedral, wrote in his *Walk in and about the*

City of Canterbury, with a proper eighteenth-century sense of self-satisfaction: 'This gate is now the city prison, both for debtors and criminals, with a large and high-pitched room over the gateway, and others in the towers. The way up to them is through a grated cage in the gate, level with the street, where the prisoners, who are not more closely confined, may discourse with passengers, receive their alms, and warn them (by their distress) to manage their liberty and property to the best advantage.' Upstairs you can still visit the room over the gateway, with a cell in each corner and the wooden condemned cell against an inside wall, and an odd collection of mantraps and boneshaker bicycles. From the roof there is an excellent view across the red-tiled roofs of the town to the west end of the cathedral.

Beyond the Westgate is St Dunstan's Street, as pretty as anything in Canterbury – at least until the level crossing is reached. Most famous, and photographed, is The House of Agnes Hotel, a gabled building reputedly the home of Agnes Wickfield, in *David Copperfield*. Over the level crossing is **St Dunstan's**, the church where King Henry II changed into penitent's clothes before walking barefoot through the streets to the cathedral, to be scourged before Becket's tomb. Another and later Chancellor who came to a violent end is associated with St Dunstan's. When Sir Thomas More was executed on Tower Hill in 1535, his daughter, Margaret Roper, obtained his head; after her death it was buried in the Roper family vault below the church.

On either side of St Peter's Street the city is an inconsequential place, little more than an unplanned island between the two branches of the Stour. Yet it has two of the riverside corners of Canterbury most worth hunting out – the **Black Friars** below the bridge, and the **Grey Friars** above it. The Black Friars (Dominicans) came to Canterbury in 1237, and got their site about twenty years later. The best view of the remaining buildings is from the bridge half way along the Friars; the guest house is on the left bank of the river, and the refectory, now used as a Christian Science church, on the right. The Grey Friars (Franciscans) had come to Canterbury in 1224, before the Dominicans, but did not have a permanent site until 1267. There is only one relic of their friary, a pretty little stone building built right over a branch of the river, and reached through a beautifully tended kitchen garden (entrance in Stour Street). The building straddles the stream, with dumpy pillars for support at either end; surprisingly, it is said never to get damp. It consists of a large upstairs room, with a smaller room opening off it, and may have been built for the provincial or head of the order. In later years it was used by Flemish weavers, and as a prison. The Greyfriars booklet refers ominously to plans for a relief road to cross the garden. If this is ever done, it will ruin one of the most tranquil corners of the city.

Before they moved to their island garden, the Franciscans lived at the **Poor Priests' Hospital**, in Stour Street, established about 1200. It continues the good work of its founder by giving a roof both to the city's health department and to the regimental museum of the Buffs – a truly medieval impartiality between peace and war. The Buffs lost their separate identity in 1961, and so this museum gives a picture of a finite period of military history from the regiment's beginnings as the Holland Regiment (formed from mercenaries fighting for the Dutch against Spain) in the 1660s to its final operations in Aden three centuries later.

Farther down Stour Street, on the corner of Hospital Lane, is **Maynard and Cotton's Hospital**, a neat little row of single-storey early eighteenth-century almshouses. All around is light industry inside the city walls – tanning, dyeing, printing, stonecutting. **St Mildred's**, originally founded in the eighth century and thus the oldest church inside the walls, is down a cul-de-sac at the end of the street; the early church was rebuilt after a fire in 1246. The Victorian church school next door is now an organ factory.

A few yards away are the remains of **Canterbury Castle**, the square buttressed keep guarding the ancient Wincheap Gate. The keep was built at the end of the eleventh century, and in the Middle Ages was used as a royal prison. In 1381 Wat Tyler and his men attacked it and burnt the prison records, and in the Civil War it was temporarily held by the Royalists. Now it is hardly more than a shell, but what survives is impressive enough.

The name 'donjon' for a Norman keep has been transferred, and altered in the process, to **Dane John Mound**, and the gardens below it. It is now thought in fact to have been a

Roman or pre-Roman burial ground, and nothing to do with defence. The mound was tidied up, terraced and surmounted with an obelisk about 1800, and the gardens, with their lime avenue, neat houses and encircling city wall, are a marvellous example of an urban open space, unplanned but just right. In the gardens is a monument to Marlowe; a bare-breasted Victorian Muse bewails the poet, on a plinth decorated with famous actors in the roles of Tamburlaine, Dr Faustus, Edward II and Barabas. The son of a shoemaker, Marlowe was educated at the King's School, and combined writing with secret service work, until he was murdered in a brawl in Deptford at the age of twenty-nine. It is now thought that the brawl was a put-up job designed to eliminate Marlowe, who was becoming indiscreet. Not far away stands the *Invicta* locomotive, bravely painted in black and red. Designed by George Stephenson, it once hauled trains on the Canterbury–Whitstable line, opened in 1830 and long since derelict.

Marlowe's name is perpetuated in the new Marlowe Theatre, in St Margaret's Street. **St Margaret's Church**, almost opposite, was badly damaged in the blitz, but has been restored and skilfully transformed into a church for the deaf and dumb, with the north aisle turned into a meeting place and canteen. The church guide must be unique in printing the deaf and dumb alphabet at the back, for the benefit of visitors.

Most of the quadrant on the other side of the High Street is taken up by the cathedral and the close, though there are plenty of other things to see: the tower of **St Mary Magdalene's Church** in Burgate, which survived the blitz and is now used as a shelter for a number of murky memorials; the noble timbered buildings of the Buttermarket; the extraordinary lopsided door of the gabled King's School shop, round the corner in Palace Street. Also in Palace Street is **St Alphege's**, an Early English church with a strange barn-like top to its tower. Alphege is one of Canterbury's own saints; as archbishop in 1012 he was carried off by the Danes, and finally pelted to death with beef bones during a drunken feast at their camp in Greenwich. Inset into the rector's chair in the choir is a fragment of wood probably from the rood screen, carved with the name 'Iohn de Cax' and below a barrel or tun – the rebus of John Caxton, brother of William, the father of English printing.

The richly-carved Norman south doorway of Barfreston Church, between Canterbury and Dover.

The inner basin and yachting marina of Ramsgate Harbour. The customs house on the right dates from the early nineteenth century.

Dover Castle, from the south. The mighty keep and much of the fortifications were built by Henry II in the 1180s.

In the **Christ Church Gateway** the cathedral has a glorious approach, 'a very goodly, strong, and beautiful structure, and of excellent artifice', as a seventeenth-century writer, William Somner, called it. A carved inscription over the main archway dates it to 1517; and though the figure of Christ was removed from the tall central niche by the Cromwellians, the front still has its rows of brightly painted shields and heraldic devices. The corner turrets were pulled down in the eighteenth century, so that a prosperous Canterbury banker could have an uninterrupted view of the cathedral clock from the door of his premises. They were not replaced until the gateway was restored in the 1930s. The gate was in fact originally dated 1507, wrongly restored as 1517. It was put up as a memorial to Prince Arthur, Henry VII's eldest son, who died in 1502.

Canterbury Cathedral – or, to give it its correct name, the Cathedral Church of Christ, Canterbury is a building of supreme poise and splendour. Externally the graceful pinnacles of Bell Harry Tower reconcile the conflicting elements of many architectural styles, and are the first glimpse of the cathedral as you enter Canterbury from any direction. Yet for all its outside beauty the chief glories of the cathedral are internal: the delicate shafts of the nave, which forms a huge vestibule to the cathedral; the powerful Norman columns of the inward-turning choir; the vast windows of medieval stained glass, which somehow survived the fanaticism of the Puritans; and the calm solemnity of the crypt, with its rows of columns stretching away from darkness into the light of the eastern end. The whole building has the unity of some great symphonic movement, yet unity here is not the work of a solitary composer but of centuries of experimentation and advance by the greatest architects of their times, and the armies of unknown masons and stonecarvers who gave their concepts three-dimensional reality.

Since Saxon times Canterbury Cathedral had been the main church of English Christendom; but without the mixture of political squabbling and clashes of personality that led to Becket's murder, and hence to the canonisation and the pilgrimages, it would certainly never have grown to its immense size and richness. There was a Saxon cathedral on the site, the successor to a church consecrated by St Augustine; but William the Conqueror's first archbishop, Lanfranc, lost no

N

Corona or Becket's Crown

St Augustine's Chair

Becket's Shrine (Site of)

St.Andrew's Chapel

Treasury

Pilgrim Steps

TRINITY CHAPEL x

St Anselm's Chapel

Water Tower

Bibliotheca Howleiana

Infirmary Cloisters

NE Transept

PRESBYTERY

North Aisle (Choir)

C H O I R

South Aisle (Choir)

SE Trans.

LIBRARY (rebuilt)

CHAPTER HOUSE

The Martyr-dom

SW Transept

CLOISTERS

North Aisle (Nave)

N A V E

South Aisle (Nave)

Pilgrim Steps

time in pulling down the building – already badly damaged by
fire in 1067 – and replacing it by one of his own. Lanfranc and
his successor, Anselm, were typical of the international ad-
ministrators appointed to high office by the Norman kings.
Both Italians, and both priors of the abbey at Bec, in Normandy,
they had the combination of religious zeal and political ambi-
tion that led to success in the eleventh century, and the equally
typical desire to build on a magnificent scale.

Lanfranc had completed his cathedral in seven years,
beginning about 1070; though his work was largely obliterated
by later building, his north-west tower stood until 1840,
when it was pulled down in a misguided desire for symmetry
and rebuilt in Perpendicular style. The present Norman parts
of the cathedral are mainly the work of Anselm, who pulled
down Lanfranc's choir and built a very much larger one of
his own. The best idea of the Norman cathedral can be got
from outside, on the south side: the south-east transept, with
its round-arched Norman windows and blind arcading, in
marked contrast to the flourishes of the Perpendicular south-
west transept below Bell Harry Tower; and the pretty little
side chapel, set at an angle, known as **St Anselm's Chapel**
(Anselm was canonised after his death). The **Crypt** is the most
miraculous of the Norman survivals. A forest of Romanesque
columns surrounds a little central chapel of far later date (it
was probably built for the Black Prince), and leads on to the
solid simplicity of the massive pillars built a century later to
support the weight of the Trinity Chapel overhead. The
Romanesque capitals are carved with an uninhibited delight
in the sculptor's fancy – a pointed-eared half-human figure
struggling with two ferocious beasts, jugglers, grotesque
human heads, weird medieval animals, or, when naturalistic
inspiration failed, delicately interlacing abstract patterns.

Such was the cathedral that Becket knew. In a niche at the
west end of the crypt he is portrayed in a gaudy piece of
Swedish fifteenth-century sculpture – the vulgarity of the
Middle Ages in decline, and a good introduction to the cult
of St Thomas which began in the church overhead. A door
leads from the north-west corner of the crypt into the corner,
known as the 'Martyrdom', where Becket was cut down. The
spot is marked by a tablet 'Thomas Becket. Archbishop. Saint.
Martyr. died here Tuesday 29th December 1170.' Behind this

simple statement lies the major conflict of mid-twelfth-century England: whether the civil courts should have jurisdiction over the priesthood. And when the two protagonists were men as self-willed as Henry II and his archbishop, and the age was one of violence, then murder was the foreseeable outcome.

Becket was born in London about 1118, of French parents. A contemporary described him as 'slim of growth and pale of hue, dark of hair, with a long nose and straightly featured face; blithe of countenance was he, winning and lovable in all conversation, frank of speech in his discourse, but slightly stuttering in his talk, so keen of discernment and understanding that he could always make difficult questions plain after a wise manner.' He began his career as secretary to Archbishop Theobald of Canterbury, went with him in exile into France in 1152, and returned with him two years later, when on the death of King Stephen Henry of Anjou succeeded to the English throne. Becket, still well under forty, was made Archdeacon of Canterbury, and in 1155 reached the highest secular post in the kingdom as Chancellor of the Realm. He lived in enormous splendour, whether he was holding court in Canterbury, or campaigning in France in the medieval tradition of the warrior-prelate, accompanied by a huge retinue which included eight wagons, one fitted up as a chapel and two carrying wine and beer. Strangely enough, he had not yet been ordained priest; and when Theobald died in 1161, Becket, the natural choice as his successor, went through the ordination ceremony only a week before being consecrated archbishop.

Now that his power almost rivalled the king's, a clash of policy was inevitable, and the two men's friendship turned to enmity. In 1164 Henry exiled Becket to France, and from his exile he sent out a stream of excommunications as he struggled to keep the clergy immune from civil law, threatening the king himself with the final sanction of the church. After six years of bickering, Henry and Becket had an uneasy reconciliation in France in November, 1170, and Becket was at last allowed to return to Canterbury. In exile he had adopted austerity with all the earlier zeal he had shown for luxury, wearing a hair shirt next to his skin and allowing his body to become lice-

ridden and verminous. Welcomed back in triumph to Canterbury, he at once showed that exile had not taught him caution.
Even before crossing the Channel he had excommunicated the
bishops of London and Salisbury, and his sermons and
general conversation on his return were as outspoken as ever.
This was the situation when Henry, listening to rumours that
came to him in France, shouted in rage 'Of the caitiffs who
eat my bread, are there none to free me of this low-born
priest?' So four knights, William de Tracy, Reginald Fitzurse, Richard le Breton and Hugh de Morville, crossed the
Channel before the king could take back his words, laid their
plans at Saltwood Castle (see p. 146), and on December 29th
rode along Stone Street to Canterbury.

In his last days Becket seems to have had a premonition of
death. On Christmas Day he preached a sermon which prophesied that there would soon be another Christian martyrdom;
and in an audience he gave the four knights on the afternoon
of the 29th he told them that he defied them to the death. This
was not long coming. That evening, in the dull winter twilight,
Becket met his murderers in the cathedral, near the cloister
door. The Martyrdom is slightly different today: Becket
confronted the knights on a small staircase that no longer
exists. When they tried to drag him into the cloister, to avoid
the sacrilege of killing him in his cathedral, he threw one of
them to the ground. Then all except Hugh de Morville drew
their swords and cut him down, slicing off the crown of his
head, and spattering the pavement with his blood and brains.
At a point where one of the swords shattered on the pavement
once stood the Altar of the Sword's Point, one of the goals
of pilgrimage. Becket was buried in the crypt, and the
cathedral's great epoch began.

Within three days came the first miraculous cure of a woman
who appealed to Becket as a saint. By Easter 1171 Canterbury
was already a place of pilgrimage; the Pope canonised Becket
in 1173; and in July the following year the remorseful king
crossed over from France and performed public penance,
walking barefoot through the streets and kneeling to be
scourged in the crypt before the tomb. That autumn Anselm's
choir caught fire; the blazing roof fell in, and the marks of the
searing heat can still be seen in the stonework of the wall of
the south aisle. With money pouring in from the pilgrims,

Canterbury could afford the best possible rebuilding. The great architect William of Sens was brought over from France, and during the next five years the **Choir** was rebuilt, resting on those magnificent columns, alternately round and octagonal, and crowned by capitals of marvellous foliation. In 1179 William of Sens, while superintending work on the vaulting, fell fifty feet from the scaffolding and injured his back, and was forced to return to France.

French William's misfortune was the great opportunity for his second-in-command, William the Englishman, 'small in body, but in workmanship of many kinds acute and honest', a contemporary chronicler called him. English William rounded off the cathedral, literally as well as metaphorically, building the **Trinity Chapel** to house the tomb of Becket and raising it high on the columns of the eastern crypt, which accounts for the final flight of steps up which the pilgrims climbed. And at the extreme east end he built the circular annexe known as the **Corona** or **Becket's Crown**, either because it was shaped like the severed top of the saint's head, or because the piece of skull was kept there as a relic. Its centre-piece is now St Augustine's Chair, a medieval marble throne, constructed in sections for ease of transport and used at the enthronement of Canterbury's archbishops. The Englishman's work is distinguished from the Frenchman's by sharper points to the arches; and a single example of a pointed arch in the blind arcading low down on the wall of the south aisle (below the Neville tomb) is thought to be a sample put there by English William to convince the authorities.

Though the patterned floor of the Trinity Chapel is now bare, the knees of centuries of pilgrims wore a narrow groove across the marble, as they peered through the grille at the marvels of St Thomas's shrine. According to the cathedral guide, this consisted of a marble table, which 'carried an oak chest shaped like an ark, strongly bound with iron. The timber-work was covered with golden plates, embossed with golden wires, pearls and precious stones. The painted wooden cover which usually concealed it was drawn up, at a signal from the guide (a monk), by pulleys from the roof.' So for three and a half centuries, until Thomas Cromwell dismantled the gorgeous trappings and carted them away to his master's coffers, the fervent, the credulous and the holidaymakers came to gaze at the shrine of the 'hooly, blisful martir', to study the windows, of a darker blue than any sky, where his miracles were depicted, and to feel, like modern visitors to Canterbury, the power of great architecture.

After the visual complexities of the eastern end of the cathedral, the **Nave** is all simplicity. Built by Henry Yevele, the greatest master of the early Perpendicular style, at the end of the fourteenth century, its calm spaciousness provides an open area where the thousands of milling sightseers can get their bearings, peering at their guidebooks or listening in to the prerecorded descriptions of the building. Yevele's trademark is the use of shaft rings to interrupt the unbroken vertical lines, but only 'a mere whispered interruption', as Newman calls it. His portrait is on one of the roof bosses in the cloister, near the door into the cathedral; he is shown with curly forked beard, and his eyes closed in death. By the same door are stones, put up in 1970, that commemorate links reforged between Canterbury and French William's home town of Sens.

The cathedral's final and greatest external adornment, the **Bell Harry Tower**, was not added until the end of the fifteenth century, when the journeys of the pilgrims had only a few decades left to run. Before the Commonwealth it was called the Angel Steeple, from the figure of an angel that crowned it. The 'Harry' after which it is now named is a bell cast in 1635, the successor to a bell called Henry given by Prior Eastry, who built the screens between choir and nave about 1300. Below the tower, at the crossing, the ceiling is magnificently fan-vaulted, a final firework-burst of decoration to mark the dying of the Middle Ages, and its blend of aspiration, greed, corruption and saintliness of which Canterbury Cathedral is the embodiment.

It is impossible to do more than scratch the surface of the cathedral in a few pages. Books have been written about it and lifetimes spent studying it. Monographs have been written on single aspects like the stained glass, which alone would take months to get to know properly. To study the **Windows** the experts recommend binoculars: nevertheless the main thirteenth-century glass – the 'poor man's bible' in the north aisle of the choir and the miracle windows round the Trinity Chapel – are all near enough to study with the naked eye.

These miracle windows were huge advertisements for the effectiveness of St Thomas's shrine, and showed the kind of cures the sick pilgrims might expect, though only if they fulfilled their side of the bargain. Thus when Sir Jordan Fitzeisulf's household was smitten with the plague, his eldest son was given holy water from Canterbury and recovered; but Sir Jordan did not pay the customary thanks-offering and so the plague broke out again, ensuring that the proper sum was offered up at the tomb of St Thomas. The windows convey something of the Lourdes-like attitude that must have prevailed at Canterbury, at least in the early days of the pilgrimages, when St Thomas, if suitably approached, could cure anything from toothache to paralysis or insanity. Thomas himself can be seen, in green-robed majesty, at the bottom of Window I (top of steps, north side).

As striking as the glass is the unrivalled series of tombs: the procession of archbishops, glowing darkly in the crypt or resplendent in the aisles; the Black Prince lying in gilded armour below a tester painted with the Trinity; pudgy, shrewd-looking Henry IV and his wife, on the other side of the Trinity Chapel. In the nave are monuments to men as diverse as the composer Orlando Gibbons, who died at Canterbury in 1625 while on his way to Dover with the Chapel Royal musicians to welcome Queen Henrietta Maria; and the Canterbury benefactor James George Beaney, previously mentioned.

All the glamour of medieval publicity makes it easy to forget that the cathedral was also the church of the largest Benedictine monastery in the country. The monastic buildings lie on the north side of the cathedral. The **Great Cloister**, reached from the Martyrdom, is not the cloister that Becket knew, but a later rebuilding of about 1400. The ceiling bosses are a heraldry-lover's delight. Opening off the east side is the **Chapter House,** built about 1300, where the monks carried on their administration. A huge empty building, with stone seating backed by arcades the whole way round and a big stone throne for the prior, it has an elaborate barrel-vaulted roof and is mainly lit by an enormous Decorated west window. From a distance it looks curiously like a Victorian market building or railway station. The medieval library next to it was destroyed by a bomb in 1942 and rebuilt in 1954. Between the chapter house and library a passage leads to what is left of the **Infirmary Cloisters**, where the monks convalesced before returning to the full rigours of monastic life. Half way along is a delightful little building, perched up on columns, which is practical as well as aesthetic – the **Lavatory** or **Water Tower**, built by Prior Wibert in the twelfth century to house the monastery's main water cistern. On the first floor of the tower (reached up stairs from the infirmary cloister or through a door in the north-east transept of the cathedral) is a copy of a drawing by the monk Eadwin, which gives a diagram of the water supply and a rough idea of the appearance of the cathedral in Becket's time.

North of the infirmary cloister you leave the shade of buildings for the sunny spaciousness of the **Green Court**, through a passage known as the **Dark Entry** because of the sudden transition from light to gloom when you go into it. It was in the Dark Entry, according to one of Barham's *Ingoldsby Legends*, that the body of Nell Cook was buried in a vault after she had poisoned a canon and the 'niece' with whom he lived. Every Friday night her ghost walks abroad.

. . . Her fatal breath is fell as death! the Simoom's blast is not
More dire – (a wind in Africa that blows uncommon hot).

But all unlike the Simoom's blast, her breath is deadly cold,
Delivering quivering, shivering shocks unto both young and
old,
And whoso in that Entry dark doth feel that fatal breath,
He ever dies within the year some dire, untimely death!

On the opposite side of the Green Court are the big arches and tiled roof of the **Norman Staircase**, which led up to a large pilgrim's hall (it now leads to the **King's School** library); and near by a great Norman gate, its archway elaborately carved, brings you to more King's School buildings and the outside world.

Another medieval building, adapted down the ages and now a school boarding house, is **Meister Omers**, at the extreme east end of the monastery ruins, beyond the Corona. (Meister Omers himself was a thirteenth-century lawyer and cathedral official.) Though it looks like a gabled Victorian house, in its main structure it is still very much as it was when it was used as a guesthouse for the prior's more distinguished visitors, in spite of Elizabethan partitioning and nineteenth-century plumbing. The King's School got its name after the old monastic school was granted a new charter by Henry VIII in 1541, but its history goes back very much further than that, possibly to the time of Augustine, who would certainly have founded some kind of academy to train boys for the expanding church. The Rev. Gostling, as a loyal King's Scholar, pushed it back to the Druids – though as he said, 'it will be in vain to continue this search any further.'

If the King's School is groaning under the weight of age, the **University of Kent**, at the top of St Thomas's Hill along the Whitstable Road, is hardly weaned yet, as it only began its career in 1965. It stands on a splendid site, with the whole of Canterbury spread out below – a place of wide concrete paths and treeless lawns, in contrast to the enclosed parkland of Sussex University outside Brighton (see p. 388). The buildings have plenty of room to stretch themselves and spread over a wide area; the individual colleges are inward-looking, built round central quadrangles (apart from Darwin College, the most recent of them). In a century or so it will no doubt have got the necessary educational mellowness, like the spiky Victorianism of St Edmund's School, built on the same hill.

Below the university is **Hackington**, a village swallowed up by Canterbury, and one of the prettiest corners of the city. The first crude attempts at cricket are said to have been carried out on Hackington green. Overlooking the green is a good row of brick Tudor almshouses, built about 1570 by Sir Roger Manwood, Lord Chief Baron of the Exchequer (see also Sandwich, p. 106). At the end of the row is an excellent pub called Ye Olde Beverlie, built as the parish clerk's house. Apart from his less worldly concerns, the parish clerk at Hackington used to sell beer to thirsty parishïoners after church. The church itself, on the far side of the green, has a strange octagonal belfry poking through the tower roof like the point of an enormous pencil. The Norman nave leads into a very fine wide Early English chancel. Sir Roger Manwood has his tomb in the south transept – a stylish affair, with the bust of this Elizabethan politician behind, and a detailed skeleton lying full-length along the tomb.

CHAPTER FIVE

Thanet and the Coast Resorts

❧

HEADING north-east along the A 28 – yet another Roman road – towards the Isle of Thanet, the first place you come to is **Sturry**, which has a curved village street bypassed by the traffic. The name comes from 'Estuari', and a branch of the Stour still flows along its western side. The church is basically Norman, with aisles added later; remains of Norman windows can be seen above the arcades. Over the churchyard wall is Milner Court, the junior school of King's Canterbury. Part of the Elizabethan house built in 1583 by Sir Thomas Smythe (see Ashford, p. 183), Customer (chief collector of customs) to Queen Elizabeth, still survives, as does a massive tithe barn, now used by the schoolboys as an indoor tennis court.

In the Middle Ages, when the Stour was wider and deeper than it is today, **Fordwich**, just south of Sturry, was the port of Canterbury, where stone from Caen was landed for the cathedral, along with hogsheads of wine for the thirsty monks of Christ Church and St Augustine's abbeys. Fordwich was important enough to be ranked as a 'limb' of the Cinque port of Sandwich, with its own mayor and jurats, who had the right to carry out such punishments as drowning criminals in the river. It is still very much a riverside place, though dinghies have taken over from the cargo boats of earlier years. At its centre is the Tudor timbered town hall; the stone ground floor was used as a storeroom and prison, while upstairs is the courtroom where criminals were tried, still with the wooden bar at which they stood to plead their case. The crest of the mayor of Fordwich included a trout on a plate – a reference to the good eating quality of fish from the Stour. The church nearby has traces of Saxon stonework in the tower. Inside it keeps its old box pews (the mayor's pew was the front left-hand one) along with two more ancient objects – a rough-hewn wooden chair, cut from the solid and unique in England,

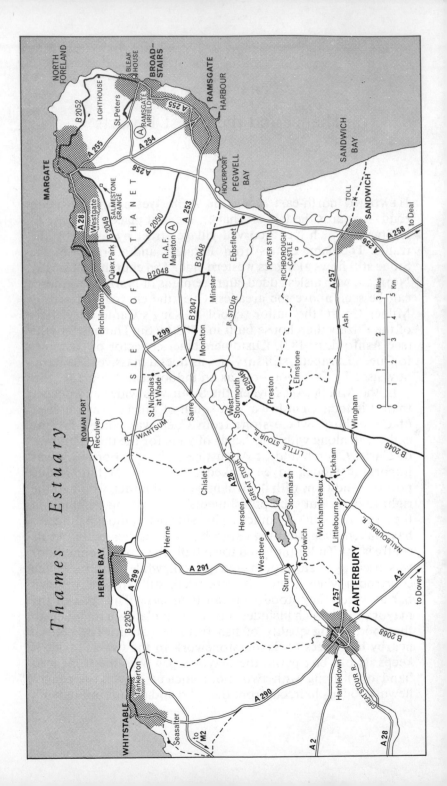

and beside it the 'Fordwich stone', carved in the form of a colonnade with tiled roof above and probably part of a Norman tomb of about 1100.

From Sturry you can continue eastwards to Thanet, or turn north along the A 291 for Herne Bay. Well inland from the coast is the original village of **Herne** – a nice curve of brick and weatherboarding climbing the steep hill, and a medieval church opposite, half hidden by tall horse chestnuts. Most of the church is fourteenth-century; the Perpendicular Lady Chapel, added a century later, is of such quality that it has been suggested that the designer was Robert Vertue, Master Mason to Henry VII and builder of Henry VII's Chapel at Westminster, who owned land in Herne. Nicholas Ridley, the Protestant bishop burnt at the stake in 1555, was vicar here in the 1540s, and it was under his direction at Herne that the Te Deum was first sung in English. Herne's black smock mill is still standing complete with sails, but in sad need of repair.

Herne Bay is a quiet, old-fashioned resort that never seems really to have got off the ground. It was laid out in the 1830s by 'two capitalists', according to a local history, and was visited by Mr Jorrocks on his voyage to Margate. The Dolphin Hotel where he stayed is still there. Herne Bay's main landmark is the clock tower on the front, given in 1837 by Mrs Ann Thwaites, 'the opulent city widow', *Punch* called her in 1842. The tower, says the article, 'seems to have been designed after one of those rolls of brawn for which the adjacent city of Canterbury has for centuries been so famous'; the pink Doric columns have been well gnawed by time in the past 140 years. The long and spindly pier is now completely bare, as the pavilion was burnt down in 1969 and has not been rebuilt. St George's Terrace opposite the end of the pier makes some attempt at seafront dignity, and just behind is the quiet (and strictly private) greenery of Oxenden Square. In the public library (High Street) is a good small local museum; the collections include finds from Reculver and pictures of the old church there, the best a naive oil painting showing the twin spires stark under the moon.

Three miles to the east along the coast the twin towers of **Reculver** stand out in brooding silhouette against the brilliance of sea and sky. The towers mark the Roman fort of Regulbium, one of the Forts of the Saxon Shore built about AD 280 by Carausius, the self-styled Emperor of Britain. Reculver stands at the northern end of the Wantsum channel, once a wide sealane for shipping; Richborough (see p. 108) guards the southern end. But whereas Richborough is stranded inland and largely survives, Reculver has been half washed away by the sea; and what remains of the ruins is now drowned in a flood of caravans. The foundations of massive Roman masonry can be followed round from the King Ethelbert inn, and inside the walls excavation has discovered the usual barracks and bath houses. Reculver's most splendid ruin is not Roman but Christian, the twin medieval towers that survive from the ancient church built as so often right at the centre of the Roman fortress. A small apsidal Saxon church was built here as early as the seventh century; the towers, known as the Two Sisters, date from a twelfth-century enlargement. For hundreds of years the church at Reculver was a landmark to shipping, but by 1809 erosion had gone so far that it was decided to demolish it. Most of it was blown up by gunpowder. The towers, shorn of their tall spires, were sold to Trinity House, who rebuilt them 'sufficiently conspicuous to be useful to navigation', as an inscription says. Two of the columns were saved and are now in the crypt of Canterbury Cathedral.

From Herne Bay you come down into **Whitstable** past the wide grassy slopes of **Tankerton**, with a ship's mast suitably marking the highest point; below the beach the long spit of Street Stones runs far out to sea. Practically every street of Whitstable is filled with the metallic slap of rigging twanged by the wind, from small boats beached in alleys or backyards. Out on the mudflats bent figures delve about for bait or shellfish; but the Whitstable oyster, which once had a whole fishing fleet dredging the offshore oyster beds, is now no more than a name. The Royal Native Oyster Stores still has the royal arms displayed above its door; but 'the natives' are now little more than a memory, and the oysters in the cleaning tanks are brought up from the West Country by lorry. Between the High Street and the sea are the 'Walls' that give Whitstable its character – rows of fishermen's cottages, the weatherboarding often painted in alternate bands of

black and white. In earlier centuries Whitstable was the port
for Canterbury, and communication between the towns was
considered so important that they were linked by the first
railway in Kent, opened in 1830, and now derelict (see
Canterbury, p. 80). Nothing survives of medieval Whitstable
except for All Saints' Church half a mile inland. Mainly
Perpendicular, it has been restored inside and out; the south
aisle was added as recently as 1962.

Seasalter, Whitstable's western suburb, perpetuates in its
name the medieval saltpans on the edge of the mudflats. And
less than two miles inland thick woodlands remain from the
ancient **Forest of Blean**, which once covered the ridge between
the Stour and the sea.

Back on the A 28 and making for Thanet from Sturry, you
come to **Westbere**, built above the marshes that fill the Stour
estuary. A combination of gravel working and mining subsidence has created an area of large lakes, now surrounded
by trees and thoroughly natural-looking, between Westbere
and the Stodmarsh promontory (see p. 111) to the south.
Westbere's fourteenth-century church is hardly more than a
chapel, yet it has some fine things in it: corbel figures below
the chancel arch, overwhelmed by the weight of stonework
above them (a similar figure, in paint not stone, is at Coombes,
in Sussex, see p. 405); and exquisitely carved sedilia. **Hersden**
nearby is a mining village; the spoil tips of the Chislet Colliery
form a manmade bluff south of the main road. Half covered
in saplings, they do not obtrude like North Country slagheaps,
but add something to the flat countryside. Seen from the main
road, the church at **Chislet**, with its odd truncated spire on
the central tower, looks like a small French château. It is a
Norman building, possibly on Saxon foundations. The Early
English chancel, longer than the nave, has a good series of
corbels on either side of the lancet windows. One pair consists
of a mitred bishop on one side and an old man in a nightcap on
the other – a sly piece of medieval humour.

As you approach Sarre, at the entrance to Thanet, there is
little to show that you are in effect leaving the mainland of
Kent for an offshore island. Yet the **Wantsum** channel, shown
on the map as a network of streams and drainage channels,
was a sealane for centuries – for the Romans and Saxons, and
right until the late Middle Ages, when the shingle built up,

the silt accumulated, and now only the watermeadows mark
where merchantmen and warships sailed in ghostly convoy.

The **Isle of Thanet** is unlike any other part of Kent. Though
the coastal strip is Kent's pleasure ground, and the lines of
semis are marching across from Margate to Ramsgate to
form a featureless suburbia, inland there are huge windswept
fields (now given over largely to potatoes), and the treeless
airy landscape has more in common with Picardy than with
the Canterbury orchard country. The name of the island is
one of the few place names that survive from the time of the
Belgae, the Celtic Iron Age race that lived in Kent when the
Romans landed. Old antiquarians had a fine time deriving it
from the Greek 'thanatos', meaning death, because as Lambarde said 'there be no snakes in Tanet and the earth that is
brought from thence will kill them.' The history of Thanet
begins by rather suspect tradition in AD 449, when Vortigern,
the king of Kent, asked the Jutish leaders Hengist and Horsa
for help against Pictish raiders, and they brought their
warriors across the sea to Ebbsfleet (see p. 103). In return, they
were given Thanet; and, having established a foothold, pro-
ceeded to conquer the rest of Kent and enslave the Britons
who lived there.

Sarre – the gateway to Thanet, where you can fork left for
Margate or right for Ramsgate – seems to consist of nothing
but hotels and pubs. One of them, the Crown, is known as the
Cherry Brandy Inn because the house still distils its own
liqueur from a recipe brought over by a Huguenot refugee who
was landlord at the end of the seventeenth century. According
to nameboards outside, it has been patronised down the years
by everyone from Kipling to Tessie O'Shea.

St Nicholas at Wade, just off the Margate road, grew up
beside a ford across the Wantsum; hence its name. It is a
windy village, with a main street in two parts called simply
'The Street' and 'The Length'. Some of the older houses have
brick gables of Dutch outline. The church is a really fine place,
big, open and flooded with light. The arcades are a jumble of
every sort of opening from Norman to Perpendicular; on the
south aisle capitals are two 'green man' heads with leaves
coming from their mouths. An ancient wooden ladder leads
to the parvise above the porch, and there is a good Jacobean
pulpit dated 1615. One of the brasses, to William Henaker,

'More than any other town Tenterden sums up the Weald.' A typical street scene of tilehung and weatherboarded houses, with the noble fifteenth-century tower of St Mildred's Church rising behind.

Mermaid Street, Rye, perhaps the most visited tourist town of the two counties.

The ruined chancel arch and choir of the Greyfriars, Winchelsea.

Medieval tomb in Winchelsea church. This effigy of a cross-legged warrior is thought to have been brought here from Old Winchelsea.

who died in 1609, has an inscription of classic simplicity: he 'lived to the age of 39 yeares or thereabouts and then died and was buried.' What more could be said? The church is made welcoming by two armchairs and a table at the back.

Margate now sprawls along almost the entire north coast of Thanet. **Birchington**, the westernmost of its satellite villages, is the only one to keep any separate character; though **Westgate**, with its wide topiary gardens above the sea and redbrick hotels, breaks the monotony of the seaward side. Birchington has a good medieval church facing a triangle of asphalt that must once have been the village green. There is an incredibly varied collection of monuments in the north chapel, memorials to the Crispes of Quex Park, the Birchington estate named after the medieval Quek or Queke family. A medieval-looking tomb with recumbent figures is in fact to a Tudor Crispe, Sir Henry, who died in 1575; Sheriff of Kent in 1546 and presumably the leading landowner of Thanet, he was known as Regulus Insulae, the King of the Island. Above is an extraordinary monument to two successive Crispes and their pairs of wives, by Joshua Marshall, Master Mason to Charles II – the only monument in England with six portrait busts. The inscription spells the name 'Queakx', which must be a phonetic approximation. The monument with kneeling husband and wife is to Lady Marie Crispe and her husband Sir Henry, who is carved in Elizabethan ruff, though he did not die until 1663. He was nicknamed Bonjour Crispe, because, after being forcibly kidnapped from Quex and held for eight months in Flanders before ransom was paid, as a true Englishman he only picked up the word 'bonjour' – but thereafter used it whenever he spoke to the villagers. Near the font is a window in memory of the Pre-Raphaelite artist Dante Gabriel Rossetti, who died at Birchington in 1882; in the churchyard a Celtic cross marks his grave.

Quex Park is a creeper-covered nineteenth-century house closed to visitors; but adjoining it is one of the sights of Thanet, the **Powell-Cotton Big Game Museum** (open Thurs. afternoons). Major Percy Powell-Cotton, who inherited Quex in 1894, spent half a century spreading alarm and death among the mammals of Africa and Asia; but he was far more than a mere trophy-hunter. In a series of enormous rooms he created tableaux showing the animals in their natural habitats – every-

C.G.K.S.   G

thing from white rhinoceros to tiny antelope standing in stuffed
verisimilitude amid jungle or savannah. He was also an
ethnographer, and since his death in 1940 the collection has
expanded in this direction into a superb display of weapons,
musical instruments and costumes from every primitive region
of the world. One of his predecessors, John Powell-Powell,
was an enthusiastic bellringer and built the Waterloo Tower
in the park to practise his hobby. The gracefully curved,
white-painted iron spire surmounting the tower can be seen
above the trees.

Inland from Quex is **RAF Manston**, one of the front-line
aerodromes in the Battle of Britain and still operational.
Beside the road is a small open-air 'museum' of aircraft – a
Spitfire, flanked by a Javelin and a Canberra, to bring home
the swiftness of technological change.

Though **Margate** is now so enormous, its centre is still that
unsurpassed crescent of sand to which Londoners have flocked
for the last two centuries. Round this have grown up the
brash trappings of a modern resort: the Dreamland amusement park, which Margate has made its symbol, a towering
block of flats by the seafront, a new shopping centre (built
incidentally on the site of Cecil Square, the first of the
eighteenth-century developments, now vanished without
trace). For all its prosperity, Margate is utterly lacking in
any sense of style. You feel that nobody cares very much
what happens to it as long as the bingo tellers are kept busy,
the fruit machines are milking the holidaymakers of their
cash, and there is enough room between the parked coaches
for the odd car to squeeze through. All of which is a pity,
as there are still parts of old Margate like Trinity Square and
Fort Crescent to show what has been lost, and what still
might be salvaged.

Until Benjamin Beale, a Margate Quaker and glover, invented the covered bathing machine about 1753, Margate was
just another fishing village. But with the machines, the sands,
and easy access from London by boat, Margate could not fail
in the early days of the seaside holiday. By 1775 there were
thirty machines in use, trundling swimmers decorously from
the bathing rooms to the water's edge, and dumping them in
the sea protected from cold winds and inquisitive stares by a
collapsible umbrella attached to the frame of the machine. In

those days of terrible roads, and before the railway reached Margate, visitors arrived from London by boat – the famous 'Margate hoy'. These clumsy craft wallowed down the Thames and back laden with seasick passengers, until the steam packet ousted them about 1815. A magnificent picture in the hall of the public library shows the steamer arriving at the jetty in 1869, in a confusion of parasols, portmanteaux, shoeshine boys, reunited families and cheerful excursionists.

In Margate, what in other places is called the pier is called the 'jetty', and vice versa. Margate's official **Pier** is the rounded stone arm guarding the harbour, built by Rennie between 1810 and 1815; the **Jetty** is the long landing stage, built in 1855 and lengthened twenty years later, which has all the amenities of the usual pier. At the landward end of the pier is the porticoed customs house building, dated 1812.

Margate's old parish church, **St John's**, lies up the hill at the south end of the High Street. It is a big gaunt building, built on the site of a Saxon church of about 1050, with an enormously long nave flanked by twelfth-century Late Norman arcading. Below the altar rails is a large and varied group of brasses, including a strange and unanatomical fifteenth-century skeleton. An unexpected survival among ramshackle buildings in the middle of the town is the Tudor timber-framed house on the corner of King Street and Trinity Hill. Now a museum, containing bygones and pictures of old Margate, it was totally derelict in 1950 and saved at the eleventh hour – one good deed to the town's credit. Half a mile inland is **Salmestone Grange**, originally a grange or farm of St Augustine's Abbey, Canterbury. The medieval buildings are now flats; the chapel survives, as does a neat little courtyard in the middle. (Grange open Sat. afternoons June–Sept.)

The chalk on which Margate is built must be riddled with tunnels and workings. The **Grotto**, at the bottom of Grotto Hill, is a nice underground folly – a network of passages and rooms, covered with an all-over decoration of thousands of sea-shells in an amazing variety of pattern and design. Discovered accidentally by schoolboys in 1837, it has led to all sorts of wild speculations about its origin, of which the theory that it was built in pre-Roman times by Phoenician traders is among the most fanciful. The Victorian novelist Marie Corelli called it 'one of the most beautiful, fantastic and interesting relics of the ancient days that exist in England or anywhere else.' The unromantic eye of the historian, however, sees it as an eighteenth-century shell grotto. Margate also has more conventional caves, at the summit of Northdown Road. Like the Hastings caves (see p. 282), they were discovered by chance about 1800 and subsequently enlarged. though they are on nothing like the same scale. It is more than likely that they were used by smugglers, and they have two circular dungeon-like pits, which could conceivably be medieval. Murals painted on the chalk in 1798 show redcoats, animals, and the Thanet Hunt galloping across the wall.

The **North Foreland** lighthouse, smartly painted in its green and white Trinity House livery, can be visited on most summer afternoons. There has been a lighthouse of sorts here since 1505, originally just a basket of blazing coals open to the sky. The present tower dates from the seventeenth century, but has been considerably enlarged and adapted down the years.

Broadstairs is a small Stratford-by-the-Sea, with Dickens instead of Shakespeare as its presiding deity. Bleak House, grimly battlemented (though this was done since Dickens's day) dominates one side of the tiny harbour; while every other house seems to have Barnaby Rudge, Pickwick or Betsy Trotwood somewhere in its name, And every year in June there is a Dickens festival, culminating in a grand assembly on the front of local people in top hats, frock coats and mutton-chop whiskers, or bonnets, crinolines and twirling parasols.

Dickens had spent a good many holidays in various houses in Broadstairs before he finally rented **Bleak House** (then called Fort House) as his summer home. When he first took the house, it was far smaller than it is today (a wing was added in the early 1900s), and a cornfield stood between it and the sea. A good deal of it is now open as a museum of Dickensiana (Easter, and May–October daily at 2). The study where *David Copperfield* was written and *Bleak House* was planned looks out to sea. In a letter to a friend Dickens described his agreeable working life at Broadstairs. 'In a bay window sits, from nine o'clock to one, a gentleman with rather long hair and no neckcloth, who writes and grins as if he thought he were very funny indeed . . . At one he disappears, and presently emerges from a bathing machine, and may be seen – a kind of salmon-coloured porpoise – splashing about in the ocean. After that he may be seen in another bay window on the ground floor, eating a strong lunch; after that walking a dozen miles or so, or lying on his back in the sand reading a book . . . He's as brown as a berry.'

The 'rare good sands' of Viking Bay are still there, as is the weatherboarded harbourmaster's office decorated with painted figureheads, and the Tartar Frigate inn, which a century ago was famous for the strength of its tobacco and rum. If Dickens were to return, he would find surprisingly little changed in the 'old-fashioned watering place' he described for his readers.

Broadstairs is full of odd corners, like the little alley of flint houses off the High Street called Serene Place, or the remains of York Gate, a Tudor sea gate at the bottom of Harbour Street. In Albion Street is St Mary's Chapel, built in 1601 on the site of the medieval shrine of Our Lady of Bradstow, from which Broadstairs takes its name. The shrine was so venerated that ships used to lower their topsails in deference as they passed.

The medieval church lies well inland. It gives its name to **St Peter's,** which is really a separate village from Broadstairs, with a little T-shaped centre of old houses and open country behind. The church is a splendid building, with a big grey battlemented tower. The Norman nave has a combination of round arches and pierced arcading; the chancel has been much Victorianised, with saints' heads painted on the ceiling and mosaics behind the altar. A local hero lies buried in the churchyard, Richard Joy, known as the Kentish Samson, who died in 1742. He showed off his feats of strength before William III; these included 'pulling against an Extraordinary Strong Horse' and 'the breaking of a Rope wich wil bear 3500 weight' (thirty-five hundredweight). St Peter's tower has the rare privilege of flying the White Ensign, dating from the Napoleonic Wars, when it was used as a naval signalling station.

Ramsgate, the third of the Thanet trinity of holiday resorts, does not thrust itself at you, like Margate, or take refuge in a Dickensian never-never-land, like Broadstairs. You either like it immediately, or you do not like it at all. It has the nicest harbour in the two counties, with two good piers to walk along, an outer harbour with fishing boats pottering about, and an inner harbour with a marina for small craft and wharves where moderate-sized boats unload their cargoes. The best way to get to know Ramsgate is by looking at it from the eastern pier, past the early nineteenth-century customs house and the obelisk put up in 1822 to mark a voyage by George IV to Hanover; on his return he raised Ramsgate's status by granting the title 'Royal Harbour'. From the pier you can see the unusual symmetry of the original resort town – to the left the tidy seaside Georgian of Nelson Crescent, to the right Wellington Crescent, elegantly colonnaded, both perched on the low cliffs that run down to the harbour and finish off the view in either direction.

The old parish church, **St Laurence**, lies well back from the harbour, at the top end of the High Street. Like the other medieval Thanet churches, it was built as a chapel-of-ease to Minster Abbey (see p. 104), probably before the Norman Conquest. It is a dark place, with two rows of Norman arcading round the centrally placed tower, and massive Norman pillars and arches inside. On some of the capitals are strange little devils' heads, which are said to represent the casting of the demon of paganism out of the English church. On the north-east pier below the tower he leers mockingly towards the altar; then, in a rake's progress, he is tamed, bridled and finally expelled through the south-west door, grimacing hideously to the last.

The present **Parish Church** was built much lower down the High Street in 1827, nearer the holidaymakers like the young Princess Victoria, who stayed at Albion House (now the council offices). It has a tall pinnacled tower, surmounted by an octagonal lantern. Far more interesting is the **Roman Catholic Church**, in St Augustine's Road behind the Regency Hotel. This is the personal testament in stone of Augustus Welby Pugin, the high priest of the Gothic Revival in architecture, whose best-known work is in the Houses of Parliament. A fervent Catholic, converted from Protestantism largely through studying medieval art, Pugin built the church at the end of the 1840s out of the money he earned as an architect. His idea was to build a typical parish church of the Middle Ages: what he actually did was to enshrine an idea in heavy masses of yellow stone, carved woodwork and stained glass. The Renaissance, with its ideals of symmetry, clarity and logic, he called 'paganism'; like William Blake in an earlier generation he loathed industrialism and tried to fight it in his own entirely different way. The best external view of the church is from the graveyard reached right through the building. It is of flint banded with stone, with a square tower intended as the base for an enormous spire, which was never built as Pugin ran out of money. In 1852 he died, aged only forty. He is buried in a chantry on the south side of the church – a delicate-featured effigy in a long robe, with his children kneeling in the medieval fashion round the base of the tomb. He lived at The Grange, over the churchyard wall, and from its battlemented tower used to watch for ships in distress at sea. Pugin was more than a mere visionary. Had his church spire been built, it would have been a landmark for shipping on a treacherous coast. After seeing an injured sailor carried ashore after a shipwreck, Pugin first of all boarded out such sailors at his own expense, and later on bought a house and equipped it as an infirmary – the start of today's Ramsgate hospital. The church and The Grange now form part of a Benedictine abbey and school.

Karl Marx, an idealist of a very different kind, stayed at Ramsgate; and Van Gogh actually lived there. In the 1870s he was a language master at No. 6, Royal Road, before he finally took up painting as a career. Surprisingly, there is no plaque on the house, though a nearby pub is called the Van Gogh.

Westwards along the coast from Ramsgate those seafaring doughnuts, the hovercraft, scutter in clouds of spray to their hoverport on the edge of **Pegwell Bay**. In 1949 a Danish crew commemorated the 1,500th anniversary of Hengist and Horsa's landing at **Ebbsfleet** by sailing a replica of a Viking longship across the Channel (in fact, they landed at Broadstairs' Viking Bay). Their ship, the *Hugin*, now makes a brave show in a field by the road, complete with fearsome dragon's head and rows of shields down either side – an ancient and effective means of sea transport next door to the hovercraft. Hengist and Horsa were followed to Ebbsfleet 150 years later by St Augustine, who landed in 597 (see Canterbury, p. 74), and was met by King Ethelbert in the open air, for fear of any magic the Christians might try to practise in an enclosed place. A Celtic cross, put up in a nearby field in 1884 to commemorate Augustine's arrival, stands on a back road near the entrance to St Augustine's golf club,

opposite a lavender farm that scents the air, and a kiosk selling
all manner of lavender products. Perhaps the lavender is
one reason why Pegwell Bay is a focus for migrating butterflies.

The rush to the coast that has swollen Margate, Broadstairs and Ramsgate into a near-conurbation has passed by
Minster, once the centre of Thanet. It is still no more than
a large village, with a long and very ordinary main street
running down to an enormous Norman church. Minster was
one of the earliest centres of Christianity in Kent; the nunnery
founded there by Domneva in AD 669 reached the height of its
fame in the time of her daughter and successor as Abbess,
St Mildred. Lambarde describes how Domneva got possession
of the land for her nunnery. King Egbert (see Eastry, p. 115)
had promised her as much ground 'as a tame deere (that shee
nourished) would run over at a breath.' After the earth had
opened up and swallowed the king's evil counsellor, Thunor,
who advised him against this method of distributing land, 'the
hinde was put forth, and it ran the space of fourtie and eight
ploughlandes, before it ceased.' The total extent was about
ten thousand acres. By the beginning of the eleventh century
the abbey had decayed and was handed over to St Augustine's,
Canterbury; nevertheless, the church was rebuilt on the
grandest scale in the twelfth and thirteenth centuries. Inside
it is huge and bare, with a great Norman arch into the tower
at the west end of the nave, wide transepts and a fine Early
English chancel. In the choir stalls are misericords with carved
heads of all shapes and sizes.

In the 1930s Benedictine nuns returned to the Minster, re-
establishing a tradition broken for a thousand years. The
Minster Abbey where they live is not in fact the original
nunnery, which was sacked by the Danes at the end of the
tenth century, but a twelfth-century grange of St Augustine's.
A certain amount can be visited, including the Norman crypt.
The ruined tower on the southern side looks far older, possibly
Saxon. The immensely thick walls are pierced with rough,
round-headed window openings, and it seems probable that
the tower was built early in the eleventh century as a beacon
to give warning of further Danish raids. Half a mile north of
Minster, where the road to Acol crosses the A 253, is the
ancient chalk quarry where Barham's Exciseman Gill and

Smuggler Bill hurtled to their deaths. Its floor is now the far more prosaic Smuggler's Leap caravan site.

From Minster you can return to Sarre and Canterbury via **Monkton**, a village with a long, featureless street and an austere twelfth-century church (kept locked); or make for the coast road and head south for Sandwich, past the three huge cooling towers of Richborough power station and a miscellaneous clutter of factories and chemical works.

Sandwich, stranded inland beside the sluggish meanders of the Stour, is in many ways the most fascinating of the ancient harbour towns. Unlike Rye, it has never really had a revival, and still looks back to the days of the Cinque Ports, rather than forward to whatever prosperity the growth of industry may bring.

The **Quay** is the natural place to begin an exploration of the town, with gardens along the town side of the Stour and timber yards on the opposite bank. The **Barbican** gate, built in 1539, still carries the traffic out of the town; the narrow passage between its twin turrets creates a bottleneck, though it also makes it easier to collect the tolls charged for crossing the bridge over the river (you pay 2s. 3d. if you have a 'Chariot, Landau, Berlin Chaise, Chair or Calash drawn by six or more horses or other beasts', but only 2½d. for a drove of calves, according to tolls of 1905 displayed under the Barbican). Far more ancient is the medieval **Fisher Gate**, built in 1384 at the time of the French raids, and the most important entrance to the town for travellers landing at the Quay. Behind it an alley leads up to the old **Customs House** (seen by request), a medieval timber building with a later brick skin. Here the 'customer' lived and carried out his duties; inside there is a splendidly painted royal arms of James I in the downstairs room where official business was carried out, and upstairs a very fine plaster ceiling modelled with the four evangelists.

St Clement's church, up Knightrider Street, is now the parish church of Sandwich and the only one of the town's three churches still in good condition. The oldest part is the massive Norman central tower built about 1100, with three rows of arcading round the exterior. As Sandwich grew, so the building was steadily enlarged; one curious feature is the addition of low pointed arches below the tower, put in to strengthen the north and south arches when the transept were removed as part of the fifteenth-century enlargement. In the chancel is a further curiosity – a medieval amplification system consisting of sounding holes cut in the stone below the choir stalls, matched by similar holes high up on the sanctuary walls. The stalls themselves may have belonged to the Brotherhood of St George, one of the town's most powerful medieval fraternities. The fifteenth-century octagonal font is carved with various heraldic shields, including the arms of the Cinque Ports. On the north wall is a tablet to William Boys, an eighteenth-century doctor and antiquarian, who wrote the history of Sandwich.

From St Clement's it is only a short step to the high embankment and ditch that still surrounds the old town; there was no town wall proper except on the harbour side. The spine of Sandwich is formed by New Street and the High Street, which bisect it into east and west halves. At the bottom of the High Street is **Strand Street**, which has the finest of Sandwich's timbered houses. This part of the town is a constant swirl of one-way traffic, which does not help sightseeing; however, there is talk of a relief road, which should alleviate matters. The **Sandwich Weavers**, part of which is used as the public library, has a long beamed front with overhangs; the name derives from the Huguenot refugees who fled from the Low Countries in the 1560s, bringing new prosperity at a time when the effects of the silting of the harbour were beginning to make themselves felt. Farther down Strand Street, behind a high wall, is the **Old House**, a timbered building where Queen Elizabeth is said to have stayed when she visited Sandwich in 1573. Though the queen ate a banquet of 160 dishes and 'was very merrye', she did nothing at all about a petition to clear the harbour that was presented to her. Nearly opposite the Old House is **St Mary's**, a wreck of a church, damaged by an earthquake in 1578; in 1667 the tower collapsed and brought down much of the rest of the building. What is left, much patched and bedraggled, is a bare damp barn, with tombs huddled at one end and a cluster of pews in the middle. At the far end of Strand Street are the crowstepped gables of **Manwood Court**, built in 1564 as the grammar school and endowed by Sir Roger Manwood (see Hackington, p. 90).

The **Guildhall** and large market square behind are the hub of Sandwich. Though the outside of the Guildhall looks bogus, the building in fact dates from 1579. On the ground floor is the old courtroom, a sombre chamber of oak panelling, royal arms, and heraldic beasts made originally for Queen Elizabeth's reception in 1573. Above is the council chamber, hung with portraits of local notabilities, like Edward Montagu, the first Earl of Sandwich, who was killed in 1672 at the Battle of Sole Bay, fought off the coast of Suffolk against the Dutch fleet. On the wall is the moot horn, which was blown before royal proclamations were read out, or as a general summons to the citizens. At the top of the building is a small museum of local history, which exhibits among other things a Puritan ordinance of 1646 ordering a day of public humiliation to be inflicted on 'saboth breakers' and other evil doers, who were held responsible for the unseasonable weather.

Near the Guildhall is the **Congregational Chapel**, one of the prettiest little buildings in Sandwich and well worth a look inside. It was built in 1706, and the roof is supported by two masts from ships in which Protestant refugees reached England after the Revocation of the Edict of Nantes in 1685. (This edict granted French Protestants freedom of worship; its repeal by Louis XIV led to a renewed influx of Huguenots into England.)

The third of Sandwich's medieval churches, **St Peter's**, is at present closed for repair. Like St Mary's, its tower fell in the seventeenth century; the ogee cupola on a rebuilt turret is one of the few tall landmarks in Sandwich. Curfew is still rung at 8 p.m. from St Peter's by thirty-one men of the town each with his own day of the month; though it is presumably no longer the signal for geese and hogs to be let loose in the streets to scavenge for refuse as it was in the Middle Ages.

If you go to **St Bartholomew's Hospital** on the saint's day, August 24, you can get a 'Bartlemas biscuit' stamped with an image of the saint and the date of the foundation in 1190. In fact the hospital (at the far end of New Street, beyond the railway) is thought to have been founded in 1217, as a thank-offering for victory over the French. It consists of a peaceful quadrangle of mainly Victorian almshouses around the thirteenth-century chapel. On each house is the name of the hospitaller who lives there, together with the date when he or she moved in.

Sandwich is famous among golfers for its three golf links

on the sand dunes towards the sea. The Sandown Road will also bring you (after paying a toll) to **Sandwich Bay,** with its wide beaches and estate of large holiday houses – a Millionaires' Row stuck down here in opulent isolation.

At the western edge of Sandwich a lane off the Canterbury Road (A 257) leads to **Richborough Castle,** one of the most magnificent Roman ruins in the country. In AD 43 Rutupiae, as the Romans called it, was the landing point for Claudius's invading legionaries. In those days a small and easily defensible island on the south side of the Wantsum channel, it made an ideal jumping-off point for the conquest of Britain. The massive walls, like those of Reculver, date from the last troubled years of Roman occupation. On one side the great square of masonry has fallen away and now lies somewhere below the river and the railway; but on the other sides, and especially the north, the wall towers up to twenty-five feet, built of flint and stones set in the iron-hard Roman mortar, with bonding courses of red tiles and a facing of dressed stone. Inside and outside the walls are the ditches of earlier fortifications, and at the centre is a cruciform foundation where an immense triumphal monument once stood. Built probably about AD 85, this was in the form of two arches intersecting at right-angles, faced with marble and topped by bronze statues – the final seal on the Roman conquest and a constant reminder of imperial might. There is an excellent small museum on the site, with the usual brooches, keys, implements and pottery, and some fine bronze figurines.

Ash, three miles along the Canterbury road, is one of those long straight places which one tends to rush through without stopping. Nevertheless, the tall Early English church is well worth a look; the needle spire above the mighty battlemented tower is a landmark out to sea, and Trinity House used to contribute to its repair. Inside it has, says Newman, 'the best collection of medieval monumental effigies of any parish church in the county'. Among them is a pretty brass of about 1450 to Jane Kerriell, wearing a strange horned headdress; a tomb with figures probably of John de Septvans, who joined Jack Cade's rebellion of 1450 (see p. 213), and his wife; and a sixteenth-century acrostic brass on which the name JOHN BROOKE reads downwards to form the first letter of each line of the inscription.

If you had lived at **Wingham** in the Middle Ages, you would have had canons to right of you and canons to left of you. So says the landlord of the Dog Inn, which is one of a row of timbered houses belonging to Wingham College, founded in 1282 by the Archbishop of Canterbury for a provost and six secular canons. Wingham is a historically-minded place: one of its restaurants is called the Tanner of Wingham, after a reference in Shakespeare's *Henry VI* to 'Best's son, the tanner of Wingham', a fictional follower of Jack Cade. The wide main street, lined with chestnuts and pleached limes, has a French look. Wingham's tall green church spire is a landmark for miles around; the church, rebuilt when the College was founded, fell into decay at the Reformation and was propped up by chestnut pillars in the sixteenth century. Wood instead of stone was used, says Newman, because a Canterbury brewer embezzled the money collected for the restoration. The whole of the south chapel is taken up by the grandiose Oxenden monument, a tall free-standing affair of 1682. The square base is inscribed with the merits of the family, and decorated with a horned ox head at each corner. Above is a three-sided obelisk carved with swags of fruit and flowers, and over the corners of the base are baroque putti in a variety of mourning attitudes. Monument and chestnut pillars make a startling contrast between the sophisticated and the simple.

At **Preston**, two miles north of Wingham along the B 2046, the remains of the palace of Juliana de Leybourne, known as the Infanta of Kent, lie under a pond opposite the village church; no visible trace remains of the home of one of the richest Kent heiresses of the fourteenth century. There is Saxon work in the tower of the homely gabled little church; and inside is a real rarity, a small white cupboard painted with the words 'Dr Bray's Parochial Library for the use of the Vicars of Preston' – a reminder of the days when a poor parson could not afford to buy books. **Elmstone's** pretty little twelfth-century church has a good Norman font of grey Bethersden marble; a medieval priest's stall made from the timbers of a boat wrecked when the priest came by river to conduct a service, as a thank-offering for his safety; and a chamber organ from Hatfield House, said to have been played by Queen Victoria.

West Stourmouth, a couple of miles to the north, is a tree-shaded village on a cul-de-sac road, which fades away into a track across the windy watermeadows of the Stour. In the small flint church, brick-buttressed and with a weather-boarded tower, is a memorial slab to Thomas Beake (died 1734), who obviously suffered the most unexpected of deaths: 'He died suddenly, in ye strictest sense being alive in Health, & dead in ye same Moment.' Beyond West Stourmouth the B 2406 brings you back to Sarre and Monkton.

The orchard country between Wingham and Canterbury is packed with villages. **Littlebourne** stretches back from the main road to its church; the heart of this red-brick village is turned over, with great practicality, to growing potatoes. The walls of the Early English church are made of a strange jumble of stone. The unusual dedication is to St Vincent of Saragossa, Spain's first Christian martyr, tortured to death under Diocletian about AD 303. He was regarded as the patron saint of winedressers; possibly the monks of St Augustine's Abbey had vineyards in Littlebourne.

A mile along the Nailbourne stream is **Wickhambreaux** (final syllable pronounced -broo), or Wickham for short, one of East Kent's beauty spots. At the entrance to the village is an old watermill, mechanised now but with the giant undershot wheel still in place. Opposite are the crow-stepped gables of the post office, and then comes a little green, with a pair of big eighteenth-century houses beside it and the church behind. This is a fifteenth-century building, with a homely wooden entrance porch; inside Victorian angels simper above the arcades, and the nave roof is painted like a starry sky. The east window is filled with lurid art nouveau glass, all heavy greens and oranges. The rest of the village is on a toylike scale. The little houses open direct on to the road, but fortunately there is nowhere for traffic to go to, so it leaves Wickhambreaux alone. A pub called the Hooden Horse is a centre of morris dancing: the sign shows the grotesque horse's head worn by the comic member of a morris team, and inside the pub is an actual example of a head. The Christmas Eve custom of 'hoodening', when East Kent farmhands would go from house to house clacking the horses' wooden jaws, ringing handbells, singing carols and generally enjoying themselves, is said to go back to the pre-Christian worship of

Woden, which involved eating horseflesh at the winter solstice, and was driven underground by Augustine and his missionaries.

Ickham, adjoining Wickham, is a quiet place, with white weatherboarded cottages and a fine Early English church set back behind a narrow green. Inside are two good fourteenth-century effigies: the scholastic world represented by William Heghtresbury, Chancellor of Oxford University; the military by the armoured figure of Thomas de Baa.

Stodmarsh, reached down zigzag lanes from Wickham-breaux, is a little hamlet whose main interest is in its name, which derives from the marshy ground where the abbots of Canterbury kept their brood mares (*stode* in Saxon, our 'stud'). Stodmarsh stands on the tongue of higher ground that separates the Great from the Little Stour.

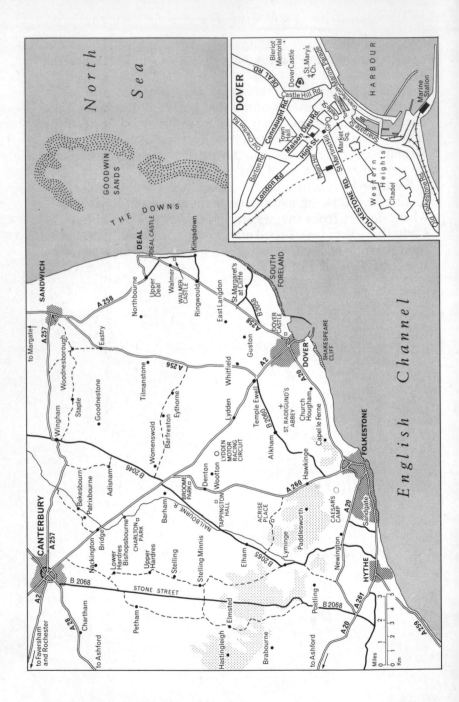

CHAPTER SIX

From Canterbury to the Coast

꙳

BETWEEN Canterbury and the populous coastal strip of Deal, Dover and Folkstone is a forgotten land of downs and the remains of great forests. The Romans built their Stone Street and Watling Street undeviatingly across it, and traffic has passed through it without stopping ever since; in the whole area hardly a single place has grown beyond the village size. Its fascination lies in its contrasts: between the open spaces of the eastern end, with its intimations of industrialisation in the pithead winding gear of the East Kent coalfields, and the hidden lanes and hamlets in the downs above Wye, fifteen miles away across the hinterland.

Patrixbourne, north of the Dover Road, a couple of miles outside Canterbury, is a gem of a place, with half-timbered houses clustered along the Nailbourne Valley, and water-splashes to cool you down on hot afternoons. The church, built about 1170, has some first-rate Norman carving; the only place to excel it is Barfreston (see p. 116). Below the centrally-placed tower the main doorway is smothered in a riot of carving – grotesque heads, animals, foliage or pattern-making, surrounded a central tympanum carved with the figure of Christ among angels. There is a smaller priest's doorway on the south side of the chancel. Almost as remarkable as the stonework is some of the stained glass, Swiss like the glass at Temple Ewell (see p. 140), and dating from the mid sixteenth to the end of the seventeenth century. The scene of Samson slaying the lion is copied from a Dürer woodcut, and shows Nuremberg in the background.

A narrow lane and yet another watersplash bring you to **Bekesbourne**, also with a Norman church (usually kept locked).

Adisham, two miles east of Bekesbourne, has a long narrow street ending at a triangular open green, with the rugged

Early English church and redbrick Adisham Court on a knoll to one side. Outside the west door of the church is a gigantic bronze statue of Thomas à Becket, too large to fit in the church, an apocalyptic figure, bearded and grasping a crozier. Even more remote is **Goodnestone**, two miles farther on, a pretty little village of redbrick houses down a cul-de-sac. The name derives from the Saxon Earl Godwin. The Early English church was largely rebuilt about 1840. One of the vicars was the Puritan Richard Culmer, notorious for his efforts to smash the stained glass windows of Canterbury Cathedral. Gostling tells the story of how Culmer, standing at the top of a long ladder and 'rattling down proud Becket's glassy bones' with a pike, was asked by a townsman what he was doing. 'The work of the Lord', replied Culmer. To which the townsman answered 'Then if it please the Lord I will help you', picked up a stone and threw it at Culmer, 'with so good a will', says Gostling, 'that if the saint had not ducked, he might have laid his own bones among the rubbish he was making; and the place perhaps had been no less distinguished by the fanatics for the martyrdom of St. Richard Culmer, than by the Papists for that of St. Tho. Becket, though his relics might not have turned to so good an account.'

In high summer the fields roundabout are ablaze with poppies along their edges. Are the farmers growing careless with their weed-killers, or do they retain a sneaking love for this flaunting redness, which keeps them from obliterating it entirely?

At the straggling village of **Staple**, two miles to the northeast, the rugged church, with battlemented west tower, has a superb octagonal font. On the sides are the symbols of the Evangelists, and on the base bearded wild men armed with clubs, and lions carved with Edward Lear-like fantasy.

The name of **Woodnesborough**, three miles east of Staple, is said to derive, like Wednesday, from the god Woden, worshipped on the hilltop on which the village is built. The church, perched up on the highest point, is basically Norman though much restored, and has a fanciful eighteenth-century wooden balustrade and cupola on top of the tower. Inside there are superb canopied sedilia, with delicately carved tracery. Down the hill the village is practically joined to Sandwich.

Eastry (East Rye, as opposed to the better known West, or Sussex, Rye) is a large prosperous-looking village a mile due south of Woodnesborough, with a church to match down a cul-de-sac of prettily terraced houses. The handsome Georgian Eastry Court, over the churchyard wall, is said to be built on the site of a palace of the Kings of Kent. It was here that the evil nobleman Thunor, wishing to ingratiate himself with King Egbert, murdered the king's two young cousins who might have overthrown him, and imprudently buried the bodies under the king's throne. The crime was revealed by a miraculous beam of light which shone down on to the throne, 'replenishing eche corner', says Lambarde, 'with such terrible and fearfull light, that the servaunts shriked at the sight thereof, and by their noise awakcd the king.' In expiation of this murder, to which he felt he had half-consented, Egbert granted Domneva the land to build Minster Abbey (see p. 104). Becket hid at Eastry before his flight to France in 1164. The Early English church, long and narrow, has a monumental west tower, with strange holes gouged in the buttresses. Inside there is a varied collection of monuments. In the chancel is a fine brass to the Elizabethan Thomas Nevynson, who among his military offices was 'scoutmaster of ye Est partes of Kent'. Captain John Harvey, who died of wounds fighting under Earl Howe on the 'Memorable First of June' (more usually called 'Glorious'), 1794, is commemorated by a relief of the naval battle. In contrast to the usual individual dedications, a window in the south aisle is a communal one, 'given by the men of this parish in tribute to wives and mothers'.

Northbourne, down byroads south-east of Eastry, and only a mile from the outskirts of Deal, looks across at the pithead winding-gear of the Betteshanger Colliery, whose spoil is carted away and dumped on the flat ground just behind Deal. Northbourne's squat Norman church, crouching above the village, has a fortress-like look about it; indeed, the early priests seem to have lived in the tower in a state of siege, conducting the services through the little window above the nave arch when the Saxons became unduly hostile. In the south transept is a vast ornate tomb to Sir Edwin Sandys and his wife. Sandys, who died in 1629, was Treasurer of the Virginia Company, and drew up the constitution of the new colony, used as a model by later colonies. It laid down among other things that the people should be governed and taxed by their own consent, and should have an assembly modelled on the House of Commons. Beside the tomb is a tablet erected by Americans in 1957, the 350th anniversary of the foundation of Virginia.

Tilmanstone is a tucked-away village of little lanes across the A 256 from Northbourne. The small, battered-looking flint church has a Norman south door, much restored, and Norman splayed windows. **Eythorne**, a mile or so away, is a coal-mining village dominated by the winding-gear of Tilmanstone Colliery. The thirteenth-century church at **Lower Eythorne** (normally kept locked) has good sedilia and an odd lead font, dated 1628, decorated with identical panels showing a classical female figure holding a torch.

Though **Barfreston** is only a mile to the west of Eythorne, it is a whole world away from coal mining and its manifestations. For sheer richness and exuberance of stonecarving there is nothing in the two counties to touch this little church, so small in scale and so richly decorated that it is more like a reliquary than a building. The village is pretty enough in its own right, and provides a perfect setting for the church on its hillock above the road. The simple Late Norman building, which reached its present form about 1180, consists of nave and chancel, without even the vestige of tower or turret. You come at once to the masterpiece of the whole church, the south doorway, which gives in a small space a microcosm of the medieval world. On the tympanum above the door is Christ in Glory, surrounded by legendary and symbolic beasts. The outermost semicircle of carving, immediately inside the dripstone, shows scenes from life on the manor house estate – perhaps that of Adam de Port, who held the Barfreston estates at the end of the twelfth century. Whether by design or accident, the topmost figure is the villein on whom the whole system ultimately depended; among the other figures are the minstrel, the cellarer and the estate steward. The inner semicircle of figures draws on the bestiaries from which the Middle Ages took their garbled ideas of natural history, making comparisons between man and the animals. A hare drinks a toast to a partridge, a monkey rides on a goat, a bear plays the harp. The blocked-up north door is also carved, but far less elaborately. At the east end is a large wheel-shaped window set high in the gable end and decorated with carvings of human and animal heads. The interior cannot help being an anticlimax, though the chancel arch and other carvings would be outstanding anywhere else.

Aylesham, a couple of miles away to the north-west, is back in the twentieth century with a vengeance. It was built in the 1920s for the miners of Snowdon Colliery near by, and consists of acres of orange-roofed semis round a central green. It would come as no surprise in Yugoslavia, but is an oddity in rural Kent. **Womenswold** (or Wymynswold), a mile away towards the Dover Road, is a complete contrast – a tight little Kentish village, with a church that has a nice Early English chancel and some good eighteenth-century monuments.

If instead of turning left for Patrixbourne you continue down the Dover Road (A 2) through Bridge, you come to **Barham Downs**, and a small side turning down to **Bishopsbourne**. This is little more than a cluster of houses by a small green, leading to the long church, with its strongly buttressed Perpendicular tower. Two very different writers lived here, Joseph Conrad, and Richard Hooker, the champion of the Church of England against both Catholicism and Puritanism, who spent the last six years of his life as rector here, completing his magnum opus *Of The Laws of Ecclesiastical Polity*. According to Izaak Walton, after arriving at Bishopsbourne in 1594, 'Mr. Hooker had not been twelve months, but his books, and the innocency and sanctity of his life, became so remarkable, that many turned out of the road, and others, scholars especially, went purposely to see the man whose life and learning were so much admired.' There is a bust of Hooker wearing a mortarboard on the south wall, and a statuette of him beside the pulpit. The west window of the church has glass by Burne-Jones (Faith, Hope and Charity), and in the south chapel are panels of sixteenth- and seventeenth-century Flemish glass, including a meticulously detailed Massacre of the Innocents.

At the south end of the village is **Charlton Park**, a long, low, ochre-painted Georgian house, which hides a Tudor manor house behind. The Georgian additions were made about 1790 by John Foote, a close friend of the Prince Regent; the huge ballroom upstairs was built specially for George, who used to relax there with amateur dramatics, after the rigours of reviewing his troops on the windswept Barham Downs near by.

Kingston, off the B 2065 south of Charlton, is a little village below the downs. Its small church may be Saxon in part. On the south wall is a fine set of funeral armour – helmet, gauntlets and heraldic tabard; and below the tower is a thirteenth-century font, rescued in 1775 by the Rev. Bryan Faussett, from a farm where it was being used for holding pigfood. Faussett was in the true tradition of antiquarian vicars. In 1771 he discovered a magnificent Anglo-Saxon gold brooch up on Barham Downs; it is now in the Liverpool museum.

The redbrick village centre of **Barham**, between the B 2065 and the Dover Road, clusters tightly below the church, with its tall green copper spire, the gift, like the similar spire at Wingham, of a nineteenth-century member of the Oxenden family. Barham disdains pavements, so it is just as well that it lies off the main roads. The late-thirteenth-century church is a fine open building, cruciform, and built without any arches at the crossing; a tall arch leads into the Perpendicular west tower. The most notable memorial is not a tomb or a brass, but a flag in the south transept – the White Ensign from H.M.S. *Raglan*, sunk by German cruisers in the Aegean in 1918. The flag was given to the church by Lord Broome, who commanded the ship; luckier than his uncle, Lord Kitchener, he was saved from drowning. In the north transept is a copy of the Barham Almanack for 1864 (price twopence, but 'to Barham Labourers Only, One Penny'), a broadsheet giving such local details as the contributions to the Clothing Club, and the times of the four vans to Canterbury per week. Over the churchyard wall is the large eighteenth-century brick-built Barham Court. An earlier building on the site was the home of Fitzurse, one of the murderers of Becket.

South of Barham the A 2 divides, where the A 260 branches off due south to Folkestone. If you continue on towards Dover, you pass the Lydden Motor Racing Circuit – a little hairpin racetrack, tucked away below the ridge, which must have the prettiest setting of any circuit in the country. **Lydden** village, two miles farther on, is the last separate place before Temple Ewell (see p. 139), on the outskirts of Dover. Its

primitive Norman church, standing by itself down a side
road, has arched recesses of unknown purpose along the side
walls of nave and chancel.

Off the A 260, just south of the junction with the A 2, is
Broome Park, now a hotel. It is notable for two reasons: it is
an outstanding example of a country house built in the 1630s,
just before the Civil War made such things impossible for
decades to come; and it was owned and adapted by Lord
Kitchener, though he never actually lived there. With its E-
shaped front and pilasters of cut brick, it has an Elizabethan
look about it. Kitchener has left his mark in his motto
THOROUGH, carved in giant capitals above the fireplaces.

South and west of the Dover Road the hills are steeper, the
villages more tucked away, and the roads even narrower, often
just single track with passing-places, as in the Scottish Highlands – though unlike the Highlands, you cannot see what is
coming at you round the next bend. However, there are a
couple of main roads before you get to Stone Street. The first
village on the Folkestone road (A 260) is **Denton**, a hamlet of
tilehung houses, with a little Early English church reached
down a grassy track. Outside the village is **Tappington Hall**,
the brick and timber Tudor farmhouse which belonged to
R. H. Barham's father, and which Barham made the setting
for several of his *Ingoldsby Legends*. The macabre whimsi-
cality and tortuous rhyming schemes tend to put off modern
readers; yet in the legends Barham made East Kent peculiarly
his own. The jest is compounded inside the house, where old
family portraits with Ingoldsby labels hang over the stairs,
and a notch on the handrail of the ancient staircase is said
to have been hacked when a Roundhead and a Cavalier
Ingoldsby met and drew their swords on each other. Born in
1788, Richard Harris Barham became rector of Snargate (see
p. 167) on Romney Marsh in 1817; four years later he moved
to London as a minor canon of St Paul's, and for the rest of
his life combined humorous writing with his unexacting clerical
duties. The legends, in which Barham drew on his memories
of Tappington and of his time on the Marsh, were mostly
written between 1837 and 1844 – those whirling fantasies of
ghosts and witches' sabbaths, of Smuggler Bill and Exciseman
Gill, of Sir Thomas Ingoldsby who drowned in his own eel-
pond and was thrown back into it by his widow because he

made such excellent bait, of poor Little Jack, killed by the buccaneer's curse.

Wootton, hidden among trees in the hills behind Denton, has the most secluded of little churches. Few rectors can have had their sermons more charmingly recorded than Edward Timewell Brydges, who died in 1807, and whose enthusiastic though ungrammatical monument reminds posterity that 'he possessed a philanthropy, which glowed with delight at all the refined pleasures of society, a mild eloquence, combined with a melodious voice, gave a charm to his oratory, which could rarely be excelled.'

From **Hawkinge,** a large main-road village four miles to the south, now virtually a suburb of Folkestone, a road leads between the Folkestone Crematorium and a derelict weed-choked aerodrome to **Paddlesworth.** The church (kept locked) has the unusual dedication to St Oswald of Northumbria, and the pub's name, the Cat and Custard Pot, is a similar rarity.

Acrise is hidden away down lanes a couple of miles north of Paddlesworth. The name has a good many pronunciations, but the one most favoured is 'Ay-cris'. As the name derives from the Anglo-Saxon 'Ac-hris', meaning oak copse, it can only be an approximation. There is no proper village – just a scattering of houses centred on Acrise Place and the church over the garden wall. **Acrise Place** (open occasionally during the summer) is a comfortable, organic kind of a house, which grew over the years from the sixteenth to the eighteenth centuries. It consists really of two houses, Tudor and Carolean blocks joined longitudinally, with Georgian portico and decorative trimmings. Acrise was bought by the Papillon family in 1666, and after changing hands several times was bought for a second time and renovated by a branch of the same family after the Second World War. The original Papillon, David, was sent over to England as a boy in 1588 by his French Protestant father; he grew up in this country and had a prosperous career as a civil engineer, being respon-sible among other things for the fortification of Northampton in 1645. His son, Thomas, was M.P. for Dover and bought Acrise, doubling the size of the Tudor building by his addi-tions. Inside the two halves are reconciled by the Adam-style decoration, done in the 1790s: the delicate plasterwork, the matching bow windows in dining-room and drawing-room, the elegant staircase, swinging round in a graceful curve, with twin recesses at the top, one of which is an ingeniously contrived door. All this forms a suitable setting for the collection of Victorian costumes upstairs, for the Meissen figurines and the china cabinets – in fact, all the daintiness of Acrise of which the butterfly family emblem forms a fitting symbol.

The church is a trim little building, surrounded by trees, with a shingled turret and spire perched on top. It is basically Norman, enlarged and altered in the thirteenth century. At the west end is a William III musicians' gallery, and at the east end of the nave the squire's pew, containing some midget Sunday School chairs. Most of the monuments are to members of the Papillon family.

West of Acrise the plateau drops steeply away to the Nail-bourne valley – one of the prettiest in the whole of Kent, with **Elham** as its fitting centrepiece. The name is pronounced 'Eelham', and this has given rise to the suggestion that eels were once caught in the Nailbourne, though this is hardly likely in such an unimpressive little trickle. Another suggestion is that it was originally Yuleham, the home of the yuletide feast. Prosaic modern minds derive it from a Saxon called Ula, since the village appeared as Ulaham in an Anglo-Saxon charter of AD 855. The Nailbourne itself is a so-called intermittent stream; though I have seen it flowing among the thick water plants on the hottest of July days. It has its own legend, going back to the beginnings of Christianity in this country. Soon after Augustine's arrival there was a drought in the valley. The locals blamed it on the Christians, so to appease them the saint knelt down in prayer, and where he had knelt a stream burst forth and watered the valley. This was too much for Woden, Thor and the rest of the old gods of paganism. They brewed up a tremendous storm, uprooting trees to block the stream and rending open the ground to swallow up its waters. But Valhalla could not be allowed to triumph completely, and so the Nailbourne flows once every seven years, bringing freshness to the parched fields.

Elham has two centres: the wide main street, and the quiet market square, a backwater of timber and tilehanging. The church behind the square is a most impressive place, mainly thirteenth-century, with a massive tower topped by a lead spire. Inside it is sumptuously decorated, surprisingly in Edwardian rather than Victorian times. The sanctuary is panelled in dark oak, with limewood embellishment by the craftsmen who restored Grinling Gibbons' carvings in St Paul's Cathedral. Below the big clerestory windows are seventeenth-century textboards, and elsewhere in the church are rarities like the embossed leather hanging above the side altar, and the English fifteenth-century alabaster panels – the outer pair showing Becket's confrontation with the king and murder, the inner one St Catherine – behind the altar in the south aisle. The Victorian glass in the chancel contains some unexpected faces. In one window David (with the face of Madame Patti, the singer) plays the harp to Saul (Thomas Carlyle); behind the throne stand Gladstone and Disraeli. The vicar himself appears in the next window with his harp, as David now grown old.

The most notable building in the main street is the heavily timbered Abbot's Fireside restaurant. It was built about 1480 as an inn, and has been dispensing food and drink ever since. Below the eaves the beam ends are carved into grotesque human figures, and inside there is a massive lintel over the fireplace, carved with fearsome dragon-like creatures. Wellington used the inn as his East Kent headquarters in the Napoleonic wars. The Abbot's Fireside is very reminiscent of the Star at Alfriston in Sussex (see p. 306); indeed, Elham and Alfriston are similar in their general atmosphere. A lane leads up beside the Abbot's Fireside to the half-timbered manor house, which once belonged to the Wotton family (see Boughton Malherbe, p. 186).

Lyminge (pronounced Limmindge), two miles south along the valley, is a large village; the oldest part, off the main road, faces a central grassy meadow. The church lies at one corner; It is ancient enough, but not nearly as ancient as what it replaces. In 633 Queen Ethelburga founded an abbey here. A plaque on the south side of the church marks her burial place, outside the walls of her own abbey church, which can be traced from its apsidal east end by the porch to its excavated west end south-west of the tower. This first church was destroyed by the Danes about 840. The present building has a good deal of later Saxon work, probably tenth-century, in the nave and chancel. The flying buttress at the eastern end was added in the late Middle Ages, and the low sturdy tower was not built until the first decades of the sixteenth century. Most recent of all is the vestry on the north side, ultra-late Perpendicular of the 1960s.

The village of **Postling**, near the southern edge of the downs, is without a pub, a shop or a 30 m.p.h. limit. But it is set in a wide sweep of magnificent downland, on one of the minor Pilgrims' Ways. Joseph Conrad chose the seclusion of Postling to write some of his greatest novels; between 1899 and 1920 he rented Pent Farm, outside the village, and wrote *Lord Jim*, *Typhoon* and *Nostromo* there. Among his visitors were H. G. Wells, who ate a revolting lunch consisting of dry bread and quinine, and Bernard Shaw, who more predictably stuck to cocoa and a biscuit. Conrad moved to Bishopsbourne in 1920. If he had followed Kipling in writing downland verse, these gentle green hills might have become as famous as the Sussex Downs. A fine row of tile-roofed barns run beside the churchyard; the shingle-spired Norman church is dedicated to St Mary and St Radegund, as at one time it belonged to St Radegund's Abbey (see p. 140). There are traces of medieval painting in the nave, and on either side of the chancel are the sawn-off ends of the roodbeam, still painted. On the north wall of the chancel is a small square stone inscribed with the date of dedication, 'the day of St. Eusebius the Confessor' (August 14), but no year to pinpoint the building.

Brabourne, lost in the downs on the other side of Stone Street (B 2068), is a compact little village, with an unexpectedly awe-inspiring church, so tall that side-on it looks almost square. The enormously wide, low tower completes the impression. The Norman chancel arch has intricately carved capitals, and the whole north wall of the chancel is Norman work. In this wall is a fine Perpendicular tomb of 'Easter sepulchre' type to Sir John Scott, a fifteenth-century Lord Warden of the Cinque Ports, who was also Comptroller of the Household to Edward IV; the helmet above the tomb was probably that of Sir Thomas Scot, commander of the forces in Kent in Elizabethan times. On the chancel floor are good brasses to the Scot family, among them Sir William Scot, with his feet resting on a greyhound. He died in 1433, and built the Scot chapel on the south side of the church. By the door opening into the chapel is a small throne-like altar, with a recess at the back for a heart encased in silver or ivory – almost certainly the 'heart-shrine' of John de Baliol, founder of Balliol College, Oxford, who died in 1269. Baliol's son, John Baliol le Scot, King of Scotland, may well have brought the heart south with him after his defeat by Edward I, and entrusted it to his brother, Alexander Baliol, who lived at Chilham (see p. 179). The eastern window on the north side of the chancel still has its original twelfth-century stained glass – a simple piece of pattern-making. Under the tower a rough-hewn medieval ladder leads to the belfry.

Hastingleigh and **Elmsted** are identical in remoteness, and in having churches that almost form a part of prosperous farms. At Hastingleigh there is an Early English chancel full of lancet windows – there are thirteen of them – and a rustic fifteenth-century rood screen. On the south aisle wall is a faded medieval painting of the Annunciation. From Hasting-leigh it is only a short run down to Wye (see p. 181), at the foot of the downs. Elmsted church has an odd little shingled belfry on top of the stone tower; inside, the building ranges from Norman (the thick-lipped heads carved below the chancel arch) to Tudor (the almost flat-topped arcading). It is full of monuments to the Honywood family. Best of all is the bust of Sir John Honywood, who died in 1781 – a humor-ous old man, who looks as though he would have justified the words of the inscription: 'Others may have moved in an higher sphere, But no man ever contributed more To the advantage comfort and happiness of the circle round him.'

Stelling Minnis, north-east across Stone Street, is a wide-sprawling place, one of several Minnises in the area. Minnis, according to a definition quoted by Walter Jerrold, means 'a wide tract of ground, partly copse and partly moor; a high common; a waste piece of rising ground'. **Stelling** church is a good mile to the north. Outside it looks like any other un-pretentious medieval church in a grassy churchyard; but once inside you are in the eighteenth century, and half-expect to see some periwigged Hogarthian cleric thundering from the three-decker pulpit, while the congregation in their Sunday smocks snore behind the tall box pews. Gallery, pews and pulpit have all been freshly painted white and grey-green – an elegant reminder of what was lost visually when the Victorians seated everyone in austere lowbacked pitchpine.

A little to the north is **Upper Hardres** (pronounced Hards) very much the small farming village; a large barn is even more prominent than the church. This is a fascinatingly bitty building, originally Norman and full of oddments – medieval tiles on the floor, medallions of thirteenth-century glass in the west window, a fine collection of funeral hatchments on the walls. A superb bracket brass shows John Strete, a rector who died in 1405, kneeling in prayer below Sts Peter and Paul balanced on their bracket. **Lower Hardres** is a straggling village with an ugly nineteenth-century church and a good eighteenth-century pub, the Three Horseshoes.

On the other side of Stone Street is **Petham**, in a broad open valley. The Early English church is a graceful place, with chancel walls that lean outwards at such an angle it is a wonder they remain standing. Above the cool whitewashed interior the beams are painted with naive floral decoration.

At **Nackington** you are almost back in Canterbury again, though you would never guess it in this cul-de-sac hamlet, consisting of a few houses and an odd little church buried among farm buildings. The top half of the tower is nineteenth-century brick, with a lead spirelet poking above the battlements; the lower half is thirteenth-century, as is the chancel, and the nave is Norman. The chancel windows contain some early medieval glass, probably made about 1180; one of them includes a portrait of Becket, done soon after his death and possibly an authentic likeness.

CHAPTER SEVEN

The White Cliffs

꙳

As you wander among the quiet back streets of **Deal**, it is
hard to believe that this was once the main harbour town of
south-east England. Yet in the days when the Downs – the
stretch of calm and shallow water between the shore and the
Goodwin Sands – was a major anchorage, filled with men-of-
war and merchant shipping, Deal was a seething centre of
Rowlandson-like marine activity. Sailors, stretching their legs
ashore after long and scurvy-ridden voyages at sea, lurched
from alehouse to alehouse; pursers stocked up with fresh
flour from the mills whose sails whirled near the beach; the
press gang roamed the streets, hated and often impeded by
Deal's inhabitants; customs and excise men fought the
smugglers – and each other; while visiting admirals, and the
families of Deal men who had become rich supplying the fleet,
picked their way on Sundays to the genteel and reassuring
classicism of St George's church in the High Street. But with
the coming of steam the usefulness of the Downs dwindled;
and Deal itself, with no harbour arm for the steamships to
anchor against, slipped into a state of picturesque somnolence.

From the end of the concrete pier (a functional structure,
built in 1957), you can see an up-and-down eighteenth-century
roofline that was hardly touched by the Victorian mania for
building urban terraces by the sea; the only typical seaside
hotel is the redbrick Queen's, at the southern end of the front.
Along the steep shingle beach rows of wooden boats are
drawn up, waiting hopefully for angling parties – direct
descendants of the Deal 'hovellers', which were often built
with hollow ribs for smuggling contraband. William Pitt,
however, in 1785 ordered all the hovellers to be burnt on the
beach. A landmark near the end of the pier is the Time Ball
Tower, used formerly for giving the correct time to shipping in

A map for this chapter will be found on page 112.

the Downs. The tower was built at the end of the eighteenth century, as the first in a chain of semaphore stations by which messages could be relayed from the Downs to London in two minutes. In 1855 the time ball was added – a replica of the one at Greenwich and connected electrically to it. At 12.55 each day the black-painted copper ball was raised half way up the shaft, at 12.58 it reached the top, and at 1 p.m. it was dropped. Still put to practical use, the tower is now Deal's information centre.

The story of Deal (or, more correctly, Deal and Walmer, which runs directly into it) begins in 55 BC, when Julius Caesar beached his galleys there after being beaten back from Dover (see p. 133). A plaque in Marine Road commemorates the landing. It would not have been made on the present shingle, which has built up in the past two thousand years, but on a vanished beach somewhere inland. The Belgic tribesmen – not savages, but the most civilised inhabitants of pre-Roman Britain – were waiting for the Romans with cavalry and chariots, and Caesar later wrote that his men were terrified at disembarking in the face of such opposition. The situation was saved by the standard-bearer of the Tenth Legion, who leapt into the water brandishing the gilded eagle standard, and shamed the rest of the legionaries into following him and engaging, indecisively, with the British.

The town's name is said to come from the Saxon 'dylle', meaning a low-lying or marshy place. Medieval Deal grew up well inland from the present town centre, at **Upper Deal**, presumably with limited port facilities down on the shore. As the Middle Ages progressed Deal grew in importance to become a 'limb' or associate of the Cinque Port of Sandwich. The main road from Sandwich passes Upper Deal, not at all medieval-looking, but a fine collection of Georgian buildings round **St Leonard's Church**. This must be one of the most extraordinary parish churches in the country, with a red-brick tower, dated 1684, topped by a trim white cupola, and a vastly inflated north aisle, looking from the outside like part of a yellow brick house lit by portholes in the north wall. In fact, the church is basically Norman; the Norman arcades survive, though a pillar on each side was removed to form a pair of wide-spanning arches. The north aisle was enlarged in 1819, and has galleries round three sides; an earlier gallery at the west end, announces that it was 'Built by ye Pilots of Deal', and displays a painting of one of the thirteen men-of-war that were wrecked on the Goodwins in 1703, with the loss of 1,200 lives. A model of the ship is on a window-sill nearby. Captains, pilots and naval gunners are commemorated on tablets in the church and tombstones in the graveyard; and a magnificent brass in the side chapel portrays Thomas Boys, armoured and bearded, who fought at the siege of 'Bullen' (Boulogne) in 1544, was made mayor of Calais, and in 1551 became Captain of Deal Castle. He died in 1562.

Deal Castle is the finest surviving example of the fortresses built by Henry VIII in 1539, at a time when fears of invasion were as real as forty years later, before the Armada. Furious that Henry had defied him over the divorce from Catherine of Aragon, the Pope preached a crusade against him, and urged the French king and the Holy Roman Emperor to invade England. The Downs were among the vulnerable places strengthened, with three fortresses built a mile from one another – Sandown, Deal and Walmer. Sandown, at the northern end of Deal's seafront, is now hardly more than a pile of stones with the remains of vaulting facing the sea, and Walmer (see p. 131) has been domesticated; but Deal Castle is still a formidable-looking and efficient place, despite its small scale. When Lambarde visited Deal the 'castles, platfourmes, and blockhouses' were still new, and he celebrated them by a doggerel couplet, translated from the Latin:

> Renowned Dele doth vaunt itselfe with Turrets
> newly rais'd:
> For monuments of Caesars host, a place in storie
> prais'd.

An earlier visitor was Henry's third wife, Anne of Cleves, who landed at Deal at the end of 1539 and dined there before going on to Dover.

These castles left the Middle Ages far behind. Built for the age of gunpowder, in place of the four-square towers and vertical walls of the Middle Ages they have curved bastions for cannonballs to bounce off, and superimposed platforms to give high firepower from a small target. Yet the Middle Ages survive at Deal Castle, in the gateway, with its Tudor brick vaulting pierced with murderholes, portcullis groove, and massive studded door. In plan it is like a six-petalled Tudor rose, built on three levels around a central staircase shaft. The outer walls are enormously thick – Henry had plenty of stone from dismantled monastic houses at his disposal – but the rooms for the Captain and his men are surprisingly domestic, with exposed beams and wattle and daub between. The upper floors of the keep were reached by an ingenious double staircase; the mortise holes for the second stair can be seen round the central stairpost. The castle was much fought over in the Civil War, but was not seriously damaged until it had a direct hit from a bomb in the Second World War. Now it is restored as near as possible to the condition it would have been in when Pepys saw it in 1660, as he sailed into the Downs with the fleet, writing in his diary that 'great was the shout of guns from the castle and ships and our answers – nor could we see another on board from the smoke among us.'

Upstairs in the keep is an excellent exhibition showing the evolution of coastal defence from the Romans to the present day; and in the gatehouse there is a small museum of local antiquities.

Behind the castle, in The Strand, is the handsome classical **Barracks** built for the Royal Marines in 1795, still an R.M. depot and the home of the R.M. School of Music. The cupola on the barracks is echoed half a mile along the High Street, in **St George's Church**, built as a chapel-of-ease in the early years of the eighteenth century. Work was held up after Admiral Sir Cloudesley Shovell, the man behind the scheme, was drowned off the Scilly Isles in 1707; and the redbrick church was finally completed in 1716. The church has galleries round three sides, and an upper gallery at the back for the boatmen, who could clump up the stairs in their seaboots without disturbing the rest of the congregation. In the churchyard is the tomb of Captain Parker, Nelson's 'dear, good little Parker' who died in Deal after being wounded in 1801 in an unsuccessful commando-type raid on Boulogne. As the coffin was lowered into the ground, Nelson leant against a tree and wept.

Next door is the brick **Town Hall**, perched up on columns, and built for some reason at an angle to the street. The council chamber upstairs contains portraits of notabilities like William

C.G.K.S.   I

III and Winston Churchill, and of that famous eighteenth-century Deal character, Mrs Elizabeth Carter. Her fine house, **Carter House**, in South Street is now a hotel. A plaque on the wall proclaims that 'Royalty and Society were her friends and visited her here.' Mrs Carter was a great bluestocking, and a friend of Dr Johnson, who found her, says Barbara Collins in *Discovering Deal*, 'as good at making puddings and pies, as translating from Greek, writing poetry, and being proficient in nine foreign languages.' She bought her house with the money she made by translating the works of the Greek philosopher Epictetus. In the eighteenth century the obscurest byways of learning could be profitable.

Carter House is at one end of **Middle Street**. This, rather than the High Street, is the true heart of Deal, and though a large section was damaged during the war and is now a car park, Middle Street and the lanes off it are the places to potter about looking for the Dutch gables or humbler weather-boarding of the old town.

The Downs are now empty, except for small cargo boats and pleasure craft, but there is a constant reminder of the menace of the **Goodwin Sands** in the jutting masts of the *North Eastern Victory*, visible from Deal at all states of the tide. She was an American cargo vessel wrecked in 1946 and thus a newcomer to the endless procession of victims that have run aground on the notorious 'swallower of ships'. At low tide you can take a boat from Deal and walk about on the Goodwins, but as the tide comes in the firm sand softens and becomes a quicksand, with such a power of suction that ships can disappear completely in a few days.

Legends of all sorts have grounded on the Goodwins – tales of the lost lands of the Saxon Earl Godwin, vanished when the sea defences were neglected for more pressing work on Tenterden church tower (see p. 152), or the island of Lomea, buried like Atlantis under the waves after a storm. Unfortunately, sample borings have shown nothing more romantic than eighty feet of sand resting on chalk. The Goodwins bred a special resourcefulness in the fishermen and smugglers who worked off the Deal coast. In their shallow-draught hovellers they could take refuge over the sands where the deeper revenue cutters could not follow them; and this knowledge handed down has been put to good use in later generations by the lifeboat crews, whose boat stands on the slipway at Walmer, brilliantly painted and ready for instant rescue.

As at Deal, the medieval village of **Walmer** was built well away from the coast; the twelfth-century church and quiet streets round it are north of the Dover Road. Built about 1120 as the chapel to the original Walmer Castle, of which one ruined wall looms at the back of the churchyard, it has a Norman chancel arch with traces of mural painting above. The walls are covered with tablets to naval officers.

While it is still possible to imagine shots being fired in anger from Deal Castle, **Walmer Castle** has had its fangs well and truly drawn. Since the early eighteenth century it has been the official residence of the Lords Warden of the Cinque Ports; and with its neat Georgian rooms tacked on to Henry's fortifications, picture windows cut in the massive walls, and elegantly landscaped garden it is more of a country house than a bastion of coastal defence. Of all the Lords Warden who have lived there, Wellington left the greatest mark on Walmer. The room where he died in 1852 has been left virtually unaltered, furnished in great austerity with the camp bed on which he always slept, the wingback chair where he collapsed, and bits and pieces like a counterpoised shaving mirror. In the next room are a pair of the original 'Wellington boots', the mask taken three days after his death showing a face incredibly gaunt and sunken, the coat he wore as Lord Warden. William Pitt, Lord Warden as well as Prime Minister, spent a good deal of time at Walmer in the 1790s, during the early tense days of confrontation with France. The room he used as a study still contains some of his furniture, and an equestrian portrait which shows him brandishing a sword, not very convincingly, in the uniform of colonel of the Cinque Ports Volunteers. The layout of the gardens was begun in Pitt's time by his niece, Lady Hester Stanhope (see Chevening, p. 222); earlier engravings of the castle show a very bleak treeless outlook. The most famous twentieth-century Lord Warden, Sir Winston Churchill, never lived there; but the present holder of the office, Sir Robert Menzies, commutes every year from Australia to this enchanting near-folly, facing the wide shingle beach and blue line of the sea.

A couple of miles south of Deal, beyond the faceless resort

of **Kingsdown**, the great chalk cliffs begin, sweeping round to Dover and beyond. Kingsdown has a few pretty cottages inland, on the steep hill up from the shore; but the first village of any consequence between Deal and Dover is **Ringwould**, a tight-knit cluster of houses off the main road (A 258). The church tower, with its lead-capped corner turret, is a great landmark; it was rebuilt in 1628 after the medieval tower and spire had become unsafe.

St Margaret's at Cliffe could not be better named, as the road down to St Margaret's Bay at the bottom of the cove is precipitously steep. Before the days of seaside holidays and cross-Channel swims the villagers sensibly stayed at the top, except for fishing voyages and smuggling forays to and from the beach. The splendid church, crouching low across the fields as you approach from inland, is virtually unaltered Norman. Outside there is superb arcading along the nave, at clerestory level; and a really fine west door at the foot of the tower, with a richly carved round arch, surmounted by naive figures possibly representing Christ and the twelve apostles, enclosed in a triangular stone framework. Inside, the solid, round-headed arcading leads to an unusually tall chancel arch; the arch into the tower is pointed, and must therefore be early Transitional, perhaps built about 1180. Around 1800 the belfry was used by smugglers to hide the ropes and tackle they used to haul contraband up the cliffs, and as a depot for their brandy and lace. During the Second World War the church was hit by a shell from a long-range gun firing across the Channel.

St Margaret's Bay is hardly more than a long seafront car-park, with cliffs rising sheer on either side. It is a marvellous place for watching the Channel shipping go by. A road half way down the steep hill leads to the **Dover Patrol Memorial** on the clifftop – a tall granite obelisk, facing a similar monument on Cap Blanc Nez across the Channel. At the end of Light-house Road diametrically opposite are the two **South Foreland** lighthouses, one high up and windswept, the other a little below and surrounded by trees; and near-by a beautifully preserved smock mill stands high above the cliffs.

Inland from St Margaret's are remote little villages like **East Langdon**, which still has geese grazing and hissing on the green at its centre; and **Guston**, which does not have geese but should do, as the name derives from 'Goose Town', after the goose fair held there in medieval times.

The only right and proper way to approach **Dover** is by sea. This is after all the traditional first sight of England – the distant view of the cliffs which seem at first to form a single wall, and then as you draw nearer separate on the right into the heights of the East Cliff, with the Castle at its summit, and on the left into the white precipice of the Shakespeare Cliff. Between the two is the traveller's goal, Dover's huge harbour, full of every sort of craft from the most ancient of tramp steamers to the most modern of hovercraft; and behind it the town, stretching in a narrow band of buildings up the valley of the Dour. As the gateway to England for over two thousand years, Dover has been a place of passage for kings, armies, embassies, pilgrims, missionaries, artists, writers, and the ever-increasing tide of holidaymakers; and it is mistakenly regarded more as a place to be rushed through on the way to or from the Continent than visited for its own sake.

Dover was the first place Julius Caesar made for when he crossed the Channel with his expeditionary force in 55 BC. In those days it was possible to sail right into the estuary of the Dour, which was navigable well inland and did not silt up until Norman times. That ancient haven between the two hills was easily defended, and Caesar had such a hot reception from the Britons on the surrounding heights that he decided against landing there and sailed north to Deal (see p. 127). Dover's subsequent history is based on this constantly evolving harbour, and on the enormously powerful **Castle** built to defend it. As the castle walls contain much of this history, it is the obvious place to begin any exploration of the town.

As you come over the hills from Deal, the stone bulk of its towers and ramparts suddenly fills the whole foreground; indeed, hardly anything else of Dover can be seen. To get to the castle by road, you have to go down the bluff on which it stands and then snake uphill again, passing through successive gatehouses up to the level of the inner bailey. Half way to the sea, surrounded by a high bank from which there is a tremendous view across the harbour, are the most ancient survivals in the castle: the church of **St Mary-in-Castro**, and the stump of a tower at its western end. This is the lower half of the **Roman Pharos** or lighthouse, built soon after the Roman

conquest in the first century AD, which blazed on the hilltop
as a beacon for the galleys coming over from Gaul, answered
by a similar lighthouse, now vanished, on the western heights.
The pharos walls are built in the typical Roman way, with
bonding courses of tiles at regular intervals up the stone walls.
The church is Saxon, rescued from near-dereliction in the
nineteenth century and restored in a singularly hideous way.
The genuinely Saxon parts of the building, like the round
arches made with tiles below the central tower, have to be
looked for among the weird mosaic with which Sir Gilbert
Scott smothered the interior. At one side of the nave is a
crudely carved Saxon slab from a child's grave; and at the
back of the church there is a collection of old pictures showing
the miserable state it was in before restoration. In the eighteenth
century it was virtually roofless and was used as a coal store.

Both pharos and church are far older than the present
castle, though the site was fortified with earthworks as far
back as the Iron Age. The Saxons had a *burh* or fortified
township, for which St Mary's church was built; and William
the Conqueror strengthened the existing fortifications immediately after the battle of Hastings. But the great keep, the
inner bailey and much of the curtain walling – in fact, the
basic Dover Castle – were built by Henry II in the 1180s, at
the then-colossal cost of £3,000. (For comparison, the chief
architect was paid a shilling a day.) The **Keep** is a classic of
castle building, combining immense strength with magnificent
living accommodation. It has three levels – a basement, and
two living storeys, each consisting basically of two enormous
rooms. Possibly for defensive reasons, the stairs in the keep
are completely illogical. There are two separate flights, and
the general rule seems to be that in order to go up you have
first to go down, or vice versa. The main flight leads past a
vaulted antechamber, and then turns up a long stairway which
brings you out into the second-storey apartments, lined with
armour and a formidable collection of pikes, maces and
muskets. These rooms are tall enough to have a gallery running
round them. A narrow and tortuous passage leads to an
exquisite chapel, still used, decorated with fine Norman
ornamentation. The chief attraction of the lower level is a
scale model of the battle of Waterloo, made in the 1830s; and
at the foot of the keep the basement rests on arches of

massive strength and thickness. During Marlborough's wars against France at the beginning of the eighteenth century the keep was used for prisoners-of-war, and the walls are covered with the names of Guillaumes and Antoines incarcerated behind these tons of stone.

The rest of the fortifications, including the lordly Constable's Tower rising sheer from the moat, were built by the middle of the thirteenth century; and anything later at Dover is mainly tinkering about entailed by changing methods of warfare.

In 1216 it proved its worth when Hubert de Burgh, the Constable of Dover Castle, held it for King John against a siege by Prince Louis of France. A tour through the underground works on the north side of the castle is well worth making, as it passes a tunnel thought to have been dug by the sappers of Prince Louis. This was the vulnerable side of the castle; it was defended by the round St John's Tower outside the main walls, and by branching tunnels connected to sallyports on the far side of the moat. In the Napoleonic Wars these defences were brought up to date, by a cunning system of spiral staircases, grenade shafts for blowing trapped troops to pieces, and remote-control doors slammed shut by iron bars for taking prisoners without danger.

Since the time of Edward I the office of Lord Warden of the Cinque Ports has been combined with that of the Constable of Dover Castle, though since 1708 the office-holders have lived in the cosiness of Walmer rather than the oppressive grandeur of Dover.

One of the best-known guns in the country stands beside the road up to the castle. 'Queen Elizabeth's pocket pistol', made in Utrecht in 1544, was given to Elizabeth by the States of Holland in gratitude for the help she had given them against the Spanish. It is a superb-looking piece, though as Mr W. Batcheller wrote in his *History of Dover* in 1828, 'it is moderately certain, that a charge of powder would not only blow it to atoms, but inflict serious injury on the individual who tried the rash experiment.'

Down a back road behind the castle is the Blériot Memorial – the granite outline of Blériot's monoplane set in the turf, on the spot where he flopped thankfully down after making the first cross-Channel flight on July 25th, 1909. It was from a spot near here that two earlier pioneers of flight, the French balloonist Jean Pierre Blanchard and his American sponsor Dr John Jeffries, had taken off for France in January, 1785. Mr Batcheller gives what must surely be an eyewitness account of their departure. On January 7th the wind was just right. 'The apparatus was prepared for the progress of inflation, and a paper kite kept flying to ascertain the direction of the wind.' By lunchtime they were ready to set off, with a cargo in the basket reminiscent of Lear's Jumblies, or Owl and the Pussycat – 'nine bags of ballast, the French edition of Monsieur Blanchard's aerial voyage with Mr Sheldon, a bladder containing several letters, a compass, a few philosophical instruments, a beautiful English and French silk flag, some refreshments, and two cork waistcoats, to guard against accidents.' In spite of such precautions, the flight nearly ended in disaster. The balloon began to lose height when only a third of the way across the Channel; and though they threw out their ballast, their food, their pamphlets, and even Blanchard's trousers, they would have landed in the sea but for a sudden air current which lifted them up and dumped them in the Forest of Guines outside Calais. They were met and congratulated by the locals, who made the balloon's car one of the showpieces of Calais town hall.

Another flier, Charles Stewart Rolls (see Eastchurch, p. 61), has a bronze statue on the Marine Parade overlooking the harbour. In 1910 Rolls capped Blériot's feat by crossing the Channel and returning in a single flight; the statue shows him wearing the flying helmet and gaiters of those incredible early days. A few hundred yards away the moustachioed bust of Captain Matthew Webb eyes the swimmers in the harbour. In August 1875, using breast-stroke and without wearing goggles, Webb made the first cross-Channel swim, spending nearly twenty-two hours in the water, and keeping out the cold, says the *Dictionary of National Biography*, 'by doses of cod-liver oil, beef-tea, brandy, coffee, and strong old ale'. Though he won his share of fame and money, Webb was a spendthrift. In a desperate effort to restore his finances, he went to Canada in 1883 to attempt the impossible, by swimming the rapids at the foot of the Niagara Falls. When he reached the central whirlpool his strength failed him, and he was sucked down and drowned in the maelstrom.

With its ultra-modern Eastern Docks complex and hoverport at the far end, and the huge Gateway wall of flats as its centrepiece, there is little enough left at **Dover Harbour** to suggest its immense history. Indeed, the vast expanse of the harbour dates only from the early years of this century, when in 1909 an anchorage was opened large enough to take the battleships and cruisers of the Grand Fleet. For centuries ships anchoring off Dover had no artificial protection at all; but steady silting-up at the mouth of the Dour made a harbour arm necessary, and about 1495 the first pier was built, forming a harbour which so delighted the sailors of the time that they called it 'Paradise'. Paradise Harbour now lies somewhere under the Western Dock area, where all the port development took place before the present century. Silting remained a constant problem, and one of the duties of the citizens of Dover was to bring their shovels to clear the harbour bar when a drum was beaten. From such primitive beginnings grew the Dover Harbour Board, formed as long ago as 1606, with the Lord Warden of the Cinque Ports at its head. The Board's headquarters is near the old part of the harbour, in the elegant white-painted **Waterloo Terrace**, which somehow survived the bombs and the cross-Channel shellfire. Travelling from Dover harbour nowadays has little of the panache of Henry VIII embarking for the Field of the Cloth of Gold, or Henry V landing after Agincourt; yet the international hordes pouring on and off the boats, and the monstrous regiment of transporter lorries, make Dover the modern meeting-place of all the world.

Dover's **High Street**, with its extensions Biggin Street and Cannon Street, runs inland at right-angles to the harbour, following the line of the Dour. **St Mary's**, in Cannon Street, is the parish church of Dover; its Norman tower, with rows of arcading and leaded spire, is the main landmark in this part of the town. Inside it keeps its Norman arches at the western end, though the rest of it was rebuilt in the nineteenth century. At the back of the church is the bench formerly used by the Barons of the Cinque Ports – an unpretentious piece of woodwork, with a central throne raised a few inches for the Lord Warden. Up the road is the hideous Victorian **Town Hall**, redeemed by the fact that it incorporates the medieval **Maison Dieu** hospital, founded early in the thirteenth century by Hubert de Burgh for pilgrims passing through Dover. The great hall, lit on the south side by a row of traceried windows, is hung with tattered banners and lined with pikes, swords and armour; at the far end, over the door into the council chamber, is a full-length portrait of Churchill as Lord Warden. Next door is the handsome brick Dutch-gabled Maison Dieu House, now the public library, and round the corner, in Ladywell, is the wonderfully disorganised jumble of the town **Museum**. A stuffed polar bear guards the entrance, and inside you can find anything from pictures of Blériot landing at Dover to figures of Buddha.

A nearby survival, so small that it is easy to overlook, is **St Edmund's Chapel**, near the corner of Priory Road. Only twenty-seven feet long by fourteen wide, it is thought to be the smallest church in regular use in England. It was built as a chapel for the cemetery attached to the Maison Dieu, and among other transformations became a naval victualling store and a house with forge, before being saved from demolition and restored in the 1960s. In 1253 St Richard of Chichester dedicated the chapel to his friend St Edmund of Canterbury, which makes it the only building consecrated by one English saint to another. The remains of Dover's great medieval priory, founded in 1131 by Archbishop Corbeuil, are incorporated in **Dover College** (entrance in Effingham Crescent). The monks' refectory, still with its Norman arcading round the base of the walls, is now used as an examination hall; the guest house has been adapted for the school chapel; and the gatehouse is a library. In Mr Batcheller's time it was a farm 'occupied by a respectable family of the name of Coleman'.

Confirmation of the enormous importance of Roman Dover has been provided by the remains uncovered during building work on the new trunk road from the end of the Folkestone Road (A 20) towards the harbour. In 1970 and 1971 the archaeologists, working frenziedly against time ahead of the road-builders, uncovered the lower part of a Roman house with the traces of superb illusionist paintings on the walls, and the foundations of two Roman forts. The earlier, built in the second century AD, has been called by Brian Philp, the archaeologist in charge, 'the finest and most complete Roman fort ever found in southern Britain' – the headquarters of the Classis Britannica, the Roman fleet in Britain. The road contractors agreed to raise the carriageway by six feet so as not to destroy the remains; and, though these are now covered from sight, they are safely buried for future archaeologists to dig up again when the age of trunk roads and traffic thundering down to the harbour is past.

Corresponding to the magnificent castle on the eastern side are the Napoleonic War fortifications on the **Western Heights** above the town. They are now largely given over to a borstal and cannot be visited; but the brick casements and redoubts are clearly visible rising above the harbour. The barracks at the top were reached from Snargate Street by a shaft cut through the rock containing three spiral staircases, with notices stating, according to tradition, that one was for officers and their ladies, the second for N.C.O.s and their wives, and the third for soldiers and their women.

In this same direction the Old Folkestone Road (blocked a mile farther on by a rifle range) climbs near the top of the **Shakespeare Cliff**, the whitest and sheerest cliff of them all. It was to this height that Edgar brought the blinded Gloucester in the fourth act of *King Lear*, making him believe that he had fallen over the edge and survived – or, if it was not this height, then everyone has been wrong for centuries. Shakespeare describes a samphire-gatherer on the cliff, and samphire (a green fleshy plant) is still said to grow there, though gorse and brambles are more in evidence.

> Ten masts at each make not the altitude
> Which thou hast perpendicularly fell,

says Edgar – a good approximation to the estimated height of 350 feet from top to bottom. At the foot of the cliff are borings for a Channel tunnel made as long ago as 1880. In 1907 Walter Jerrold wrote of the tunnel as 'an inevitable coming event as soon as timid opposition shall have been worn away', but after sixty-five years it seems as problematic as ever. It now seems probable that the tunnel, if it is ever constructed, will emerge in the northern suburbs of Folkestone.

In its spread along the Canterbury road, Dover has swallowed up the village of **Temple Ewell**, which nevertheless has managed to keep its identity. It is a little maze of a place, near the source of the River Dour, which runs through the middle of it past an old watermill. The name derives from the Knights Templars, who had a preceptory there and founded the village church, which still has its original Norman north doorway. In the chancel windows are brilliant little inset panels of Swiss seventeenth-century glass, showing scenes from the life of Joseph in a strange mixture of mock-medieval townscapes, turbans and Roman armour. By contrast, **Whitfield** is a suburb of little character, though **Church Whitfield** outside has a Saxon church (kept locked), much restored. In the Middle Ages the tenant of Archer's Court, a Whitfield manor house, had the dubious privilege of holding the bowl into which the king was sick on his sea voyages – a royal cupbearer in reverse.

You can get from Dover to Folkestone by either of two parallel routes – the main road (A 20) along the coast, or the much quieter and more delectable B 2060 through **Alkham,** lying deep in its valley. Alkham is a sheltered little place, clustered below a long low church on the hillside. The Early English church was built early in the thirteenth century by the monks of St Radegund's Abbey near by; its chief glory is the wide and graceful north chapel, arcaded the whole way on slender Bethersden marble shafts, perhaps built by Canterbury Cathedral masons at the end of the century. **St Radegund's** is well worth the backhanded journey down minute country lanes from Alkham; or you can get to it direct from Dover. Founded by Praemonstratensian monks (from Prémontré, in France) about 1191, the abbey was on a fairly large scale. The creeper-covered gatehouse was originally the tower of the church, and the pretty Elizabethan farmhouse behind was made out of the refectory; Henry VIII had most of the stone carted away to build Sandgate Castle (see p. 143). Radegund was a German princess born about AD 520. When she was ten she was carried off by Clothaire, King of the Franks, and was later forcibly married to him. However, she must have been an uncomfortable lady to live with, as she wore a hair shirt under her royal robes; and Clothaire was no doubt secretly relieved when she left him, took the veil and founded an abbey at Poitiers. Here, according to an eighteenth-century writer, 'the care of lepers and persons afflicted with the most nauseous distempers, constituted her greatest pleasures'. She survived until 587, abstaining from meat, fish, eggs and fruit.

If you go to Folkestone by the main road, you pass **Church Hougham** (pronounced Huffem), a few hundred yards off the

road. The most noticeable thing about it is the soaring ITA
transmitter mast near by. The church has a hefty tile-hung
broach spire, and is much-restored Norman; inside there are
blocked Norman arches on the south side of the chancel.
Even more remote is the church of **Capel le Ferne**, tucked
away behind Capel Church Farm a good mile from the
bungalow sprawl of the village, and with sheep grazing in the
churchyard. Though it is usually kept locked, it is worth the
effort to get in, as it has a rare stone screen across the chancel
instead of the usual wooden one – three simple pointed
arches, with a round-arched opening above for the rood or
figure of Christ.

From Capel the road coils steeply down Dover Hill into
Folkestone. This is as good a side as any from which to
approach the town, as you arrive almost in the middle of it,
and can get a panoramic view by making a short detour to the
green slopes by the martello tower, high above the East Cliff
sands. From here the resort area of Folkestone is invisible;
at your feet is the harbour, with small craft lolling on the
low-tide mudflats and a British Rail ferry moored against the
mole outside, while behind rises the steep hill of old Folkestone,
crowned by the battlemented tower of the parish church. The
name in Saxon times was 'Fulchestanc', presumably from
some prominent lump of rock where the folk assembled. In
the Middle Ages it was important enough to be made a 'limb'
of the Cinque Port of Dover; but until the nineteenth century
it was hardly more than a few rows of fishermen's cottages
down by the harbour, and a scatter of houses up the hill
between the harbour and the church.

The steep, narrow **High Street** survives from this earlier
age, though many of the cottages have been gutted to make
restaurants or souvenir shops. It is now closed to ordinary
traffic, which has brought it back to the state it was in when
Richard Barham wrote that 'its streets, lanes, and alleys –
fanciful distinctions without much real difference – are agreeable enough to persons who do not mind running up and down
stairs'. The church on top of the hill stands in the middle of a
nice group of Georgian redbrick and weatherboarding; near
by is a neat little square called The Bayle, with a good pub,
the British Lion.

Seen from close to, **Folkestone Church** is much larger than distant views suggest. It is basically an Early English building, with Perpendicular chapels and central tower added in the fifteenth century. The dedication, to St Mary and St Eanswythe, commemorates Folkestone's patron saint. Eanswythe, the grand-daughter of Ethelbert, the Kentish king converted by St Augustine (see p. 74), founded a nunnery at Folkestone in AD 630; the site is thought to have been on the clifftop east of the present church, but all traces vanished during the great storms and cliff erosions of the Middle Ages. When Eanswythe died in 640, the nunnery was sacked by the Danes, and was probably never restored, though the church was rebuilt by King Athelstan in 927. According to Lambarde, her miracles ranged from lengthening a roof beam by three feet when the carpenters had sawn it too short, to forbidding 'certaine ravenous birdes the countrey, which before did much harm thereabouts'. Her relics are kept in a shrine behind an elaborate little door in the north wall of the sanctuary – the bones of a young woman about thirty, who died in the seventh century, discovered in the wall when the Victorian alabaster arcading was being installed. This was part of an extraordinarily complete scheme of decoration, which gives Folkestone church a feeling of lush sumptuousness. Individual details like the painted angels may be insipid enough, but the overall effect has an Albert Memorial kind of impressiveness.

West of old Folkestone are the unruffled Victorian squares and hotels, which grew up when the railway came to the town in the 1840s. (William Cubitt's superb viaduct, best seen from Foord Road, is as fine as Brighton's much more famous structure; Newman calls it 'the most exciting piece of architecture in the town'.) Between the hotels and the sea is that unique Folkestone creation known as **The Leas** – a clifftop expanse of lawns and flower gardens, with a Riviera-like tangle of pine and broom tumbling down to the sea-level promenades. For any South Coast resort to compare itself to the Bay of Naples may seem far-fetched; yet if you look over the treetops on a sunny afternoon to some lonely fisherman in a dinghy far below, the scene is far more Mediterranean than English Channel. Then you turn round and it is back to Strauss waltzes bouncing from the blue curlicued bandstand, the rows of deckchairs, and the terraces behind, now disrupted by a lumbering modern office block. A little way along the Leas is a statue of Folkestone's greatest man, William Harvey, discoverer of the circulation of the blood, holding a heart in his hand. Harvey was born in Folkestone in 1578 and died in London in 1657, reputedly by taking poison after he found that he was going blind.

Beyond the Leas Folkestone turns into **Sandgate**, which still has a few weatherboarded cottages left in its High Street. Down on the beach is Sandgate Castle, one of Henry VIII's fortresses, neglected and with its front side washed away by the sea. Presumably in a century or so it will have vanished, like Sandown round the coast. The main road inland from Sandgate leads through the militarised wasteland of **Shorncliffe Camp**, passing a redbrick garrison church of cathedral-like dimensions.

Farther inland, beyond the bypass that skirts Folkestone to the north, are the remains of far earlier fortifications, on the top of the chalk hill known as **Caesar's Camp**. The ditches round the top may be Iron Age or medieval; the one thing that is certain is that they are not Roman. The Camp is a place of painful memory to me, as on a climb up to the top I was bitten by a malevolent horse; Kent also has its wild animals. A few hundred yards to the east is the smooth cone of **Sugarloaf Hill**, man-made, but no one knows why or when.

Newington, just north of the A 20, is still a remarkably countrified little village, in spite of its nearness to Folkestone. The church tower, topped by an ogee-shaped cap, is a landmark from the main road. The church has a Norman chancel arch and is packed with monuments; on the south wall is a brass to Dr Christopher Reittinger, a Hungarian who was physician to the Tsar of Russia, and died at Newington in 1612. Four centuries earlier, in 1201, the Lord of Folkestone and the Earl of Guisnes fought for the village in a trial by battle. The Earl won, and Newington was granted to the Abbey of Guisnes, in Flanders.

CHAPTER EIGHT

The Borders of Romney Marsh

꙾

THE crescent of land that stretches behind Romney Marsh from Hythe round to Rye marks the ancient southern coastline. At the eastern end, round Hythe, the gentle contours of the greensand ridge cram themselves into a steep escarpment above the levels of the Marsh; and beyond Appledore you are in an estuary area, where old maps show wide tongues of water stretching inland to Tenterden, isolating Oxney as a real island, and splitting Romney Marsh into separate fragments. This coastal strip is clearly defined by the waters of the Royal Military Canal. At the heart of the area is Tenterden, once a harbour town though now ten miles from the nearest sea. There are no trunk roads to speak of, apart from the A 20 skirting Hythe, which makes the district ideal for haphazard exploration.

Hythe itself is built on a succession of parallel terraces, rising from the canal to the parish church. The canal gives central Hythe much if not all of its character; shaded by tall trees it runs through the heart of the town, an ideal spot for a stroll or splashing about in a rowing boat. Though now isolated from the sea by the silting up of the estuary and the accumulation of shingle, Hythe was an important harbour in former centuries – the central Cinque Port, geographically speaking, between Sandwich and Dover to the east, and Romney and Hastings to the west. The coast is now a smooth stretch of shingle, and any trace of the harbour has long ago vanished.

The High Street is long and narrow. Half way down is the eighteenth-century town hall, perched on columns and with a clock jutting over the street. From the High Street narrow alleys lead up to the higher levels, where traffic should be deterred (but isn't) by the difficulties of squeezing through. The church, soaring over the town, is a big medieval building;

the tower was destroyed by an earth tremor in 1739 and re-built in 1750. Inside it is remarkable for its tall chancel, built about 1220 but not finally vaulted until 1886. From the nave you climb nine steps into the chancel, and the feeling of height is enhanced by a triforium gallery and clerestory windows above. Shafts of grey Bethersden marble add the finishing touches to this slightly dead elegance. Below the chancel is a vaulted crypt (reached from outside the church) lined like a catacomb with skulls and thighbones. They were formerly thought to have been placed there after a battle, but were probably dug up in the Middle Ages when fresh burials were made and laid finally to rest in the crypt. There are said to be 2,000 skulls and 8,000 thighbones; presumably these were the parts of the skeleton thought most worthy of preservation, ribs or vertebrae being thrown back into the ground.

When Cobbett visited Hythe in 1823, he could afford to make light of the Napoleonic threat, and disparage all the military preparations that had been made against it. The martello towers (there are two good examples at the end of the front at Hythe) came in for his special scorn – 'these ridiculous things, which I dare say cost five, perhaps ten, thousand pounds each'. Hythe itself 'is half *barracks*; the hills are covered with barracks; and barracks most expensive, most squandering, fill up the side of the hill' (they are still there, beside the canal). As for the canal, 'those armies who had so often crossed the Rhine and the Danube, were to be kept back by a canal, made by Pitt, thirty feet wide at the most!' What would he have said about the hideous concrete pillboxes that are dotted about the countryside? Perhaps, like the martello towers, they will be tourist attractions in a century or so, though it seems unlikely.

Up behind Hythe is the village of **Saltwood** – a small green, a medieval church lonely in a field, and the high walls of **Saltwood Castle,** until recently the home of Lord Clark, the art historian, and now occupied by his family (castle may be seen by special arrangement). The first castle here is said to have been built by Aesc, the son of Hengist, in 488; but Saltwood's chief claim to historical fame, or notoriety, came seven centuries later, in 1170, when the murderers of Becket met there to plot their crime. As an added irony, the castle previously belonged to Becket, as Archbishop of Canterbury and had been taken from him; the plotters probably met in the ruined Norman hall on the south side of the courtyard. The present owners live in the great gatehouse, whose towers are thought to have been added by Henry Yevele, the architect of the nave of Canterbury Cathedral, in the fourteenth century. The enormous room known as the Archbishop's Hall of Audience is now a library. Saltwood is an attractively romantic place to wander about in, as the ancient masonry is still largely creeper-clad, with flowers and even small shrubs growing between the stones of the battlements.

A couple of miles west of Hythe, along the B 2067, **Shepway Cross** marks the site of the Court of Shepway, where the authorities of the Cinque Ports met to carry out their official business. The name derives from 'Shipway', as before the channel silted up boats used to come up to West Hythe, and in Roman times even farther, to Lympne.

Lympne (pronounced Limm) was the Roman Portus Lemanis, one of the Forts of the Saxon Shore built against Saxon sea-raiders at the end of the third century AD. It stood on the now-vanished arm of the Rother that entered the sea at Hythe; indeed, the river itself was called the Limen or Limene, and is so marked on old maps. A Roman road, Stone Street, now the B 2068, leads due north from Lympne to Canterbury. If you walk down the steep path beside the present Lympne Castle, you will see the remaining fragments of the Roman fort in a field. The Saxons called it the 'stout wale' or strong fortress, a name down the years transmuted to Stutfall. **Lympne Castle** was built overlooking Stutfall about 1360, using stone from the Roman walls below; a previous house on the site was built for the Archdeacons of Canterbury by Lanfranc, William the Conqueror's Archbishop. The Castle was restored early this century. Though of no great interest, apart from a fine hall with kingpost roof, it stands in a superb situation, with wide-ranging views across the rich farmland of Romney Marsh to the hulking blocks of the Dungeness atomic power station in the distance – a lookout point from Roman days down to the Second World War. Next door to the castle is Lympne's medieval church, looking a good deal more fortress-like than the castle. The early Norman tower was built about 1100.

Lympne Airport, recently rechristened Ashford Airport, is the oldest airfield in regular airline service in the country. It was used by the R.F.C. in the First World War and the R.A.F. in the Second, and in between was the base for such record-breaking flights as Amy Johnson's to Cape Town in 1932. In the 1950s it was used for the first British car-air cross-Channel ferry.

Aldington was the home of one of those victims of delusion thrown up by the uneasy mental climate of the Reformation, Elizabeth Barton, the 'Holy Maid' or 'Nun of Kent'. A maid-servant at the Archbishop's manor house, she seems to have suffered from something like goitre ('a great infirmitie in her bodie,' says Lambarde, 'which did ascend at divers times up into her throte and swelled greatly'), leading to fits in which she prophesied and described events that were happening elsewhere. Her fame soon spread beyond Aldington to Canterbury. Archbishop Warham set up a commission to examine her on points of doctrine, which she answered successfully. If she had confined herself to miracles – 'lighting candels without fire, moistning women's breasts that before were drie and wanted milke, restoring all sorts of sicke to perfect health, reducing the dead to life againe' is Lambarde's comprehensive list – all would have been well. But she tried to intervene in Henry VIII's divorce proceedings against Catherine of Aragon, possibly instigated by the anti-divorce party, prophesying that he would lose his throne if he went ahead with the divorce. For this unwise remark she was executed at Tyburn on a charge of high treason.

Aldington's magnificent church (usually locked because of vandalism) stands on a high point above the scattered village. The tall Perpendicular tower is sixteenth-century, but the main building is much earlier, of the twelfth and thirteenth centuries. Inside there is some very fine woodcarving – fourteenth-century choirstalls, with floral carving below the misericords, and a flamboyant pelican on the front of the pulpit. Erasmus, the great Renaissance scholar from Rotterdam, appears on the list of rectors, for the year 1511–12. He is said to have resigned from the living because his English was not up to preaching a sermon; but it is most unlikely he ever came to Aldington.

In complete contrast to this lofty building is **Bonnington's** church, St Rumwold's, down by the Royal Military Canal.

Newman describes it in a pretty simile, 'like a plump little grey hen'. St Rumwold must qualify for the title of most improbable saint. Born in Northamptonshire in AD 662, he had the power of speech at birth, preached at Brackley on the second day of his life and died on the third. This was the saint whose image was such a money-spinner at Boxley Abbey (see p. 201). The church is said to be the oldest on the Marsh; it has a curious flat ogee cap on the shingled belfry, and the remains of a precipitously high musicians' gallery at the west end. Fortunately the lane beside it carries little traffic and nothing disturbs the quiet setting of trees and water.

At **Bilsington** a stone obelisk, half chewed away by time, stands on a rise overlooking the Marsh. This was put up in 1835 in memory of Sir William Cosway, M.P. for the district, who was killed falling from a stagecoach. The small, stumpy church is on the other side of the road, behind a well-preserved moat with farm buildings in the middle. A large bell, presumably too heavy for the flimsy bellcote, stands in a frame at ground level outside. Inside the church there is a good set of biblical texts painted in roundels. North of the village are the remains of **Bilsington Priory,** of which a fine hall and undercroft survive (can be seen on application to the owners of the modern Priory next door). The Priory, founded for Augustinian canons in 1253, was used as a lodging by the Archbishop of Canterbury on his periodic visits to Romney Marsh; he was allowed to stay there 'two nights and a day, but nothing more.'

On the outskirts of **Ruckinge** a field is edged with a row of ploughs and other Kentish farm implements – part of the collection of Mr Collick, a local farmer. Thomas Aveling, the pioneer of the steam traction engine in the 1860s, came from Ruckinge, and the village sign reproduces the smokebox door of an Aveling and Porter steam road roller. The church has a Norman tower with a weird lead spire poking through the usual conical roofcap. In the graveyard a plank with an illegible inscription marks the grave of the two Ransley brothers, notorious smugglers who in 1800 were hanged on Penenden Heath outside Maidstone for highway robbery.

Warehorne is a remote hamlet, built round a midget green. The church is large for so small a village; the tower was struck by lightning in 1770 and rebuilt in brick to the old battle-

mented medieval shape. Inside it has hardly been touched
since that date, and with its box pews and mouldering portrait
of some forgotten rector would still seem like home to R. H.
Barham, who lived in the village when he was rector of
Snargate (see p. 167).

Lightning must be a hazard along this exposed edge of the
Marsh, as **Kenardington** church across the field was struck in
the sixteenth century and severely damaged. The nave was
pulled down, the fine Decorated tracery of the south aisle
blocked up, and the aisle transformed into the nave. With its
bare interior it has a desolate air. In the fields below are the
remains of earthworks traditionally said to have been built
by King Alfred at the end of the ninth century to keep out the
Danes. The squarish enclosure can still be traced, and at the
lowest level is an entrance that in those days would have
opened on to the shore.

Woodchurch, a few miles inland, is a much more conse-
quential place than these quiet hamlets. The big church with
its tall broach spire is a landmark for miles around, partnered
by a derelict smock mill nearby. It is a straggling village, as
big in area as many small towns, built round a large triangular
green. The name presumably derives from the first Saxon
wooden church on the site. The present building is mainly
Early English, of the early thirteenth century, with arcade
columns alternately round and octagonal, and three tall
lancet windows in the east wall. The tower has enormous
buttresses because of subsidence; in spite of them the spire is
getting on for two feet out of true. In the south aisle is a
thirteenth-century medallion of glass showing the Entomb-
ment of the Virgin, a wonderful Rouault-like composition of
dark blue and brown. The Bonny Cravat pub opposite the
church is said to get its name from a French fishing boat used
for smuggling; 'Bonne Crevette' or 'Good Prawn' seems a
likely derivation.

From Woodchurch you can continue west for three miles
to Tenterden, or head south for **Appledore** on the edge of the
Marsh. Appledore was once a busy shipbuilding centre, but
it is now a quiet place, with a wide village street, and a church
with a squat battlemented tower. It has had its wild past: in
the ninth century it was captured by the Danes, who built a
fort where the church now stands; and in 1380 it was sacked

by the French. The church was rebuilt after this raid with the former north aisle and nave as a single unit, which accounts for the curious appearance of a wide nave leading to a far narrower chancel. Much of the wooden screen across the church dates from this rebuilding. The National Trust owns the stretch of the Royal Military Canal between Appledore and Warehorne.

The **Isle of Oxney** still has a cut-off island feel about it, and is still completely surrounded by water; though round much of the perimeter only ditches and streams remain of the wide waters that once covered the Rother Levels. The name 'Stone Ferry' is a reminder of the days when you had to take to the water to cross from the island village of Stone to the mainland. Outside the Ferry Inn is a list of the tolls that had to be paid until the 1930s to cross the bridge to Oxney, ranging from 1s. 6d. for a charabanc to 1d. for a pig or a Bath chair. **Stone** is a small scattered village; the square fortress-like tower of its church is a landmark as you approach Oxney from Appledore. The church was completely rebuilt after a fire in 1464. Inside, below the tower, there are far more ancient survivals – iguanodon bones dug up in a nearby quarry, and a misshapen block of stone that was once a third-century altar to Mithras, the god of the Roman legionaries. This may well have been the garrison altar of Stutfall Castle (see p. 147); the figure of a bull, the emblem of Mithras, can still be traced on the front.

Wittersham, the 'capital' of Oxney, is a largish village with a long, low church, mainly fourteenth-century. The massive battlemented tower was added at the end of the fifteenth century. In the Middle Ages Wittersham was famous locally for the quality of its miracle plays.

Heading north from Wittersham, you cross the Levels to **Smallhythe**, the ancient harbour of Tenterden. Like Appledore, it was a shipbuilding centre. Henry VIII visited Smallhythe in 1538, to inspect one of his warships under construction there. But now Smallhythe is visited for the **Ellen Terry Museum** (National Trust) in Smallhythe Place, down on the levels. This timber-framed yeoman's house was built about 1480 for the harbourmaster; on the lawn just below is a large rectangular pond, formerly the repair dock and now loud with the croakings of bullfrogs who have begun to colonise the marshes. Ellen Terry lived here for nearly thirty years, from 1899 until her death in 1928; the house is partly a museum and partly rooms preserved as she left them. Before films or recordings there was no way for an actress to pass on to the future her particular qualities, so for Ellen Terry we have to rely on the mute and static evidence of pictures of her most famous roles, or of the clothes she wore. Her first husband, the artist G. F. Watts, painted her as a young girl with flowing pre-Raphaelite hair, before the breakdown of their shortlived marriage; and subsequent drawings and photographs right through to old age show the same straight nose and determined chin. Her great days as an actress came in the last twenty years of the nineteenth century, when she played opposite Sir Henry Irving at the Lyceum; but of those glittering performances only the brocaded clothes survive, and the superlatives of Shaw and other writers.

A few yards up the road is another fine half-timbered house, the Priest's House, beside a small church rebuilt in brick after being burnt down in 1514. Apart from the gables, stepped in Dutch style, the church is hardly more than a brick barn.

More than any other town **Tenterden** sums up the Weald, both in the beauty of its buildings and in its general air of unruffled relaxation. The great pinnacled tower of its church, which from a distance dwarfs everything else into insignificance, retires into the background once you actually get into Tenterden, as it is set back a little from the High Street. This is the heart of Tenterden – wide and lined with grass and trees at the western end, then narrowing to the main centre of Georgian or half-timbered houses, shops and pubs. In Saxon times Tenterden belonged to Minster-in-Thanet (the name means '-den belonging to the men of Thanet'), which accounts for the rare dedication of the church to St Mildred. This lady, an Anglo-Jutish princess of Kent descended from King Ethelbert and Queen Bertha (see Canterbury, p. 74) was the daughter of Domneva who founded the nunnery at Minster in AD 669. In course of time Mildred succeeded her mother as abbess, and Tenterden was among the lands granted to Minster either before her death or soon after.

The tower is the manifestation of Tenterden's prosperity as a wool town in the fifteenth century. When the sea came

right up to Smallhythe Tenterden was a harbour town as well –
a 'limb' of Rye and thus a corporate member of the Cinque
Ports – and the church was worthy of such a centre of trade.
Inside it is an uncomplicated building, with a twelfth-century
nave, thirteenth-century south aisle, and fourteenth-century
north aisle. In the Lady Chapel is a fine seventeenth-century
monument to Robert and Martha Whitfield. Though the
figures kneel demurely enough, Martha at least was not
as meek as she appears, as records show her 'chiding
and brawling' in the church with another Tenterden house-
wife.

It is worth walking a little way along the Ashford Road to
the Unitarian meeting house. Built in 1746, it still has the
original pulpit and galleries. A painting on the wall shows
Benjamin Franklin attending a service in 1774.

Tenterden is well supplied with pubs. At one end of the
High Street the William Caxton perpetuates the now suspect
theory that the pioneer of printing was born in Tenterden.
The White Lion is a coaching inn with courtyard at the back;
while the Eight Bells looks the oldest of all, with an enormous
stretch of timbered wall along a side lane, and the ostler's bell
still hanging in the yard.

Tenterden's little station, at the end of Station Road, is the
headquarters of a band of enthusiasts who are working to
revive a ten-mile stretch of the Kent and East Sussex Railway
between Tenterden and Bodiam. The waiting room has been
turned into a museum of photographs and other historical
material relating to the line, and beside the road to Rolvenden,
at Rolvenden Station, a wonderful collection of old engines
awaits the reopening. Several of them were built in the 1870s
and '80s, but they are still perfectly capable of hauling their
loads along what was – and will be again – the most enchanting of country railways.

The Ashford Road leads through St Michaels, Tenterden's
northern suburb, to **High Halden**, a long, wide and rather
featureless village. The church, down behind the central
green, has an extraordinary octagonal wooden belfry tacked
on at the western end. Built in the late thirteenth or early
fourteen century, it is cunningly braced and buttressed with
timber; a cross-sectional plan inside the church reveals its
complex construction.

Rolvenden, back through Tenterden along the A 28, is like a small-scale version of Tenterden – brick and weather-boarded houses, a wide village street with a grass verge, a tall church tower. The church is mainly fourteenth-century, with columns alternately round and octagonal, as at Woodchurch. Over the south chapel is a large squire's pew, at first-floor level, set out like a comfortable room with carpet, table and chairs. In the sanctuary is a tablet to John Frankish, Rolvenden's martyr vicar, who was burnt at the stake in Canterbury in 1555; and over the door to the north chapel is a memorial by Sir Edwin Lutyens to Lt Henry Tennant, killed in the First World War. The Tennants lived at **Great Maytham Hall,** a neo-Georgian mansion designed by Lutyens and built in 1909–10 on the site of an eighteenth-century house that had largely burnt down. Great Maytham is now split into flats and run by the Mutual Households Association; the Lutyens entrance hall and main rooms, all fairly dull, and the old vaulted cellars can be visited. In the Middle Ages the estate was owned by a baron who rejoiced in the name of Orable de Maytham; and in Victorian times the Hall was let to Frances Hodgson Burnett, author of *Little Lord Fauntleroy*.

The road past Maytham brings you back across the Levels again to Wittersham. South from Wittersham you join the main Rye road (A 268) near **Peasmarsh,** an attractive switch-back of a place which tends to become a racetrack in summer. The Norman church, shapely and isolated, is down a lane south of the main village. It still has its round Norman chancel arch, carved with splendid heraldic animals; the chancel, enlarged two centuries later, has beautiful Early English lancet windows.

Iden is a quiet little village, with a small bright church tucked away behind the houses. The wide north aisle and chapel beyond have the effect of a second nave; on the aisle wall is a large oil painting of the Prodigal Son by Hans Feibusch, dated 1950. Iden church has unusually elegant roof timbers. Alexander Iden, the Sheriff of Kent who killed Jack Cade (see p. 269), is said to have come from here.

At the top of the hill down into Rye is **Playden.** Its church, battered and unrestored in an area where smartness is the general rule, has an exceptionally tall and graceful spire above a centrally placed tower. From the choir a long and

ancient ladder leads up into the tower; and in the north aisle
is a small sixteenth-century slab to a Flemish brewer, Cornelis
Roetmans, carved with barrels and mash forks as emblems of
his trade. He was a refugee from the Spanish persecutions in
the Low Countries, who settled along with the Huguenots at
Rye Foreign outside the town. Perhaps a Flemish mason
carved the inscription '*bidt voer de siele*' ('pray for his soul').

It is not surprising that tourists flock to **Rye**, as it might
have been planned to the specifications of the tourist industry.
First of all, it is indisputably a most beautiful town, full of
half-timbered and Georgian buildings that would be exceptional anywhere else, but in Rye hardly get a second glance.
Then it is built on a hill, as all good towns should be, so that
you can make a satisfying gentle progression from river level
up the cobbled streets to the church on the crest of the hill,
never in a straight line but always coming to sudden right-
angled bends, with some new vista of gable ends and tiled
roofs to lure you on. It has small boats to look at when you
are tired of buildings, forming a link with Rye's seafaring
and piratical past; and a history rich in raids, disasters,
smuggling and general villainy, scarcely credible among the
genteel antique shops, tearooms and small potteries that
mark the tourist transformation.

Most people approach Rye from London, down the main
road, and thus miss the superb distant view of the town
across the flats of Walland Marsh to the east. On no two days
does this prospect of the town seem the same. When the cold
east wind whistles across the marsh the red roofs and low-
towered church crouching on the hilltop stand out brilliantly
against the backcloth of hills; on hot, still days Rye is almost
hidden behind a veil of heat haze; and at dusk on a stormy
winter's day it looks unbelievably dramatic, hunched up
and twinkling with a few lights under a furious red-streaked
sky.

On signs beside the roads into the town the date 1289 is
prominently displayed (inevitably the signs are placed in the
far-from-medieval outer subtopia of Rye). It was in that year
that Rye was raised to the status of a royal borough; it was
already an 'ancient town' linked with the Cinque Ports and
equal in status, not just a mere 'limb', like so many of the
lesser ports around the south coast. In those days Rye really

looked like a port. The sea flowed right up to the foot of the cliffs, with the wide inlets of the Tillingham and Rother guarding the town on either side. Rye stood on an easily defended peninsula, entered through the frowning **Landgate** which still confronts the traffic, with other gates now vanished, and a strong town wall of which sections survive.

Though Rye was never affected by the sea to anything like the extent of Winchelsea, a great bite was taken out of the eastern cliff during the terrible storms towards the end of the thirteenth century, and a whole area of the town disappeared below the waves. In the days of its greatness Rye contributed five ships to the Cinque Ports fleet – as many as Romney, Hythe and Sandwich, but only half the number of Winchelsea; and it had the right of supplying fish direct to the king's table, carried up to London by special carriers known as 'rippiers'. It was the French, not the sea, that really finished Rye. In 1377, as the culmination of a long series of attacks, they swept down on the south coast, making Rye one of their chief targets. The town was burnt to the ground, and though it managed a slight recovery during the next two centuries the relentless silting of the estuary prevented it from ever again approaching its former status.

Rye had its share of famous visitors in pre-tourist days. Queen Elizabeth came there on a royal progress in 1573, and, according to tradition, was so pleased with her welcome that she granted the town the right to call itself 'Rye Royal'. No doubt this was more due to the gift of a hundred gold angels she received than to the townsmen's loyal if banal verses, which began

> O happy town, O happy Rye:
> That once in thee ye Queen doth ly,

and ended

> O God that givest life and breth:
> Preserve our Queen Elizabeth.

A century and a half later George I came to Rye a good deal less willingly. Early in 1726 he was blown ashore on Camber Sands and made his way to Rye, where he stayed four days with the mayor, James Lamb, in Lamb House, and stood godfather to Lamb's child, who was born the night of his arrival.

By this time smuggling was in its heyday. It was still flourishing when in 1773 John Wesley preached to the people of Rye, who were quite 'willing to hear the good word', but in spite of all his powers of persuasion 'will not part with the accursed thing smuggling'. Not surprisingly; as smuggling was highly profitable, and Rye might have been built for the purpose, with vaulted cellars below many of the houses for storing contraband, and interconnecting attics so that a smuggler could make his getaway below the eaves while the exciseman was banging on the door half a street away.

Rye has been an artist's delight since Van Dyck sketched it in the seventeenth century. It produced its own famous literary figure in the dramatist John Fletcher, born in 1579 possibly in the building called Fletcher's House (now tea-rooms) beside the church. But its greatest ghost is an American, the novelist Henry James, who fell in love with Rye at first sight, and from 1897 until two years before his death in 1916 lived at **Lamb House** (National Trust). This superb Georgian house, looking down a quiet cobbled lane, had been built by James Lamb shortly before George I's surprise visit; and its comfortable opulence exactly suited Henry James. The small garden building where he wrote *The Ambassadors* and *The Golden Bowl*, booming out those rolling sentences to his secretary, was destroyed by a direct hit in 1940. The only room that is anything like a literary shrine is the 'Henry James Room', with his writing desk, books by contemporaries and younger writers, and portraits which show him evolving from brooding youth to self-satisfied Master. One revealing exhibit is a page proof of *The American*, in which James reverses the usual progress of compression by putting six words in the place of one. (Only the Henry James Room and the garden are open to the public.)

James Lamb, the builder of the house, founded a family which ran Rye for well over a century, holding the office of mayor almost nonstop and in strict control of the parliamentary voting in those days of small electorates and rotten boroughs. In 1742 Lamb was involved in Rye's most notorious murder case – the killing of Allen Grebell by John Breeds or Breads, a 'sanguinary butcher'. Breeds had been fined by Lamb, who was mayor at the time, for giving short weight. Burning with resentment, he lay in wait for Lamb late one

night in the churchyard, and stabbed a figure he thought was
the magistrate with his butcher's carving knife. However, it
was not Lamb at all, but his brother-in-law Allen Grebell, who
had borrowed Lamb's cloak for the evening. Breeds was soon
arrested, as on the evening of the murder he had been roaming
about the streets shouting that 'butchers should kill Lambs',
and his bloodstained knife was found lying in the churchyard.
He was hanged, and left to rot on a gibbet, which can be seen
upstairs in the **Town Hall**. Only the skull is left; the rest of
the skeleton was removed by superstitious old women, who
boiled up the bones to make an infusion against rheumatism.
Also kept in the Town Hall are Rye's four maces: a small
sixteenth-century pair obviously descended directly from the
medieval fighting mace, and dented where they were used to
knock recalcitrant Ryers out of the way; and a splendiferously
massive Georgian pair, which could not have left the beadles
energy for anything more active than staggering beneath
their weight.

Round the corner from the town hall the huge Perpendicular
window of the **Church**'s north transept fills the end of Lion
Street. Set back above it is the low tower, dominated by the
gilded quarterboys who strike the bells over the clock (it is no
use looking hopefully towards the clock on the hour, as they
only bang their hammers on the quarters). Inside, the church
is far older than an outside glance would suggest. The transepts
are Norman, built about 1120; the nave, slightly later, provides
an evolutionary study, from the round arches by the crossing
to the full-fledged pointed Transitional at the western end.
The clock dominates the inside as it does the outside; the
first thing you see as you go in is the gilded pendulum swinging
overhead, and in the north chapel are the two original quarterboys of 1760, pensioned off in 1969. The modern replicas on
the tower are made of fibreglass, though you would never
know it. I was told that someone mathematically minded had
worked out that between them the old quarterboys had more
than twenty-one million hammer-blows to their credit. The
clock mechanism, still going strong after more than four
hundred years, can be seen in the belfry, on the way up the
tower. Made in 1560 by Lewys Billiard for £31, it is said to be
the oldest clock with its original works in any English church.
From the tower battlements there are wide-sweeping views

across the red roofs of the town to Romney Marsh and the Channel.

Rye is famous for its pubs. There are estimated to be seventeen of them (excluding clubs with bars); and I was told by the landlord of the Union that the record for the shortest time taken for a drink in each of them stands at twenty-three minutes. They range from the ultra-picturesque and half-timbered, like the Mermaid and the Flushing, to the dignified, white-painted Georgian of the suitably-named George, which has its own assembly room, complete with musicians' gallery. One of the excellent monographs published by the Rye Museum is entirely devoted to the old inns and ale-houses.

The Museum is well worth a visit, apart from its monographs. It is in the Ypres Tower, the thirteenth-century castle of Rye, and is full of every sort of bygone from mesh 'glasses' for protecting hop-pickers' eyes to Rye's eighteenth-century fire engine. Below the tower is the green open space called the Gun Garden, where in Elizabethan times 'good ordnance of Her Majesty' threatened the sheep and seagulls on the flats below.

The museum has pottery made in Rye as long ago as the thirteenth century, forerunners of the ware produced in a host of small potteries that have proliferated in the last few years. Best-known is the Rye Pottery, just outside the town, which reached its centenary in 1969. Its most typical local products are the 'Sussex pigs', which date back to the eighteenth century and were used at weddings. The head was removed, stood snout down and filled with beer, and the guests could thus each manage a hogshead without difficulty. The pig was taken as the stubborn symbol of the county:

> And you can pook and you can shove,
> But a Sussex pig he won't be druv.

So runs the old verse.

There is no room here to catalogue Rye's fine buildings: Rye's own guidebooks do this very adequately. But it is worth mentioning the ancient black-painted wooden warehouses along the Strand; and the extensive use of 'mathematical tiles'. These were tiles made to look like bricks, and used as cladding on half-timbered or plastered houses to give them an air of Georgian solidity. A good place to see them is on the

Conduit Street wall of the stationers in the High Street; the tiles are coming away here and there to reveal the deception. The George owes its eighteenth-century appearance to the tiles, though underneath there is a Tudor timber-framed building.

Though quite large boats still moor in the Tillingham beside the Strand Quay, the modern **Rye Harbour** is out towards the sea, reached down a dreary road lined with gravel workings. It has a spiky Victorian church, and a few old houses including one with a watchtower on one corner. Across the fields to the south are the low, rounded walls of **Camber Castle** (at present being restored and not yet open to the public). Like Deal Castle and its fellows round the coast (see p. 128), this was one of a chain of castles built during the invasion threat of the late 1530s. It is stranded hopelessly far inland today; but when it was built it was placed strategically on a spit of land commanding one side of the Rother estuary.

Winchelsea, hardly more than a mile away across the Brede, is in complete contrast to Rye. Rye seethes with tourist bustle, but at Winchelsea all is quiet, with hardly a shop to be seen among the red brick and white weatherboarding. Rye is so built up that it is bursting at the seams, whereas beyond Winchelsea's few streets of old houses there is nothing but grass, marked with the ghostly traces of the buildings that once stood there. Winchelsea is a disaster area from the distant past of English history. The blows that fell on it were the same as those suffered by Rye, though more severe. Both were 'ancient towns' with large fleets; but Winchelsea was more exposed to the sea, standing originally on a shingle spit running north-east from the cliffs near Fairlight. Throughout the thirteenth century the spit was gradually eroded, until a great storm in 1287 finally breached it and washed away much of the town. All the townspeople could do was to abandon it completely and move to higher ground; the old town became the 'Old Winchelsey Drowned' of early cartographers, and was finally forgotten.

Winchelsea was so important a part of the country's defensive system that there were none of the delays usually met with when a complete rebuilding is involved. Public buildings were put up on the new hilltop site; cellars were built for important merchants; and wharves were provided for them on the banks of the Brede. The grid layout of Winchelsea still betrays the hand of the town planner after seven centuries. Though the new town was safe from the sea, it was vulnerable to the French, who attacked and pillaged it seven times in the fourteenth and fifteenth centuries. In one of these raids the magnificent **St Thomas's Church** was largely destroyed. All that remains of this cathedral-like building, the centrepiece of Winchelsea, are the choir and side chapels. To left and right of the present west front, which is roughly where the rood screen would once have stood, are the weathered arches and buttresses of the transept walls, marking the limits of destruction. No one knows when the great west tower and nave were finally thrown down – perhaps not until the final French attack in 1459. An eighteenth-century print shows the two lower levels of the tower still standing, but they have since been pulled down.

What remains inside is of great beauty. Most notable are the superb tombs in the north and south aisles, with their stone canopies of pinnacled tracery. There are three tombs on the north side: the figures are older than the canopies and are believed to have been brought from Old Winchelsea church. They are of a cross-legged warrior in armour, marvellously preserved, a lady in a head-dress, and a scholarly-looking young man in a long robe. The two tombs on the south side are even more sumptuous, with canopies so lofty that they half obscure the windows. That on the left is thought to be of Gervase Alard, Admiral of the Western Fleet under Edward I, whose effigy lies in complete armour, the hands clasping a heart. The main gable of the canopy is supported by small heads of Edward I and Queen Margaret. The other tomb, only a little less grand, is probably of Stephen Alard, Captain and Admiral of the Cinque Ports and of the King's Western Fleet. The small heads are of Edward II and Isabella. For those who might be tempted to add their initials to the already well inscribed Alards, there is a notice of 1902 prominently displayed which warns that those who injure tombs are 'liable to imprisonment for not exceeding six months with or without hard labour and if a male under 16 with or without whipping.'

As striking in their way as the tombs are the stained-glass windows. They form an unusually unified set, as they are all by the same artist, Dr Douglas Strachan, and all date from round about 1930. Their style is half way between the simpering naturalism of most Victorian glass and the chunky abstractions of today; and apart from their decorative function they tell the history of Winchelsea in true medieval manner.

Across the road is the old **Court Hall**, with a museum on the upper floor. The lower floor was once the town gaol. In the museum is a model of the town in its prosperous days, and such strangely assorted exhibits as an old church barrel organ and an iguanodon's footprint from the bottom of Fairlight Cliff. Of great local interest are the boards painted with the names of Mayors of Winchelsea since 1295, beginning with Gervase Alard. A new Mayor is elected every Easter Monday, and Winchelsea is the smallest town in the country to have its own mayor and corporation.

Wandering about Winchelsea is an unworrying business, as there is no traffic to speak of, except on the main road. On the west side of the churchyard is **Wesley's Tree**, a small ash descended from the tree where Wesley preached his last open-air sermon in 1790; a pretty little Wesleyan chapel lies on the westernmost of the Winchelsea roads, opposite the ruins of the medieval Black Friars' house. A short way down this road is the **Pipewell Gate**, at the top of a steep cliff about thirty feet high where Edward I's horse shied and leaped over when the king was at Winchelsea to review the fleet. Amazingly, both horse and rider were uninjured, and the king rode calmly up the hill again and through the gate.

In its great days, before the French destroyed its buildings and its harbour silted up, Winchelsea had about six thousand inhabitants; now it is down to a tenth of that number. To get an idea of its decline, you can walk across the fields to the black hulk of the post-mill, across bumps and hollows that mark vanished streets and buildings. Best of all is to leave the town by the south exit, continuing down the road that leads past Wesley's Tree. On the left are the ruined chancel arch and choir of the **Grey Friars**, across a field which was once the town's market place. The road turns sharp right to Hastings, but a narrow lane straight ahead leads between fields full of small mounds and depressions down to Winchelsea's loneliest and most evocative ruin, the **New Gate**. It was through this gate that the French are said to have been treacherously admitted in 1380, and one can imagine them systematically pillaging their way northwards through the town, leaving devastation now covered by the grass. Beside the gate is the deep town ditch; but neither gate nor ditch could save the ancient town of Winchelsea.

CHAPTER NINE

Romney Marsh

❧

EARLY in his clerical career R. H. Barham was rector of Snargate, on **Romney Marsh**, and had no doubt of the supreme importance of that unique peninsula. 'The World', he wrote in one of his *Ingoldsby Legends*, 'according to the best geographers is divided into Europe, Asia, Africa, America, and Romney Marsh. In this last-named, and fifth, quarter of the globe, a Witch may still be discovered in favourable, i.e. stormy seasons, weathering Dungeness Point in an egg-shell, or careering on her broomstick over Dymchurch wall.' Witches are now hard to find, though an occasional warlock can be seen emerging on to the main road from the Dungeness atomic power station. But Romney Marsh is still as fascinating as ever: a fascination made up of the flatness and openness of the place after the little tucked-away lanes of the Weald; of the feeling that Dungeness is the Land's End of the south-east coast – far more so than Beachy Head or the North and South Forelands; and of the impermanence of an area wrested from the sea by dyke and sea-wall, which is yet steadily growing eastwards with the shingle carried along the coast by wind and tide.

Romney Marsh proper is bounded on the south by the road from Appledore to New Romney, which follows the line of the Rhee Wall, the Rivi Vallum of the Romans. South and west of the Rhee Wall is Walland Marsh, almost equally large; nevertheless, the whole expanse is generally known as 'Romney Marsh'. Denge Marsh, east of Lydd, gives its name to Dungeness – the 'ness' or point of land of Denge.

Since the Romans, every age has left its mark on Romney Marsh. The Saxons carried on the work of 'inning' or bringing the marshland into cultivation. The Normans and their successors built the superb churches which are astonishingly

A map for this chapter will be found on page 144.

thick on the ground for so small a population. Farmers bred the famous Romney Marsh sheep, which still dot the fields all over the Marsh, though many of the water-meadows are now ploughed up for potatoes and wheat; and if you drive down any of the little byroads the odds are that you will have to pull in for a few minutes while a farmer and his collie work the sheep from one field to another. Then came the holiday-makers, fringing the coast with bungalows and chalets at Camber on the southern side and along practically the whole eastern side. And finally within the last decade the Central Electricity Generating Board decided that Dungeness was remote enough for an atomic power station, and built alongside the lighthouses the great grey blocks which loom in the distance across the fields, and which are the focal points for the line of pylons striding westward towards the Kentish hills. Yet in spite of the pylons and gravel workings, the tourists and the holiday camps, Romney Marsh remains a secretive place, its essential character unaltered by this multifarious human activity.

At the heart of the Marsh lies the Romney Marsh group of parishes – not the towns like Lydd and New Romney, which have an almost metropolitan air among so many tiny places, but the hamlets centred on Ivychurch, with ten parish churches and a couple of ruins thrown in They lie so close together that they can all be visited in a day, and they form a unity in diversity, with brightly coloured royal arms on the wall, biblical texts gold-painted on oval boards, and clear glass windows letting the Marsh light stream in.

A mile north of the main road from Rye across the Marsh (A 259) is the little church at **Fairfield**, dedicated to St Thomas à Becket. Becket is said to have had lands round here, and the farm where the church key is kept is still called Becket's Barn. The church lies a couple of hundred yards from the road along a grass causeway surrounded by sheep and sheep's droppings: sheep, water, grass, wind and solitude make Fairfield the quintessence of the Marsh. Before the causeway was built parishioners had sometimes to come to church by boat, and a photograph inside the church shows it on a little island surrounded by flood waters in every direction. There was a church here early in the thirteenth century, but the present brick cladding dates from early this century.

Inside are tall grey-painted box pews, and a three-decker pulpit. The rector preached from the top level of the pulpit and read the lessons and prayers from the middle level, while his clerk sat in the cramped lowest compartment. The font is a numerical curiosity. The basin has seven sides, the base of the column on which it stands has five, and the plinth has ten.

Brookland is the largest of these Marsh villages. It has the most famous of all churches, and the most obvious, as it stands right beside the main road. The detached octagonal wooden belfry, looking like three candle-snuffers fitted one inside the other, has attracted various explanations: that it blew down off the church roof twice and after the second occasion was allowed to stay on the ground; that Cardinal Wolsey brought it to Brookland from Lydd; or that it was so astonished when a virgin came to be married at the church that it jumped off the roof of its own accord. In fact it has probably been there as long as the church. The lowest of the massive timbers, stretching tier on tier up into the gloom, are thirteenth-century, as is the church itself. It contains all sorts of interesting bits and pieces. Most notable is the lead font, Norman in provenance as well as date. It is a cylinder decorated round the outside with the signs of the Zodiac – a complete year from March round to February, and then the first eight months repeated, making twenty panels in all. Below each sign is the work for that month: in June (Cancer) a man mows with a scythe; in September (Libra) corn is threshed with a flail; in December (Capricorn) a man brains a pig with an axe. No one knows how the font got from Normandy to Brookland. One theory is that it may have been seized by English sailors in a raid on the French coast.

On the south wall are fragments of a wall painting of the murder of Becket, with a knight's sword raised over the saint's head. At the west end of the south aisle is a wooden enclosure known as a 'tithe pen', where the parson's corn, wine, cloth and other contributions from his parishioners used to be weighed out. The weights and measures for the purpose, beautiful precision objects dated 1795, stand in a glass case against the wall. Brookland church has a reminder of the eighteenth century's care for the comfort of the clergy: a wooden sentry-box known as a 'hudd' or hood, in which the

parson protected his wig from wind and rain while conducting
the burial service at the graveside.

In the late Middle Ages Brookland was the centre for games
and wrestling on the Marsh, and was also renowned for its
strolling players, whose Passion plays were much in demand.
Like the other Marsh villages, it became a centre of smuggling.

Snargate's sonorous name has a prosaic origin in the 'snare-
gate', or sluice-gate, which controlled the supply in the waterway leading to Romney Harbour. The big church, built on a
mound, dates from the thirteenth century, and has a simple
four-square stone tower built about 1400. On the north wall
are two lead sheets dated 1700 taken from the roof, one of
which shows that church repairers have been known to enjoy
themselves. On it appear the names of the churchwarden, the
plumber, and 'T. Apps, carpenter, and all his jolly men'.
Near by is a red wall painting of a galleon in full sail. Inevitably Snargate church was used by smugglers. In 1743 revenue
men seized a quantity of tobacco in the belfry and a cask of
Hollands gin under the vestry table. The north aisle was sealed
off from the rest of the church and was a regular smugglers'
hide. When Barham was rector here in the 1820s he was often
challenged by smugglers on the lanes to his home at Warehorne
a couple of miles away.

Brenzett church is a much smaller affair, and is the only
church in England dedicated exclusively to St Eanswith or
Eanswythe (Folkestone church shares the dedication with St
Mary, see p. 142). Its long porch has curious glazed window
arcades. Brenzett's chief historical claim to fame is that in
1381 it was the rallying point for Wat Tyler's Romney Marsh
supporters, armed only with pitchforks.

The largest and most prosperous of these buildings is at
Ivychurch; the name has nothing to do with creeper-clad
connotations, but means 'the church on the island in the
waters'. It is a Decorated church of complete uniformity, as it
was all built in the decade 1360–70. The stone entrance porch
is battlemented like a castle gatehouse; above is a parvise or
upper room, where a chantry priest may have lodged, and
which was put to use as a secret food store during the Second
World War. The Marsh has always been a possible landing-
point for an invader, and during earlier centuries the beacon
turret on the corner of the lofty tower was a watchman's

lookout post. Inside the church there is a feeling of great
spaciousness, as the nave is completely bare, with seats in the
choir alone. Along part of the south wall run stone seats,
reserved for the aged and infirm before the days of pews –
one explanation of the expression 'Let the weakest go to the
wall'. In the nave is a hudd, as at Brookland.

The north aisle is now partitioned off along its whole length.
Cromwell's soldiers are said to have stabled their horses on
its rough brick flooring, and in later centuries smugglers used
a vault below to conceal brandy, gin, tea and tobacco, hiding
the contraband in coffins emptied for the purpose. One Sunday
the rector was even turned away from the door by his own
sexton with the words 'Bain't be no service, parson. Pulpit
be full o' baccy, and vestry be full o' brandy.' Tea was so
expensive that the locals had to make their own out of marsh
herbs, and a jug of Hollands was cheaper than a pot of China.

Snave church, north along the road towards Ashford, is a
forlorn place, and is the only one of the group that recalls the
dilapidation of all of them remarked on by travellers a generation ago. You can only reach it on foot, down a grass track
between tall trees. The south porch seems to be crumbling
away; the whitewashed interior is of puritanical austerity.

The church at **Newchurch**, three miles to the north-east, has
a similarly forlorn, neglected look. It stands in an overgrown
graveyard, with bushes forcing their way between the bars of
family tomb enclosures. The battlemented tower leans away
from the body of the church at an angle of at least five degrees.
Inside there are unusually wide aisles, with the north aisle the
same width as the nave.

Most easterly of the group is **Burmarsh**, only a mile outside
Dymchurch. This is one of the earliest of the Romney Marsh
settlements, the name deriving from the Saxon Bur-wara-
mersce, the 'men of the burgh of the marsh'. The little church,
reached by a footbridge across a stream, is largely Norman,
with a good rustic Norman south doorway. The tower was
rebuilt in the fourteenth century.

Dymchurch, on the coast a mile to the south, crouches
behind the massive sea-barrier of Dymchurch Wall, first built
by the Romans. Dymchurch strikes a balance between being
a seaside resort and an unspoilt little town. In spite of the
holiday camps at adjoining St Mary's Bay and an amusement

arcade, the centre of Dymchurch, with its curving main street, and church and town hall down a side road, has very much the Kentish village feel. The church is an enlargement of 1821, and much of the old Norman work remains hidden inside; the original Norman west door now forms the inner arch under the tower.

Opposite the church are the local authority offices in an eighteenth-century building. Upstairs is the old Court Room, which can be seen on request; it still has high box seating and the Royal Arms of George II, together with a small museum of Romney Marsh exhibits. Especially interesting are the old maps of the area, showing Dungeness much blunter than it is today, and the Marsh subdivided into sections called 'waterings'. Down by the wall is a martello tower full of exhibits showing the preparations against invasion during the Napoleonic wars; it also has a cannon mounted in a suitably anti-Bonaparte position on the roof. The tower was built where it is to protect the sluice controlling the water level of Romney Marsh – of paramount importance, as the whole of the Marsh is below mean high tide level, and Dymchurch itself is more than seven feet below.

The legendary exploits of smugglers, excisemen and red-coats in and around Dymchurch have been celebrated, and glamourised, in Russell Thorndike's series of novels about Dr Syn, a fictional vicar of Dymchurch at the end of the eighteenth century. Dr Syn himself has the best of both worlds by leading a Jekyll and Hyde or Scarlet Pimpernel life as both parson and smuggler; the sordid and brutal realities of the constant war of attrition between lawbreakers and revenue men are transmuted into a gentlemanly contest by the novelist's skill. Every other year in the summer Dymchurch is turned over for a day to a Dr Syn carnival, when cargo is landed on the beach, battles are staged, and the present rector leads the proceedings disguised as Dr Syn and his alter ego, the smuggling Scarecrow.

At **St Mary-in-the-Marsh**, a couple of miles inland to the west, you are back among the churches of the central Marsh. The building is simple and remote. Inside the door on the west wall is what seems to be a medieval altarpiece, with three scenes separated by carved wooden saints, and by the door is a tablet to E. Nesbit (1858–1924), the writer of *The Railway*

Children and other children's books, who is buried in the churchyard.

Old Romney church, the last of the central group, lies down a little side road, and is separated from the main road by a field full of sheep. There may well have been a church here since Saxon times, as the Saxons reclaimed or 'inned' a large area where Old Romney now stands. Originally there was a single port of Romney – the ancient Cinque Port, called by the Saxons Rumenea – but as the sea retreated the seaward part grew in importance, and Old and New Romney were being differentiated by the early thirteenth century. This church is the most delightful of all the Marsh group. It stands in a beautiful setting, with a giant yew in the churchyard, and has a sturdy tower with a squat spire on top, and a higgledy-piggledy roofline which reflects its gradual growth from the thirteenth century on. Inside there is an air of homely tidiness. The box pews are trimly painted pink, as is the splendid minstrels' gallery at the west end, which still has the minstrels' pews in place. Pews and gallery were restored by the Rank organisation, who used the church in a film about Dr Syn. The roof beams are rough-hewn, and the stonework is equally massive.

The altar in the north chapel is a smooth black stone slab, marked with five consecration crosses – the original medieval *mensa*, discovered during restoration work in use as a step. It is an extremely rare survival, as both Edward VI and Queen Elizabeth ordered all stone altars to be destroyed as undesirable links with pre-Reformation days. In the chancel floor a stone slab commemorates John Deffray, rector for nearly half a century. He was a French Huguenot who fled from France after the Revocation of the Edict of Nantes in 1685, and ended up as rector of Old Romney in 1690. Ten years after his arrival he wrote how he had found the church and services neglected, but instituted a choir and set up a 'religious society'. The outcome of his labours was that 'to the joy of all pious souls, our shepherds, ploughmen and other labourers, at their work perfume the air with the melodious singing of psalms.'

New Romney is the capital of the Marsh. It has a long, straight country-town High Street, with a grey-painted town hall on the south side. Farther up on the north side the imposing red-brick front of Priory House keeps its Dickensian shop windows on either side. New Romney church, built about 1100, is one of the glories of the Marsh. Before the great storms at the end of the thirteenth century altered its course, the River Rother ran into the sea in a large bay with New Romney at its apex; and ships could moor beyond the churchyard walls. The land still drops away below the walls, but it needs the eye of faith to see a harbour in the haphazard collection of bungalows and yards that now stand there; though there is still a narrow, sluggish watercourse under a bridge.

As you come down the street towards the church, the massive tower looms over you, bewildering in its variety of stonework and window pattern, like some textbook of late Norman masonry. Steps lead down into the church; presumably with the years the roadways to north and west have been gradually built up. Inside, the church has the Marsh pattern of nave and aisles of equal length, and no transepts. The tower was a little later than the original church. If you walk through the high arch beneath the tower and look upwards, you can see the patterned arcading which decorated the original west front, and was cut through or blocked up when the tower was added.

In earlier times the church was a centre for local government, with the sessions of the Jurats, the yearly Cinque Port meetings and the election of the Mayor all taking place there. It is worth looking downwards as well as upwards, as the floor is a grand mix-up of tiles of all periods, surrounding black memorial slabs whose beautifully incised inscriptions are a copybook of seventeenth- and eighteenth-century lettering. Above one of the sedilia is a carved stone head of a tonsured priest, individual enough to be a portrait.

A mile from New Romney, where once the sea flowed in between two spits of land, are the two resorts of **Littlestone** to the north and **Greatstone** to the south. Littlestone has an air of faded Victorian gentility, with a large pink granite Diamond Jubilee fountain on the sward in front of the hotels. Greatstone forms part of the largely bungalow sea frontage which stretches south as far as Dungeness. At low tide a sunk section of the Second World War Mulberry harbour which never got to France can be seen offshore.

If Romney Marsh is a world on its own, then **Dungeness** is a world within that world. It is a place where incongruities meet on a few square miles of windswept pebbles – a pair of lighthouses, the bird sanctuary at Boulderwall, sea anglers shoulder to shoulder, the vast masses of the atomic power station, gravel pits, the Pilot Inn with a cluster of houses round it, the lifeboat brightly painted and ready for emergency at the top of its slipway, a shanty town of old railway carriages. A good first impression can be got from the top of the old lighthouse, which is open on most summer afternoons. The view takes in the whole coastline from Fairlight round to Folkestone. Immediately at the foot of the lighthouse, and beyond it to the shore, the grasses have colonised the shingle in successive waves, with bare patches between, so that waves of green seem to be reflecting the grey of the sea. The line of the derelict railway can be followed, converted along some of its length into the road to the power station. Most obtrusive of all is the power station itself, only a few hundred yards away on foot, yet a good three miles by car, as you have to go half way back to Lydd and then double back on your tracks to get there by road.

A light of sorts has stood on Dungeness Point since early in the seventeenth century, when an open coal fire was kept alight there, financed by dues levied on passing shipping. By the mid eighteenth century the sea had receded considerably, and there was obviously need for a large and permanent structure. This need was met by Samuel Wyatt, who in 1792 built a tower over a hundred feet high, lit by eighteen sperm oil lamps instead of a coal fire. An electric light was installed as early as 1862, and the lighthouse continued in use until the beginning of this century, when it too had been stranded inland by the build-up of shingle. Its circular base has now been turned into the lighthouse keepers' homes, neatly painted in the Trinity House livery of white, green and black. The black tower which superseded it, and which visitors now climb, operated from 1904 until 1961, when the atomic power station obscured its light, and it had in turn to make way for the elegant black and white minaret of the new automatic lighthouse, worked from complex control panels in its base.

The new tower is floodlit, which makes it more visible to shipping, and also reduces deaths among migrating birds which might otherwise collide with it. The ground floor can be visited in the afternoon, but 'only if the fog signal is not sounding'.

The shingle movement that makes lighthouses obsolete could leave the atomic station on an island, and means that for much of the year lorries are kept busy carting shingle westward from the point to the far side of the station, in a perpetual motion of stone. At the moment only Dungeness 'A' is in operation: Dungeness 'B', which will be considerably more powerful, is still being built. Dungeness 'A' can be visited on Wednesday afternoons in summer (tickets must be got beforehand from local electricity showrooms), or at other times by special arrangement; though it is a schoolboy's delight, no child under fourteen is allowed round. Going round Dungeness is like a conducted tour of the temple of an esoteric religion, with clicking geiger counters to measure the strength of the invisible power. The fact that it is like any other power station, except that it uses atomic fuel instead of coal, tends to be overlooked. The tour takes in one of the reactors; through a window you look down into an enormous hall, where white-clad figures pad silently around below a gigantic gantry, which rolls gently forward laden with fresh fuel elements for the living heart of the reactor. In the central control rooms banked dials monitor every activity of the uranium core, of the gas that is heated by the energy produced in the reactor, and of the steam that drives the turbines; while computer printouts snake on to the floor. A concrete-sided whirlpool outside marks the return to the sea of the huge quantities of water used for cooling purposes – one reason that led to the choice of Dungeness as a site. The rows of sea anglers on the steep shingle seem singularly unworried by the much publicised risks of atomic power stations; and you can buy superb fresh-caught fish at many of the roadside shanties.

Before the present network of little roads the locals had to walk everywhere on the shingle, and for this evolved their own footwear – the 'backstays' or 'backsters', wooden over-shoes rather like snowshoes.

Dungeness has lost much of its ancient windswept solitude; yet if you stand on its eastern shore, with nothing between you and the sea except a few fishing boats and black-painted huts standing out against the shingle, you can recapture that sense of remoteness, until the damp mist blows in from the sea and the world shrinks to the pebbles round your feet.

Anyone with children will certainly want to see Romney Marsh from the Romney, Hythe and Dymchurch Railway, which has one of its termini – if that is not too pretentious a word – at Dungeness. On its thirteen-mile journey the railway passes over roads, dykes and ditches, and gives a complete picture of the Marsh terrain, from the naked shingle of Dungeness to the meadows round Hythe. For enthusiasts, there is a 'model land' at New Romney. The main section of the railway, covering the eight miles between Hythe and New Romney, was opened as long ago as 1927, to link up the Southern Railway terminals at each of those towns. The five-mile extension out to Dungeness was opened two years later. Though the gauge is only fifteen inches, the railway can carry an amazing amount of traffic; motorists are liable to be held up while the *Green Goddess* or *Samson* chugs slowly by (maximum speed of trains at level crossings, 5 m.p.h.), bursting with an axle-bending load of holidaymakers. The R.H. and D. was considered of such strategic importance that it was requisitioned by the army in the Second World War, and carried much of the material for Pluto – the pipeline under the ocean from Littlestone to France which supplied our forces in Europe after D-Day.

With its nearness to Dungeness power station, **Lydd** now rivals New Romney in importance. Yet it is still hardly more than a village, overshadowed by its enormous church which has been called the 'cathedral on the Marsh'. Thomas Wolsey, the future Cardinal, was vicar here early in the sixteenth century. The noble pinnacled tower, 132 feet high, was built in the 1440s and looks as though it should belong to an Oxbridge college rather than a parish church. At the foot of the tower are twin pairs of doors set in the base of a single arch. Originally a Saxon basilica stood on the site, and there is still some Saxon stonework in the north aisle. A plan inside the church shows its conjectural Norman predecessor completely engulfed by the present long, low bulk of nave and aisles. Much of the fabric, including the chancel, is new, as the church suffered a direct hit in the Second World War, which destroyed the chancel, and damaged the chapels and roofs. A painting under the tower inside the west doorway shows the extent of the damage. The new chancel ceiling is white, with coloured oak leaves and Tudor roses; and the new east window has three narrow lancets, full of glowing purple and red glass. As at New Romney, the church at Lydd was used for local affairs. The Jurats and commons of Lydd used to meet around the Stuppeny tomb, in the North Chapel, to elect their Bailiff – a custom that carried on until 1885.

Behind the church there is a pretty little triangular green surrounded by small shops and houses, and near it on the main road some big eighteenth-century houses. Down towards the coastal firing ranges Lydd peters out in a waste of derelict army hutments. Lydd gave its name to the explosive called Lyddite, which was first tested here towards the end of the nineteenth century.

Along the southern side of the Marsh the steep shingle beach of Dungeness merges into the huge level expanse of Camber Sands. Camber is a holiday village built among or on the sand dunes, and when the wind blows hard from the south you may find yourself in a whipping hail of sand which is the nearest approach to a Sahara sandstorm the South Coast has to offer. The vast dunes, topped with marram grass and gorse scrub, are a favourite with film-makers. Outside Camber the dunes provide natural bunkers for the Rye golf course, one of the finest championship links in the country.

CHAPTER TEN

Ashford and the North Downs

❧

SOUTH-WEST of Canterbury the valley of the Great Stour cuts through the North Downs, and gives easy access to Ashford and the farmlands of central Kent. The main road (A 28) takes the line of least resistance and follows the same course, through a landscape of hill and woodland, seldom more than a few hundred yards from the waters of the river.

Chartham, the first separate village beyond the outskirts of Canterbury, reconciles the medieval and the modern in an unusually successful way. From the main road your eye is caught by the enormous church, with its row of Decorated windows down the side; but it is not until you have crossed the railway into the village that you realise there is also a large paper mill on the other side of the Stour. Chartham has two village greens – a large open space directly in front of the church, and behind it a smaller triangular green forming the heart of the village. The church belonged to the monks of Christ Church, Canterbury, which accounts for its great size; it dates mainly from the 1290s, with a Perpendicular tower added about two hundred years later. The magnificent chancel windows are of the type known as 'Kent tracery', in which the stonework in the upper part seems to burst apart into starlike shapes. The roof is equally splendid – a forest of close-set beams, linked at the crossing by a carved boss. In the north transept is a very fine early brass to Sir Robert de Septvans, who died in 1306. He is shown in chain mail, with head uncovered and curling hair (the absence of a helmet may mean that he died in his bed rather than on the battlefield), and his legs crossed in a balletic, even yoga-like, position. On his shield and surcoat are the seven winnowing fans ('sept vans') which form a rebus on his name.

Above the village the brick buildings of St Augustine's Hospital sprawl across the hillside. The road over Chartham

Downs, below the hospital, is one of the most spectacular couple of miles in the whole of Kent.

From Chartham you can continue along the main road to Chilham (see p. 179), or turn off through the delightfully named **Old Wives Lees** for the villages on the northern slopes of the downs. None of them is of particular importance individually, but jointly they make a composite picture of quiet remoteness. There is not a single east–west road along the downs, and finding your way from one place to another can be a time-consuming business.

Selling straggles up and down the hills; its cruciform church, with commanding brown-rendered central tower, has a fine Early English chancel and chapels. The church at **Sheldwich** has a unique fourteenth-century window high above the chancel arch, a wild triangular affair with blob-like excrescences on the whirling tracery. The tiny Early English church at **Badlesmere** (down a road signposted Fisher Street) has hardly been touched since the eighteenth century. It still has box pews, three-decker pulpit and textboards painted in cream on brown; the pew-ends nearest the altar were carved about 1415.

Throwley is right up on the high downs. Its stark Perpendicular church tower is visible miles away across the fields; in the north chapel is a statue to George, first Lord Harris, a tough campaigner who captured Seringapatam in 1799, during Wellesley's victorious campaign against Tippoo Sahib in India.

Eastling is an open little village, with a good pub called the Carpenters Arms. Two miles to the south is **Otterden Place**, run by the Mutual Households Association and divided mainly into flats, which still keeps the look of a Tudor brick mansion, though it was largely rebuilt in the early nineteenth century. The main rooms can be seen (Wed. and Thurs. afternoons, May–Sept.). Downstairs there are a large number of portraits of the Wheler family, who bought Otterden early in the eighteenth century and still own it. Most interesting of them was the Rev. Granville Wheler, Prebendary of Southwell, whose sharp-featured clerical face gazes down from the library wall. In 1729 he carried out electrical experiments in the long gallery upstairs, charging a glass rod by rubbing it with a silk handkerchief, and holding it near one of the

C.G.K.S.   M

Otterden pageboys to make his hair stand on end. His son, another Granville, gambled away much of the Wheler fortune. At his death in 1786 Otterden was ruinous, and could only be salvaged by pulling down much of the Tudor courtyard house and remodelling what was left. The house has a very rare survival: in a back courtyard is a donkey wheel used to draw water from the well.

Otterden Place has its own small church – an eighteenth-century redbrick barn on a medieval site. Inside there are three remarkable tombs from the years around 1600, on a lower level than the present floor, and presumably at the level of the floor of the original church. Most impressive is the ponderous monument to Sir Justinian Lewin (died 1620), an armoured effigy with his wife kneeling beside him.

Newnham has an unspoilt village street, with one outstanding half-timbered house decorated on its plaster panels with red swirls of foliage. The church at **Doddington** is worth a short detour up a tree-lined lane. It has an exceptional dedication to the Beheading (Decollatio) of John the Baptist. Externally its oddest feature is the pretty west tower, white weatherboarded up to the battlements. It is largely Norman, with the original east window arrangements of three small openings and another above. One of the main piers has been cut away to form a 'double squint' giving views of the main altar and the altar in the Early English side chapel; fortunately this tunnelling does not seem to have affected its usefulness as a support. In the chapel a monument to George Swift, a young law student, records an early road fatality. He died in 1732, 'By an Unfortunate Fall from a Chariot'.

Milstead has a good village centre; the church faces across the road to the superb half-timbered manor house. **Bredgar** is larger, with a good deal of modern building going on, and a neat village pond in the middle. The name derives from the 'broad gore' or wide forest clearing of a Saxon settlement, and there was probably a church here in Saxon times. The present church is mainly fourteenth-century, though the Norman west door survives from an older building. On the other side of the Sittingbourne road (A 249) is **Stockbury.** From a distance the church tower, solitary on a bluff overlooking the valley, looks like the keep of a fortress; and in fact it stands near the site of a vanished castle. Below the church the orchards tumble into the valley, and behind it the road slopes down to Stockbury village, built round a tiny green.

From here you can head back for Canterbury along the M 2, joining it at the Stockbury interchange.

Chilham, back again in the Stour valley, is one of Kent's most self-conscious beauty spots. Isolated from through traffic, its enchanting square of half-timbered houses is now a large car park, and the houses are mainly tearooms and antique shops. The village stands, in proper feudal manner, between the churchyard and the gates of the castle. The church has a fine Perpendicular tower, built in a flint and Caen stone chequering; the nave is fifteenth-century, while the transepts are a hundred years older. For a few years after St Augustine's Abbey, Canterbury, was dissolved, the gilded shrine that contained St Augustine's body was kept in the church, but in 1541 it was removed and disappeared. It is a simple and stately building, with several remarkable tombs to members of the Digges family. Largest of all is the tall black marble column in the south chapel, commemorating Lady Mary Digges, who died in 1631 and was the wife of Sir Dudley Digges, builder of the present Chilham Castle. The column, eleven feet high, is surrounded by figures of the cardinal virtues – Justice, Prudence, Temperance and Fortitude. In the north aisle is a more typically seventeenth-century monument to Sir Dudley's sister, Lady Margaret Palmer, who died in 1619 and was, according to the inscription, 'fayrer then most women wiser then most men'. Here the polished Bethersden marble has been cut away in an intricate pattern to give a luxuriously inlaid effect. Such tombs are a whole world away from the Victorian pathos of the memorial in the chancel to the two little Hardy boys, sons of the owner of the Castle. With their arms round each other, they are reading the *Babes in the Wood*, while their battledore and shuttlecock lie on the ground beside them.

The Castle is not open to visitors; but the grounds are, and enough can be seen to get a fair idea of the building. The Norman keep of the original castle is hidden away round the back of the house. Below it Saxon construction has been discovered, and there may well have been some kind of fortress on the site even in pre-Roman times. Sir Dudley Digges completed his brick Jacobean mansion in 1616; he was a highly successful diplomat and lawyer, who in 1618 went on an embassy to Moscow for James I, and when he died in 1639 held the office of Master of the Rolls. His house is a typical assemblage of gables, tall chimneys and stone-mullioned windows, and has been attributed to Inigo Jones. What is not typical is the ground plan, which forms five sides of a hexagon, with an open side at the back, enclosing a central courtyard. This shape accounts for the strange angles the sides of the house make with one another. Below the Castle the gardens fall away in a series of terraced lawns towards the Stour valley, with an aviary and lake on the valley floor, and a heronry at the western end of the park. On summer afternoons there are usually displays of falconry in the gardens, when you can put on a gauntlet for a falcon to land on your wrist, or buy jesses, bells, bewits and other accoutrements to take home with you.

The downs hereabout are poor in prehistoric remains. There is, however, one impressive example, the long barrow known as **Jullieberrie's Grave**, across the Stour from Chilham. The track below the Jullieberrie Downs runs fairly close to it, but the barrow takes a bit of finding. To get to it you have to skirt a field and come down almost to the banks of the Stour; the barrow is there right enough, but is heavily overgrown with thorn bushes. A copse of tall trees grows along one side of it. The strange name Jullieberrie is said to be a corruption of the name Julius Laberius, one of Julius Caesar's tribunes killed in a battle near Chilham in Caesar's second expedition in 54 BC.

At **Godmersham**, set in the rich parkland of the valley floor, there is no village to speak of. A semicircle of road crosses the Stour, which meanders through watermeadows studded with enormous oak trees, and brings you to Godmersham Park, a wide Georgian brick mansion. In the 1790s Godmersham was inherited by Jane Austen's brother Edward; she often stayed here, and may well have drawn on her memories of this idyllic place when she wrote *Mansfield Park* (though the story is set in Northamptonshire). In order to inherit Godmersham and other properties, Edward had to change his name from Austen to Knight, which seems a small enough price to pay for so many pastoral acres. The church, outside the brick wall of the park, has a Norman tower built on the north side; the tower has its own eastern apse, showing that it was used as a separate chapel. There is a strange Victorian screen perched up on tall wooden pillars; and in the chancel a naive medieval relief carving shows a mitred bishop, possibly Becket, seated below his own cathedral.

On the other side of the main road is **Crundale**, up terrifyingly narrow lanes in the heart of the downs. Its isolated church, backing on to a wide downland valley, has a good deal of Norman work remaining, including the arcade cut through the nave wall into the north aisle. Inside the door is a huge fifteenth-century stone graveslab, incised with the figure of a priest in full canonicals.

A stretch of the downs between Crundale and Wye is now a national nature reserve, famous for orchids and rare butterflies and moths.

Wye is now chiefly known as the home of one of this country's main agricultural colleges, but it is in addition a smart little country town, between the placid waters of the Great Stour and the steep scarp of the downs. Its most prominent landmark is up on the hillside – a large crown, carved in the chalk by students of the college to commemorate Edward VII's coronation in 1902. The churchyard and the college fill the centre of the town, looking across to the Green with its timbered houses, and the Georgian dignity of Church Street. Wye's church is an odd-looking building, reflecting the disasters of its history. It was originally a large cruciform building of about 1300; the nave and aisles survive from this period. In 1572 the steeple was struck by lightning and set on fire, and in 1686 the tower collapsed, bringing down the whole east end. This was never rebuilt; instead, in the eighteenth century, the present little apsidal chancel was built where the old tower once stood, and the massively buttressed and pinnacled tower was built in the south-east corner. There are hardly any monuments, but there is a good set of funeral hatchments below the big clerestory windows.

Wye was the birthplace, in 1640, of Mrs Aphra Behn, the Mata Hari of Restoration England, who spied for Charles II on the Continent, and had a second career as the first woman novelist.

Wye College has now expanded far beyond its medieval

beginnings at the corner of the churchyard. It was founded in 1447 by Cardinal John Kempe, who was in his time Lord Chancellor to Henry VI, Bishop of Rochester, Chichester and London, and Archbishop of York and Canterbury. At the Reformation the college for secular priests was disbanded, but Kempe's grammar school survived until 1893, when the buildings were turned into an agricultural college for the south-east, and later into the agricultural branch of London University, including a 720-acre farm.

The college has a museum (open p.m. Wed. June–Sept., Sat. Aug.) at the village of **Brook**, three miles outside Wye. A vast medieval barn houses a collection of every sort of farming bygone, from carts and ploughs to a land-measuring wheel that turns three hundred times per mile. An oasthouse at the back has smaller exhibits like sickles and bird scarers. The labour-saving thistle tongs could surely be adapted for lazy gardeners by some enterprising maker of garden tools. Brook, in a fine open situation below the downs, gets its name from the stream that runs along the edge of the road. The Norman church, next door to the museum, has an enormously wide, square west tower; apart from the windows, the whole building has remained unaltered since early Norman times. Above the tower arch two windows, from a chapel or priest's room in the tower, look down into the nave. There are remains of medieval painting right along the south wall, and in the chancel are scenes from the life of Christ, set in painted roundels to separate them from one another.

Ashford stands at the hub of all the communications of central Kent. From it roads radiate in six different directions and railways in five; and it has recently drawn Lympne Airport (see p. 147), rechristened Ashford Airport, into its orbit. It has been designated one of the chief growth areas under the Strategic plan for the South East, so what the town and the villages round it will be like by the end of the century is anybody's guess. At the moment it is expanding fast, and swallowing up outlying places in a sea of industry and housing development. But it still has a recognisably Georgian town centre – made a good deal more tolerable since the by-pass was built – which stands on a spur of high ground above the Great Stour, and is separated from most of the later suburbs by the river and its tributary streams.

The High Street, at the heart of old Ashford, is very much the main street of a country town, a place of small shops rather than supermarkets, with some good Georgian buildings left, like the three-storey red-brick County Hotel. Half way down is the little rabbit warren of gabled shops called Middle Row, all overhangs and unexpected corners. At one end of the High Street is Castle Street, worth the short stroll to have a look at the green-painted First World War tank preserved there as a memorial; and at the other end East Hill, dropping steeply down to the river, has some of the best Georgian houses in the town. These are incorporated into Ashford girls' public school, whose main buildings take up much of the north side of the hill.

Away from the High Street, on the south side behind Middle Row, is the calm of the churchyard, surrounded on all sides by good brick or white-painted houses. On the west side is the single tall brick gable of the old grammar school, dated 1635. The church's soaring tower, with a gilt-vaned pinnacle at each corner, is a landmark for miles around; it formed part of a major rebuilding scheme for the church begun and financed by Sir John Fogge about 1470. Fogge was a leading Kentish landowner, who served in Parliament and became Treasurer of the Royal Household to Edward IV. After weathering the storms of Richard III's reign he held office under Henry VII, and died in 1490. His huge stone table tomb is in the chancel, north of the altar. Fogge's additions were the final stages of an overall reconstruction that had been going on for well over a century. Nave and aisles are wide, with galleries round all three sides. The elaborate nave ceiling, panelled and embossed, is dated 1638. Even finer is the ceiling below the tower at the crossing, part of the original Fogge decorative scheme of the 1470s, painted in grey and black, with gold rosettes. In the south transept are three enormous effigied tombs to Sir Thomas Smythe (see Sturry, p. 91) and two of his sons. Smythe, who died in 1591, is carved reading a book. Known as 'Customer' Smythe because he was in charge of the Port of London customs, he was a man of great wealth; under the tax-farming system of the day he paid the Queen an annual rent of £30,000 for the customs and no doubt made a handsome profit. The Latin inscription commends him for his 'singular liberality towards those of the higher rank and love for the trading interests'. In short, a Customer who was always right. Also in the transept is a superb Charles II royal arms, put up in 1660.

After centuries of somnolence as an agricultural centre, Ashford was dragged into the industrial world with the coming of the railways in the 1840s. The locomotive works down Newtown Road were opened in 1847 and are still one of British Rail's chief construction and maintenance centres for rolling stock. The works, reached past a typical Victorian campanile, and the yellow brick houses built for the maintenance men, still form a mid-nineteenth-century enclave that can hardly have altered externally, except for the modern signs reading 'Cyanide Hardening Shop' or 'Sheet Metal Shop', and the occasional fork-lift truck staggering past under a load of axles and wheels. (Visits on Tues. and Wed. afternoons, by arrangement with the Works Manager.)

East of the town a string of villages leads you into the open country. **Willesborough,** now embedded in Ashford, has a church with a 'candle-snuffer' spire like the one at Upchurch (see p. 52). **Sevington** is hardly more than a hamlet, with an isolated medieval church. **Mersham** (pronounced Merzam) is a good deal larger; its church, down a cul-de-sac, has a spectacular west window, with a row of thirteen lights along the bottom, presumably for glass depicting the apostles with Christ in the larger central panel. It is full of Knatchbull tablets and memorials. The epitaph on the tomb of Lady Bridget Knatchbull (died 1625) in the chancel begins with the unforgettable couplet:

> The dust closed up within this Marble Shrine
> Was (when it breath'd) a Blossome feminine.

A mile west of the town, off the A 20, is **Godinton Park,** set comfortably in a hollow, with topiary yew hedges of monumental thickness between the house and the noble trees of the park. The greatest of these, on the side opposite the entrance front, was the Domesday Oak, which split asunder and collapsed on September 3rd, 1939, while Chamberlain was making his broadcast announcing war with Germany. The outer appearance of Godinton, with its rounded Dutch-style gables, and stone mullions setting off the mellow brickwork, is due to Captain Nicholas Toke, who remodelled the old house in 1628 – at least, that is the date on the rainwater heads. The fifteenth-century Great Hall, spanned by an enormous chestnut tiebeam, is still medieval in character, despite the plaster ceiling put in by the Captain, and the flamboyant chimneypiece surmounted by a Lely portrait of James, Duke of York, later James II, as Lord High Admiral. The hall's rich panelling is a foretaste of the incredible woodcarving found elsewhere in Godinton. The most sumptuous is on the staircase, which is lit partly by fretted arcades opening from the Great Hall. As at Knole, there are heraldic beasts on the elaborate newel posts, above near-human figures – 'barbarously carved', says Newman – and on the upper landing three female figures, usually interpreted as Faith, Hope and Charity, though Christopher Hussey suggested three of the Captain's five wives as a possible alternative.

Upstairs the Captain left a permanent record of his military leanings in the carving and panelling of the Great Chamber, the showpiece of Godinton. Below the ceiling a carved wooden frieze depicts in a series of panels the complexities of musket and pike drill, carried out by little soldiers in the padded trunk-hose of Queen Elizabeth's reign. Hasted called these militiamen 'a very droll exhibition', as indeed they are; but they are of historical interest as well, and the pikemen's drill is still performed by the Honourable Artillery Company today. Above the fireplace the frieze shows the Captain's non-military interests – hunting, pig-sticking and bear-baiting. Captain Nicholas lived on until 1680; he survived five wives and died at the age of ninety-three while on his way to London to look for a sixth. He is buried in the church at Great Chart (see p. 190).

Downstairs, the Priest's Room, opening off the hall, may have been the chapel of the medieval house. Fittingly, it has a carved confessional box, turned into a cupboard. This room was used by the Victorian artist R. B. Martineau as the background for his painting 'The Last Day in the Old Home' (Tate Gallery).

West of Godinton you can make your way from village to village by the back roads, keeping roughly parallel to the A 20. **Hothfield** has a long, low thirteenth-century church, down a cul-de-sac and beside a vast kitchen-garden wall that is about all that is left of Hothfield Place, apart from a fine park. The church was struck by lightning and largely burned to the ground in 1598, and five years later it was rebuilt by Sir John Tufton – hence the very late Perpendicular windows which flood the church with light. The Tufton tomb, between the chancel and the north chapel, is a magnificently pompous object, made of different kinds of marble. At the feet of the effigies of Sir John and his wife are their respective crests: his a mythical, rather than a naturalistic, sea-lion; hers a lion's paw. Sir John, who died in 1624, 'lived peacefully in this country and was allwayes ready and well furnished to defend ye same'. So the inscription runs.

On the other side of the Great Stour from Hothfield a high ridge gives the villages built along it magnificent views across the plain of the Beult to the south. **Pluckley** owes much of the consistency of its appearance to the whim of a nineteenth-century squire, Sir Edward Cholmeley Dering, who had every window in the village altered, giving them rounded lights under an overall exterior arch, in the curious belief that this shape would bring luck. Outer arches and window frames are all white-painted, which makes Pluckley's houses look as though they have their eyebrows permanently raised in surprise. You can see similar windows at **Little Chart**.

Egerton is an unassuming village, with no such special characteristics, dwarfed by the tall Perpendicular west tower of the church. Inside a lofty arch runs the full width of the tower. The most noticeable fitting is the enormous multi-branched eighteenth-century chandelier, hanging from a cherub's head. The fifteenth-century octagonal font is carved with symbols of the evangelists; and an armorial wooden memorial panel to Henry Hussey (died 1694) makes a fine splash of colour by the door. The modern altar rail is supported by figures of Becket, Augustine and other saints.

There is no village at all at **Boughton Malherbe** – only an austere stone church superbly placed above the valley, and backed by dour farm buildings. The chancel is raised high, five steps above the nave; on the walls and floor are brasses to the Wotton family, and in a recess three domesticated-looking marble lions, which once formed part of a monument. The farmhouse is all that is left of the Elizabethan mansion of the Wotton family, the birthplace in 1568 of Sir Henry

Wotton, a diplomat who described an ambassador as 'an honest man sent to lie abroad for the good of his country', and a poet best known for the lines beginning

> How happy is he born and taught
> That serveth not another's will,
> Whose armour is his honest thought,
> And simple truth his utmost skill.

Harrietsham, two miles to the north, is a good tile-hung and weatherboarded village cut in two by the A 20. There are fine Georgian houses in the southern part; but best of all are the low brick almshouses, built originally for Mark Quested, of the Fishmongers' Company, in 1642 and rebuilt in 1770. A stream fed from a reedlined lake flows through the northern half of the village. The grey-brown stone church, battlemented all round, is a little north of the village, near the Pilgrims' Way; it has a tall Perpendicular west tower and an Early English chancel. It is worth going round the back of the church to see the massive square tower, possibly Saxon, on the north side. The sundial above the porch, put up in 1853, is accurate to within five minutes. A short way beyond the church, north of the main road, is Marley Court, and the Marley Tile factory which takes its name from the house.

Lenham is bypassed by the A 20 and can enjoy being a beauty spot. The square is a fine mixture of building styles from medieval to Georgian. At one corner is the Saxon Pharmacy, named after a Saxon grave discovered outside in the course of restoration work. The Pharmacy is part of a typical wealden timber-framed house, with a tall medieval window, and a kingpost roof rising above the glowing glass bottles and blue drug jars of an old-style chemist's shop. It was restored from dereliction in the 1940s by Robert H. Goodsall, that most erudite of delvers into the byroads of Kent history, who had previously bought and restored Stede Hill, above Harrietsham. The long white Dog and Bear inn has a brilliant royal arms over the door, to commemorate Queen Anne's stay there. Another small square forms a kind of antechamber to the churchyard; on one side is a long tiled barn, with a pond in front, and a farmhouse dated 1672 in the background.

The original church was maliciously burnt down in 1297,

and though the incendiarists were excommunicated by the Archbishop, they were never discovered. The present building consists of nave and north aisle, with a good Perpendicular west tower. It still has its medieval stone altar slab, which was let into the floor and thus survived the destruction of the Reformation. North of the altar is the tombstone to the prolific Mary Honywood, who died in 1620 aged ninety-two, leaving behind her a village-sized population of 367 descendants – sixteen children, 114 grandchildren, 228 great-grandchildren and nine great-great-grandchildren. The ornately carved pulpit is probably Elizabethan, and the medieval lectern may have once been a 'singing desk' or music stand for the choristers. On the south wall of the nave is a faded medieval mural showing St Michael weighing souls.

Above Lenham a crest of pines runs along the ridge of the downs above the Pilgrims' Way – more like Ashdown Forest than the chalkland. Half way up the ridge the wide windows of the Lenham hospital gaze out across the valley.

The magnificent Perpendicular church tower of **Charing** is one of the landmarks on the A 20 between Maidstone and Ashford. Fortunately for this delightful little town, the main road splits to the west of it and the heavy traffic pases by on either side, leaving the High Street to wander gently uphill between the two halves. Charing's prosperity had two causes: it lies by the Pilgrims' Way, and so its guesthouses were always put to good use; and it had belonged to Canterbury since Saxon times. The Archbishop's Palace (in fact the manor house), where Henry VIII was entertained by Archbishop Warham in 1520 on his way to the Field of the Cloth of Gold, is beside the road down to the church. The ivy-covered remains of the gatehouse are still standing, and across the courtyard a Tudor brick farmhouse dated 1586 has been built among the ruins of the palace's medieval stonework. The huge barn was once the banqueting hall.

The church itself is a good deal older than the tower; it has no aisles but consists of a nave and transepts, with windows ranging from Early English lancets to the latest of square Perpendicular shapes. The arch from tower to nave is enormously high and graceful. The roofbeams, elaborately carved and painted, were put in after a fire that destroyed all the woodwork in 1590, caused, says a contemporary account, 'by means of a birding-piece discharged by one Mr Dios, which fired in the shingles, the day being extreme hot and the same shingles very dry.' The Church guide suggests that the Spanish nature of the roofbeams may be due to Mr Dios making amends for the damage he had caused. Like Ashurst, Sussex (see p. 368), Charing church has an eighteenth-century vamping horn, in its original case (kept in the vestry). It still makes a most efficient megaphone. Until the Reformation the stone block on which John the Baptist was supposedly executed was kept in the church, but it has never been seen since.

Behind the church is the medieval vicarage. A plaque attached to the ancient yew tree near by has given two centuries of vicars something to think about on their journeys past the church. Dated 1772, it reads: 'O Vicar, who ever thou art, reflect and profit by the reflexion how small the distance and perhaps quick the transition from yon house thou inhabitest to the caverns of the Dead.'

The High Street provides a good amble of ten minutes or so – unpretentious brick or black-and-white timbering, broken here and there by grander places like the gabled Peirce House set back a little from the road, or the fine Georgian Wakeley and Ludwell Houses.

From Charing a lane full of right-angled kinks brings you to **Westwell**, a pretty little village miles from anywhere. The church is a curious muddle from outside, cement-rendered, with brick buttresses and a broach spire awkwardly perched on the narrow tower. But inside it is a wonderful forest of stone columns, alternately round and octagonal in the arcades, leading to a stone-vaulted Early English chancel, with an additional pair of columns in the chancel arch to take the weight of the vaulting. In the chancel are fine sedilia, and a memorial to the infant son of R. H. Barham, author of the *Ingoldsby Legends*, who was curate here from 1814 to 1817. **Eastwell** is even more remote – a ruined church right by the Pilgrims' Way, with nothing left except the tower at the edge of a romantic lily-covered lake. Eastwell Park's monstrous flint and stone gatehouse, built in the 1840s, is an unforgettable sight as you leave Ashford on the A 251.

The broad green of **Boughton Lees** is a good mile from the fortress-like church of **Boughton Aluph**. The Saxon village was known as Boctun, and in the thirteenth century the manor belonged to the sonorously named Alulphus of Boctune – hence the present name. He is thought to have replaced the Saxon church by a building of his own; this was in turn greatly enlarged and adapted in the fourteenth century by Sir Thomas de Aldon, King's Yeoman to Edward III. The armorial glass of the Black Prince and other members of Edward III's family dates from his time. The church is still undergoing heavy restoration after incendiary bomb damage in 1940 and later weather deterioration. Its bare interior is acoustically perfect for music; when I went there the Deller Consort were recording renaissance polyphony, and the strands of sound formed an aural reflection of the intricacies of the stonework. At the back of the church is a little brick porch with a Tudor fireplace, traditionally said to have been adapted for travellers along the Pilgrims' Way, who would rest there before the final stage of the journey to Canterbury. It makes a nice fancy to imagine the weary pilgrims warming their hands in front of a blazing fire before pressing on through robber-infested woods above Godmersham (see p. 180); though as both porch and fireplace look Elizabethan if not later, it may be only a fancy.

South-west of Ashford, the Tenterden road (A 28) brings you first to **Great Chart**, a good solid Kentish village. Its grey stone church, a little way out of the village, stands out strikingly on the skyline. In Saxon times Great Chart was far larger than it is today, but it was burnt to the ground by the war-party of Danes who established themselves at Appledore (see p. 150) in 893; the destruction of Great Chart led to the early growth of Ashford. At the entrance to the churchyard is a small white-painted timber-framed building, with widely overhanging eaves – the fifteenth-century predecessor of countless modern bungalows. It may have been built for a chantry priest, or as an office for church business.

The church itself dates mainly from the fourteenth century, when a small Norman church was rebuilt; finally, after a fire in the mid fifteenth century, there was a major restoration in which the Perpendicular aisle windows and clerestory were added. The man responsible for the building's ultimate grandeur was James Goldwell, who was rector at Great Chart before becoming Bishop of Norwich in 1472. He is portrayed

Water, grass and solitude: Fairfield Church, on Romney Marsh.

The atomic power station built on the shingle of Dungeness. The old lighthouse in the foreground is no longer operational.

The Medway at Aylesford, flowing past the backs of houses below the commanding church.

in the stained window at the east end of the south chapel; much of it is the original fifteenth-century glass. In the north chapel is a large altar tomb to his parents, William and Avice Goldwell, who died within a month of each other in 1485. In the same chapel are brasses to members of the Toke family, who lived at Godinton near by (see p. 184): two sixteenth-century brasses to John Toke and his son, also called John; and a very late brass to Captain Nicholas Toke, who died in 1680 and is shown in a full suit of armour – the latest brass on which such armour appears.

Bethersden, four miles towards Tenterden, was famous in the Middle Ages for its marble, used as embellishment in Canterbury and Rochester Cathedrals, as well as smaller churches. It is a typical wealden village, with plenty of good weatherboarded houses, built tidily around an oval arrangement of roads. The church is a big Perpendicular building, with tall battlemented west tower and an uncomplicated interior. A modern stained-glass window in the south chapel shows Bethersden's farming concerns of cabbages, chickens and oasthouses.

CHAPTER ELEVEN

Maidstone and District

⚜

FOR a county town, **Maidstone** (nowadays easily reached from London along the M 2) is a haphazard, incoherent place. This is due partly to its plan, as it is bisected by the Medway, with only a single bridge over the river, and thus has not grown in a unified way; and partly to its history as a small market town. The old town lies east of the river, on either side of the High Street which runs uphill from the bridge. Maidstone's eighteenth-century Town Hall stands on an island site at the top of the High Street, right in the centre of everything; while the bulky County Hall from which Kent's affairs are run is out of the main swim, along the road to Chatham. The river that severs Maidstone is the most attractive feature of the town, especially upstream from the bridge, where you can stroll along the riverside walk below the stone walls of the medieval Archbishop's Palace, looking over the pleasure boats on the water to the stalls of the market across the river.

Maidstone pushes its prehistory back a hundred million years or so, when iguanodons plodded about the shores of the great Wealden lake. When the town was granted a new coat-of-arms in 1949, on the four hundredth anniversary of its incorporation, it chose as one of its supporters the unlikely-sounding 'Iguanodon proper collared gules'. (Maidstone also commemorated its brewing history by its crest, a horse's head 'gorged with a Chaplet of Hops fructed proper'.) The Medway valley was a natural site for Stone Age settlement. Stone implements are constantly being found, and the area was an important one for Neolithic burials. In spite of Maidstone's commanding position at the upper end of the Medway gap in the North Downs, the Romans do not seem to have built any kind of township there though an important Roman highway ran through it, giving access to the Weald. Even in Norman

A map of this chapter will be found between pages 177-8.

times it was little more than a manor and associated farming community. Its prosperity began in the late Middle Ages, when it became the focus for Wealden agriculture and an industrial centre. Ragstone quarried near by was shipped down the Medway for such buildings as Hampton Court and Eton College, and was also shaped into cannon balls; fuller's earth was both exported and used for Maidstone's own cloth industry; and local sand was used by glassmaking pioneers. In the seventeenth century what are still Maidstone's main industries began – papermaking, and especially brewing. Fremlin's vast concern dominates the roads immediately north of the High Street, and directly opposite the red and yellow brick mock medieval walls of the Courage brewery rise sheer from the river.

The oldest buildings in Maidstone are in the cluster by the Medway south of the High Street. Most prominent is the **Archbishop's Palace**, which consists of a stone Elizabethan E-shaped front on a medieval building; the bulk of the palace was moved here from Wrotham (see p. 207). It is now owned by the Corporation, and its rooms can be hired for receptions and other functions. The rooms on the lower floor have huge beams and blocked-up medieval fireplaces; the upper rooms, reached by outside staircases, are heavily panelled. The finest of them has a big oriel window overlooking the river. The Palace is gauntly furnished with steel-framed chairs and little else, but at least it is kept in constant use. On the river side are the buttressed dungeons in which John Ball is said to have been imprisoned. Ball, the 'mad priest of Kent', is famous for the lines 'When Adam delved and Eve span, Who was then the gentleman?' He was released when Wat Tyler and his followers seized Maidstone in 1381. The palace's small stone gatehouse is now used by the Department of Weights and Measures. Near it a wide stone flight of stairs leads down from the gardens to the River Len, a tributary of the Medway, with a medieval bridge cowering in the darkness below the concrete span of Mill Street.

Across Mill Street is a long low stone building, with external staircase, once thought to have been a tithe barn, but now called with more probability the **Archbishop's Stables**. If this is correct, it is back to at least part of its original function, as it houses the Tyrwhitt-Drake collection of carriages. Both floors are crammed with painted and polished triumphs of the carriage-maker's art, from an Italian gig of about 1670 which perched its driver among a riot of carved wooden dragons and centaurs, to the sober blue and black landau still used by the Mayor in Maidstone's annual carnival. A comfortable-looking travelling coach has a sad story attached. It was built at great expense for the Earl of Moray's honeymoon, in about 1840, but the girl called off the wedding, and the disappointed earl shut the coach away in his coach house for good, and shot the six white horses that were to have hauled it.

Maidstone's **Parish Church** (usually locked because of vandalism) is upstream from the Archbishop's palace. It was built by Archbishop Courtenay at the end of the fourteenth century, and is an enormously wide Perpendicular building, with spacious aisles and narrow chapels on either side of the chancel, and sumptuously ornate roof beams. There was originally a spire, which rose nearly a hundred feet above the tower; it was destroyed by lightning in the eighteenth century. The north aisle is the regimental chapel of the Royal West Kents, and is hung with tattered banners. On the west wall are monuments to the Astley family; one of them, commemorating Sir John Astley, who died in 1639, is a very strange affair on two tiers, each tier with standing statues of a man and a woman wearing shrouds. Sir John was Keeper of the Jewels under Elizabeth, and Master of the Revels to James I and Charles I. Near the tower door is a tablet to Laurence Washington, related to an ancestor of George Washington, chiefly interesting for the Stars and Stripes appearing on the family arms. One of the choir misericords is carved with a grinning cook flourishing a meat hook in one hand and a ladle in the other – presumably the cook at the **College of Priests**, which lies across a green lane leading down to the river. It was founded in 1395 by Archbishop Courtenay, for a master and twenty-four chaplains and clerks. The tall gatehouse faces the church; the outer stonework has seen better days, but the vaulting over the entrance is still good. The gabled Master's House is now the home of the Kent Music School, and another ancient building in the precinct is used by the local sea cadets.

The streets of Maidstone's inner rectangle have plenty of worthwhile things to look at, though large areas are falling before the march of steel and concrete. William Shipley, founder of the Royal Society of Arts, lived at Knightrider House in Knightrider Street, a tall three-storeyed building now the offices of the Maidstone and District bus company. Along Lower Stone Street and up Gabriel's Hill there is the occasional half-timbered or weatherboarded building. Besides the **Town Hall,** the High Street has most of Maidstone's hotels, and a cannon captured at Sebastopol, pointing down the hill towards the bridge. North of the High Street is Earl Street, with the medieval Brotherhood Hall, which belonged first to the Corpus Christi Fraternity, then to the grammar school, and is now part of Fremlin's. Higher up is the large white house of Andrew Broughton, Mayor of Maidstone during the Civil War, a Roundhead who read out the death sentence on Charles I. Though a regicide, he survived the return of Charles II, and lived on until 1688. Maidstone was the scene of a major Parliamentary victory in 1648, when Fairfax defeated the Royalist forces under Lord Norwich in a battle which was fought right up through the streets of the town and ended at midnight after five hours of conflict.

Maidstone Museum is in St Faith's Street, opposite some handsome almshouses of 1700. The actual museum building, Chillington Manor, is worth more than a passing look; it is an E-shaped red-brick Elizabethan manor house, with long gallery and bewildering staircases, and gives the museum authorities all sorts of interesting rooms and passageways to play around with. The collections naturally concentrate on Kent, with displays beginning in the Palaeolithic age, including stone implements collected by Benjamin Harrison, the archaeologist-shopkeeper from Ightham (see p. 218). The museum has portraits of Kent writers and their families, like William Hazlitt (who has a theatre in Maidstone named after him), and Edward Hasted, the historian of Kent; a costume gallery; musical instruments including Marie Antoinette's guitar and Handel's travelling clavichord; and the museum of the Royal West Kents, full of uniforms, pistols, medals and trophies.

Seven major roads converge at Maidstone, and the town is spreading rapidly out along all of them. At the south end of Sandling Road (which becomes the Chatham Road) are the County Hall buildings, with a grandiose pedimented front facing the roundabout and a white crescent stretching behind. Most of the square island on which the County Hall stands is taken up by Maidstone prison, of which nothing can be seen but a blind white stone wall. Off the Sittingbourne Road is Penenden Heath, now a public open space, where in Saxon and later times the shire court was held, chosen for its central position in Kent. Maidstone's finest open space is Mote Park, south of the Ashford Road. The white eighteenth-century Mote House is now a Cheshire Home; it stands on a rise overlooking a large artificial lake, used for boating, formed by widening the River Len. Behind a wall in Mote Park is the Turkey Mill, converted from fulling to papermaking by James Whatman in 1739, and the origin of 'Whatman' and 'Turkey Mill' first-class papers. The main entrance is under red-brick railway arches on the Ashford Road.

Maidstone has no castle of its own, except for **Allington**, built on a bend in the Medway half way between Maidstone and Aylesford. You get to it from the London Road, turning off by an ultra-modern supermarket. Like The Friars at Aylesford (see p. 199), Allington Castle is now owned by the Carmelites; they bought it in 1951, and run it as a religious retreat, and for conferences and study sessions. It is a comfortable place, in spite of its thick stone walls, battlements and arrow slits, and in its setting of lawns and trees makes a soothing contrast to the clatter and dust of the gravel pit half a mile up the road. In 1282 Sir Stephen of Penchester (see Penshurst, p. 235), Warden of the Cinque Ports, was licensed to fortify his manor house at Allington, and built most of what we see today, notably the east wing, with its great hall now austerely furnished with refectory tables and presses, and the west wing, with Solomon's Tower, the strongest fortification at Allington, at its southern corner. Allington passed to the Cobhams, and in 1492 was bought from them by Sir Henry Wyatt, who restored it, built a Tudor range with a long gallery right across the courtyard, and settled down to a life of prosperous entertainment. In the time of Richard III Sir Henry was imprisoned in the Tower and is said to have been racked in the presence of the king. The brown pigeons that flutter about the castle (incidentally, their feathers are the same colour as the Carmelites' habit) may be descended from birds brought back from the Near East by Sir Thomas

Wyatt, Sir Henry's son. According to legend, during his imprisonment Sir Henry was kept alive by a cat which brought a pigeon to his cell every morning, and Sir Thomas introduced the brown pigeons as a living reminder of his father's sufferings.

Sir Thomas Wyatt (often called the Elder, to distinguish him from his son, also Sir Thomas) was born at Allington in 1503. He was the archetype of the Tudor courtier – diplomat, musician, linguist, jouster, and above all poet. Some of his love poems are supposed to have been addressed to Anne Boleyn, who often visited Allington, as did Henry VII and VIII, Katharine Parr, Cardinal Wolsey and Thomas Cromwell. He died in 1542, from a fever caught while on his way to the West Country to meet the ambassadors of the Emperor Charles V. His chief claim to fame as a poet is that he introduced the Italian sonnet into England; but he left an enormous quantity of poems apart from his sonnets. In spite of his worldly success, Wyatt was basically a disillusioned man, as is shown by his *Penitential Psalms*, or even the love poems, of which the theme is

> Payne of all payne, the most grevous paine
> Is to love hartelye and cannot be loved againe.

Sir Thomas Wyatt the Younger's life was a brief chronicle of disaster. Born in 1521, he succeeded to his father's Kent properties; but on the accession of Queen Mary in 1553 feared for the estates acquired at the Dissolution and led the men of Kent in revolt, with the object of replacing Mary by the Protestant Lady Jane Grey. He had some success at first, including the bombardment of Cooling Castle (see p. 41), but his defeat was inevitable, and he was captured and executed in 1554. With the downfall of the Wyatts Allington fell into neglect. In the seventeenth century it was rented by the Bests, a recusant family said to have used the priests' hiding hole behind the linenfold panelling in the chapel. (Also in the chapel is a 'black Madonna' carved from Irish bog oak by Clare Sheridan.) When Lord Conway bought the castle in 1905 it was virtually a ruin; he spent a quarter of a century and £70,000 on its restoration. His signature is the statue of St Martin on horseback, set in a niche above the courtyard, and Allington as it is now bears witness to that 'flood of delight' he felt when he first passed under the gatehouse into the peaceful courtyard.

To get to Aylesford, on the other side of the Medway from Allington, you have to come back on the main road. On the outskirts of Maidstone the familiar lion's head of the British Legion badge proclaims the **British Legion Village**. In 1925 the Legion took over Preston Hall, a stone Victorian mansion on the north side of the road, as a chest hospital for tuberculous ex-servicemen – there were 55,000 of them after the First World War. It has now expanded far beyond that original medical aim into a rehabilitation and employment centre for disabled ex-servicemen and women, making wooden sheds and metal road signs, and equipped with its own printing works. Severed from the Hall and workshops by the A 20 traffic is a crescent of Legion houses, centring on a restaurant and village hall.

Aylesford, across the river, suffers from being the home of the vast Reed paper works (the successor of a mill founded in the seventeenth century), and of all the small towns in Kent must be the one least adapted by its layout to heavy modern traffic. The graceful five-arched medieval bridge over the Medway is constantly blocked from side to side by buses and lorries, the overhangs of the timbered buildings are battered by tall vehicles, and there is no pavement at all up the hill at the end of the High Street. Aylesford has been called the place where English history began, as it was at 'Aegelsthrep' (one of the multifarious old spellings of the name) that the Saxons under Hengist and Horsa defeated the British under Vortigern in AD 455.

The church stands commandingly above the bridge; it has a square tower with a Norman base, and a pair of naves of equal size, built in the early fifteenth century. High on the chancel walls are swords, helmets and gauntlets, the funeral armour of the Colepeppers and other local magnates. Sir Thomas Colepepper (died in 1604) is buried in the ornate altar tomb between the two chancels, with coloured alabaster figures of Sir Thomas and his wife on top, and sons and daughters kneeling at the sides; but their sober tomb is overshadowed by the pompous arrogance of the Banks memorial, which fills the whole corner of the north chancel. Sir John Banks, who died in 1699, stands in full-bottomed wig on one side of an urn, with his wife on the other; at the foot lies their son Caleb Banks.

Sir John lived at **The Friars**, beside the river, and Pepys has left a lively description of a visit to Aylesford in March 1669 to see him on Admiralty business, though Banks was away. 'A mighty cold and windy but clear day, and had the pleasure of seeing the Medway running, winding up and down mightily, and a very fine country.' Pepys found The Friars 'mighty finely placed by the river; and he keeps the grounds about it, and the walls and the house, very handsome.' Very handsome it still is, back in the hands of its original occupants, the Carmelite friars, who built themselves a priory in 1242, were expelled by Thomas Cromwell in 1538, and returned four centuries later in 1949. After the suppression, the priory passed briefly to the Wyatts of Allington. Sir John Banks did a great deal to it in the seventeenth century; but most of its present appearance is due to the past twenty years of work by the Carmelites. The centre of the complex is now an arcaded shrine, with seating in the open air for a large congregation of pilgrims. Off the main shrine, which is on the side of the medieval monastic church, are a number of smaller shrines, remarkable for ceramics by Adam Kossowski. This Polish artist has worked steadily at Aylesford like some medieval illuminator, taking concentration camp heroes as well as biblical themes as materials for his inspiration. Of the buildings the free-standing gatehouse still survives, as well as part of the cloisters. The pilgrims' hall has been reconstructed with two galleries; its windows look out on the Medway's swans and mudflats. From the other side of the Medway The Friars appears as a harmonious range of gables, tiled roofs and stone walls, and would not seem alien to the medieval traveller, arriving footsore in the evening from the Pilgrims' Way.

From Aylesford you can get to Rochester along the still-countrified eastern bank of the Medway; though the villages – Eccles, Burham and Wouldham – have little to offer, apart from **Wouldham** church. This has a battlemented tower with outsize turret, abutting the church on the north side. There was a Saxon church on the site, and there are twelfth-century chalk pillars inside. The whole place has a rough-hewn effect, with the chancel walls leaning alarmingly outwards. Below the west window of the south aisle are two cannon balls said to be from the *Victory*, and just outside the church is the grave of Walter Burke, purser on the *Victory*, who stayed with Nelson after he was mortally wounded, and held him in his arms as he died. Burke himself died ten years later, aged seventy; which means that he must have been sixty at Trafalgar, well past the normal age of active service.

North-east of Aylesford, just off the A 229 to Chatham, is **Kits Coty**, a Neolithic tomb of three large upright stones and a single huge horizontal, standing on an open slope of the downs and reached by a steep track with hedges joining to shut out the light overhead. At the foot of the hill is **Little Kits Coty**, or the Countless Stones, a much less impressive affair. The story goes that a local baker vowed to count the stones of Lower Kits Coty by placing a loaf on the top of each one, but every time he started, the devil knocked off the loaves and foiled the attempt.

At the foot of the downs a string of villages marks the line of the Pilgrims' Way. **Boxley** consists of little more than a church, a pub and a group of old houses. The church lies well back from the road, at the end of a long narrow green; a stone path points straight as an arrow from the church entrance to the pub door. You go into the church through a narthex or vestibule, with its outer door and window asymmetrically placed. On either side of the door from the narthex into the tower are corbels of a bishop and a king, probably Edward II. The thirteenth-century pillars and arches of the nave are made of chalk. Genealogists with patience and good eyesight could spend a long time on the tablet of the Wiat (more normally Wyatt) family on the chancel wall, put up in 1702; this includes the story of how Sir Henry Wyatt was saved by a cat (see Allington, p. 197).

In the Middle Ages Boxley was famous for its Cistercian **Abbey**, founded in 1146 by William of Ypres. What remains can best be seen from the minor road that runs parallel to the M 20 half a mile south of Boxley village – broken, creeper-covered stone walls, with a red-brick house built inside them, and an enormous and magnificent tithe barn thought to be thirteenth-century. Boxley Abbey owed its prominence to two miracle-working images. First and foremost was the Rood of Grace, a figure of Christ on the Cross, which Lambarde, almost frothing at the mouth in zealous indignation, described as follows (spelling modernised). 'A cunning carpenter . . . compacted of wood, wire, paste and paper a rood of such exquisite art and excellency that it not only matched in comeliness and due proportion of the parts the best of the common sort; but in strange motion, variety of gesture and nimbleness of joints passed all other that before had been seen; the same being able to bow down and lift up itself, to shake and stir the hands and feet, to nod the head, to roll the eyes, to wag the chaps, to bend the brows, and finally to represent to the eye both the proper motion of each member of the body, and also a lively, express and significant show of a well-contented or displeased mind.' In a darkened church, in an atmosphere of chanting and incense, this rood must surely have given the pilgrims their money's worth.

The other image was simpler – a statue of St Rumwold, the child saint (see Bonnington, p. 149), which could only be lifted from the ground by those of pure life. According to Lambarde, if a pilgrim had not offered them enough money the monks kept the statue on the ground by means of a pin running into a post, while if they were satisfied they lifted the statue themselves by a crank mechanism. As a result, 'chaste virgins and honest married matrons oftentimes went away with blushing faces, leaving (without cause) in the minds of the lookers-on great suspicion of unclean life and wanton behaviour, for fear of which note and villainy women stretched their purse strings.' Boxley was dissolved in 1538, and the rood was publicly burned in St Paul's churchyard the following year. Perhaps St Rumwold is somewhere among the abbey ruins, waiting for a lady archaeologist of blameless life to lift him up.

From Boxley eastwards the Pilgrims' Way can be driven along for several miles, though it is extremely narrow, needing the passing places provided at intervals. **Detling** has an unobtrusive church on its outskirts, with a sumptuous medieval lectern, thought to have been carved about 1340 and to have come from Boxley Abbey. The intricate design is made up of foliage, flowers, abstract patterning and animals, including an elephant with a howdah on its back. Beside the main road, on the downs high above Detling, is the Kent County agricultural showground. In the distance, on the other side of the road, the bat ears of an early-warning radar station jut up on the skyline.

In the quiet churchyard at **Thurnham** is the grave of Alfred Mynn, one of the fathers of Kent cricket, who died in 1861. The inscription says that 'four hundred persons have united to erect this tombstone, and to found in honour of a name so celebrated the Mynn Memorial Benevolent Institute for Kentish Cricketers.' With Victorian thoroughness the amount raised is specified – £121 10s. invested in India 5 per cent stock.

Hollingbourne is a long village rambling uphill from a stream, with some fine half-timbered houses by the flint and ragstone church.

Leeds Castle, south of Hollingbourne across the A 20, should surely be as well known as Knole or Penshurst, both for the grandeur of its buildings and the beauty of its setting. Unfortunately, apart from the grounds, it is strictly and unrelentingly private. It can be seen in flashes from the A 20 and the minor road to Broomfield; or at greater leisure by entering the grounds on foot through the main gate on the Broomfield road and walking round the lake – a natural moat, with the castle built on two islands in the centre. A Norman castle was built here at the beginning of the twelfth century by Robert de Crevecoeur, probably on the smaller of the two islands. Under Edward I at the end of the next century it became a royal castle, and from his time date the walls and turrets whose bases rise sheer from the waters of the lake. The older building on the small island is called the Gloriette, the French for arbour or summerhouse, joined to the main island by a two-storey stone bridge, the Pons Gloriettae. The main building on the large island, though built as recently as 1822, fits in remarkably well with the spirit of the whole place, with its unadorned stone walls and battlements. Edward I's gatehouse still stands at the inner end of the bridge, and on the landward end are the ruined walls of the barbican which guarded the roads in medieval times. The park, laid out by Capability Brown in the eighteenth century, is a marvellous place to wander in, with its giant horse chestnuts, oak and beech, and its fine turf shorn by the golf club. The reed-fringed lake is full of duck, moorhens and gliding black swans.

The village of **Leeds** lies west of the park, straggling uphill from the church. This has one of the oddest towers in Kent: a squat thirteenth-century stronghold, which looks as though a giant fist has come down on a tower of normal proportions and flattened it out. Inside there is a finely traceried fifteenth-century rood screen right across the church; and on the outside of the north wall is a blocked-up window said to have belonged to an anchorite's cell – a tame hermit like an Indian holy man, who was kept at public expense because of the benefits arising from his spirituality.

In spite of its small size **Otham** has more than its share of good half-timbered buildings. **Stoneacre** (open Wednesday afternoons) is a fine yeoman's house of about 1480; the great hall is lit by two-tiered windows and has an oak screen across one end, and the ceiling has a rare kingpost made of a cluster of four engaged shafts.

Bearsted, across the main road from Otham, is a growing suburb, but still manages to keep an attractive unity of its own. Round the enormous village green are some really good half-timbered and Georgian houses, with a glimpse of tall oasts behind. The church stands on a hill at the end of a dogleg road, and is not at all obvious from the village; it is remarkable for the stone beasts, including a lion with paw raised and an eagle, that peer over the parapet of the Perpendicular tower like sinister watchmen. The rest of the church is mainly fourteenth-century, built on the site of an apsidal Anglo-Saxon basilica. Behind a glass panel at the west end of the nave is part of an Anglo-Saxon arch, which was painted in the twelfth century with a red consecration cross, said to be the earliest example of a painted cross in this country.

West of the British Legion Village (see p. 198), the A 20 takes you past the two Mallings, both a little way south of the road. The road to **East Malling**'s neat village centre runs past the trees of a leading fruit-growing research station. **West Malling** is far larger, and qualifies as a small town; it is a fine place to stroll about in, with a High Street that is unusually wide for this part of Kent, lined on either side by mainly Georgian houses. South of the town is **St Leonard's Tower**, a square eleventh-century building with arcaded windows, like a keep without a castle to go with it. It is ascribed to Gundulf of Rochester, the leading tower-builder of the region (see also p. 43). The church, at the south end of the High Street, has a tall spindly spire on a sturdy medieval tower; apart from the chancel, the rest of it dates from a rebuilding in 1901.

At the bottom end of the High Street, Swan Street leads down to St Mary's Abbey, an enclosed community of Church of England Benedictine nuns. The medieval gatehouse (now a private dwelling) leads to a large open space, with a free-standing tower on the far side. This tower, with pyramidal pinnacles and Norman blind arcading, bears a strong resemblance to the west front of Rochester Cathedral, and must be a survival of Gundulf's Benedictine nunnery founded here in the 1080s. Behind the tower is the modern abbey.

West Malling aerodrome, along the road to Mereworth (see p. 207), was one of the centres of fighter resistance in the Battle of Britain. Towards the end of 1972 its deserted hutments were put to good use when West Malling became one of the resettlement centres for Asians driven out of Uganda by General Amin.

Offham's open triangular village green has a quintain in the middle, consisting of a white-painted upright with a centrally pivoted horizontal piece of wood on top. The quintain was originally used by knights practising for tournaments, but simple contraptions like this one were used at village merry-makings. The quintain in action had a target board attached at one end and a sack of sand suspended at the other. The competitor rode or ran at it, trying to hit the target with his spear; he might hit it squarely, miss it altogether, or not get out of the way in time and be struck on the back of the neck by the rotating sack.

North of West Malling, the main road along the west bank of the Medway (A 228) to Rochester runs through an industrialised landscape of cement works and their belching chimneys. Near the new M 20 flyover are the ruins of **Leybourne Castle** – the bases of rounded towers, and an entrance gateway – with a 1930s house tacked on the front. Leybourne was the castle of Sir William de Leybourne, friend of Edward I, who visited him in 1286 and awarded him the title of '*Admiral de la Mer du Roy d'Angleterre*' – the first time an Englishman had been given the title of Admiral. A Victorian squire of Leybourne, Sir Joseph Hawley, won the Derby four times with horses trained there; he engaged Sir Arthur Blomfield to restore the church in 1874. Blomfield's raw-looking stone encases the Norman tower of the medieval church. Inside it consists of a nave and narrow aisle. On the north wall are two iron crowns, said without much confidence to have been presented by Edward I and Queen Eleanor after their visit to Leybourne. The window-like opening in the chancel wall is the 'heart shrine' of Sir Roger de Leybourne; the left-hand of the two little stone caskets contains the embalmed heart of this famous crusader, who died about 1271.

Towards Rochester the cottages of **Snodland** and **Halling** are strung out along the narrow main road like Yorkshire industrial villages, facing the cement lorries thundering by. Snodland is redeemed to some extent by the side street that leads down to the medieval church, which is built on a mound directly above the Medway (and next to the tall chimneys of a paper mill). The pinkwashed, classical station building might have come straight from central France.

On this side of the river there are several villages below the downs, near the Pilgrims' Way though not actually on it. **Birling**, a mile east of Leybourne, consists largely of stone Victorian cottages with pinched-up gables. **Addington** is a rapidly expanding place, with a small green, and a remote church, built on a mound and hidden among tall trees. Two fifteenth-century chapels give the building an unusual T-shape. In the south chapel are some fine brasses, notably one on the wall to William Snayth (died 1409) and his wife; above it is an overbearing seventeenth century tomb to the Watton family. Across the road north of the church is the prehistoric burial chamber known as the **Chestnuts** – a group of leaning sarsen stones that once formed the centre of an earth-covered barrow. Directly behind is the enormous new gash in the ground made by the M 20 extension.

Near **Trottiscliffe** (pronounced Troslif or Trosley, but never as spelt) is one of the finest Neolithic remains on the North Downs, the **Coldrum Stones** burial chamber. It consists of a chalk mound surmounted by a group of large stones, mainly fallen, a stone circle and a ditch round the outside. Looking eastward from the main group you can see for miles across the valley to the next spur of the downs in the distance – as nobly sited a burial place as a king could wish for. It is now a permanent memorial to Benjamin Harrison (see p. 218).

In Trottiscliffe church is a case containing human and animal bones from Coldrum. Study of the bones has revealed a good deal about the physique of these ancestral Kentish

Men. They were, says Ronald Jessup in his *South East England*, 'long-headed and short in stature, good-looking and of moderate muscular strength with wide feet free in movement; they had healthy teeth with an edge-to-edge bite; the aged suffered from rheumatism which was not helped by the constant squatting posture.' The church also has an incongruously large pulpit, with grotesque columns supporting the sounding board; it was built for Westminster Abbey in 1781 and ended up here about forty years later. It is worth looking at the outside of the west wall of the church, which was rebuilt in 1885 from flints meticulously cut square by a local craftsman. The church forms the centrepiece of a group of farm buildings and a big rectory, outside the residential sprawl of the village. The artist Graham Sutherland lives in Trottiscliffe.

High up on the other side of the Gravesend road is **Stansted**, the perfect downland hamlet, built on a switchback of hills, with a large village green in the valley, and an impeccable flint church, complete with giant yew tree outside the door. At the edge of the churchyard an art nouveau black granite memorial, surmounted by scroll-carrying angels, commemorates Sir Sydney Hedley Waterlow, one of the founders of the great Waterlow printing firm, who lived at Trosley Towers near by. Waterlow's was a typical Victorian success story. Born in 1822, he began printing in 1844 in partnership with his brothers, starting with £120 from their father. They made their fortunes from cornering the market in railway printing and stationery. Waterlow was a philanthropist as well as a businessman. As Lord Mayor of London in 1872, he was responsible for opening the Guildhall Library to the public. He held many offices in the City, and found time to be Liberal M.P. for Maidstone and then Gravesend.

Wrotham (pronounced Rootam), at the foot of the hill, is bypassed by the A 20, though its narrow High Street gets a lot of heavy traffic to and from Gravesend. At its centre it widens out into a little square, with the church looming over the north side, the Tudor brick gables of Wrotham Place appearing above the wall opposite, and a cluster of pubs and back streets of cottages, some opening straight on to the pavement. The church is magnificent, and has all sorts of unusual things about it. The big fifteenth-century tower has an

The village-like complexity of Knole, the great house of Sevenoaks.

Penshurst Church from the gardens of Penshurst Place.

The Pantiles, Turnbridge Wells, a perfect example of a traffic-free shopping precinct, built mainly in the eighteenth century.

A magnificent group of oasthouses, at Beltring, near Paddock Wood.

outside passage right under it, perhaps made for processions around the church, with a stone which may once have held a sanctuary ring granting safety to criminals who grasped it. Inside it is most spacious, with wide aisles and some finely traceried windows; the east window was brought from St Alban's, Wood Street, in the City, and is thought to have been designed by Wren. At the corner of the south aisle and chancel is a bulging turret staircase; this climbs above the rood loft exit to a passage joining the two aisles, which has openings east and west into the church and is known as the 'nuns' gallery'. Those who have been up there say that they must have been very thin nuns. In front of the rood screen are some good brasses, and in the north aisle is a tomb said to be that of Richard de Wrotham, founder of the church.

On the corner of White Hill, the old main road, is an inscription to Lt.-Col. Shadwell, 'shot to the heart by a deserter' in 1799; there is a memorial to him in Maidstone church. Beyond is the Bull Hotel, an old coaching inn, and next door on the edge of the town (easily seen from the road) is what is left of the Old Palace, after most of it was carried off to Maidstone to make the Archbishop's Palace there. The surviving part, now inhabited, may have been the kitchen quarters; on the right as you look at it is another wing cut off below roof level, now little except a stone wall with bricked-up windows. The fields beyond the Palace used to be famous for their partridges.

The grandest house hereabouts, **Mereworth Castle** (pronounced Merryworth), five miles south-east of Wrotham, is unequivocally not open to visitors, writers of guidebooks included. However, you can get a good view of it through the main gates on the A 26; and occasional glimpses as you approach it from the north. Mereworth, with its grey dome, orange walls and Ionic columned porticoes, is nothing less than a complete Italian villa stuck down in the Kentish countryside. It was built in the 1720s for John Fane by Colen Campbell, one of the leaders of the Palladian revival, and is a direct copy of Palladio's Villa Rotonda at Vicenza. As a concession to the British climate, Campbell used the lantern on top of the dome as a gigantic chimney-pot, carrying the flues up between the inner and outer skins of the dome. (The interior of the castle, with its plasterwork, illusionist paintings and long

C.G.K.S.   O gallery, is fully described by Newman.) The two lodges are now on the opposite side of the road to the castle, as the road was shifted after they were built.

Unlike the castle, **Mereworth Church** can be seen. In its way it is as unusual as the castle: a hybrid of London churches, the main body with its huge overhanging eaves copied from St Paul's in Covent Garden, and the west end crowned with a replica of the steeple of St Martin-in-the-Fields. There is also a semi-circular columned porch to the main entrance below the tower. John Fane (by this time Earl of Westmorland) built it here in the 1740s, after he had pulled down the medieval church near the castle. No one has ever dealt so high-handedly with their architectural neighbours as these Georgian grandees. Inside, there are elephantine grey columns, painted to look like marble, and a barrel-vaulted roof painted with coffering. The best thing about the church is a semi-circular lunette at the east end, glowing with golden sixteenth-century armorial glass.

Wateringbury, back towards Maidstone, is half way between a village and a small town. The main street has some good Georgian houses, and arcaded shops with slim cast-iron pillars. There is a Whitbread brewery half way down the hill towards the Medway. The church is reconstructed, slate-roofed and ugly; what it was once like can be seen from a drawing inside, dated 1852. Over the door is a unique object called a 'dumb borsholder' – a staff of office dating back to Saxon times, carried to the Court Moot and in use until about 1740. It has a spike at one end for breaking down the doors of suspected wrongdoers.

Wateringbury's most interesting character was Edward Greensted, parish clerk and schoolmaster at the end of the eighteenth century, and author of a local history. He is commemorated on a sandstone tablet (seriously flaking) on the outside wall of the tower. He has left a vivid description of the great storm of August 19th, 1763, when hailstones up to ten inches in diameter hurtled down on the houses, orchards and livestock of Kent. 'The storm over, how shocking was the prospect! Our houses flowing with water, scarcely a pane of glass to be seen, the roofs and walls of our houses shatter'd, the waters roaring in torrents down the streets, the surface of the earth covered with the prodigious hailstones and water, the corn, fruit and hops destroy'd, scarcely any saved.' Not surprisingly, it took the farmers years to recover.

Another place that suffered severely in the storm was **Nettlestead** church near by. This extraordinary church is nearly all window – a nave with enormous Perpendicular windows, tacked on to a simple thirteenth-century tower. The nave was built by Reginald de Pympe in the first half of the fifteenth century; he campaigned at Agincourt with Henry V, and it is thought that he saw in France what could be done with stained glass. There are six windows in the nave, and three in the chancel added about 1465 by John de Pympe. Several of the saints survive in softly coloured blue or red robes on an architectural background. The 1763 storm wrecked all the windows on the south side, but much of the shattered glass has since been cleverly replaced or restored. The painted and gilded memorials on either side of the chancel arch commemorate the two wives of Sir John Scott, an Elizabethan soldier. The Scotts took over Nettlestead Place from the de Pympes in the sixteenth century; the grey stone house, a product of successive rebuildings from the Middle Ages on, can be seen over the churchyard wall. A later Scott was a strong Parliamentarian, and took his politics so seriously that he besieged his Royalist wife in the house for four days in 1646.

Yalding, where the Teise and Beult join the Medway, is a place of boats, locks, islets and medieval bridges. By the Anchor Inn there is a superb bridge, made of stone with a brick parapet, with sharp cutwaters, and passing places in the narrow roadway. The waters here are deceptively inviting on a hot day; but there are weirs and a lock as well as the bridge, with 'danger of drowning' signs everywhere. Yalding runs uphill from the Medway. Big oasthouses stand right in the village, and the main street has the usual nice Kentish mixture of red brick and weatherboarded houses. The church has a square tower, which looks strange as it is without battlements, and even stranger because of an onion dome on its turret, like something strayed from Austria, made of lead and dated 1734. The poet Edmund Blunden lived at Yalding; a verse from his poem *Forefathers* epitomises a vanished rural past, and could stand for any village of the Weald.

From this church they led their brides,
   From this church themselves were led
Shoulder-high; on these waysides
   Sat to take their beer and bread.
Names are gone – what men they were
These their cottages declare.

Downstream from Yalding, a superb medieval bridge, with no houses anywhere near, crosses the Medway between West Farleigh and Teston.

East Barming's isolated church lies down a lane; the tower with its spindly spire is a landmark from the main road. There has been a lot of restoration, but the east end still keeps its three little arched Norman windows. The carved bench ends are thought by Newman to be German about 1300; he calls them 'very wild', and certainly Samson rending the lion and St George spearing the dragon (or St Michael the devil) are explosively energetic. The altar is modern, well carved in traditional linenfold style.

The medieval bridge at **East Farleigh** was where General Fairfax crossed the Medway before taking Maidstone in 1648. Above the river, with its boats, locks and weirs, the shingled spire of the church stands out on the skyline, looking down on a vast hopfield.

A couple of miles away is **Loose,** on the southern outskirts of Maidstone – a secretive little place, tucked away in a valley off the A 229; it is perched on a hillside, and is full of the sound of running water, with a causewayed path running between two streams. Richard Church in *The Little Kingdom* gives chapter and verse for a sign which read 'Loose Women's Institute'; but it is no longer in evidence. The **Wool House** can be seen by appointment; it has long, low beamed rooms inside, and close vertical timbering on the walls outside. The stream that splashes down beside it still looks sparkling even in this age of pollution.

CHAPTER TWELVE

The Sevenoaks Ridge

❧

THE main road from London to Hastings (A 21) enters Kent five miles north of **Sevenoaks**, swinging down the steep slope of the North Downs at Polhill, crossing the Darent valley, and climbing to central Sevenoaks high on the greensand ridge. A cheerful, breezy commuters' town, Sevenoaks consists mainly of successive generations of businessmen's houses spreading north from the old town centre, and expanding into the area between the London road and the splendidly landscaped new bypass. On the south it ends abruptly south of Sevenoaks School, where the grass and trees of Knole take over from the houses. Knole still dominates Sevenoaks; the school and the church lie across the park from the great house, and the main entrance road to Knole is right in the middle of the town.

It seems likely that the name means exactly what it says – that in Saxon times a clump of seven oak trees made a good meeting-place in this heavily wooded area, and the name stuck. At any rate, belief in this origin was perpetuated a few years ago, in 1955, when seven young oaks were planted on the southern edge of the town. The trees (in a row, not a clump) are on the west side of the Tonbridge road, south of the White Hart; they are now about twenty feet tall. The town was put on the map by Sir William Sevenoke or Sennocke, a foundling who rose to be Lord Mayor of London. Said to have been found in a hollow tree, or, less romantically, lying in the street, some time in the 1370s, he became an apprentice in the City, joined the Grocers' Company, and made a fortune. He endowed Sevenoaks School by his will in 1432, though it had been founded some years earlier; today's sober ragstone building, with almshouses on either side, was designed by Lord Burlington about 1724. The tall Perpendicular church tower opposite is a great landmark; part of the building goes back to the thirteenth century, but it is much restored. A new roof was built a few years ago, after the old one caught fire from a workman's blowlamp. Inside there are monuments to Sevenoaks's varied collection of notabilities: Lord Amherst, who captured Montreal and accepted the surrender of the French in 1760, at the end of the campaign in which Wolfe was killed; William Lambarde, author of the *Perambulation*; Dr Thomas Fuller, an eighteenth-century investigator of flea bites and eruptive fever. A tablet to John Donne records that the great love poet and Dean of St Paul's was rector here from 1616 to 1631. The Sackvilles of Knole are not buried here but in the family mausoleum at Withyham (see p. 322).

Lambarde himself was lukewarm about Sevenoaks; the only 'memorable thing' he could find to say about it was its connection with Jack Cade. During his short-lived revolt in 1450 – largely brought about by the repressions of Lord Saye and Sele, owner of Knole and Lord-Lieutenant of Kent – Cade defeated Henry VI's troops at Solefields, south of the town (there is a plaque commemorating the battle on the corner of Solefields Road). He and his followers marched to London, dragged Lord Saye from the Tower, where the king had put him for safe keeping, and hacked off his head. Cade was finally killed near Heathfield (see p. 269).

Going north into the town from the church and school you pass any number of fine old buildings, among them The Chantry, a brick house with two projecting wings, built about 1700, and the Red House, the home of Dr Thomas Fuller and later of Francis Austen, the uncle of Jane. The old trading area of the town was built at the junction of the High Street and the London Road. The Old Market House, an unpretentious 1840s building decorated with swags made of red tiling, has come down in the world since the J.P.s used to meet in its upper room to sentence local malefactors: its ground floor is now a public lavatory. Beyond is a little alley leading through a tunnel to The Shambles. Much of this warren of cobbled lanes and cottages has been knocked down and cleared right through to the High Street, but enough still remains to give an idea of the cramped conditions under which the ordinary townspeople lived.

Farther up the High Street is Bligh's Hotel, built as a farmhouse about 1600. In the eighteenth century it became known as Bedlam Farm, as it was used as a country home for insane patients from Bedlam Hospital in Moorfields. Near by is the Vine cricket ground, the original home of Kent cricket. The earliest recorded match was played on the ground in 1734, when the home side of Kent defeated Sussex. The ground was given to the town by the cricket-loving third Duke of Dorset in 1773; in those days it was right in the country, with one or two houses to the north. It is a smallish and rather sloping pitch, with a tremendous view away to the North Downs. The cricket pavilion, built in 1850, is an elegant single-storey white wooden building, looking far more Regency than Victorian, with pediment and sash windows.

Though modern Sevenoaks is expanding northwards along the roads to London and Dartford, its centre of gravity is still very much **Knole** (National Trust), on its southern side. If a house can be said to have a character, then Knole has more character than any other house in the two counties. It is often linked with Penshurst (see p. 235) near by; but by comparison with Knole, Penshurst is a straightforward, open house, with none of the twists and turns, the dark corners, the sense of mystery that give Knole its endless fascination. You can see Knole in the distance from the Tonbridge road; but when you drive towards it through the park it is hidden behind the tree-covered hills or knolls (on one of which the house stands, hence its name), until you round the last bend and the jumble of stone walls and turrets lies close before you. Before going into the house, it is worth getting an idea of its scale and complexity by walking a short way on to the golf-course, on the left-hand side as you stand facing the house. Over the high stone garden wall rise gables and oriel windows, and a bewildering series of stone towers and long tiled roofs; while through the gates set here and there at odd angles you catch glimpses of workshop yards and storage sheds.

Knole is intimately bound up with the history of the Sackville family, as the title of Victoria Sackville-West's lovingly detailed chronicle, *Knole and the Sackvilles*, implies. Yet though the Sackvilles transformed the interior, adding the rich decoration, furnishings and pictures down the centuries, the external appearance is due to an earlier owner, Thomas Bourchier, Archbishop of Canterbury. Bourchier bought it in 1456 from Lord Saye and Sele, and turned it from a medieval muddle into the Oxford college-like appearance it has today. In Archbishop Cranmer's time Henry VIII coveted the palaces at Knole and Otford, remarking to Cranmer that Otford was damp and would do for his retainers, but 'as for Knole, it standeth on a sound, perfect and wholesome ground; and if I should make abode here, as I surely mind to do now and then, I will live at Knole.' Naturally Cranmer complied; and Knole remained almost continually in royal hands from 1536, until in 1566 Queen Elizabeth gave it (subject to lease) to her cousin, Thomas Sackville. In 1603 Sackville bought the freehold, and from then on it was firmly in the Sackville family.

Whether by accident or medievally astrological design, Knole is linked to the passing of time; it is said to have seven courtyards corresponding to the days of the week, fifty-two staircases for the weeks of the year, and 365 rooms for the days of the year, no doubt involving some cheating with anterooms and lobbies. You go under the outer gateway into the Green Court, an austere quadrangle at present undergoing wholesale restoration of the stonework. (Though the official guidebook attributes this courtyard to Bourchier or his successor, Newman puts it as late as 1540.) Facing you is yet another gatehouse, indisputably Bourchier's, which brings you into the Stone Court, at the heart of Knole. All the great staterooms lie behind or beside this court. Below the flagstones are huge reservoirs of water. The court carries reminders of the first and the last of the Knole Sackvilles: the initials T.D. (Thomas Dorset) and the date 1605 on the beautifully shaped lead water pipes; and the name Shelley's Tower for the square gate tower on the left looking back towards the entrance. 'Shelley' was the nearest the Knole retainers could get to the name of the third Duke's mistress Giannetta Baccelli, an Italian dancer whom he met while ambassador in Paris just before the French Revolution and kept in style at Knole.

You go into the medieval Great Hall under a Jacobean colonnade surmounted by a Georgian balcony – a mingling of the centuries typical of Knole. The bulbously carved oak screen was put in by Thomas Sackville, who sat down to dinner on the low dais at the opposite end, surveying a small army ranging in importance from the chaplain to the scullery-maid. Sackville was created first Earl of Dorset in 1604; his portrait, painted about 1600, hangs in the hall. He was a sober politician, Lord Treasurer under Elizabeth and James I, and died in harness at the Privy Council table in Whitehall in 1608. Knole was his passion: after getting full possession in 1603, he spent thousands of pounds on beautifying it, importing craftsmen from Italy to work on the magnificent carving and plasterwork. Earlier in his life he had been a poet, author of *Gorboduc*, the first English tragedy, performed in 1561, and of poems which influenced Edmund Spenser. From this many-sided man stemmed the owners of Knole for more than two centuries – 'a race too prodigal, too amorous, too weak, too indolent, and too melancholy' (*Knole and the Sackvilles*).

Behind the hall the Great Staircase – a Jacobean *tour de force* of heraldic carving and grisaille wall painting – leads to the galleries and state bedrooms. At the foot of the stairs is a life-size nude carving of the seductive Gianetta Baccelli, a plaster copy of an original which was banished to the attics when the third Duke brought a wife home to Knole. John Frederick Sackville preferred cricket to politics or diplomacy, though this did not prevent him from being sent as ambassador to France, a suitably frivolous envoy during the final frivolous days of the old régime. After his return from Paris in 1789 he sobered up, married, had a family, lost his good nature, and died only ten years later at the age of fifty-four.

At the top of the staircase is the Brown Gallery, the most typical gallery of Knole. The sombre room stretches into the distance, lined with a double row of portraits in identical frames. This part of the house has no heating and no artificial light, and in the dusk of a late autumn day these rows of gloomy historical personages gaze down with hypnotic effect. Below the paintings stand rows of seventeenth-century chairs; even their brocade has been preserved in the uncorrupting timelessness of Knole.

In complete contrast are the small rooms opening off the end of the gallery, where Lady Betty Germain, an eighteenth-century friend of the Dorsets, lived for forty years, engaged in needlework, letter-writing, and making pot-pourri to sweeten the air of Knole (you can still find bowls of it here and there, made to her recipe). On the other side of the gallery is the Spangle Bedroom, whose giant four-poster once sparkled with sequins, now turned black with age; this great bed is challenged by the huge green-velvet-hung four-poster in the Venetian Ambassador's Bedroom, across the Leicester Gallery. The focus of interest in this gallery is the original drop-end Knole sofa, the Jacobean original of countless modern settees. In the gallery annexe is a Charles I billiard table, with curved ivory-tipped cues laid idly down, as though half way through some ghostly game.

All these rooms are at the back of the Stone Court. Another vast suite opens off the top of the staircase, leading along one side of the court towards the front of the house. The huge ballroom was decorated by Thomas Sackville with a sumptuous frieze of gryphons, mermaids and monsters; below are portraits of all the Sackvilles, ending, as did the direct line, with the young fourth Duke of Dorset, killed in a hunting accident in 1815, soon after his twenty-first birthday.

The Reynolds Room takes its name from the portraits by Sir Joshua that line the walls. Among them is a delightful painting of the third Duke's Chinese pageboy, Wang-y-Tong, who was taught at Sevenoaks School across the park, and was called Warnoton, as the locals could not manage his outlandish name. Below the ornate Jacobean chimneypiece are ostentatiously elaborate silver firedogs made about 1680 – a far cry from the sober ironwork of earlier generations. The last and most formal of the galleries is the Cartoon Gallery, so called because one long wall is covered with dull copies of the huge paintings by Raphael done for a series of tapestries on the lives of Saints Peter and Paul. And finally comes the grandest of all the bedrooms, the King's Bedroom, reputedly prepared for James I, with a tall four-poster crowned with ostrich plumes. This room houses the extraordinary silver furniture – everyday objects like mirrors and tables, transmuted to a degree beyond vulgarity by a heavy silver overlay, and teased by the silversmith's art into a riot of swirling ornamentation.

Though part of Knole is still occupied by the Sackville family and life goes on there, the vast house gives off a feeling of time transfixed that is almost palpable. A return to the broad daylight of the park breaks the spell; yet behind those grey walls the ghosts of Knole linger on, staring down from the walls on to the sombre opulence that they created, and we can wonder at.

South and east of Knole Park are noble woods for picnicking or walking in, and tucked-away little hamlets like **Godden Green**. At the foot of the steep hill towards Underriver is **Black Charles** – a far from sinister house, despite its sinister-seeming name. This derives in fact from the Blaccherl ('Black Ceorl', or swarthy man) family, who came there in the fourteenth century. Besides its superb oak beams and timber framing, Black Charles is a treasurehouse of craftsmanship in wood, including seventeenth-century doors from France, and a fourteenth-century oak carving of an indeterminate figure, said to be a butcher.

Seal is the first largish village on the main road east from Sevenoaks, notable for Old Seal House, a handsome half-timbered building, now shops and offices, which stands at the central crossroads. Seal church, begun in the thirteenth century, has a fine Perpendicular tower. A little statue of St Peter, complete with keys, stands in a niche over the entrance door. Inside is the bewigged stone head of Lord Camden, Attorney-General and Lord High Chancellor in the reign of George III, who lost his job for opposing the American War of Independence.

Oldbury Hill (National Trust) is the most impressive earthwork of the Sevenoaks ridge. It is on the north side of the A 25, above Ightham, and is so heavily wooded that you have to use the eye of faith to convince yourself that it is an ancient site at all. The main entrance is from a small layby, where the road widens briefly into a dual carriageway. You walk up a steep track, and after a minute or two stone steps to left and right lead to the dip that marks the Oldbury ramparts. These were constructed about 100 BC by Iron Age tribes, and may have been defended against the Romans during Claudius's conquest of Britain in AD 43.

Below Oldbury is **Ightham**, a delectable village, which rambles up and down, and has a superb cluster of half-timbered houses at its centre. For many years the village shop was kept by Benjamin Harrison, who became internationally known in Victorian times as an archaeologist; the Coldrum Stones burial chamber (see p. 205) is now a permanent monument to him. He died in 1921 aged eighty-four, and is commemorated by a tablet in the church. This is notable for its brickwork: the north aisle was constructed entirely of brick in 1639. These seventeenth-century bricks are longer than later varieties (ten inches as opposed to nine). Harrison's modest tablet is overshadowed by the monuments of the Cawnes and Selbys, who owned Ightham Mote near by. In the chancel, life-size in full armour, lies the stone effigy of Sir Thomas Cawne, who died about 1374; the window above, with strange cork-shaped carving in the tracery, forms part of the tomb. More eye-catching are the seventeenth-century Selby monuments: the double memorial to an uncle and nephew, both called Sir William; and a smaller but far more interesting wall monument to Dame Dorothy (died 1641), wife of the younger Sir William. She was a great needlewoman; two of her pictures, 'The Gunpowder Plot' and 'The Golden Age' (Adam and Eve), are depicted on the monument, though they are hard to see without extra lighting. The final couplet of her epitaph,

> Whose Arte disclos'd that Plot, which had it taken,
> Rome had tryumph'd & Britan's walls had shaken,

was at one time taken to mean that Dame Dorothy had something to do with unmasking the plot, but is now thought to refer simply to her needlework.

Ightham Mote (open Friday afternoons), the home of Mr C. H. Robinson, lies hidden away down side roads a couple of miles south of the village. Through the hamlet of Ivy Hatch, you suddenly plunge down a steep-sided lane with hardly room for two cars to pass, and ahead of you is the grey stone manor, with a small lake beyond. Though the house is surrounded by a moat, the name 'Mote' probably means the place where the moot or Saxon council met. There can be few places in this country more peaceful or unspoiled after six centuries.

Though it now appears as a single harmonious building, in the form of a hollow square with a moat around it and an imposing gatehouse leading to it, in fact the construction spans about three hundred years, from the Cawnes in the fourteenth century to the Selbys in the seventeenth. Across the courtyard is the old core of the house – the Great Hall, probably built by Sir Thomas Cawne about 1340. As well as the huge oak beams, the ceiling is supported by a stone arch resting on comic little human corbels. In spite of its comparatively small size, Ightham Mote makes room for two chapels: a medieval one above the hall, connected with the solar or ladies' retiring room by a squint through which services could be watched; and the Tudor chapel built about 1520, complete with linenfold panelling, pews and pulpit, and with a sanctuary ring at which criminals could take refuge. Ightham has its stories connected with religious persecution, its priest's holes, and even a cupboard in the Great Hall where a walled-up skeleton is said to have been found; but though a member of the Allen family who owned the Mote in the time of Elizabeth was described as keeping 'a vile and papisticall house', search parties discovered nothing treasonable there.

Plantagenet stonework and Tudor timbering form such an integrated whole that it is strange to find a Palladian window in the drawing-room, especially noticeable from outside the house. Apart from odd bits of carving like the Saracen's head on the staircase, the drawing-room is the only light-hearted thing about Ightham, which tends to the rich and melancholy. A flamboyant Jacobean oak frieze, carved with Saracen heads, vultures, fruit and flowers, runs round the room below the ceiling; and there is a huge, almost obese overmantel. Frieze and overmantel were put in by the younger Sir William Selby, husband of the needlewoman Dame Dorothy; her portrait gazes disapprovingly down the main staircase. Before they came south to the soft airs of Kent in the 1590s, the Selbys were Lords of the Marches on the Scottish Border. Their talent for rough justice is commemorated on their monument in Ightham church, which mentions that the younger Sir William executed or exiled '1,500 wicked and desperate thieves' in that wild region.

Below the Palladian window on the north side of the house is a little water gate opening on to the moat. Legend links this with the Cromwellian suit of armour in the Great Hall. A soldier of the time, the story goes, fell in love with one of the Selby ladies, but while trying to get into the house through the water gate he slipped into the moat and drowned. But peaceful rather than tragic memories rule over this beautiful house, in its calm setting of hill, water, grass and huge dark trees.

Two of the prettiest villages in the Sevenoaks area lie on the Pilgrims' Way, north of the A 25 – Kemsing, right off the main road, and Otford, where the old travellers crossed the Darent. Kemsing's chief claim to fame is St Edith's Well, at the junction of the road from Seal into the village. It stands in a little lawn by the war memorial, and feeds a small stream. St Edith, daughter of King Edgar the Peaceful and Lady Wulfrith, was born in Kemsing in AD 961; she lived most of her life at the Abbey of Wilton, in Wiltshire. After her death at the age of twenty-four a cult grew up round her, a shrine with a miracle-working statue was built in the churchyard, and the church prospered from the offerings of pilgrims. Lambarde tells how for a consideration the priest at Kemsing would bless corn and other grain in the name of St Edith to protect it from mildew and blight. The church, with its wood-shingled spire and belfry, and white doves cooing on the buttresses, is as pretty as the village.

Otford has been much more in the mainstream of history. It is strategically placed at the crossing of the Darent; Roman remains have been found here; and it was the site of battles in 774 and 1016. In medieval and Tudor times the Archbishops of Canterbury had a palace here. The remains of the Tudor palace lie back from the main road. They consist of a single-storey building used as a storehouse, a gallery, now turned into cottages, and a three-storey brick tower. Round the back, the carved brickwork of the gallery windows is still in good condition; they look on to a stream which runs through a watermeadow. This, the last of the Otford palaces, was built by Archbishop Warham early in the sixteenth century in preference to Knole. Becket is reputed to have started the palace's water supply by striking his staff into the ground at St Thomas's Well, now in a private garden; and Lambarde tells how Becket 'was much hindered in devotion, by the sweete note and melodie of a Nightingale', and at once put a miraculous ban on birdsong in the palace park.

Otford church has a magnificently sturdy twelfth-century tower, covered in an ugly layer of cement. There was originally a Saxon church here, and much of the masonry in the nave dates from about the time of the Norman Conquest. On the west wall of the nave are eight sombrely painted funeral hatchments in memory of members of the Polhill family (after whom the steep hill up the downs north of Sevenoaks is named).

In the middle of Otford is a tidied-up village pond, with weeping willows on either side, and ornamental waterfowl swimming about on it.

Chevening, off the B 2211 north-west of Sevenoaks, is little more than the great mansion, a few small houses built against the high outer wall, and an ancient church. The house cannot be visited, but the north front, facing up the slope of the Downs, can be seen by walking a short way up the footpath to Knockholt. The nucleus of the present house was built between 1616 and 1630; the architect is said to have been Inigo Jones. It was bought in 1717 by General James Stanhope, George I's Foreign Secretary and Head of Government. In 1718 he was made Earl Stanhope, but died only three years later, leaving the vast alterations he planned to be carried out by his widow. These included the two pavilions on either side of the house, far more attractive than the main house as it now stands.

Its appearance is largely due to Charles, the third Earl, who was a vintage example of the wealthy English eccentric. He was a keen republican, and his sympathies with the French Revolution gained him the nickname 'Citizen' Stanhope. He was also a scientist, who experimented with steam-driven ships, and invented the first iron printing press and a machine to do multiplication and division, now on view in the London Science Museum. He added an attic storey to Chevening in 1795-96, and covered the exterior with 'mathematical tiles'.

Eccentricity continued in the next generation with Charles's daughter, Lady Hester Stanhope, who kept house for her uncle, the Prime Minister William Pitt the Younger, until his death in 1806. Thereupon she travelled to the Near East and built herself a castle on the slopes of Mount Lebanon, where she bossed the Arabs, surrounded herself with vast numbers of cats and other animals, and lived like an Oriental princess for nearly thirty years.

Chevening was left in trust by the seventh Earl Stanhope to be occupied by a descendant of King George VI, a cabinet minister, the Canadian High Commissioner, or the United States Ambassador. It is at present undergoing major repairs: the mathematical tiles have been removed, the whole house is being refaced with brick, and the attic storey is being replaced by a mansard roof.

The church is a pretty little thirteenth-century building, thought to have been built here because at this point the east-west Pilgrims' Way crossed the north-south main road; but both sections where they ran through the park were closed by the eccentric third Earl, who built the present road

Old Scotney Castle, near Lamberhurst, a romantic ruin reflected in the waters of the moat. In the background is the stone house built for Edward Hussey in the 1830s.

Bateman's, Burwash, where Rudyard Kipling lived from 1902 until his death in 1936. It was built in 1634 for a wealthy Sussex ironmaster.

The main gatehouse of Bodiam Castle. (Since this photograph was taken the moat has been drained and the waterliles cleared.)

from Sundridge at his own expense. Inside the church is the Stanhope Chantry, kept locked since visitors started removing armour and other mobile trophies from the walls. The most notable memorial is the white marble figure of Lady Frederica Stanhope, who died in childbirth in 1823, aged twenty-three. Carved by Sir Francis Chantrey, she lies quietly asleep, cradling the child who killed her.

West of Sevenoaks, Sundridge and Brasted now form an almost continuous village along the A 25. **Sundridge**'s tall-towered church (usually locked) is on the hillside south of the main road; the finest house in the village is Sundridge Old Hall (now an antique shop), a Kentish yeoman's timber-framed house built about 1458. The great hall is lit by a superb oak twelve-light window. Inside you can still see the circle of rough stones where the open fire blazed, and the soot on the blackened plaster between the beams is so hard that a wire brush will not shift it.

Combe Bank, the big house of Sundridge, is a large white Georgian building, now a girls' convent school (open Sat. afternoons, May–Sept.), and well worth seeing for its magnificent internal decoration. The 'Adam Room' has been recently restored to its original eighteenth-century colour scheme; but far richer and more strange is the 'Walter Crane Room' (now the school library), decorated by Crane about 1880 with spikily metallic Seasons and Signs of the Zodiac, against a background of dark green and bronze. This was commissioned by Dr William Spottiswoode, a mathematician and physicist who combined the job of Queen's Printer with that of President of the Royal Society. The great scientists of the period – Darwin, Huxley, Herbert Spencer – used to meet in this room; not only was Combe Bank the first house in the neighbourhood to be wired for electricity, but the work was carried out under the supervision of Michael Faraday himself. A later scientific owner of Combe Bank was Robert Mond, one of the founding fathers of I.C.I.

Brasted's old name, Bradestede, may derive from Bredsted in Jutland, where the original Jutish settlers came from; or it may simply be the 'broad steading', or sprawling village, which it still is. Half way along the straight High Street is a pretty green, backed by some fine old buildings, including a row of Tudor cottages. A side road leads down to the church, on the other side of the Darent. The medieval tower is still standing, but the rest of the church was pulled down and rebuilt in the 1860s, in a discreet and non-Gothic-Revival way. In 1944 it was badly damaged by a flying bomb, which blew out all the glass and cracked the chancel walls. The original church's great age is recalled by a Saxon tombstone below the tower, discovered during demolition in 1865.

About 1840 Napoleon III lived for some time at **Brasted Place** (now a Church of England training college), before returning to France as emperor.

For a practical demonstration of the steepness of the sandstone ridge, you can take the **Toys Hill** road in the middle of Brasted. This shoots up to 770 feet, and the high point is marked by the Fox and Hounds pub. There is marvellous National Trust woodland up here for walking and picnicking.

The **Ide Hill** road, running parallel to the east, will also take you up and over the ridge. Ide Hill village is not much more than a green and a few houses, with a spiky little Victorian church; but the view across the Weald from the car park below it must be one of the most spectacular anywhere in England. Two or three miles to the south the landscape is dominated by a huge sheet of water – not a flood, as you might legitimately think, as it does not yet appear on any of the maps, but the new Bough Beech reservoir. This caused an outcry when it was proposed, as it inevitably drowned houses and good farmland; but on the credit side it enhances the landscape as only water can do, and is used for fishing in summer and boating in winter. No swimming allowed.

As its name implies, **Westerham** is the westernmost town in Kent. Like every other place on the appalling A 25, it has to suffer the relentless pounding of coaches and heavy lorries; though relief is in sight with the proposed M 25 motorway. On the green at the top of the hill are statues of Westerham's most famous men, General Wolfe, who spent his childhood at Quebec House, and Sir Winston Churchill, who lived at Chartwell a couple of miles to the south. Wolfe's statue, put up in 1911, shows him leading his men to victory with drawn sword, while Churchill, in a bronze by Oscar Nemon, slumps back in a chair, with his chin thrust aggressively forward.

Behind the green is an attractive group of old houses, mainly antique shops, pubs and tearooms. The church still keeps its Early English tower and chancel, though most of it was reconstructed at the end of the fifteenth century. Inside there is a splendid fourteenth-century timber spiral staircase running up into the tower. Only one other like it is known, in Hemel Hempstead church, Hertfordshire. Hexagonal in shape, it still looks as sound as ever, and seems to have undergone very little repair. As you would expect, James Wolfe is well commemorated in the church of his youth. In the north wall is the Wolfe Memorial window – a glowing Pre-Raphaelite Annunciation scene designed by Burne-Jones and made in the William Morris workshops. Over the south door is a memorial tablet, with a pompous poem thought to have been written by the Rev. George Lewis, vicar of Westerham at the time of Wolfe's death in 1759.

Wolfe was born in January, 1727, at Westerham Vicarage, not at Quebec House; his mother stayed at the vicarage for her confinement, while her husband was away with his regiment. The Wolfes had moved to **Quebec House** (National Trust) the year before, and lived there until 1738. In those days the house was known as Spiers, possibly from its twelve steep gables or 'spires'. As it lies so low it is liable to flood; during the disastrous floods of September, 1968, the waters of the Darent poured in at the back and out at the front, leaving damage that took eighteen months to put right. The downstairs rooms are full of Wolfe relics – portraits, caricatures, his massive field canteen, the dressing gown in which his body was brought back to England. Though he died in a blaze of glory, Wolfe's military success only came at the very end of his life. After a swift rise to the rank of lieutenant-colonel by the age of twenty-three, he spent seven years stagnating in Britain; but in 1757 this period ended when Pitt the Elder came to power, and Wolfe was sent out to Canada. Throughout the campaign he was ill with the gravel and rheumatism, and was already broken in health when he defeated the French spectacularly on the Heights of Abraham, falling mortally wounded at the moment of victory, and dying with a smile on his face. He is buried at Greenwich.

You can follow Wolfe's trail along the dogleg of Westerham High Street to **Squerryes Court**, on the west side of the town. Wolfe is said to have received his first commission, at the age of fourteen, in the garden of Squerryes; the spot is now

marked by a small classical urn at the top of the garden
terraces. Squerryes is the ideal middling-sized country mansion,
red brick and welcoming, with a small lake in front and a
garden and park behind. It dates from the 1680s; in 1731 it
was bought by John Warde, and has remained the Warde
family home ever since. As a boy Wolfe became friendly with
the Warde children, who all appear in a conversation piece in
the drawing-room, painted by Wootton in 1735. The Wolfe
Room contains documents and pictures, including the only
portrait for which Wolfe is known to have sat, probably
painted about the time he received his commission at Squerryes.
His mother's recipe book is on view; among other things, it
tells you how to make 'a good water for a consumption' from
ground snail shells, sliced earthworms and herbs, simmered in
milk and served two spoonfuls at a time.

Squerryes is full of good pictures, from simple family
portraits to the huge equestrian figure of Philip II of Spain,
partly by Rubens, which dominates the Picture Gallery.
Prominent among the Warde portraits is the glum, red-robed
figure of Sir Patience Warde, Lord Mayor of London in
1680; he was given his strange name because his father was
fed up with having a string of sons and only one daughter.
Far more cheerful is the Falstaffian portrait of a later John
Warde, painted in 1829 sitting ponderously on the back of his
favourite horse Blue Ruin, so called because he bought him
from a gin merchant. Warde has been called the father of fox-
hunting, and was a master of foxhounds for fifty-seven years.
The first John Warde was a racing enthusiast; the gazebo he
built about 1740 to watch his racehorses at their training
gallops still stands on a hill overlooking the lake, on the other
side of the road.

The Darent's source is in Squerryes park; at any rate, one of
the two streams that meet in Westerham rises there, so it can
claim half the source at least.

South of Westerham the roads run up on to **The Chart**, a
wide expanse of mixed heath and woodland that stretches
over the county border into Surrey, and is a splendid place
for walks, with its alternation of trees and open ground. The
Chart gives its name to **Chartwell**, which you can find easily
enough on summer weekends by following the nose-to-tail
queue of cars and coaches through the back roads. Chartwell

(National Trust) is built on the side of one of the combes which cut into the southern side of the ridge, and give magnificent views across the fields and woodlands of the Weald. It was certainly the views rather than the house that appealed to Churchill; when he bought it in 1922 it was a gloomy, creeper-covered Victorian barn of a place. There has been a house on the site since the Middle Ages, built near the 'well on the Chart' – the spring that now feeds the swimming-pool and lake.

As it now stands, Chartwell is nothing special in the way of English country houses; but for its association with one of the giants of the twentieth century its plain façade would hardly deserve more than a glance through the open front gates. Though Chartwell has the elements of a shrine, it is far too much of a home to let the reverential aspects get the upper hand. In the entrance hall you are immediately confronted by an umbrella stand full of walking-sticks; and in the drawing-room, the first large room you come to, a pair of splendid George II mirrors and a glowing pink and yellow Monet painting of London Bridge look down on a small card table set for bezique. Upstairs, several bedrooms have been converted into display rooms for various aspects of Churchill's life. The Anteroom is full of medals, photographs of the generals of both World Wars, and fine china; while the Museum Room is remarkable for the hideousness of many of the gifts it contains, including two silver and crystal bowls from Stalin. Of far greater interest is the famous Boer War poster offering £25 for Churchill's capture 'levend of dood', dead or alive. The Uniform Room is bright with the fancy dress in which Churchill delighted, like the full dress of a Privy Councillor and of the Lord Warden of the Cinque Ports, and the ultra-Churchillian assemblage of green velvet siren suit, ten-gallon hat, and Turkish-looking slippers. The literary side of Churchill is centred on the study, a magnificent room where Philip Tilden, Churchill's architect, removed the Victorian ceiling to show the great beams and rafters of an older Chartwell. Here Churchill wrote much of his life of Marlborough, his chronicle of the Second World War, and his *History of the English-speaking Peoples*. A vast painting of Blenheim hangs above the fireplace, and on the left is a small portrait of his father, Lord Randolph Churchill, who died a disappointed man in 1895, and whose life formed the subject of an early book by Churchill, written in 1906.

Much of the real character of Chartwell is concentrated in the garden: in the lawns and terraces where Churchill strolled with his dog – or on occasion a pet sheep – at his heels; in the pond where he fed the golden orfe; in the orchard whose trees he planted; in the Golden Rose Garden planted to mark the Churchills' golden wedding in 1958. Round this part of the garden runs the wall with which Churchill busied himself during his years in the wilderness, a relaxing contrast to the frustrations of the 1930s. It is a copy of the wall round Quebec House. Far from being some little piece of do-it-yourself bricklaying, it is enormous, about eight feet high, built stepwise down the hill round all four sides of the kitchen garden. Typically, Churchill sparked off a union uproar when in 1928 he took out a card as an adult apprentice in the Amalgamated Union of Building Trade Workers; just as typically, he finished the wall.

At the far end of a little group of cottages near the wall is Churchill's studio, lined with paintings and with an unfinished canvas still on the easel. He describes how he was inspired to start painting by watching the wife of Sir John Lavery. 'Splash into the turpentine, wallop into the blue and white, frantic flourish on the palette – clean no longer – and then several large fierce strokes and slashes of blue on the absolutely cowering canvas. Anyone could see that it would not hit back.' Churchill seized a brush, did likewise, and so began his career as the patron saint of amateur artists.

Crockham Hill, the nearest village to Chartwell, is another place of spectacular views; Samuel Palmer is thought to have drawn the landscape here, though his viewpoints cannot be identified exactly. Suitably enough for a village so embedded in beautiful countryside, the church contains the tomb of Octavia Hill, one of the founders of the National Trust. 'Noble in aim, wise in method' as the inscription calls her, her recumbent effigy lies in the sanctuary, a smiling female crusader in a stone-carved shawl.

CHAPTER THIRTEEN

The Eden and the Upper Medway

❧

THE illogicality of county boundaries is nowhere shown more clearly than in the corner where Kent, Sussex and Surrey join together. A mass of roadside nameboards make sure that you do not forget whose authority you are in, road surfaces constantly change both in colour and quality, and it seems surprising that the hedgerow plants and the style of buildings do not alter in sympathy. In fact, the divisions follow for a good way the streams that once separated the kingdom of Kent from its neighbours – Kent Brook from Surrey, and Kent Water from Sussex.

Edenbridge, five miles south of Westerham, is strung out along the Roman road which led south across the Weald to Lewes and north to London. At its northern end fields have given way in the past few years to factories, and its population has grown enormously with the building of two G.L.C. overspill estates; but its centre still keeps something of the feeling of an old market town. In summer the dead straight road is jammed with cars making for the coast; but what Edenbridge could be like, given the chance, was shown in the festival held in 1970 to commemorate the town's seven hundredth anniversary, when the road was closed to traffic, and the centre was given over to people listening to the band, watching the medieval-type booths, or drinking outside the pubs of which Edenbridge has its fair share. The sign of one of them, the Crown, an old coaching inn, stretches right across the road in the middle of the town. The central square – little more than a widening of the High Street – is unusual in having industry or its relics as its main feature. Set back on the west side are the black-painted wooden sheds of a tannery which has been there since the seventeenth century and probably much earlier, approached past half-timbered

A map for this chapter will be found on page 212.

medieval buildings; and opposite is a white-painted eighteenth-century watermill, with the undershot wheel and a good deal of the grinding machinery still in place. The modern factories up the road carry on Edenbridge's tradition as a town where things are made, and saves it from being just another feature-less commuting dormitory, or sheltered monument to the past.

The name of the town looks as though it should derive from the River Eden; but in fact it is the other way round. In Norman times the name was Eadelmsbrege, or 'Eadhelm's Bridge', after a Saxon who had rebuilt the Roman bridge across the river – which was not called the Eden until some centuries later. The church is north of the river, set back from the square and built on the site of a Saxon predecessor. Some Norman work survives, but it is mainly Early English, with a heavily buttressed tower that seems to grow from the soil, topped by a well-proportioned shingled spire. Inside, the wide south aisle has almost the effect of a double nave. The monuments are not particularly noteworthy; though there is one curiosity, a memorial window in the south wall com-memorating a bewhiskered Victorian station master, who gazes down from the glass disguised as a prophet.

The Roman road was used to bring iron down from the hills to the south, and round Cowden (accent on the -den), one of the local beauty spots, there are visible reminders of the time when the skies were red with the glow from primitive blast furnaces. West of Cowden down a small lane is Furnace Pond, now a quiet thirty-acre stretch of water surrounded by trees and lined with bulrushes. This supplied the water power for the furnace of Richard Tichborne, who built **Crippenden Manor**, north of Cowden, in 1607. In the garden of Crippen-den is the 'Cowden gun', made at Furnace Mill and the only local gun known to survive. The Tichbornes were strong Parliamentarians and the gun, a small type known as a falconet, may have been made for Cromwell but never supplied because it was faulty.

Cowden village – a short street of white-painted and half-timbered houses – is tucked away from the outside world. The church has an unusually tall spire (127 feet), and both spire and tower are shingled. The building is mostly fourteenth-century, with a nineteenth-century north aisle added. Inside it is remarkable for the timbers below the tower, and for the fine kingpost roof. Before the Reformation it housed an image of St Uncumber, the popular name for St Wylgeforte, to whom wives wishing to get rid of their husbands – 'uncumber theym of theyr Housbondys', wrote Sir Thomas More – used to make offerings. As a girl she was beautiful, but so pestered with suitors that she prayed to be rid of them, grew a flourishing beard, and passed the rest of her life in hirsute sanctity. By the church is one of the few local smithies where you can actually see horses being shod. When I went there the smith was dubiously looking at the latest product of technology, a plastic horseshoe.

At **Holtye**, a little east of the White Horse Inn, a sign by the road marks a stretch of the Roman road where it continued south from Edenbridge. At the bottom of the hill, down a footpath, the Sussex Archaeological Trust have uncovered and protected a few yards of the original surface, made of rammed iron cinders. Unfortunately much of the exposed section is now green with moss, and grass is starting to re-invade it.

East of Edenbridge the Eden meanders through a broadening plain, full of villages but preserved from major expansion by lack of anything that can be called a main road. Immediately downstream is **Hever** (pronounced Heaver). The much-filmed **Hever Castle** is largely the creation of an American millionaire early this century. Its toy-like fortifications, artificial lake and Italian garden make a perfect film set, complemented by the trim village church outside the gates and the old pub, the Henry VIII Inn, opposite. There is no village to speak of; Hever exists by virtue of its castle, with the pale ghosts of Anne Boleyn and her grasping father flitting somewhere in the background. The castle started life in the thirteenth century, as a fortified manor house inside a moat. From the de Hever family it passed to the Cobhams, and in the mid fifteenth century was bought by Sir Geoffrey Bullen, a former Lord Mayor of London. His ambitious grandson, Thomas, inherited Hever in 1506, and a few years later was well on the way to advancement; as a reward for encouraging Henry's infatuation for his daughter Anne he was created Earl of Wiltshire and Ormond. Anne – who adopted what she thought was the more elegant spelling of

'Boleyn' – became Queen in 1533, but only three years later was executed on Tower Green. In 1538 Thomas Bullen died at Hever, broken and neglected by his friends. Henry took possession of Hever and gave it to Anne of Cleves, his fourth wife, whom he had recently divorced; and on her death it passed into three and a half centuries of mouldering obscurity.

In 1903 it was bought by William Waldorf Astor and completely transformed. With his architect, F. L. Pearson, he filled the interior with fake Tudor plasterwork and wood-carving; built a village of bogus Tudor cottages beyond the moat for guests and servants; and created a splendid garden centring on an artificial lake where the Eden flows through the grounds. The Astors have owned Hever Castle ever since, in a placidity broken only by appalling floods, the first in 1958 and the second ten years later, when the Eden, polluted with oil and sewage, swirled through the castle to a depth of over four feet, leaving a devastation that took three and a half years to put right.

Though Hever has a moat (now filled with waterlilies), a drawbridge and a neat stone gatehouse, it is hard to imagine them ever being used for defence; fortunately, they were never put to the test. The inner courtyard, with its timbering, gabled windows and giant climbing plants, is small; an elongated Burgundian wine barrel almost fills one side of it. Inside, the house is chiefly remarkable for its portraits, as magnificent a gallery of sixteenth-century royalty and notables as you could find anywhere. In the entrance hall facing you are the three great Tudor sovereigns: a canny Henry VII, by Mabuse, a majestic Henry VIII, by Holbein, and a hawk-eyed and forbidding Elizabeth, by Geerarts. The best portrait of Anne Boleyn herself (by an unknown artist) is upstairs, in the long gallery. With her parchment skin and hair drawn severely back, she hardly looks the *femme fatale* of legend. The Venetian ambassador said of her: 'Madame Anne is not one of the handsomest women in the world. She is of middling stature, swarthy complexion, long neck, wide mouth, bosom not much raised, and in fact has nothing but the king's great appetite, and her eyes, which are black and beautiful.' Only a few months after her marriage Henry was being unfaithful to her, and warned her to 'shut her eyes as her betters had done.' In spite of his treatment of her, she prayed for that bloated ogre just before her execution.

Hever gardens have an autumnal melancholy about them, and are best seen on an afternoon of Indian summer, when the leaves of the vast horse chestnut trees in the park are beginning to turn. The formal Italian gardens are like an open-air museum, crammed with busts of emperors, giant jars, sarcophagi, urns and fragments of pillars, all collected in Rome by Mr Astor when he was American Minister there at the end of the nineteenth century. Beyond the formality the reed-lined lake stretches away into the distance.

Hever church, like the castle, is of sandstone, with a tall shingled spire visible a couple of miles away across the meadows. The earliest parts of the building are late thirteenth-century. The most important memorial is the tomb of Anne Boleyn's father, Sir Thomas Bullen, north of the altar; the brass on top shows him in the robes and insignia of a Knight of the Garter.

The story goes that the Henry VIII was originally called the Bull, but that after the execution of Sir Thomas Bullen's son and daughter it became known as the Bull and Butcher (or 'Bullen Butcher'). But Henry, as always, had the last word.

A mile and a half to the east, down winding byroads, is **Chiddingstone**. When you walk down the short village street you feel like a time traveller visiting the Tudor world; it is now preserved from everything except traffic by the National Trust. Some of the houses, with their overhanging first storeys and heavy beams, are known to have been there since the fifteenth century. Built and owned mainly by small farmers and tradesmen, they epitomise the rural affluent society.

The church is a serene sandstone building, with a Perpendicular pinnacled tower. It was largely rebuilt by Sir Bartholomew Burghersh, a famous soldier of his day, about the middle of the fourteenth century, with further reconstruction after 1624, when it was struck by lightning and severely damaged. The interior is spacious, with nave and aisles of the same length. The south aisle is almost a private memorial chapel to the Streatfeilds, the neighbourhood's leading family for over four hundred years. Sophia Streatfeild, who has a small tablet on the wall, was a friend of Dr Johnson, a bluestocking, and well known among her friends for her ability to weep to order – a useful attribute in the age of sensibility. She died in 1835 aged eighty-one.

At the end of a pathway that leads round behind the houses opposite the church is the 'Chiding Stone', a bulbous lump of sandstone to which scolds were brought to learn the error of their ways, and which is supposed to have given the village its name. More prosaic etymology derives it from 'Cidd-ingas', the people of Cidd.

Chiddingstone Castle, the Streatfeild family home, lies on the other side of the tall gates at the end of the village street. The first Streatfeild settled here in the early sixteenth century, in a Tudor house where the castle now stands. In 1683 a descendant built a new brick house, in the latest Carolean fashion, called High Street House, which lasted until Henry Streatfeild came into some money at the end of the eighteenth century and turned High Street House into a mock-medieval castle. He added battlements, towers and turrets, and Gothick doors and windows; and in a high-handed way diverted the High Street to run north of his property, dug a three-acre artificial lake, and knocked down a few cottages that spoilt the view. The building was completed by his son about 1835. The entrance hall and unpretentious staircase of High Street House still hide inside all this fake grandeur. When the last Streatfeild died in 1936 the castle became a school, and during the war it was occupied by troops. It is now once again privately owned, with the rooms given over to Jacobite relics and Oriental objets d'art, including a fine collection of Japanese lacquer.

The lake in the grounds is very popular with local anglers; in 1945 it produced the largest bream ever caught in the British Isles. Across the lake are tunnels cut in the sandstone, which are said to have been used by brandy smugglers in the great days of contraband.

Leigh (pronounced Lye) consists mainly of bogus Victorian half-timbering, but is full of character nevertheless, and has an excellent village green. North of the road the grounds of Hall Place run the whole length of the village. The park and lake can be seen here and there over the wall, and there is an assortment of turreted and gabled entrance lodges. The church is on a rise looking across the green; it is basically medieval, but much of it, including the tower, is Victorian. Inside on the north wall there is an odd Tudor brass showing a woman rising from the tomb at an angel's trumpet call, leaving her shroud behind her. In 1971 Leigh won the title of 'Best-kept Village in Kent'.

Penshurst, best reached down the side road a little west of Leigh, clusters round a T-junction, at the gates of Penshurst Place. At either end are bridges, one over the Eden and one over the Medway, and in between are houses of Kentish brick and weatherboarding, a garage (once the smithy) with a horseshoe-shaped door, the big village hall, and the creeper-covered Leicester Arms Hotel. Opposite the hotel is the prettiest corner of Penshurst – a group of half-timbered cottages shaped like a hollow E, and forming a large inhabited lychgate at the entrance to the churchyard. The eye-catching feature of the church is the Perpendicular tower, with vast pinnacles on the corners; the rest of the building is twelfth- and thirteenth century, much altered by the Victorians. The interior has been brightly painted in places, especially the roof of the Sidney chapel, which was reconstructed about 1820, and the medieval font. The main memorials in the Sidney chapel include the mutilated thirteenth-century effigy of Sir Stephen de Penchester, and the altar tomb of Sir William Sidney, the first of the Penshurst Sidneys. (The most famous Sidney of all, Sir Philip, was buried not here but in St Paul's.) An ancient rarity which somehow ended up in Penshurst is the medieval coffin lid under the tower, carved with the figure of a woman known as the 'smiling lady', with the foliated Albigensian Cross superimposed. This was the symbol of the Albigenses, a French sect savagely suppressed by the Pope in the thirteenth century. In the west wall is a new window, full of Becket references, installed in 1970 to mark the eight hundredth anniversary of his murder. It is by Lawrence Lee, who designed the nave windows for Coventry Cathedral and lives near Penshurst.

At first glance **Penshurst Place**, with its vast stone west front rising from a broad expanse of grass, may seem on the dull side. But a longer look shows that the uniformity of a first impression is in fact an illusion: the walls themselves separate into a number of distinct parts, and above them gabled roofs lead the eye back into the hinterland of the great house. Sir Philip Sidney wrote that it was 'built of fair and strong stone, not affecting so much any extraordinary kind of fineness as an honourable representing of a firm stateliness; handsome without curiosity and homely without loathsomeness.' When Sidney described Penshurst towards the end of the sixteenth century it was already old. The centrepiece then, as it still is today, was the magnificent medieval hall, built by Sir John de Pulteney about 1340. Visitors approach the house from the south side – a viewpoint which breaks it up into its component parts. Seen from the formal garden the Pulteney's hall and its associated rooms are on the right; to the left of them is the fifteenth-century addition known as the Buckingham Building with the Elizabethan galleries built on at right-angles to form the western side of the forecourt. There is no particularly striking feature, yet it all fits comfortably together.

Sir John de Pulteney, who bought Penshurst from the Penchester family in 1338, was a medieval magnate on the grand scale, four times Lord Mayor of London, and buried in the church of St Lawrence Pountney, which was named after him. His Great Hall is the first place you enter, after passing through the Garden Tower and across the forecourt. Over sixty feet long and nearly forty wide, and lit by tall traceried windows, the hall has hardly been altered in more than six centuries, apart from the blocking of the central roof vent that carried the smoke from the central hearth. The massive beams are of chestnut instead of the more usual oak, and are supported by grotesque human figures carved in wood – the peasants on whom the whole social structure ultimately rested. At the far end of the hall is one of Penshurst's most fascinating relics, the helmet carried at Sir Philip Sidney's funeral in 1587, surmounted by a porcupine, the Sidney family crest. A staircase leads down from the hall to a vaulted crypt, crammed with armour and weapons.

Elizabethan and medieval Penshurst meet in the State Dining Room, up a flight of stairs from the hall. This was the solar of Pulteney's house; it still keeps the small window where the ladies could keep an eye on the goings-on in the hall below. The walls are hung with Sidney portraits, starched and ruffed, in the stylised postures of the Elizabethan studio.

Penshurst came into the Sidney family in 1552, when Edward VI granted it to Sir William Sidney, Chamberlain and Steward of the Household, who years before had fought at Flodden, and gone with Henry VIII to the Field of the Cloth of Gold. Sir William died soon after taking over Penshurst, and it was his son Sir Henry who really established the Sidneys there.

Henry Sidney was brought up with Edward VI; 'as the prince grew in years and discretion, so grew I in favour and liking of him', he later wrote. He was something of a prodigy. The chronicler Holinshed praised his 'comeliness of person, gallantness, and liveliness of spirit, virtue, quality, beauty and good composition of body'. Among his strangely assorted court offices were those of Chief Cupbearer, Otter Hunter and Chief Cypherer; and as early as 1550 he was sent as ambassador to France. He remained in favour in Mary's reign, and was Elizabeth's Lord Deputy in Ireland. His campaigns there wore him out physically and financially, and he met the usual lack of appreciation from the Queen. To add to his worries his wife caught smallpox after attending Elizabeth when she had the disease. 'I left her a full fair lady,' he wrote, 'in mine eye at least, the fairest; and when I returned I found as foul a lady as a small-pox could make her.' Little wonder that his portrait at Penshurst (in the Panelled Room next door to the Nether Gallery) shows a thoroughly despondent face beneath the luxuriant beard. When he was fifty-four he described himself as 'toothless and trembling'; and he died shortly after, in 1586. Nevertheless, he found time from his burdensome public life to build the north and west fronts to the house, and the fine gatehouse on the northern side.

Ironically enough, in 1554, when his eldest son was born, he named him Philip after the Spanish king, who was the boy's godfather. Perhaps Elizabeth's harsh treatment of Sir Henry was partly due to this. Sir Philip Sidney's life was a contrast to his father's in every way, brilliantly successful, and cut off in its prime before court envy and intrigue could exact their toll. As a courtier he knew how to win round the queen; after being banished from the court for speaking his mind, he gave her, says the Hon. Mary Sidney in her 1903 guide to Penshurst, 'a whip, to show he had been scourged, a chain, to chain him to Her Majesty, and a heart of gold, to show he was now entirely hers.' As a poet he was famous for his 'Arcadia', inspired by the country round Penshurst and written in conjunction with his sister Mary, and above all for the sonnets he wrote to Penelope Devereux, calling himself Astrophel and her Stella. His death from a wound received before the walls of Zutphen in the Low Countries has been told and retold, but still remains a classic parable of heroism and waste. After his thigh had been shattered by a bullet from a musket he rode from the field; then, as his friend Fulke Greville put it, 'being thirsty with excess of bleeding, he called for drink, which was presently brought to him; but as he was putting the bottle to his mouth he saw a poor soldier carried along, who had eaten his last at the same feast, ghastly casting his eyes at the bottle, which Sir Philip perceiving, took it from his mouth before he drank and delivered it to the poor man with these words, "Thy necessity is greater than mine".' After undergoing the crude surgery of those days he lingered on for a few weeks at Arnhem until gangrene set in, and then quietly died. His portrait is in a corner of the State Dining Room, sandy-haired, thin-faced and pensive.

On Sir Philip's death in 1586 his younger brother Robert (subsequently made Earl of Leicester) took over Penshurst, adding the Long Gallery, and the Nether Gallery on the floor below, in a southern extension to the house. Lord Leicester had a remarkable quartet of grandchildren. The only girl, Dorothy, inspired the Roundhead poet Edmund Waller, who addressed her in his verses as 'Sacharissa' in the stilted manner of the seventeenth century.

> Ye lofty beeches, tell this matchless dame,
> That if together ye fed all one flame,
> It could not equalise the hundredth part
> Of what her eyes have kindled in my heart.

A portrait of her in the Queen Elizabeth Room shows a plump middle-aged lady, good-natured but no longer inspirational. Two of her brothers, Philip and Algernon, fought for the Parliamentarians. In later life Algernon became friendly with William Penn and helped to draft the Pennsylvania constitution. As a prominent Whig he was accused of joining in the 'Rye House plot' of 1683, which aimed to assassinate Charles

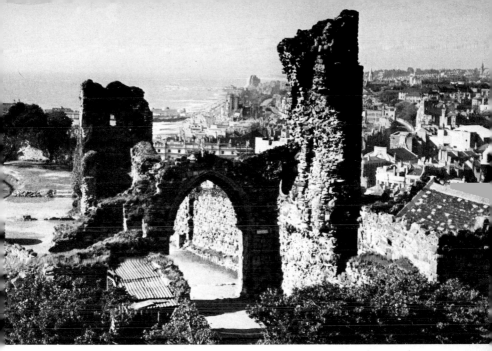

The ruins of Hastings Castle, with the seafront framed between the remains of medieval masonry.

The Seven Sisters, a spectacular succession of chalk cliffs between Birling Gap and Cuckmere Haven.

Sunset over Camp Hill, on Ashdown Forest. 'A tract of sandy heathland, where bracken, heather and scrub form an oasis of wildness amid the rich farmland that lies all around'.

II, was tried and condemned before Judge Jeffreys, and died stoically on the block. The youngest brother, Henry, was instrumental in the accession of William III; but perhaps his greatest claim to fame lies in the fact that, as Master of the Ordnance, he adopted the broad arrow or 'pheon' of the Sidneys as the mark of government property. A combined portrait of Philip, Algernon and a fourth brother, Robert, painted in boyhood, is in the Long Gallery.

In the eighteenth century the male line of the Sidneys died out, and Penshurst decayed. Fortunately, as has so often happened, new owners revitalised and restored it. These were the Shelleys (related to the poet), who inherited the house at the end of the eighteenth century; Sir John Shelley Sidney, who took the old name, his son the first Lord De L'Isle and Dudley, and their successors restored and rebuilt, in a style as near the 'firm stateliness' of the ancient building as the nineteenth century could provide. Their alterations were mainly to the north and west sides, and so do not concern visitors to Penshurst, except in so far as they affect the external appearance of the house. The present owner, Viscount De L'Isle, has carried on the work of his predecessors by restoring the Nether Gallery.

The fifteenth-century Buckingham Building, a much altered fragment of medieval Penshurst, links Pulteney's hall with Leicester's galleries. The state rooms on the upper floor – the Queen Elizabeth and Tapestry Rooms – contain the finest furniture at Penshurst, together with the hangings from which the Tapestry Room takes its name. Finally, and very much of the twentieth century, is the toy museum recently opened in a converted stable at the back of the house.

Penshurst, like Knole, is set deep in parkland. North of the house a ride between tall trees leads to a small reed-fringed lake – perhaps one of the ponds referred to by Ben Jonson, who loved Penshurst, and wrote of it in 'The Forest':

> Thou hast thy ponds, that pay thee tribute fish,
> Fat aged Carps, that run into thy net,
> And Pikes, now weary their own kind to eat.

Over the fence the wide expanse of grass beyond the north front is the local cricket pitch; and on the other side of the great house the orchard mixes apple trees and roses behind a massive yew hedge, like a garden in a medieval illumination.

Bidborough, across the Medway two miles east of Penshurst, consists mainly of prosperous-looking houses running along the ridge, and wide views northwards across the valley from it. The old village and the partly Saxon church are down a side road. The church still has its tiny children's pews, installed about 1790 at the beginning of the Sunday School movement.

Two miles to the south is **Speldhurst**, a neat village on top of a hill. The half-timbered George and Dragon claims to date from '*c*. 1212' and might even do so. The original church was struck by lightning in 1791 and burnt down; the present Victorian building does not look much at first sight, but has windows – a number of them designed by Burne-Jones – which are among the masterpieces of the William Morris factory. With the sun behind them, the saints in the south aisle windows stand out almost three-dimensionally against their dark backgrounds.

Ashurst, on the East Grinstead–Tunbridge Wells road, is little more than a hill down which lorries thunder, a stretch of river and weir popular with fishermen, a station and a pub. But it has a dainty little church perched up above the road, with a white weatherboarded bellcote on top. There has been a church of sorts here since the tenth century; no one seems to know the date of the present building, though the porch is dated 1621. In the Middle Ages there was a miracle-working rood here; Lambarde tells us that it 'did by certaine increments continually wax and growe, as well in the bush of hair that it had on the head, as also in the length and stature of the members and bodie itself.' Near the porch is a pillar sundial made in 1634 by Elias Allen, the most famous instrument-maker of his time.

Groombridge, a couple of miles to the south, is half in Sussex and half in Kent. The Sussex part, which grew up when the railway came, is nothing special, but the Kent part, across a tributary of the Medway, is an attractive spot – a triangular green with weatherboarded and tile-hung houses along two sides, the red-brick symmetry of Groombridge Place, a superb Charles II manor house, across a moat, and a chapel-of-ease, in similar brick, at its gates. The name is said to derive from a Saxon, Gromen, whose name means simply 'the man', as in 'bridegroom', and who built a moated castle where the Place now stands. A Norman castle was later built on the site; in the fifteenth century it passed to the Wallers, one of whose descendants was Edmund Waller, the seventeenth-century poet (see Penshurst, p. 238); and in 1618 it was bought by Charles Packer, who built the Jacobean house which can be seen from the public footpath beside the lake. As Clerk to the Privy Seal, Packer accompanied Charles I to Spain in 1623, on his unsuccessful mission to seek the hand of the Infanta in marriage. Packer built the chapel as a staunch Protestant's thankoffering for the expedition's failure; as the Latin inscription dated 1625, above the door says, 'Because of the happy return of Charles our Prince from Spain.' It is Late Perpendicular in style, with big traceried windows, one of which has magnificent armorial glass designed in part by Packer himself.

Between Eridge Green, south-east of Groombridge, and Frant is the expanse of **Eridge Park**, which takes the form of a rough circle about three miles in diameter. Eridge Castle is the home of the Nevills, Lords Abergavenny, who were originally tycoons of the Tudor iron industry (spelling their name Bergavenny). Around the whole circumference of the estate are small cottages and lodges in every variety of Gothic, all emblazoned with the letter A, used by the nineteenth-century Abergavennys to sign their properties. In the park's south-west corner is the Iron Age Saxonbury Camp, with an easily traceable defensive ditch round the summit. At the top, within a tangle of pines, oaks and rhododendrons, is a vintage folly – a round tower, complete with arrow slits, machicolations and conical roof. Over the door is a coroneted 'H.A.' and the date 1828. A perfect place for the Sleeping Beauty to lie imprisoned.

Frant is built round a vast irregularly-shaped green, with plenty of large Victorian and neo-Georgian houses for commuters. The village nucleus is at the northern end. A short street leads from the green to the dark stone pseudo-Perpendicular church dated 1821, with tall pinnacles on the tower and a slate roof. What was once the local mansion is now a veterinary research station. The little village school, built in 1816 and rebuilt in 1852, is inscribed with a quotation from the Book of Proverbs, as a reminder of the days when educationalists knew what they wanted, if not necessarily how to get it: 'Train up a child in the way he should go; and when he is old he will not depart from it.' Frant station, over a mile away, is a Victorian railway gem.

Tunbridge Wells has become a byword for quiet gentility. Even the revivalist names of the main districts – Mounts Sion, Ephraim and Pleasant – conjure up a vision of the sort of place where you would not be surprised to meet John Wesley on the street corner. But nowadays it is something of a boom town, with new office blocks going up in the centre.

The beginnings of Tunbridge Wells were not all that respectable. It owes its existence to a jaded young courtier in the time of Charles I, Lord North, who in 1606 was riding back to London from Eridge Castle after convalescing with his friend Lord Bergavenny. North rode past a spring of reddish-coloured water, tasted it, took a sample up to London to have it tested, received glowing reports of its health-giving properties, and returned the following year after another round of dissipation. By 1620 the wells at Tonbridge, as Tunbridge was then spelt, had become a popular summer resort for the courtiers. In 1630 Queen Henrietta Maria came there to recuperate after the birth of the future Charles II, camping in tents on the common, and Tunbridge Wells was made. (The 'Royal' was added to the town's name much later, by Edward VII in 1909.)

Though the town's centre of gravity has shifted north up the hill to the administrative centre and the large stores, the **Pantiles**, where the red water still trickles, remains the heart of Tunbridge Wells. This is a town-planner's dream which has grown up by chance, a pedestrian traffic-free precinct, surrounded by harmonious buildings some of which go back to the seventeenth century. The actual spring is in a recess below ground level, beside Boots the chemists; under a canopy is a bust of Lord North. Fifteen of the original pantiles (large roofing tiles) from which the precinct takes it name can be seen near by, at the foot of the steps that lead up to the arcaded upper level. These were laid after a complaint by Queen Anne in 1698 that the walks were unpaved; the work had still not been done when she returned the following year, and she never came back again.

The Pantiles reached their heyday in the mid eighteenth

century. In 1735 Beau Nash arrived at Tunbridge Wells, established himself as Master of Ceremonies, and remained in charge for a quarter of a century. His innovations were a recognised and rigidly enforced code of behaviour, and the introduction of organised gambling. Nash was accompanied from Bath, his previous kingdom, by a forbiddingly effective lady called Sarah Porter. Known as the 'Queen of the Touters', she used to pursue visitors around the Pantiles until she had worn down their resistance to entering the gambling rooms. But with the increasing popularity of the seaside in the second half of the century Tunbridge Wells lost its appeal as a summer resort for the jaded, and raffishness gave way to respectability.

Across the road on the north side of the Pantiles is the **Church of King Charles the Martyr**, whose plain brick walls, gabled roof and wooden clock tower hide a sumptuous interior. It dates from 1678; most of those who took the waters and subscribed to the church were royalists, which accounts for its dedication to the king. It is square in plan, with dark-stained galleries on either side, and a plaster ceiling of great panache, decorated with cherubs' heads, flowers, fruit and leaves. Before Tunbridge Wells was a properly defined unit, the altar was in Tonbridge, the pulpit in Speldhurst, and the vestry in Frant.

From the Pantiles, Tunbridge Wells grew northwards. Off the High Street, there are cobbled and brick-paved alley-ways of small eighteenth-century houses, leading purposefully up Mount Sion. Past the station, at the top of Mount Pleasant, is what is left of one of the most ambitious development schemes of the early nineteenth century – Decimus Burton's Calverley Estate. Half way down Crescent Road a large stone archway complete with lodges and Doric columns leads into Calverley Park, a curve of big widely spaced houses, separated from the public park by mighty shrubberies. Far more attractive is the sweeping curve of Calverley Park Crescent, with its colonnade of white-painted iron pillars. Burton's largest building is Holy Trinity Church, beyond the civic centre; its pinnacled tower is a local landmark.

The neo-Georgian town hall is worth going into for a look at the portrait of Beau Nash at the head of the stairs. In wig, flowered waistcoat and brown velvet coat, with his cocked hat under his arm, he looks every inch the man who drove into

Tunbridge Wells 'seated in a magnificent post chaise drawn by six greys, with outriders and postillions blowing French horns, and every appendage of parade.' The same building complex includes the town museum. Apart from the general historical and bygone exhibits, it has a large collection of Tunbridge Ware – an art which consisted of decorating boxes or trinkets with mosaics built up of minute squares of different types of wood.

West of the town is the common, crisscrossed by roads and footpaths, and studded with the strange rock outcrops that jut from the earth for a mile or two around. Most impressive of all are the **High Rocks**, which cover several acres and include such a variety of chimneys, overhangs, crevices and other formations that, though hardly fifty feet high, they are used for practice by local mountaineers. Those less strenuously inclined can amble along a 'scenic walk' among oaks, pines and rhododendrons, crossing the gorges by walkways.

Eastwards, Tunbridge Wells runs virtually without interruption to **Pembury**, a swollen village astride the traffic torrent of the A 21. Pembury's nucleus is a small triangular green on the north side of the road, surrounded by big Victorian houses. Opposite is a large stone church with a tall spire, quite medieval-looking but in fact built in the 1840s. The medieval church is through the modern housing and past the waterworks, well over a mile from the village. It is a lonely and impressive stone building, with a good kingpost roof and a vast and hideous marble reredos.

Capel, a mile and a half away down winding lanes, is a church virtually without a village, as the houses are said to have been deliberately burnt after the Black Death to prevent further infection. Inside, the north wall is covered with medieval paintings. The Last Supper can still be made out fairly easily.

Tudeley, a mile towards Tonbridge, is another tiny hamlet with a church worth looking at. Reached past farm buildings, it is mainly eighteenth-century red brick with a squat tower; its uniqueness lies in its east window, which is by Marc Chagall, and is his only stained-glass window in this country. In memory of Sarah d'Avigdor Goldsmid, who was drowned in a sailing accident in 1963, it shows Christ on the cross looming above the waves, where the girl lies as if asleep – a gentle lullaby rather than a harsh lament.

Though **Tonbridge** is far more ancient than Tunbridge Wells, it is a good deal less interesting to wander about in. The Saxons had a fortress on the castle mound, and this is perpetuated in the town's name, which comes from 'Dun-burh', meaning 'Hill-castle'. To the Normans it was a strategic point for controlling the tribes of the Weald, so important that the lands around it had the special title of 'lowy', meaning the league of ground in every direction which formed the castle's domain. The castle is now a peaceful enough place, overlooking the Medway on the west side of the main road and reached by a riverside walk. On top of the 'motte', or mound on which the Saxon fort and the first Norman castle stood, is the base of a round tower, with a well shaft down through the motte. The great thirteenth-century gatehouse, on the landward side of the castle, survives up to three storeys. In the early Middle Ages the castle was owned by the de Clares, rebellious barons who often came into conflict with the king. The fortifications were slighted (made undefendable) by the Parliamentarians in the Civil War, and the castle was finally tamed at the end of the eighteenth century by a Mr Hooker, who built beside the gatehouse a smart Gothic mansion, now used as the municipal offices.

The rest of old Tonbridge also lies north of the river. On the west side the High Street widens slightly by two fine gabled Tudor black-and-white buildings, the Chequers Hotel, and a clothing shop with rows of suits hanging among some superb internal timbering. The parish church, down an alley across the street, is built on the site of a Saxon church, and is mainly fourteenth-century, enlarged in the nineteenth. Inside it gives a feeling of enormous width, enhanced by the double south aisle. The east window is an ambitious composition of modern glass by Leonard Walker, dating from 1954: Christ together with saints and prophets, thrown confusingly together in big pieces of brilliantly coloured glass. There is a good array of funeral hatchments on either side of the nave.

The main buildings of Tonbridge School are in the form of an open E facing directly on to the High Street. It was founded by Sir Andrew Judd, ex-Lord Mayor of London and Master of the Skinners Company, in 1553. Old prints show a long range of buildings fronting the street; the present strenuously worthy Gothic block, set back behind a courtyard,

is mid-Victorian and later. Behind are the playing fields, and
the imposing orange brick chapel built in 1902. Its entrance
door is under a massive bronze war memorial of St George;
inside there is a strange and lofty combination of barrel-
vaulted roof and hammer-beams. On the north wall is a copy
of the memorial to Judd (the original is in St Helen's,
Bishopsgate) which tells, in excruciating and unpunctuated
doggerel, of his voyaging life:

> To Russia and Mussova
> To Spayne Gynny without Fable
> Traveld he by land and sea
> Bothe Mayre of London and Staple.

Judd School, the boys' grammar school founded in 1888 at
the southern end of the town, perpetuates his name.

The traffic that used to suffocate Tonbridge has been
siphoned off by a splendid new bypass, opened in 1971 and
joined to the Sevenoaks bypass.

Downstream from the bridge the Medway is lined with
timber wharves and sawmills; the ground there is low-lying
flood land, mainly unbuilt on and bringing fields almost into
the heart of the town. Tonbridge is the country's main supplier
of cricket balls, and a centre of up-to-date printing.

Shipbourne (pronounced Shibburn), due north of Tonbridge on the A 227 and half way to Ightham (see p. 218), is
sandwiched between acres of Forestry Commission conifers
and the park of Fairlawne, the home of the Cazalet racing
stables. The village centre of Shipbourne – a Victorian feudal
creation of church, pub and cottages – was built about 1880
by Edward Cazalet. The hefty stone church, on the site of a
former chapel of the Knights Hospitallers, has vast gargoyles
protruding from the tower. The pub, called the Chaser, has a
sign showing horse and jockey, painted by the present landlord. The few houses that make up the rest of Shipbourne are
along the sides of an enormous undulating common that forms
the village green.

Shipbourne was the birthplace in 1722 of Christopher
Smart, a poet who was befriended by Dr Johnson, and finally
went mad from a combination of religion and drink. He wrote
an enormous blank verse poem called 'The Hop Garden', which
painstakingly sets down the details of a craft unaltered until

the recent advent of hop-picking machines and electric drying plant.

The road to **Plaxtol** runs along the north side of Fairlawne Park, and there are generally a few thoroughbreds looking pensively over the wall. Plaxtol is very much a beauty spot, with a crossroads church and a village street running down to a small tributary of the Medway. At the bottom of the hill, on the stream, is the medieval half-timbered Spout House, which is now used as the showrooms for a wrought iron factory and has a small museum of Wealden craftsmen's tools. The church is said to be the only complete seventeenth-century church in Kent, and has no dedication. It was commissioned by Archbishop Laud, and is dated 1649 above the inner door in the porch. The interior is simple – apart from the roof, which is a forest of hammerbeams – with light flooding in through the clear window glass. A Victorian stone reredos makes an incongruous background for medieval oak carvings of the crucifixion and other scenes.

Isolated in the undulating orchards a mile east of Plaxtol is **Old Soar Manor** (National Trust), a thirteenth-century stone solar block, with a red-brick Georgian farmhouse attached. The house is on the site of the medieval hall; and what is left is the first-floor solar, with garderobe (lavatory) at one corner and chapel at the other. Below are vaulted undercrofts, and a garderobe pit that could be cleaned out when need arose. For all its two-light windows and king-post roof, Old Soar must have been uncomfortably primitive to live in.

The main landmark of the flat Medway plain below Tonbridge is **Hadlow**'s fantastic folly tower. Hadlow, three miles south-east of Plaxtol, is an attractive village, with a core of good eighteenth-century brick and weatherboard, a medieval church down a back street, and an up-to-date horticultural college on the outskirts. But the tower, soaring up in a forest of crockets and pinnacles to 170 feet, is the one thing you cannot get away from, in Hadlow itself or in the countryside for miles around. The tower is all that remains (apart from a Gothic coach house and other outbuildings converted into private houses) of Hadlow Castle, a vast house pulled down in 1951. It was begun by Walter May about 1790; and the tower was built half a century later by his son, Walter Barton May, inspired by the tower of William Beckford's palace at

Fonthill, in Wiltshire. It was a good deal better constructed, as Fonthill fell down in 1825. According to local legend, May built the tower to keep an eye on his wife's comings and goings after she left him, or alternatively so that he could see the sea – presumably to the south-east, over Romney Marsh and Dungeness. It was used by the Royal Observer Corps as a watch tower in the Second World War.

CHAPTER FOURTEEN

The Heart of the Weald

✤

EAST of Tunbridge Wells lies the '-den' country, where names like Marden, Biddenden and Horsmonden perpetuate the clearings in the thick Wealden forest where the Saxons fattened their pigs in summer. Now in place of the forest it has some of the best of the Kent orchards, white and pink with blossom in the spring; yet in spite of its prosperity and accessibility, hardly any of the dozens of tile-hung villages have grown even as far as the small-town stage. At the entrance of the orchard country the River Teise wanders gently along through woodland, before swinging north to join the Medway near Yalding.

The monks, as always, picked the most beautiful place on the river to build **Bayham Abbey**, whose ruins lie four miles east of Tunbridge Wells, north of the road from Frant station to Lamberhurst (B 2169). The abbey dates from the earliest years of the thirteenth century. Much of the gatehouse survives, facing north over the river; as does the roofless east end of the great church: the transepts, still with unworn faces on the corbels; and the grass-lined chancel, its stones clutched by the roots of a vast beech tree. The ruins have been recently restored, and are open the whole year. As the Teise forms the boundary between the two counties, the ruins are in Sussex, while the new Bayham Abbey – a gabled stone Victorian house on the slope north of the river – is in Kent, which must lead to problems with the local authorities.

Bayham belongs to the Camden family; and their arms, an elephant's head, can be seen on many of the Victorian cottages round about.

At **Lamberhurst** the Hastings-bound traffic thunders down the A 21 to a bridge over the Teise, which has been recently widened, no doubt better for the motorist, but no improvement for Lamberhurst. However, much of this good old Kentish

A map for this chapter will be found between pages 177-8.

village is spared, as it lies on a bypassed loop of what was once the main road. The church is down a minor road north of the village; it is fourteenth- and fifteenth-century, much restored. An innovation in these days of smaller congregations is the transference of the main altar to the north wall of the nave, with the seats running north and south, and the chancel turned into a transept. On the south wall are tablets to the Hussey family, of Scotney Castle; and in the churchyard a tombstone to a couple who died aged ninety-six and 101, with the somewhat inapposite inscription 'Surely I come quickly.' Lamberhurst was an ironworking centre, with a foundry on the Teise near Bayham. Hasted wrote that the iron railings round St Paul's – 'the most magnificent balustrade perhaps in the universe' – were cast there; but Straker thought they were probably made in conjunction with other furnaces.

There are two **Scotney Castles**: the austere stone house built for Edward Hussey at the end of the 1830s; and the romantic ruin at the foot of the hill, with its single round fourteenth-century tower reflected in the still waters of the moat. Apart from the tower and medieval stone approach, old Scotney is mainly seventeenth-century. Edward Hussey deliberately knocked it about to make it still more picturesque; then all around, and especially in the quarry from which the stone for the new house was excavated, he planted the forest trees and the brilliant rhododendrons and azaleas which are the glory of Scotney in early summer. Old Scotney and the gardens were left to the National Trust by Edward Hussey's grandson, Christopher Hussey, who died in 1970. Through his articles in *Country Life* and through his books, for more than forty years Christopher Hussey was a pervasive influence on the growing appreciation and love of English architecture and the landscape in which it was set; and Scotney is his finest memorial. Another Lamberhurst garden worth a visit is that of **Owl House**, off a minor road north-west of the village. With its water garden, wide lawns and woodland ride it makes a spacious setting for the modest tilehung house.

Three miles south of Lamberhurst down the A 21, a backhanded turn along the B 2079 brings you to the Bedgebury Pinetum, which forms part of the 2,000-plus acres of **Bedgebury Forest**, run by the Forestry Commission since 1924. Bedgebury is an open-air laboratory of tree-growing, where you can wander among forest plots, comparing growth rates of trees of all sorts, or stroll round the pinetum, which was begun as an offshoot of Kew Gardens after increasing London pollution started to kill off Kew's conifers. The pinetum is planted on a hilly site, with broad avenues leading through the cypresses, spruces and pines, and narrow paths among the rhododendron undergrowth. The trees sprawl, or tower, or droop, with an infinite variety of greens and silvers in their foliage; the few specimen oaks that stand here and there are modern interlopers, botanically speaking, into this ancient coniferous world. At the end of an avenue stands a vast monkey-puzzle, with a bole like the leg of an elephant eighty feet tall; beyond is a lake, with rhododendrons crowding to the edge, and a stand of swamp cypresses, pale green in spring and glowing brilliantly russet on an afternoon of pale autumn sunshine. (The ground at Bedgebury gets extremely wet and slippery after only a small amount of rain, so it is worth taking an extra pair of shoes.)

Kilndown, on a back road a mile or so from Bedgebury, is an unremarkable small village, except for its grey stone church, austere on the outside but startlingly decorated within. This Gothic Revivalist's ideal was consecrated in 1841, and during the next few years was painted, gilded and enriched to the specifications of Alexander Beresford Hope, who lived at Bedgebury Park and was one of the leaders of the Revival movement. Gold, red and blue are the dominant colours, on the chancel screen, on the font cover, on the pulpit. Kilndown displays an intensity of self-righteous worthiness that opens an unbridgeable gulf between the Revivalists and their medieval originals.

Goudhurst stands at the summit of a steep spur of land rising from the Teise, with magnificent views, especially to the west over the river valley, and south to the Hawkhurst ridge. The village street proper begins at the pond; the houses, half-timbered, tilehung and weatherboarded, climb stepwise to the church at the summit. You walk through Goudhurst at your peril, as for much of the way there is no pavement on either side of the street. At the top the road seems to end abruptly, with the churchyard on one side and a tilehung house with vast overhanging eaves on the other; the illusion is caused by a bend so sharp that the traffic disappears from view. Near the top the street widens a little, with the Manor House facing straight up the hill, and two pubs opposite, almost next door to each other; one of them, the Star and Eagle, adjoins the churchyard and is thought to have had monastic connections.

There was a church here as early as 1117; the present building is thirteenth-century, enlarged in the fourteenth when the population grew with the influx of weavers from Flanders – the medieval influx, as opposed to the sixteenth-century flight that followed the Spanish domination of the Low Countries. The medieval tower was destroyed in a storm in 1637 and replaced the following year by the present stocky structure, with its squarecut window and classical doorway. The top of the tower is over five hundred feet above sea level, and was used as a lookout point in both World Wars. The stained glass was blown out by landmines in 1940. Goudhurst church is a treasury of splendid monuments. Best of all is the table tomb in the south aisle to Sir Alexander Culpeper and his wife, dating from the 1530s. On top the two figures lie side by side; unusually, they are carved in wood, he in armour, with head bare, wearing a red and gold surcoat, she in a red cloak over a black dress, with a Holbein head-dress fastened under her chin.

Goudhurst church saw the last act of the fight against the Hawkhurst gang of smugglers (see p. 278). Their leader, George Kingsmill, was a Goudhurst man; and another local, William Sturt, formed a militia to deal with him. After capturing a member of the militia and torturing him to get information, Kingsmill sent him back with the message that he was coming to attack Goudhurst. Sturt evacuated the women and children and posted his militia in the church tower. Swearing that he would 'boil four of the militiamen's hearts and eat them for his supper', Kingsmill led 150 of his gang to the attack; but the militia beat them off and routed them. The church register laconically records the burial of Kingsmill, 'leader of the scoundrels killed by the discharge of a lead bullet.'

Finchcocks, a couple of miles west of Goudhurst, is a large and striking red-brick Georgian house among the meadows by the Teise; Newman calls it 'the most notable Baroque house in the county'. It consists of a central block, with symmetrical wings, three storeys high, and was built for Edward

Bathurst in 1725. A battered statue of Queen Anne, rescued from the old Royal Exchange, stands uncomfortably in a niche over the front door. An enormous hall, bigger than any of the other rooms, runs from front to back. The house was until recently a ballet school, and is now being restored. It is hoped eventually to open it to the public, and to give occasional concerts in the hall during the summer months.

As you come into **Cranbrook**, four miles east of Goudhurst, you pass a painted sign punning on the town's name, showing a crane standing in a brook. Neither bird life nor water are particularly obvious today; yet it was to its water as much as anything else that Cranbrook owed its vanished prosperity. In spite of its present air of a sleepy backwater (even the main roads pass it by), Cranbrook is a town built by industry. It was the centre of clothmaking in Kent; the industry began in the fourteenth century, when Edward III lured clothmakers from Flanders to break the Flemish monopoly and make England self-sufficient in cloth manufacture, and lingered on into the eighteenth. Cranbrook was the ideal centre for the trade, as there were plenty of streams which could be dammed to provide power for the fulling mills, oak trees from which the mills could be built, and fuller's earth to clean the cloth.

The most lasting reminder of this trade is the magnificent **Parish Church**, a gloriously wide and airy place, which dates almost entirely from the fifteenth and sixteenth centuries, with elegant Late Perpendicular columns and clerestory windows. Above the tower clock is a figure of Father Time, who, according to legend, jumps down from his perch at midnight and scythes the churchyard grass; the legend is said to have been started by a former rector, who could not afford to pay for the grass to be cut and did the job himself under cover of darkness. Another rector left a unique and useless addition to the fittings of the church – the tall stone 'tub' for total immersion, standing against the south wall and reached by a flight of steps. This was installed in 1710 in an attempt to lure Baptists back to the church on the grounds that 'anything you can do we can do better'; but it was only used once. It is certainly an uninviting bathing-place.

Next door to the churchyard are the very varied buildings of **Cranbrook School**, founded early in the sixteenth century and granted a royal charter by Queen Elizabeth in 1574. On the left is the handsome Georgian School House; in the middle is the tall block of Big School, where the charter is displayed; and behind are more modern buildings, including an ultra-modern science block named after Lord Rootes, the school's most prominent recent pupil. In conjunction with the local historical society, the school runs a small museum, notable for an outstanding collection of Kent and Sussex birds. These were assembled around the turn of the century by the African explorer Boyd Alexander, who seems to have shot anything that flew in the two counties, including an osprey killed on Bedgebury lake. The birds were expertly stuffed and mounted by the local bootmaker.

The rest of Cranbrook is typical Kent weatherboard and tilehanging, with the narrow Stone Street turning a corner into the gentle slope of the wider High Street. On the corner is the long low George Hotel, where Queen Elizabeth stayed on her visit to Cranbrook in 1573; the town's many pubs are relics of the thirsty days of the clothiers. Up the hill at the eastern end of Stone Street is Cranbrook's stately **Windmill**, a tall smock mill on a high brick base, built in 1814 for Henry Dobell. The mill was restored in recent years by experts from Holland, and though the grinding gear is disconnected, the sails still whirl around on most Friday afternoons. You can climb up the inside by ladders worn smooth by grain dust, to the topmost level where the driving shaft enters and meshes with the cogs high up in the roof. The mill is still partially operational, with an electrically driven machine for rolling barley, and grain stored in sacks – far more than a mere museum piece.

Benenden, three miles south-east of Cranbrook, is mainly known for its girls' public school, founded in 1923. Its premises are a large red-brick mock-Tudor building, quite handsome with its stone-mullioned windows, built in 1859 for Lord Cranbrook and bought and modernised by Lord Rothermere in 1912. The house was originally called Hemsted, and superseded an Elizabethan house of the same name. Benenden village is a single straight street, with a long tongue-shaped green leading up to the church. Outside there is still plenty of the medieval church remaining, but inside it is an object-lesson in nasty restoration, with sharp-sawn Victorian pillars between nave and aisles. In fact, these replaced classical rather than medieval columns, as the church was largely destroyed by a storm in 1672 and rebuilt in the next few years. Lightning set fire to the steeple (there is now only a tower), and the flames spread to the roof and all the other timber work. A board inside the north door commemorates the storm.

Sissinghurst Castle (National Trust), off the Goudhurst–Biddenden road (A 262) is a marvellous fragment set in a beautiful garden. It is a memorial to the creativity of Harold Nicolson and his wife Victoria Sackville-West, who found the place a wreck when they took it over in 1930. Over the next decade they restored the Tudor buildings and made a garden which expressed their personalities by means of planning and planting, a place of controlled romanticism where one open-air 'room' leads inevitably into another. Victoria Sackville-West describes how she came upon it. 'I fell in love; love at first sight. I saw what might be made of it. It was Sleeping Beauty's Castle: but a castle running away into sordidness and squalor; a garden crying out for rescue.' Harold Nicolson's diaries give a running commentary on the progress of this rescue operation, which provided an idyllic refuge from the threatening international scene of the 1930s. A photograph of Sissinghurst taken in 1932 shows a scene of virtual dereliction, with the long entrance block in decay and the tower standing gauntly behind; a few walls form the skeleton of the garden still waiting to be born.

The existing buildings – low entrance block, tower and two cottages – are all that remain of a great Tudor manor house built in the sixteenth century by the Baker family of Cranbrook, whose most famous member, Sir John Baker, was a highly successful politician and acquirer of property in the reigns of Henry VIII, Edward VI and Mary. Beyond the tower was a vast courtyard building stretching well back into the present orchard; the south cottage stands at the bottom corner of the courtyard. Sir John became known posthumously as 'Bloody Baker', because of his persecution of Protestants, and all sorts of horrors, including rape and murder, were attributed to him. However, he seems now to have been the typical grasping and self-seeking man of his age, who used the offices of Attorney-General, Chancellor of the Exchequer and

Speaker to his advantage. Scruples got you nowhere in Tudor times. It was probably his son, Sir Richard, who built the gate tower and mansion early in Elizabeth's reign. In the following century the Baker fortunes declined and Sissinghurst began to slide downhill with them. The final degradation came in the 1750s, when it was used as a prison for French sailors captured in the Seven Years War. An unlikely officer on guard duty there was the historian Edward Gibbon, who wrote that 'the duty was hard, the dirt most oppressive.' The prisoners were jammed together; they murdered their guards and were murdered in reprisal, and tore out all the woodwork to burn as fuel. Sissinghurst was left a wreck, and the main mansion was finally pulled down about 1800.

Though it now leads nowhere except to the garden, the tower with the Sackville-West flag flying above it makes a fine sight. The first floor was Victoria Sackville-West's study, and is still furnished as she left it, with writing table, books and souvenirs. On the second floor are photographs showing the transformation of the house and garden. In the middle of the room is the clumsy hand printing-press of the Hogarth Press, used for the first edition of T. S. Eliot's *Waste Land* and works by Graves, Forster and other *avant-garde* writers of the 1920s; with splendid impracticality this was the first piece of furniture to be brought to Sissinghurst in 1930. The book-lined library in the entrance block can also be seen; with its Sackville portraits and silver mirror it is like a small offshoot of Knole. But it is the garden of Sissinghurst that most people come to see: the White Garden planted entirely with white or grey plants; the walk of pleached limes; the herb garden with a medieval profusion of herbs, such as caraway, fennel, tansy, borage and woad; the roses in formal beds or clambering over the warm brickwork of the gateway.

The French prisoners at Sissinghurst are said to have given its name to the Three Chimneys, a pub on a bend in the road half way between Sissinghurst and Biddenden. The inn sign shows a soldier looking at a signpost, and wondering which of the 'trois chemins' he should take. However, as the name Three Chimneys was current two centuries earlier, the bewildered Frenchman is just another local myth.

Frittenden, in the hinterland north of the Sissinghurst–Biddenden road, is a quiet village on a hillside, with a tall-spired church and a pub called for some reason the Bell and Jorrocks. It is full of ponds and streams which flow down to join the Beult in the valley below.

Biddenden's most famous residents were the two 'Maids of Biddenden', Eliza and Mary Chulkhurst, twins joined at hip and shoulder. Though they are supposed to have been born about 1100, the sign on the village green shows them dressed in blue Elizabethan costume. They died aged thirty-four, within a few hours of each other. The Maids are perpetuated in an Easter charity which provided cheese and two four-pound loaves to be distributed to each poor parishioner of Biddenden, paid for from twenty acres of ground called the 'Bread and Cheese Lands'. Nowadays on Easter Monday visitors can eat biscuits embossed with images of the Maids. It is not surprising that Biddenden is touristy, full of antique shops, pubs and restaurants in the fine half-timbered buildings of the main street. The pavements on either side are made of irregular ankle-twisting slabs of Bethersden marble. A little way north of the green is the magnificent six-gabled Old Cloth Hall, the centre of the local cloth trade in prosperous medieval and Tudor times. The house contained workshops for the weavers, and was probably the collecting point for cloth to be taken to Cranbrook for final inspection and sealing. This is one of the grandest of the Biddenden houses; and you cannot go down a side road without seeing some splendid example of a half-timbered house built by the proceeds of the cloth trade.

Biddenden church separates the old village from the lapping tide of modern housing. It is mainly thirteenth- and four-teenth-century, with a later tower, begun about 1400. The tower, like the village pavements, is made of Bethersden marble (see p. 191) – a misnomer for anyone expecting gleaming white walls, as it looks much like any other building stone. Inside there are some fine brasses, mainly quite late; to see them you have to roll back the carpet below the chancel step. Several of these sober clothiers in their ruffs and long robes are portrayed with two or more wives; 'cocks with their hens', as Newman aptly puts it. The brasses have not been immune from theft in recent years; indeed, on one occasion Biddenden lost much of its church treasure, and even the carpets were rolled up and taken. In the churchyard is a simple wooden cross to the film-maker Richard Massingham (died 1953).

Smarden, three miles north-east of Biddenden, is high on the list of villages that should be banned to heavy traffic. A small village, built on a dogleg, it is loud with the noise of lorries negotiating its angles; and the walker who tries to cross the village street to get to the churchyard is literally in danger of his life. Apart from that, it is a most beautiful spot. Coming from the west you suddenly see a compact cluster of tiled roofs and weatherboarded walls; then round the corner the main street widens out, with a few hundred yards of old houses juxtaposed in casual perfection. The village name derives from the Saxon 'Smeredaenne', meaning 'butter valley and pasture'; and sheep still crop the orchard turf right in the centre of Smarden, though I saw no cattle. You enter the churchyard below the first storey of an overhanging building (as at Hartfield, see p. 322), called the Pent-house. The church looks ordinary enough from the outside – early fourteenth-century, with a Perpendicular tower of about 1475 – but inside it is structurally very unusual. The single aisleless nave, thirty-six feet wide, is spanned by a timber roof of great ingenuity, known as a scissors-beam roof, because the timbers intersect. The church has been called the 'Barn of Kent' for this reason. The south window of the chancel is a jigsaw puzzle of bits of old stained glass: half a face, part of a hand, a bird's wing, fragmentary inscriptions, in a surrealist montage of colour. On the south wall is a copy of the charter granted by Queen Elizabeth in 1576, allowing Smarden to hold a weekly market and annual fair; this confirmed an earlier charter granted by Edward III in 1332. On top of the sixteenth-century oak alms-box is a panel of deep blue Limoges enamel (now protected under glass), probably made in the thirteenth century.

Immediately behind the church are some good timber-framed houses, still with brown timbers and ochre infilling, as in Normandy, rather than the almost universal black-and-white.

Though **Headcorn** is quite a commuting centre, it still keeps the feel of a small town based on agriculture. This is due to some extent to the large agricultural merchants whose premises dominate the south side of the High Street. Headcorn

is at the heart of the rich watermeadows along the river
Beult; Queen Elizabeth is said to have been so impressed by
the crops grown locally that when she visited the town she said
it should be called 'not Hedecron' – the old name – 'but
Hedecorn', and the anagram has stuck. The High Street has
several half-timbered houses; the most prominent is Shakespeare House (no connection with the poet except for the
period), with an excessively tall and startled-looking gable.
At the corner of the churchyard is the old Cloth Hall, now
estate agent's offices. Behind the church is Headcorn Manor
(in fact built in 1516 for the parson) with a noble two-storey
oriel window lighting the central hall.

The church is set right back from the end of the High Street
behind a large and well-filled graveyard; on the north side a
nice row of cottages leads to the Manor. By the south porch
is a vast hollow oak tree, nearly fifty feet in circumference,
and venerable enough to lend credit to the story that King
John held a bull-baiting below it. From the north side the
Perpendicular church, with its massive battlemented tower
and severe roof line, looks like a fortress. Inside, the wide nave
and south aisle are darkened by the Victorian stained glass.
There is a battered wall tomb decorated with the Culpeper
arms; and inside the door are two curious paintings on wood,
more like icons than anything else, one showing a turbanned
priest swinging a censer, and wearing a robe fringed with bells.

Outside the town, on the road to Frittenden, is the narrow
medieval Stephen's Bridge, possibly built by and named after
Stephen Langton, Archbishop of Canterbury at the beginning
of the thirteenth century.

Ulcombe, along byroads three miles north of Headcorn,
has a fine church, isolated high above the village at the foot
of the hill. This is one of a whole row of churches, beginning
at Boughton Malherbe (see p. 186), that run at about the
same level along the slope of the greensand ridge; it is thought
that an old road to Canterbury, now vanished, may have
linked them. The churchyard has two vast yews; the church
interior has been stripped of choir stalls and provides an
austerely modern setting for the medieval painting on the
walls: red, black and yellow chevrons under a north aisle
arch; a corresponding pair of outline crucifixions in the south
aisle; and two fragmentary scenes, one of Dives and Lazarus,

and one of St Michael fighting a fiercely horned and winged devil. In the north chapel is a splendid brass to Ralph Sentleger (died 1470) and his wife. He wears fanciful and most un-military armour, while she is wasp-waisted, and elegantly coiffed and mittened. The church's setting is spoilt by a vast blue-painted corrugated iron barn directly behind.

A mile to the west as the crow flies, though at least three times the distance as the lanes wander, is **East Sutton**. Its little gem of a church is virtually the private chapel of East Sutton Park, whose red-brick gables can be seen over the churchyard wall. The Park was the home of the Filmer family, Royalists who were besieged there by General Fairfax in the Civil War; though the house hardly looks martial enough to stand up to a siege. Sir Robert Filmer, friend of Charles I and author of a book on the divine right of kings, was captured by Fairfax and imprisoned in Leeds Castle. The north chapel, added to the thirteenth-century church about 1345, has two delicate windows which show perfectly the change from the Decorated to the Perpendicular style. Inside there are numerous Filmer memorials, including a very large brass, about seven feet long, on the floor of the north chapel, and a stained-glass portrait of Sir Robert, the last baronet, in the east window of the south chapel; he was killed in the First World War, and is shown in his red full-dress uniform.

Below **Sutton Valence** the main road falls steeply away down a one-in-eight slope to the plain of the Beult. Most of the little town lies east of the road, terraced on different levels to give wide-ranging views across the plain. The centre is dominated by the grey stone walls of the boys' public school, founded in 1576 by William Lambe, the town's most famous citizen. Lambe, born in Sutton Valence in 1495, was a wealthy clothmaker, whose school was an extension of the almshouses he had founded some years previously; Victorian successors to the original almshouses stand at the far end of the elliptical green. His portrait hangs in the main school building, entered from the main road a short way up the hill: a benevolent face with an iron-grey beard, topped by a flat Tudor black hat. He is also commemorated by a London street, Lamb's Conduit Street, north of Theobald's Road, marking the place where Lambe brought fresh water to the people of Holborn in 1577. Sutton Valence is an attractive place to wander about in, with its different changes of levels; it is free of traffic, as the side roads on which it is built lead nowhere in particular. The church is on the other side of the main road, a stone Victorian building with a well-scrubbed look, on the site of an older church.

The line of hillside churches continues westwards with **Chart Sutton**; and **Boughton**, crouching against the slope and surveying immense views southward, a harsh Victorian reconstruction redeemed by a medieval lychgate. Beside Boughton church is the driveway leading to **Boughton Monchelsea Place**. This is the back entrance through the stables; the main driveway runs through immensely tall beech trees from the road at Boughton Green. The name Boughton (pronounced Borton) in fact derives from the Anglo-Saxon for beech tree, 'boc-tun' being a 'clearing among the beeches'. The rest of the name comes from the Montchensies, a Norman family who built the original manor house in the thirteenth century. The present house is basically a dullish stone Elizabethan mansion, with projecting porch and a neat row of dormer gables, completed in 1575 by Robert Rudston, who had joined Wyatt's Kentish rebellion in 1554 but was for some reason pardoned, perhaps on the grounds of his obscurity. The house was added to by later owners: a fine broad staircase was put in about 1685, and a century later the hall was given fashionably Gothic pillars and vaulting. For a house that has been inhabited for so long Boughton Monchelsea has an oddly unlived-in feeling, perhaps because during nearly two centuries, from 1728 to 1903, there were children about the house for only twenty years; for ninety-eight years it belonged to two bachelors. Inside there is some splendid old furniture, including a seventeenth-century bed, and a superbly carved Flemish dower chest. In the drawing-room are two good little Lucas Cranach portraits, one of Martin Luther; the sumptuous blue and silver cloth hangings in one corner of the room were made originally for Augustus the Strong of Poland, and were rescued from destruction at the hands of the Russians by the present owner of Boughton Monchelsea, Mr M. B. Winch, who was in Poland at the end of the Second World War. A room on the first floor is now a costume museum, and there is a small display of carriages in one of the stables in the back courtyard.

Linton is the westernmost of these hill villages. The church has a chapel full of tombs, and on the other side of the road is a nice group of old buildings, including the Bull Inn, dated 1574. North of Linton it is only a mile up the road to Loose (see p. 210), and the outskirts of Maidstone. To the south the road divides just over the Beult. The A 229 brings you to **Staplehurst**, built on either side of a switchback rise in the dead-straight Roman road. The gaunt church, built right at the summit, has a tremendously high opening to the rood loft, and some simple modern windows in the north wall, plain glass, with shields at the centre. In 1865 Staplehurst was the scene of one of the worst railway disasters of Victorian times, when the Dover–London boat train was derailed there. Charles Dickens was on board but unhurt; though severely shocked, he went to the help of the injured.

Marden, three miles west of Staplehurst, is as ancient a Kentish village as any, going back to Saxon times; though rows of Edwardian and later semis are now more prominent than timber or tiling. The church stands right at the centre of the straggle, a big building, with a tower capped by a white weatherboarded belfry, and a pyramidal slate roof. It is mainly thirteenth- and fourteenth-century, much enlarged about 1400 with the influx of Flemish weavers. Inside, the most immediately striking thing is the glass in the chancel, both the east window and the two side windows – harsh gashes of reds and blacks and greens that make the rest of the glass seem placidly insipid by contrast. Dating from 1962, they are by Patrick Reyntiens, who has worked with John Piper and has been greatly influenced by Graham Sutherland; the theme is St John's vision in *Revelation*. The font has a massive seventeenth-century cover which does not lift off but has opening panels. Beside the porch stand the old village stocks, moved here from outside the wooden lockup in the village square.

Horsmonden, across the Teise south of Marden, was a centre of ironworking. Near by is one of the finest of all the iron-masters' artificial lakes, a great sheet of water over a quarter of a mile long. The beauty of this Furnace Pond is that the footpath takes you right over the spillway, with the water cascading down from step to step, and a circular basin at the bottom where the giant wheel (now vanished) once turned. The overgrown mounds on either side would surely give the

industrial archaeologist something to get his spade into.
Horsmonden village is large and not particularly memorable,
except for the square green at the centre, which gives it the
feel of a small French town (though in France it would be
paved). If you follow the footpath sign pointing to the church,
you will have a walk of a good two miles, as it is so far from
the village that it seems to have nothing to do with it. But it is
well worth driving along the narrow lanes to get there. The
tall embattled tower, rising from a cluster of barns and oasthouses, looks across orchards, hopfields and water meadows
to the Teise. Inside the church is very plain, apart from a
magnificent chandelier, the gift of the rector of 'Horsmonden'
in 1703. (The final syllable of the name is still stressed,
Horsmondén, as are most of the -den names.) Behind the
church you can look across to Goudhurst, perched compactly
on top of its hill.

On the outskirts of Horsmonden the grounds of **Sprivers** –
over a hundred acres of park and woodland – are owned and
run by the National Trust.

A couple of miles west of Horsmonden two vintage villages,
Brenchley and Matfield, almost run into each other. **Brenchley**
is self-consciously perfect, with a notice on the outskirts proclaiming that it was the best-kept village in Kent in 1970. The
centre is full of weatherboarding and pubs, built round a small
triangular open space where the village pound once stood. The
Old Palace, across the road from the church, is the most
prominent of the secular buildings; there certainly was a Tudor
house there, but most of its heavily timbered appearance is
due to the modern restoration which turned it into cottages.
The church has a curious concave-sided pyramid cap on its
corner turret. Most of the exterior is hidden as you approach
it by a double row of tall yews clipped into cylindrical shape.
The original foundation is said to have been in 1233; the tower
is probably fourteenth-century; and the Victorians did a great
deal of restoration. The first immediate impression is of
width and light, as there is hardly any stained glass in the
main windows or clerestory. Round the chancel arch and
easternmost aisle arches texts are painted, picking up the far
older texts and decoration on the beams and kingposts; above
is an area of roof boarded in and painted blue – the 'celure'
decorated to honour the rood which once stood below it. The

linenfold panelling along the organ loft at the back of the church may have come from the rood screen. Though Brenchley hardly looks an industrial area, in the last century it was famous for its beaver hats; and nowadays snakeskin is dressed there.

Matfield is completely different, wide open rather than cosy, built round an enormous village green. At its northern end is a pond full of ducks and swans, and behind it Matfield House, the height of Georgian elegance, with a large stable block set back on one side. The clock tower on the coach house says 'Mind the time' in large letters. The rest of the green is surrounded by smaller Georgian houses; and it is no wonder that on a fine day the photographers are as thick on the ground as the admirers of the ducks. As Matfield was part of Brenchley parish until the 1870s, it has to be content with a little Victorian church, attractively set in trees at its southern end.

North of Matfield, dreams of the idyllic country life are shattered by the housing estates of **Paddock Wood**. By the railway is the huge square yellow box of the Hops Marketing Board building, and behind it the taller though less bulky grain silos of the Southern Counties Agricultural Trading Society (SCATS). At least Paddock Wood's industries are rooted in the area; the hop theme is taken up by the pub sign of the Hop Pocket (a pocket is an outsize sack) next door.

Through Paddock Wood, on the low-lying fields near the Medway at **Beltring**, is a monumental cluster of oasthouses – the ranks of pyramid roofs and white-painted vanes of the Whitbread Hop Farm, rising over acres of hopfields.

CHAPTER FIFTEEN

The Rother Valley

✤

BOTH East Sussex and West Sussex have a River Rother, and neither will agree as to which *the* Rother is. I am naturally prejudiced, as I lived for nearly ten years near Bodiam, where the eastern Rother emerges from hill-surrounded seclusion and ambles through an ever-widening spread of water meadows to Rye and the open sea. In addition, the western Rother is a mere tributary of the Arun, and even rises over the border in Hampshire. Finally the eastern Rother is the most typical river of the Weald, cutting a deep channel which is still only crossed in its upper reaches by twisting steep lanes, and with its tributary the Dudwell producing a landscape of dramatic ridges which is amazingly spacious despite its small size on the map.

Rotherfield, seven miles south of Tunbridge Wells, is a suitable place to begin, as the Rother is said to rise in the cellar of one of its houses, and several of its small tributaries rise near by. It looks westward across a narrow valley to Ashdown Forest and the creeping expansion of Crowborough (see p. 323), but has so far managed to stay compact, built round an irregular crossroads, with plenty of good tile-hung houses and a tall-spired church. Rotherfield has its fair share of comfortable pubs; one of them, the King's Arms, conceals the Manor House, which can be seen over the wall of the garden.

The church is a big friendly building, with a complete array of old box pews inside. The dedication to St Denys pushes the foundation of a church here back to the eighth century, when Bertwald, Duke of the South Saxons, was cured by the monks of St Denys near Paris and built a church as a thank-offering. A small monastery was also established, and it is thought that the remains lie under fields south of the church. A track called

'Chant Lane' is by tradition named after the chanting monks of St Denys.

The present building dates from the twelfth century on. Apart from the pews, there is some fine woodcarving, especially a Perpendicular screen between chancel and side chapel, a Jacobean pulpit complete with sounding board, and a sixteenth-century font cover which is incongruously raised and lowered by a World War II bomb hoist – a strange example of swords into ploughshares. The Burne-Jones east window, showing drooping musicians surrounded by a jungle of climbing plants, was put in about 1860. Sussex iron can be seen in the grave slab bearing a double cross by the north door; this may be fourteenth-century, about the same date as the medieval frescoes which survive, especially over the chancel arch. Old Rotherfield can just be deciphered from a painting on the wall of the north aisle, which shows the village, with a good deal of artist's licence, as it was about 1711.

As this is a land of hills, it used to be a land of windmills as well. More survive here than anywhere else in the two counties. There is a well preserved post mill half way between Rotherfield and Mayfield, on a high point with the improbably Greek name of **Argos Hill**. From it you can see Mayfield with its church tower a little to the south-east, and due south across the Rother valley to the Heathfield ridge.

Round Rotherfield and Mayfield you continually come across the broken-down bridges and derelict cuttings of the branch line that once ran from near Eridge to Heathfield. Though **Mayfield** is now railwayless, it is still the most prosperous-looking place in the neighbourhood. Coming from Rotherfield, the most prominent feature of Mayfield is the cluster of buildings that form the Roman Catholic convent school, at the eastern end of the main street. The school is built around the remains of **Mayfield Palace**, one of the great residences of the medieval Archbishops of Canterbury and an important administrative centre for church affairs. The first in the succession of archbishops to live at Mayfield was St Dunstan, who in the tenth century built a small wooden church there. It was at Mayfield that his famous encounter with the devil took place. As a good blacksmith the saint was forging a horseshoe when the devil visited him. He seized the devil's nose with his red-hot tongs, whereupon the Prince of Darkness leapt in a single bound to Tunbridge Wells and plunged his nose in the water to cool it. Hence the sulphurous (and health-giving) qualities of the water. Visitors to the convent are still shown the tongs, the well supposed to have flowed when St Dunstan struck his staff on the ground, and his anvil, kept in the wellhouse.

The finest part of the palace still survives – the fourteenth-century great hall, now used as a chapel. It is built on an enormous scale (seventy feet long and forty wide), with three giant stone arches supporting the roof and resting on grotesque corbels which are themselves of unusual size. In a recess off the hall is the tomb of Cornelia Augusta Connelly, who died in 1879 and was the American foundress of the Society of the Holy Child Jesus. After the Reformation, the palace eventually passed to Sir Thomas Gresham, the Elizabethan financier and founder of the Royal Exchange; his grasshopper crest is carved on one of the fireplaces shown to visitors. After changing hands a good many times the palace fell on hard times. In the mid eighteenth century the roof was stripped off the great hall, and for the next hundred years the palace mouldered away as a picturesque and much visited ruin. In 1863, on an outing from her school in St Leonards, Mother Connelly saw the palace; later the Duchess of Leeds, an American friend, bought the property and gave it to her. Edward Welby Pugin was commissioned to design the restoration, and only two years later the hall was reroofed and in use as a chapel. The stone tower west of the hall is medieval; the gatehouse to the main street is Tudor, probably built by Archbishop Warham. (The palace is open to visitors at most reasonable times, though notice is appreciated.)

Apart from the palace, Mayfield was prosperous in its own right as a centre of wealden ironworking. The main street is dignified, with wide brick pavements and some good timbered buildings, notably Middle House, built by Sir Thomas Gresham for his retainers and now a hotel, which has the date 1575 carved on the bargeboards. The tall village sign in the middle of the pavement has reached the respectable age of half a century; it won the second prize of £500 for a competition for village signs run by the *Daily Mail* in 1920. The figure of a girl on top refers to the origin of the town's name from Maghfeld or Maid's Field.

The **Church**, naturally dedicated to St Dunstan, is set back a little from the street, with open country behind. The greater part of it was built after a fire in 1389, in which much of the village was destroyed. It has an odd-looking interior, with some late Perpendicular arcading cut short where it meets the chancel. There are two very fine eighteenth-century candelabra, a rustic octagonal font with the date 1666 carved on it, and two cast-iron grave slabs in the nave, one by an obviously inexperienced founder, as several of the figures and letters have come out the wrong way round.

South of Mayfield a pretty road leads direct across the Rother valley to **Heathfield**. The main road makes a wide loop via **Cross In Hand**, an important road junction, with a post mill on its central triangle, not as good as the one on Argos Hill but worth a glance.

Heathfield is undistinguished, with no character either of Sussex or anywhere else. About twenty years ago the best thing about it was its fire station; it still is. East of the town is the wide expanse of Heathfield Park, behind a seemingly endless wall. Over the wall down a side turn you can see the round castellated folly known as Gibraltar Tower, built in honour of General Sir George Augustus Elliot, Governor of Gibraltar, who successfully defended the Rock against combined French and Spanish attacks from 1779 to 1783. Old Heathfield, at the south-east corner of the park, consists of a church, a pub and a few cottages. At **Cade Street** nearby, an inscribed monument north of the road to Battle marks the spot where Jack Cade, leader of the Kentish rebellion of 1450, was killed by Alexander Iden, Sheriff of Kent (see also pp. 108, 154, 213). The inscription ends with the moral: 'This is the Success of all Rebels, and this Fortune chanceth ever to Traitors.'

The most memorable thing about **Horam**, a couple of miles south of Heathfield, is a large cider press beside the main road. This belongs to the makers of Merrydown cider, who took over Horam Manor in 1947; their premises can be visited in the morning or early afternoon.

To the east is a jumble of inconsequential lanes and small villages, reminiscent of the North Downs. **Warbleton** is hardly even a village – just a large and noble church, set in magnificent country, with a farm next door and a long low house opposite. The interior is dominated by a galleried manorial pew, dated 1722, with two compartments at first-floor level, ideal for sleeping during sermons or keeping a check on church attendance among the tenantry. Hanging on the wall is a Victorian engraving which shows Richard Woodman, an ironmaster of Warbleton, being burnt at the stake with nine others at Lewes in 1557. When the rector handed him over to the authorities, Woodman rebuked him for 'turning head to tail' to satisfy the Catholics. An iron-bound door in the church may come from the strongroom where Woodman kept his workmen's wages.

Another village well off the beaten track is **Dallington**, which has some old half-timbered buildings and a church with a spire covered in stone slabs instead of the usual shingle. The nave is a Victorian rebuilding, with turned beams like enormous chair legs stretching right across.

At **Wood's Corner**, half a mile east of Dallington on the road to Battle, is a folly built by Mad Jack Fuller, the squire of Brightling, who died in 1834 aged seventy-seven. It stands near the Ordnance Survey triangulation point (558 feet), and takes the form of a cement-rendered sugar-loaf, put up after Fuller had bet a friend that the spire of Dallington church was visible from the Grecian temple in the grounds of Brightling Park (then known as Rose Hill). When Fuller found he was wrong, he had the sugar-loaf built on the skyline. Inside it is reminiscent of a Mycenean beehive tomb; it was inhabited until 1880 and could still make a bizarre weekend cottage.

From Wood's Corner a side road leads up to **Brightling Needle**, an obelisk built on the highest point for miles around (646 feet), and the most prominent of Mad Jack's constructions. Brightling Park's broken-down stone wall runs from near the beacon to Brightling village; the dignified two-storey house can be seen over the churchyard wall. Fuller lies buried underneath the massive pyramid in the churchyard. According to legend, he sits inside wearing a top hat and holding a bottle of claret; but the church guide punctures this story by stating that 'he died a natural death and is buried in the ordinary recumbent position beneath the floor of the pyramid.' Inside the church is a tablet to Fuller on the south wall of the nave; the bust shows the fleshy face of a man who enjoyed the

Shipley Mill, once owned by Hilaire Belloc. In recent years it has been restored and is now in full working order.

The centre of Arundel, with the turrets of the Castle looming behind.

The Great Hall of Parham Park, near Storrington. The Hall is decorated with elaborate Renaissance plasterwork and lined with Elizabethan portraits.

good things of life. He was interested in music, and in science, as is shown by the observatory he built on a hill near Brightling Needle, still used for amateur astronomy. Fuller bought Bodiam Castle (see p. 274) when it was about to be demolished, and commissioned a number of paintings of Sussex from Turner. He sat as M.P. for Sussex from 1801 to 1812, after an election that cost him and his supporters a total of £50,000. On one occasion he was ejected from the House for calling the Speaker an 'insignificant little fellow in a wig'. A window in the north wall of the church contains the coat-of-arms of the Fullers, with the motto 'Carbone et Forcipibus' ('by charcoal and tongs'), referring to their trade as ironfounders.

Before his great building programmes at Winchester and Oxford, William of Wykeham was rector here in 1362. His coat-of-arms can be seen outside the church on two shields above the small door in the south wall of the chancel.

East of Brightling the road passes over the aerial ropeway of British Gypsum, with endless chains of containers gliding silently by. Apart from occasional glimpses of this nature, the biggest industrial concern in the area is virtually invisible.

From Brightling a lane runs north of Hastings Corporation's **Darwell Reservoir**, a brilliant sheet of water seen here and there through the trees or across a field, and then swings down to **Mountfield**, the quintessence of a forgotten Sussex village: a big house set in a park full of old oaks; a few cottages; and a small church with squat tower, simple nave with Norman chancel arch, and organ gallery at the back. Beyond Mountfield a dead straight road leads south to Battle (see p. 286), a couple of miles away.

Robertsbridge, north of Mountfield, on the main Hastings road, used to be called Rotherbridge; the road runs uphill from the Rother and the level crossing between a jumble of old houses, many of them half-timbered. At the top of the hill there is a small green with a varied group beside it, and the red tile-hung bulk of the George Inn facing down the street. This was an old coaching inn; in more recent times W. G. Grace stayed there, as did Hilaire Belloc, who began his tramp through Sussex described in *The Four Men* at the George, 'drinking that port of theirs and staring at the fire' on October 29th, 1902, as he precisely dates it. Robertsbridge used to be the junction for the Kent and East Sussex Railway, used in the summer by hop-pickers making for the hopfields round Bodiam (see Tenterden, p. 153).

Robertsbridge grew as an appendage to a Cistercian abbey, founded towards the end of the twelfth century. The ruins are now part of a farm at the end of Fair Lane, about a mile east of the town. The farmhouse has an inordinately high-pitched roof, protecting what remains of the abbot's house, including the tall west window; and in the garden are the ruins of the refectory.

Across the river from the abbey is **Salehurst**, whose large gaunt church is used by Robertsbridge, which has no church of its own. The name comes from the Anglo-Saxon 'sealh' meaning willow and 'hurst' meaning wood, and the area is still famous for its cricket bat willows. In medieval times Salehurst was on the main road to London, and until the Reformation was more important than Robertsbridge. The present church was begun in the thirteenth century, and greatly enlarged by the abbots of Robertsbridge in the fourteenth. Inside is a remarkable font, carved with salamanders running round the foot; by tradition it was given to the church by Richard Coeur de Lion in gratitude for being released from imprisonment in Bavaria by Abbot William of Robertsbridge.

From Heathfield to the Hastings road at Hurst Green, the A 265 runs along the crest of the high ridge that separates the Rother and the Dudwell. **Burwash**, five miles east of Heathfield, consists of a single main street, with the church at the eastern end and an exceptionally harmonious collection of houses, which can all be seen by five minutes' walk along the brick pavement. Most imposing of all is the high-roofed Carolean house near the church, which according to Pevsner is timber-framed under the elegant brickwork. However, charming though Burwash is, it is not the village that most people come to see so much as **Bateman's** (National Trust) just outside, the house where Kipling spent the last three decades of his life. Bateman's is a handsome stone house built in 1634 by a wealthy ironmaster; aptly enough, the stone from which it was built has rusted in places where ore runs through it.

Kipling came here in 1902 from Rottingdean (see p. 379), and tells of his first visit with his usual whimsy. 'We had seen an advertisement of her, and we reached her down an en-larged rabbit-hole of a lane. At very first sight the Committee of Ways and means said: "That's her! The Only She! Make an honest woman of her quick!" We entered and felt her Spirit – her Feng Shui – to be good.' Kipling was thirty-seven at the time and at the height of his fame. At Bateman's he wrote *Puck of Pook's Hill, Rewards and Fairies* and above all the Sussex poems; and he lived there until his death in 1936. Among the relics in the drawing-room is a small water colour of Lake Rudyard in Staffordshire, where Kipling's parents met and which no doubt they remembered nostalgically when they christened their first-born out in Bombay. Kipling's father, Lockwood Kipling, was by profession an architectural sculptor and went to Bombay as the principal of an art school there; he was later curator of the Lahore Museum. He carved the terracotta plaques which were used as illustrations for *Kim* and other books, and which hang on the walls at Bateman's.

Over the wide staircase are several portraits of Kipling, the best painted in 1891 and showing him in a white Nehru-type jacket. Upstairs is his study very much as he left it: the long table still with ink well and pipe cleaners; the chair raised on blocks for his short stature; the novels, histories and books of travel and poetry lining the walls; the personal oddments picked up in the course of a wandering life. From the bedroom across the corridor can be seen the small dome-shaped rise which was the original of Pook's Hill. A large room with powder closet leading off it is used as an exhibition room, with early magazine editions of the short stories, more plaques by John Lockwood Kipling, and a remarkable seventeenth-century Sussex fireback showing an ironmaster, Richard Lenard of Brede, holding a hammer and surrounded by his wares.

The garden was largely planned by Kipling, and leads down to the banks of the Dudwell, with a derelict watermill that Kipling harnessed for electricity when he first came to Bateman's. In one of his poems he personified the mill.

> See you our little mill that clacks
>   So busy by the brook?
> She has ground her corn and paid her tax
>   Ever since Doomsday book.

The mill is now being restored by the Sussex Industrial Arch-aeology Study Group.

Kipling's only son John was killed at Loos in 1915, aged eighteen. There is a tablet to him on the south aisle of the church, which also has a fourteenth-century iron grave slab, said to be the oldest in existence. The church tower was built about 1090, and in spite of much Victorian rebuilding the graceful chancel arch was left untouched.

Like Heathfield, which used to be pronounced 'Heffle', Burwash was 'Berrish' to the locals. A Victorian rector of the village, John Coker Egerton, left a marvellous picture of Burwash life a century ago in *Sussex Folk and Sussex Ways*. In his day the roads were so bad that six horses had to be used to pull a two-wheel cart; and a farm labourer's life was no rustic idyll, but was summed up in the rhyme

> Pork and cabbage all the year,
> Mouldy bread and sour beer,
>   Rusty bacon, stinking cheese,
>   A chaff bed full of fleas –
> Who do you think would live here?

Etchingham is a scattered village, with a commuter station and a massive fourteenth-century church. In the Middle Ages the fortified manor of the de Echyngham family stood roughly where the station is now, guarding the crossing point of the Rother, which was navigable as far as here for the ships of the time. The manor has disappeared, but Sir William de Echyng-ham's baronial church still stands, with its centrally placed tower held together by metal cramps, its flowing tracery which suggests a French architect, and its brasses. In front of the altar lies Sir William (headless now) in chainmail, over an inscription 'Of earth was made and formed, and to earth returned, William de Echyngham was his name. God on my soul have pity.' The copper vane on the tower is the original fourteenth-century one.

The road to **Bodiam** branches off the A 21 a mile south of Hurst Green; or you can get there from Salehurst by twisting back lanes. Though **Bodiam Castle** seems remote and pointless today, it was built to guard an important crossing of the Rother, which in the Middle Ages was a navigable river and a possible invasion route for the French right into the heart of

Kent and Sussex. The castle is a classic of medieval fortification, austere in the symmetry of its walls, round corner towers and square-cut gatehouses. In the summer it dozes peacefully above its reflection in the moat; but a better time to see it is on a lonely winter afternoon, with a cold rain whipping the water and battering the walls – a reminder of the chill grimness of the Middle Ages that lay behind the pageantry. It was built by Sir Edward Dalyngrygge in 1385, at a time when the French fleet had virtual command of the sea, and is thought to be unique as a combination of private dwelling and part of the national defence system. Fortunately, it was never attacked, though it was held by an opponent of Richard III during the Wars of the Roses, and was probably slighted (made undefendable) by Cromwell in the Civil War. By the mid eighteenth century its teeth had been so thoroughly drawn that it was used to grow vegetables. It belonged to various owners, including Mad Jack Fuller (see p. 270), before its final restoration by Lord Curzon, who bought it in 1917 and left it to the National Trust when he died nine years later.

The main entrance to the castle is on the north side, through the gatehouse which still has its portcullis, now rusted into place. Inside there is a single large courtyard, with buildings round all four walls: great hall, chamber, ladies' bower and chapel for Sir Edward; servants' hall and massive kitchen; household offices. By the standards of the time it must have been comfortable, though damp; looking up the south-east tower, for example, you can see three storeys of bedrooms each with its own shapely fireplace. The south-west tower is also worth a close look, as it houses the castle's well, and cut in the stone round the upper levels are rows of nesting boxes for pigeons. A small museum in the curator's cottage has a model of how the castle looked in its prime – like a college quadrangle of the same date, crouching behind a shield of stone. A rectangular depression between the southern side of the moat and the Rother marks the site of the harbour, and a flat area towards the village is said to have been a tilting yard (though more prosaically it is now thought to have been the village mill-pond).

Apart from the castle, Bodiam is the centre of the Guinness hop gardens, which stretch along the south side of the river. From Bodiam the most prominent landmark is the spire of

Ewhurst church on the ridge to the south. Ewhurst used to be a complete backwater, but has lately undergone an arty transformation right in its centre.

The centre of **Northiam** is full of character, though the outskirts down towards the Rother are unprepossessing. Not all that long ago the name was pronounced 'Norgam', as Bodiam was 'Bodgem', and a local rhyme testifies to patriotism if not to any great poetic talent:

> O rare Norgam, thou dost far exceed
> Beckley, Peasmarsh, Udimore and Brede.

Northiam's showpiece is the ancient battered oak on the village green, now held together by chains and clamps, under which Queen Elizabeth I dined in August 1573, on her progress through Kent and Sussex. She took off her green shoes there and let the people of Northiam keep them; they are kept at Brickwall, the home of the Frewen family, and are put on show when the house is open to the public. All round the green are fine examples of weatherboarded eighteenth-century houses. The church, with its tall stone spire, lies hidden away behind; the base of the tower is Norman, and the rest of the building was built at various times in the Middle Ages. In early Victorian times it was considerably altered, and the Frewen mausoleum was added on the north side.

Northiam's two main houses are at opposite ends of the village. **Brickwall**, now a boys' school, takes its name from the high walls that surround the gardens. The front has a close-set pattern of elaborate timbering, with the date 1633 on the bargeboards of the central gable. The walls of the drawing-room are lined with Frewen family portraits, which must be among the most comprehensive collection of any prosperous squirearchal family in the country. The first Frewen came to Northiam as rector in 1573; the portraits begin in the seventeenth century, and include paintings by Cornelius Jansen of Lord Keeper Coventry and his wife. Thankful Frewen was secretary to Coventry in the reign of Charles II; his brother had the equally Puritan and worthy name of Accepted Frewen and became Archbishop of York. (Northiam went in for original names. When vaccination became compulsory in the last century one furious inhabitant saddled his daughter with the name Annie Antivaccinator.)

Also in the drawing-room is the sedan chair belonging to Martha Frewen, who burnt to death in her bedroom in 1752, while passengers in the Rye coach listened helplessly to her screams.

Great Dixter, at the end of a lane off the main street, is of more architectural but less personal interest. It is largely the creation of Nathaniel Lloyd, who in 1910 bought a ramshackle fifteenth-century hall house and in the following years employed Lutyens to restore it, and to add the tile-hung extension on the left as you face the building. At the back of the extension is the third section of the house, a yeoman's hall brought timber by timber from Benenden and re-erected at Dixter. The great fifteenth century hall is a magnificent room, with an enormous central beam supporting a kingpost, and hammerbeams on either side; the hammers are carved with armorial bearings, including those of the Dalyngrygges who built Bodiam Castle. The hall leads into a ground-floor parlour with solar above; on a beam in the parlour is an inscription carved by a tenant of Dixter, who 'came the ferst of Elisabethe rain' (in 1558) and lived there for over thirty years. Above the porch is a small bedroom, with its own little kingpost, structurally unnecessary but in keeping with the superb timbering of the whole place. The gardens at Dixter have an incredible amount of topiary-yew clipped into birds, pyramids and battlemented walls. They are presided over by the gardening writer and expert Christopher Lloyd.

Towards the end of the Second World War Northiam had a brief taste of world-shattering affairs, when on May 12th, 1944, four Allied prime ministers met on the playing fields before D-Day, and held an inspection of the troops of Southern Command. Their names are recorded on a plaque on one of the gates: Churchill of Great Britain, Mackenzie King of Canada, Smuts of South Africa, and Huggins of Southern Rhodesia.

Beckley, on the road to Rye, is a pretty, strung-out village, with a grouping of medieval church and Georgian houses at the Northiam end. Alfred the Great, who died in AD 900, referred in his will to lands at 'Beccanleah' (Beckley), and there was certainly a Saxon church on the present site. With its homely dormer windows breaking the roofline, squat Norman tower and topheavy spire, it is a church full of character. Inside, there are two 'jack-in-the-green' corbels (grotesque stone heads with leaves growing from their mouths) and a dug-out oak chest that may be eight centuries old. On still nights the quiet of Beckley is said to be broken by the hoofbeats of Sir Reginald Fitzurse, riding unavailingly to the church for sanctuary after the murder of Becket. From Beckley it is only a couple of miles to Peasmarsh (see p. 154), on the road to Rye.

Newenden, over the Rother from Northiam across a narrow humpbacked bridge, is a trim little place, with a good pub, the White Hart, which was the *Evening Standard* Country Pub of the Year in 1967. The church is a fragment of a much larger medieval building; it has a fine Norman font, carved with a design of dragons and other fabulous beasts. According to Lambarde, in 1241 the first Carmelites to arrive in England 'made their nest at Newendene, which was before a wooddie and solitarie place'.

Two miles to the west is **Sandhurst**, not much to look at except for its church, which is a mile away from the village down the back road to Bodiam. The original village is said to have been near the church, but after the Black Death of 1349 the surviving inhabitants moved to healthier ground up on the ridge. Part of the churchyard is still reputed to be a plague pit where victims were buried. The church has a massive stone tower, built in the fourteenth century and perhaps used as a watch tower for Bodiam Castle below. Half a century ago Sandhurst had a mill claimed to be the only five-sailer in Kent. Now only the brick base is standing.

Hawkhurst has grown considerably in the last few years, and is now at the uneasy half way stage between village and town. It reached the height of its fame, or rather notoriety, in the first half of the eighteenth century, when the 'Hawkhurst Gang' of smugglers held a reign of terror over much of Kent and Sussex. They regularly murdered or tortured opponents, and were so self-assured that after a successful smuggling run to Rye they would celebrate at the Mermaid there with their loaded pistols lying on the table in front of them, without any interference from the magistrates. The old part of Hawkhurst, known as The Moor, lies half a mile south of the main crossroads, round a large triangular green. The long, low ragstone church has magnificent Perpendicular window tracery in the aisles, which were added about 1450. Finer still is the Decorated east window dating from the previous century, a five-light masterpiece rising to a star at the apex. The glass was blown out, and the church put out of action for thirteen years, by a flying bomb which landed in the churchyard in 1944. One of the new windows on the south side commemorates Sir John Herschel, the nineteenth-century astronomer, who lived at Hawkhurst for the last thirty years of his life; the fitting subject is the Wise Men and the Star. Church and green are surrounded by prosperous brick and weatherboarded houses. Up the hill, in the more recent part of Hawkhurst, is what looks from a distance like a large wealden church, with a spire dominating the Hawkhurst ridge; a closer look shows it to be Victorian Gothic (built by Sir George Gilbert Scott in 1861). Opposite is a civilised country-town row of shops, with weatherboarding above and an arcade of cast-iron pillars below.

At **Flimwell**, where the A 268 crosses the Hastings road, you pass an extraordinary collection of steep-gabled Victorian farm cottages, set well back from the road behind gardens crammed with vegetables. Obviously no one is ever going to schedule them, yet they are as much a part of the history of the countryside as any half-timbered cottage. On the brow of the hill behind, at the southern edge of Bedgebury Forest (see p. 250), is a recent landmark, the lattice tower and saucer aerials of a television relay station.

Ticehurst, a couple of miles beyond the crossroads, is a good tilehung village. Down the road to the church is an unusual little row of shops with an arcade of spindly iron pillars leading to the church. The church is thirteenth- and fourteenth-century, and still keeps some of its medieval glass, originally in the east window but now in the north wall of the chancel. One of the lights is a 'doom window', showing souls being trundled off to hell in a tumbril by grinning devils. On the outskirts of the village is Ticehurst House, a dour Victorian mansion, now a private clinic.

Wadhurst, a good deal larger than Ticehurst, was a centre of the iron industry. The big Queen Anne vicarage which dominates the High Street was built by John Legas, chief ironmaster of the town; and if the church is not actually built of iron it is largely floored with it. The tall slender spire, nearly 130 feet high, which shoots up behind the main street, has been struck by lightning six times down the years; the tower is Norman, and the rest of the church Early English or later. On the floor of the chancel, nave and aisles are thirty iron grave slabs, mainly of the seventeenth century. The earliest ones have a simple repetitive design of shields; but as the century progressed the founders grew more assured, and by the end of the century were producing complex and ornate designs, like the embossed slab of William Barham in the chancel, dated 1701. Recent examples of ironwork are the cast iron cross and candlesticks on the altar, made in 1967, and the wrought iron and glass screen protecting the bell-ringers, decorated with lambs, hops and flowers and presented in 1958. In the porch are memorials to the Luck family, one of which is decorated with terracotta plaques made by Jonathan Harmer of Heathfield, an early nineteenth-century potter whose work can be found on monuments here and there in East Sussex. At the Tunbridge Wells end of Wadhurst is a group of Victorian workshops with walls largely of glass – an early example of a factory estate, looking like a set from a Keystone comedy.

The last important prize fight in England was held at Wadhurst in December 1863, with enthusiasts catching a special train from London Bridge at six in the morning.

CHAPTER SIXTEEN

The Norman Shore

✢

THOUGH William the Conqueror landed his army along the coast in Pevensey Bay, and defeated Harold and the Saxons six miles inland, at Battle, Hastings has appropriated for itself the name of the most crucial conflict in English history. Hastings, now the terminal point of the A 21, was an important port in Saxon times; the name Haestingas is a Saxon tribal name, and in Edward the Confessor's reign the town was renowned for its sailors and ships. It was the first place William made for on his landing. The Bayeux Tapestry has a scene of Normans throwing up a motte or earth mound, and constructing one of William's prefabricated castles – wooden structures, brought over in sections from Normandy – on top of it. It was from this strongpoint, where the ruins of Hastings Castle now stand, that the Normans marched along the high ridge to Battle on the morning of October 14th, 1066.

Nine centuries later it needs an effort to visualise that early Hastings. The topography is now quite different, as the sea has carried away much of West Hill, and over half the stone Norman castle which was built almost immediately after the Conquest. It is thought that the Saxon harbour was in the centre of the modern town, roughly on the site of the cricket ground, with a creek leading out to sea along the line of Harold Place; West Hill would both have protected the harbour from the wind, and dominated it as a site for fortification. Old Hastings is across to the east of the castle, in the sheltered valley between West and East Hills. The inland harbour gradually fell into disuse as the creek became blocked by shingle, and was finally abandoned after the colossal storms of 1287 (see Winchelsea, p. 160). From being one of the most powerful of the Cinque Ports, Hastings fell into decay.

The combined outcrop of West Hill and Castle Hill, a

A map for this chapter will be found on page 266.

rolling stretch of mown grass, is the natural place to begin an exploration of Hastings, as it gives a bird's-eye view of the layout of the place, from the fishing boats drawn up on the shingle below, to the looming bulk of the St Leonards Marine Court building two miles to the west. The **Castle** itself is fragmentary. All that remains is part of the curtain wall, the lower sections of the western gatehouse, and a few arches and part of the tower of the collegiate church, begun about 1070 by the Norman governor, Robert d'Eu. (William entrusted the whole of Sussex to six of these great barons, dividing the county into six administrative areas, or 'rapes', each with a port defended by a castle, and extending inland from south to north. Hastings was the easternmost of the rapes, the others being Pevensey, Lewes, Bramber, Arundel and Chichester.) The original motte survives in the angle of the curtain wall, but there is no trace of a keep. Presumably it was built in the southern part of the castle, and collapsed and fell as the cliff eroded. Outside the curtain wall is a honeycomb of passages in the sandstone, shown to visitors as dungeons, but thought by experts to have been used as storehouses. However, they have the extraordinary property of making even the smallest whisper audible along all their twists and turns, and would have made excellent oubliettes for political prisoners.

West Hill also contains some far more extensive underground passages, the **St Clement's Caves**, a naturally formed network of tunnels with a good deal of man-made embellishment. In the nineteenth century they were leased by a Mr Joseph Golding, who spent years underground, hewing galleries, arcades and statues from the sandstone, and producing one of the commercial wonders of Hastings. During the war the caves were used as air raid shelters, and are now hired out for dances, soundproofed by eighty feet of rock.

From West Hill steep alleys lead down to the old town. This consisted originally of two main streets, All Saints Street and High Street, running roughly parallel down to the shore; but about ten years ago a third street, The Bourne, was brutally gashed through the old buildings to take the increase of traffic – 'the Rape of Hastings indeed', as Pevsner savagely puts it. Fortunately it is easy enough to forget this miserable assemblage of neo-Georgian housing while exploring the streets around it. Near the southern end of the High Street is

St Clement's Church, one of the two medieval churches surviving from Hastings' original total of seven. This is the borough church of Hastings, containing the mayoral pew, marked by a gilded rail; it was begun about 1270, suffered severely in an attack by the French in the 1370s and was largely rebuilt soon afterwards. The west end is cut off at an angle, to fit in with the hilly site. It is the only church in Sussex dedicated to St Clement, the patron saint of blacksmiths and sailors. (Old Romney in Kent has the same dedication.)

The other medieval church, **All Saints,** is at the north end of All Saints Street, at the entrance to old Hastings. It stands on a bluff overlooking the town, and was rebuilt like St Clement's after the French raids, probably a few decades later. Though it is not a particularly large building, it has a feeling of great spaciousness, with lofty vaulting under the tower. Over the chancel arch is an extensive piece of medieval wall painting, much better preserved than most – a 'Doom' painting, showing Christ in judgement, seated on a rainbow. On either side of the central figure are the Virgin and St John, with the New Jerusalem in the background, and in the lower right-hand corner damned souls hanging from gallows. A brightly painted rhyme under the tower, dated 1756, tells of the joys of bellringing, with a warning to the would-be ringer:

> But if you ring in spur or hat
> Sixpence you pay be sure of that.

The most famous character connected with All Saints was Titus Oates, who was curate there; later in his career, in 1678, he took advantage of a surge of anti-Catholic feeling and concocted his notorious 'Popish Plot', which led to a wave of persecutions.

All Saints faces directly across the road to the Catholic church of **St Mary Star of the Sea,** a timelessly Gothic nineteenth-century building with walls of rounded pebbles. It was founded by the poet Coventry Patmore, who from 1876 to 1891 lived in the splendid Georgian Old Hastings House near by. The red brick stables of this house are now the Stables Theatre.

An alley beside All Saints churchyard leads up to the **Tackleway,** one of the prettiest streets in any of the South Coast resorts – a row of small weatherboarded houses, painted white, blue, orange or green, facing on to the gorse-covered slopes of East Hill. The name has nothing to do with fishing tackle, but comes from an old French word, *tegill*, meaning tile. From the Tackleway a number of steep alleys lead down to **All Saints Street**, the best preserved street in the old town, full of half-timbered houses, with occasional unexpected patches of wilderness. Shovells, a fifteenth-century house with jutting upper storey, was the home of the mother of Sir Cloudesley Shovell, the seventeenth-century admiral (see also p. 47). The **High Street** has a dignified Georgian look; many of the houses have been turned into antique shops, and the old town hall is now a museum of local history (open summer only). A final reminder of antiquity is a fragment of the medieval town wall, marked by a plaque, in Winding Street.

In George Street you are out of the antique selling area and into that of shops that stock oilskins and waders, and restaurants that specialise in mussels and jellied eels. Hastings is still very much a fishing town, centred on the tall black 'net shops' of the Stade. These unique wooden structures, used for storing nets and tackle, are thought to date back in general design to Elizabethan times. Built of tarred wood, they are about eight feet square and three storeys high, with the upper floors reached by internal ladders. The nets drying in the sun outside them are nowadays mainly of orange nylon; but the sailors mending their nets or busying themselves about the boats may still have a piratical gold ring in one of their ears – like their ancestors who, says Augustus Hare, were known as 'Chopbacks' from their habit of chopping an axe down the backs of their enemies.

Next to the net shops is the **Fishermen's Museum**, built in 1854 as a chapel. Its central exhibit is the *Enterprise*, the last of the Hastings sailing luggers, built in 1909. The walls are hung with faded photographs of ancient mariners with white fringe beards; and as a fitting companion there is an enormous stuffed albatross. There is also a picture of Churchill being given a gold winkle by the secretary of the Hastings Winkle Cjub.

Like Brighton, Hastings owed its beginnings as a resort to an eighteenth-century medical man, a certain Dr Baillie; and by 1800 it was already becoming popular. The two miles of sea front, from East Parade down to the far end of St Leonards, now form a single unit; but in fact the twin resorts of Hastings and St Leonards grew gradually outwards, until they coalesced in the 1870s. One of the earliest developments was Pelham Crescent, built in 1824 by Joseph Kaye – a grey row of buildings directly below the castle, with a grey classical church in the middle. The best part of early nineteenth-century Hastings is Wellington Square, built on a steep site west of Castle Hill.

Hastings pier is nothing much in the way of piers, though it has all the necessary adjuncts, including a new 'zooquarium'. Opposite is one of the town's showpieces, the **White Rock Pavilion**, built in the 1920s and faintly Oriental looking, with pink-washed walls, and tiled pyramidal rooflets, surmounted by green spikes, at either end. It has a fine concert hall, and a large room where the Hastings Embroidery – a latterday Bayeux Tapestry nearly 250 feet long, made in 1966 to mark the nine hundredth anniversary of the battle – is on view from May to September. The original White Rock was a prominent landmark which blocked the promenade near where the pier now stands. As it was very much in the way and, according to Mr W. H. Dyer's guidebook, 'gave the young Princess Victoria a hazardous passage when she came to the town', it was broken up and carted away in the 1830s. Across the White Rock Gardens is the town's main museum and art gallery; among the paintings of old Hastings is an especially evocative one by C. Powell, showing the shore as it was in 1790: a sea like a mirror, fishermen wading in the shallows, and grass stretching from the foot of Castle Hill to the shingle of the beach.

The only layout of any character west of the White Rock is Warrior Square, spaciously green and a welcome break in the monotony.

St Leonards was the first, and remains the best, of the host of exclusive seaside residential developments where speculation and amenity make uneasy bedfellows. In 1828 the builder and architect James Burton, together with his more famous son Decimus, began to lay out a new resort at what was then a respectable distance from Hastings. The centrepiece of the scheme, the white stuccoed Royal Victoria Hotel, is still there; but the symmetry has been spoiled by the vast 1930s bulk of Marine Court, fourteen storeys high and designed to look like the sun decks of an ocean-going liner. Behind the Royal Victoria is the classical block of the Assembly Rooms (now a Masonic headquarters). A little entrance lodge leads to the landscaped valley of St Leonards Gardens, still with a good many Burton houses surviving on either side. Over a fence, in the gardens of Gloucester Lodge, a memorial portrait plaque of James Burton benevolently surveys his garden city by the sea. Visitors coming to St Leonards from the north used to have to pay a toll before being allowed under the arch of North Lodge, at the upper end of this highly desirable piece of marine exclusivity.

St Leonards church was destroyed by a flying bomb in 1944 and rebuilt in safe modern style in 1961. Inside it is impressive, with lofty paraboloid arches round the windows, and dark blue glass of saints and prophets by Patrick Reyntiens.

To get to **Battle** by the route William took, you should not go by the London Road from St Leonards, but take the Old London Road, and turn east in Ore, along The Ridge. If the Normans did not keep exactly to this line they must have stayed very near it, as in 1066 it was the only practicable route to Telham Hill, where William drew up his troops that October morning. It was not until late in the afternoon that Harold the Saxon died from blows to the head and body – not, according to recent studies, from an arrow in the eye. This theory, handed down from generation to generation, is said to be due to a misinterpretation of the Bayeux Tapestry in which a spear passing behind Harold's head has been taken for an arrow protruding from his eye, but it is the kind of story that can withstand any amount of scholarly carping. The battle can be easily visualised from the terrace in the grounds of **Battle Abbey**, and followed in miniature from the diorama in the town museum. The Saxons were drawn up on Cald-bec Hill, barring William's advance to the north. They must have been exhausted after their long forced march down from the north of England, where they had defeated the Norwegian army under Harold Hardrada at Stamford Bridge, near York, less than three weeks before. Nevertheless they were so sure of victory that they spent the previous night drinking, unlike the dour Normans, who had passed the time in prayer. According to one account, the battle started when the Norman minstrel

Looking towards Chanctonbury Ring from the foothills near Washington.
The trees of the Ring were planted by a local landowner in the eighteenth
century.

The queen of the South Coast resorts. Brighton's Palace Pier, beach and seafront buildings, with modern skyscrapers towering above the Georgian terraces.

The Royal Pavilion, Brighton, a riot of mock-Oriental extravagance built by the Prince Regent (later George IV) in the early years of the nineteenth century.

Taillefer made a suicide charge against the Saxon ranks; and with shouts of 'Dieu nous aide!' from the Normans and 'Out! Out!' from the Saxons the slaughter began.

In fact, Harold should have won the battle by wearing the enemy down, as the Norman strength lay in their heavily armoured mounted knights, who could not penetrate the strong Saxon shield line. But late in the day the Normans on the right flank (seen from the Saxon side) made a feint retreat. The Saxons on that flank charged into the valley in pursuit, defying Harold's orders to stay put, and were slaughtered by the Norman cavalry. The Normans now had a way open up the hill and came in behind the Saxon army; and the battle was over. True to their practice, the Normans butchered anyone they caught, leaving the Saxon bodies to rot. It is not known what happened to Harold's body. According to one story, Harold's mother buried it at Waltham Abbey, in Essex; while another account says that William wrapped it in purple linen and buried it on the cliff at Hastings.

Before the battle William had vowed to build an abbey in the event of his victory, and it was in fulfilment of this vow that the Abbey of St Martin was founded, with the high altar on the spot where Harold fell. The original abbey, consisting of church and monastic buildings, was completed by the end of the eleventh century; but the magnificent remains we see today are what is left of later rebuildings. Most splendid of all is the great gatehouse, built about 1338, which looms over the market square of Battle and closes the vista when you look down the High Street. At the height of its glory the abbey had a long church with numerous side chapels, together with a cloister and the usual monastic buildings; but at the Dissolution in 1538 it was granted to Sir Anthony Browne, 'Master of the Kings Majestes Horcys' as his tomb in Battle church describes him, and was largely demolished by him.

However, a good deal still remains, notably the monks' dorter or sleeping quarters over a series of beautifully vaulted common rooms, and a row of cellars built into the side of the hill up which the Normans advanced. It was above these cellars that Sir Anthony Browne began the so-called 'Princess Elizabeth's Guest House', of which two corner towers now remain. As one of the executors of Henry VIII's will, Browne was put in charge of Princess Elizabeth; but he died in 1548, the year after the king, and Elizabeth never came to live there. Browne converted the abbot's house to his own use. Much altered and added to down the centuries, it is now a girls' boarding school. A melodramatic curse was laid on Sir Anthony as he feasted in the abbey: one of the dispossessed monks marched up to him with the prophecy that his line would end 'by fire and by water'. In 1793 the curse was finally fulfilled. Cowdray House, the home of the Montagues (Sir Anthony's son was the first Viscount Montague), was burnt to the ground, and the last Lord Montague was drowned in the Rhine (see Cowdray, p. 446).

During the Middle Ages the abbot was a man of tremendous consequence, with absolute power within his 'lowy' or area of sway, and able to pardon any criminal throughout the whole of England. He was expected to be as much of a soldier as any baron; in 1377 it was the Abbot of Battle, Hamo de Offington, who finally succeeded in beating off the French after they had sacked the Isle of Wight and carried off the Prior of Lewes. It was almost certainly during their retreat from the abbot's troops that the French burnt much of Hastings (see p. 283).

In the Abbey precincts is a monument put up in 1903 by the French in honour of '*le brave Harold*'; it stands on the spot where the Saxon king stood to command his army.

The town of Battle is an attractive place. A mainly Georgian High Street slopes up from the abbey, leading to Mount Street (the original road to London), with a white-painted windmill at its summit. Outside the abbey gates, set back from the market square, is the timbered Pilgrims' Rest, fifteenth-century and possibly built for the abbey's cellarer. The **Parish Church** is very much in the shadow of the abbey walls. It was begun soon after the abbey, at the beginning of the twelfth century; the tower was added in the fifteenth century, and the whole thing was restored by Butterfield in Victorian times. In the sanctuary is the ornate tomb of Sir Anthony Browne and his wife, with a frieze of winged cherubs' heads round the side and alabaster effigies on top. On the north wall is a copy of the Roll of Battle Abbey, a document of dubious authenticity on which the sonorous Norman names of William's knights are listed – Columber, Grendoun, Malebraunch, Wardebois. Besides the diorama already mentioned, Battle Museum (in Langton House) has a reproduction of the Bayeux Tapestry.

As a final reminder of Battle's past, a brass plate in the market square marks the spots where bulls were tethered for baiting.

Round Battle the country is still heavily wooded, mainly with Forestry Commission conifer plantations, like the Great Wood south of the Sedlescombe road. Near the junction of this road with the main London road (A 21) acrid smoke drifting with the wind marks the kilns of the Sedlescombe charcoal burners; the kilns are low cylinders of iron, filled with slowly burning wood from the forests round about. In the Landes, near Bordeaux, the same technique is used by itinerant burners up from Spain. The iron kilns are a modern refinement; traditionally, turves were piled over the heaps of smouldering wood.

Sedlescombe is a pretty village, with its share of tearooms and antique shops, and a long, narrow green running up its gently sloping hill. The church is north of the village, end on to the road, and was greatly enlarged and restored in 1868. The hierarchy of rural society three centuries and more ago is well illustrated by a church seating plan of 1632 that hangs inside. Sir Thomas Sackville, family and retainers sat in the front; behind were pews of villagers like the Widows Van, Stint and Sloman, and right at the back Youths and Strangers. At the south end of Sedlescombe is the Pestalozzi Children's Village (visits by appointment). It was opened in 1959 as an international home for children from displaced persons' camps in Europe, and now has children not only from Europe but from Korea and Tibet. Its nucleus is an undistinguished but adaptable nineteenth-century country house, round which a colony of low-built cedarwood homes has grown up. Each is a 'national house', where children keep their own customs while at the same time integrating themselves with the life of the village outside. Johann Heinrich Pestalozzi (1746–1827) was a Swiss educationalist who took charge of orphans during the Napoleonic wars. After the Second World War another Swiss, Walter Robert Corti, founded the first Pestalozzi village at Trogen in Switzerland, and Sedlescombe is its English offshoot. It has now largely outgrown its original purpose, and is an expanding centre for training children from the developing countries.

When Battle Abbey was built, stone for its construction is said to have been brought by boat as far as Sedlescombe along

the River Brede, then much wider and navigable far inland.
Brede village, three miles east of Sedlescombe, perches on a
spur of land north of the river; its large church has a fortress-
like appearance as you come up the hill towards it. Brede is a
compact little place, with a typical mixture of brick and
weatherboarding at its centre. The church is a vast enlarging
of a small Norman building of about 1140; the tower is mid
fifteenth-century, and a chapel with fine tracery in the east
window was added as late as the 1530s. In this south chapel
are tombs of the Oxenbridge family, notably that of Sir
Goddard Oxenbridge, who died in 1537 and probably built
the chapel. In effigy Sir Goddard looks harmless enough, but
like Col. Lunsford of East Hoathly (see p. 290), he is said to
have eaten children for his supper. The children of Sussex
finally got their own back by making Sir Goddard drunk with
beer and then sawing him in half with a huge wooden saw,
the children of East Sussex sitting on one end and those of
West Sussex on the other. Near Sir Goddard's tomb is a tall
and gentle Madonna, carved in oak by Clare Sheridan, the
sculptress cousin of Winston Churchill, who died in 1970
aged eighty-four. A woman of extraordinary persistence, she
travelled to Russia soon after the Revolution and carved
portrait busts of Lenin and Trotsky, staying for two months in
the Kremlin and provoking Lenin to get the expression she
wanted. She learnt to carve oak during a six months' stay on a
Red Indian reservation; this Madonna was in memory of her
son, drowned while sailing before the mast in a windjammer.
Like the Oxenbridges, she lived at Brede Place, a small brick
and stone manor on a terrace overlooking the river valley.
Brede church has a series of grey-looking paintings of the
Stations of the Cross, by Sir W. T. Monnington, the current
President of the Royal Academy.

Westfield is largely a red-brick eyesore in a fine high position.
Its church has a solid tower, Saxon in origin, with vast buttresses, and a perfect Norman chancel arch with squints on
either side. It suffered greatly at the hands of the Victorians,
notably in its hideous columns between the nave and new
north aisle. Hastings is creeping out so rapidly towards
Westfield that it will soon be swallowed up.

The eastward expansion of Hastings along the coast is
blocked by the sandstone cliffs that begin at East Hill and

stretch right round to Fairlight Cove. Unlike the grass-covered chalk cliffs beyond Eastbourne, which fall sheer to the sea, the Hastings cliffs are split by sloping glens, full of gorse and bracken, and overhung by trees. Most beautiful of all is **Fairlight Glen,** where a stream runs between huge boulders below the tangled woodland. The Lovers' Seat perpetuates the memory of a girl who waited here for her lover to be rowed ashore from his ship. Unlike many such stories, this one ended happily, as the girl's parents finally consented to a marriage.

Fairlight itself is little more than a collection of old coast-guard cottages, and a ponderous grey stone church in a breathtaking position. The church is a complete nineteenth-century rebuilding, but it has a grandeur that suits the place. The tower is a landmark for miles out to sea; when the weathervane blew down a few years ago the village was inundated with anxious enquiries from sailors asking when it was going to be replaced. The churchyard has a luxuriant collection of tombstones, including one, sadly neglected, to Richard D'Oyly Carte, founder of the opera company.

From Fairlight the road drops steeply down to **Pett Level,** a flat expanse of watercourses and meadows, dotted with small lakes that are sanctuaries for wildfowl. The beach hereabouts is held in place by a barricade of groynes and cross timbers. **Pett** village lies well inland on top of a hill; its spiky Victorian church has a curious octagonal tower and spire, and a complement of large and sinister gargoyles.

Icklesham, two miles north of Pett along winding lanes, is the only substantial village in the area, and marks the eastern end of the Hastings peninsula, which William made the bridgehead for his invasion. It has a fascinatingly irregular Norman church, with a centrally placed tower rising in three successive steps. The Norman capitals on the nave columns are all different; the finely carved roof corbels above, in the forms of flowers and fruit, are Victorian work. The whole place is an architectural textbook of Norman and Early English styles. Icklesham was first mentioned in 772, in a royal charter granting land to the Bishop of Selsey (see Bexhill, p. 293). From Icklesham it is little more than a mile to Winchelsea (see p. 160).

Guestling, three miles back towards Hastings, has no village centre. The isolated church, Saxon in origin with a squat tower built about 1100, is down a side road beside a farm. It was largely rebuilt after a fire in 1890, but still has a good Norman arch, with chevron moulding, in the north aisle. Guestling was probably the meeting place of the governing body of the Cinque Ports, known as 'Court Guestling'; off the beaten track and on neutral territory, it would certainly have been a suitable spot.

The main road from St Leonards to Bexhill (A 259) is now so built up that you can get little idea of the local topography as you drive along it. In medieval times an area of undrained and overgrown marshland stretched inland as far as Crowhurst (see p. 299), protecting the Hastings peninsula on its western side; hence the strategic importance of Battle, half way between the Crowhurst gap and the Brede levels. The pub called the Bo-Peep, at the west end of St Leonards, is said to be named after the games of hide-and-seek the smugglers played with the revenue men. According to a notice inside, the famous nursery rhyme was written by 'Old Humphrey', a Hastings character, after watching the landlord's little daughter playing in the fields.

At **Bulverhythe** the wreck of the Dutch East Indiaman *Amsterdam* is visible occasionally at extremely low tides. There was a port here in the Middle Ages. In the last century the noise of the sea shifting the shingle was called 'Bulverhythe bells' by the local fishermen, and was a portent of bad weather.

Bexhill is a latecomer to the status of a seaside resort, and has never summoned up the self-assurance to build itself a pier. Development began only in 1885, when Lord De La Warr gave the first impetus by building on a large tract of his land between old Bexhill and the sea. Bexhill is a featureless place. Its pride and joy is the De La Warr Pavilion, built in the 1930s by Erich Mendelsohn and Serge Chermayeff, apostles of the then-revolutionary functional style of architecture. With its great bows of glass and spacious stairway, it is still way ahead of most other buildings on the South Coast. Next door to the pavilion are two groups of buildings in delightful contrast to it, Marina Arcade and Marina Court Avenue. With their green onion domes and glimpses of inner courtyards, they are like small great-nephews of Brighton's

Royal Pavilion. They were built at the beginning of this century for the Maharajah of Cooch-Bihar.

Bexhill's beach requires the services of a 'mud-man', whose job it is to mark mudholes with flags as a warning to bathers.

The old village is inland, north of the railway at the top of Upper Sea Road – a small oasis of weatherboarding, round the ancient parish church. Though the church was vastly expanded in the nineteenth century, it still has traces of Saxon work, a powerful tower of about 1070, and Norman arches at the west end. Bexhill is first mentioned, along with Icklesham, in a charter of 772, recording the grant of land at 'Bexlei' by Offa, King of Mercia, to Bishop Oswald of Selsey. In its homely attention to detail, this charter takes us back beyond the harsh efficiency of the Normans to the 'good time of the smaller things' whose passing Chesterton lamented. 'These are the bounds of the 8 hides of inland of the people of Bexhill. Firstly at the servants' tree, from the servants' tree south to the treacherous place, so along the shore over against Cooden cliff, eastward and so up on to the old boundary dyke, so north to Kewhurst, and so to the Benetings' stream, and so north through Shortwood to the boundary beacon, from the beacon to the bold men's ford, from the ford along the marsh to the road bridge, from the bridge along the ditch to Beda's spring, from the spring south along the boundary thus to the servants' tree.' The church's chief treasure is an eighth-century Saxon stone, probably carved at much the same time as the charter was written. It is decorated with crisply carved interlaced cable ornament, and may have been the lid of a reliquary placed there when the church was consecrated. About 1750 the medieval glass depicting saints in one of the north windows came by devious means into the possession of Horace Walpole, who incorporated it into his jackdaw's nest of antiquities at Strawberry Hill, Twickenham; it was finally restored to Bexhill in 1921. Over one of the nave arches is a mural of saints and angels, painted in 1951 by Alan Sorrell, best known for his imaginative reconstructions of buildings and towns of the past.

Across the main road from the church are a few ruined walls surviving from the old manor house, and a large and much-altered stone barn.

Bexhill straggles westwards along the A 259 as far as the

prison; and then you are away from buildings and in the flat expanse of **Pevensey Levels**. Half a mile north of the road is the small village of **Hooe**, with a medieval church at the end of a farm track, dozing in an unenclosed and peaceful churchyard. Inside is a rough-hewn muniment chest, supposedly Saxon. An alternative route from Bexhill to Pevensey is along the coast road, through the smart resort of Cooden, and skirting the not-so-smart shanty town of Norman's Bay.

When William landed in 1066 this area of dyke and meadowland was a swampy inlet of the sea; the ancient names – Manxey, Rickney, Chilley and Pevensey – all have the Saxon '-ey' suffix meaning 'island'. The Bayeux Tapestry shows the Normans landing at Pevensey on September 28th; some of the ships are already unloaded, while elsewhere sailors are lowering the masts or leading the horses through the shallows. Apart from being a convenient landing-point, **Pevensey** had the great advantage from William's point of view of having a ready-made **Castle** – the Roman fortress of Anderida, built about AD 280 as one of the 'Forts of the Saxon Shore' (see Richborough, p. 108). The Roman walls are not built to the usual rectangular plan, but in a rough oval, corresponding to the raised ground of the 'island' of Pevensey. They are still remarkably well preserved round three of the sides, especially the massive west gateway, with its rounded stone buttresses, striped every few feet with courses of thin Roman brick. When the Romans left Britain in 410, the Romanised Britons occupied the castle; but in 477 the Saxons under Aella attacked Anderida and slaughtered every man, woman and child within the walls. The Saxons took over the name and applied it to the thick forest that spread north into Sussex and Kent – the Andredsweald, or Forest of Andred, shortened in course of time to the Weald.

The Normans built their own castle in the south-eastern corner of the walls. Much of the inner bailey survives, including the base of the gatehouse, the foundations of the chapel, and the lower levels of the keep, strengthened by gigantic semicircular bastions. The keep was built about 1100, the gatehouse about 1220. Unlike so many medieval castles, Pevensey seems to have been really defensible, withstanding sieges by William Rufus in 1088 and Simon de Montfort the Younger after the Battle of Lewes in 1264. It was even incorporated in the South Coast defences in 1940: a camouflaged gun emplacement is marked by a notice as prominently as the Roman postern and medieval oubliette.

Like all self-respecting castles, Pevensey has a ghost, reputedly of Andrew Borde, a Pevensey character who lived in the fifteenth-century **Mint House** (now an antique shop) outside the castle gates. Borde was court physician to Henry VIII and Edward VI, and was Henry's unofficial jester, reputedly the original 'Merry Andrew'. Born in 1490, he took orders, studied medicine on the Continent and acted as secret agent for Thomas Cromwell. His sense of humour is typified by the punning Latin name he made up for himself – 'Andreas Perforatus', Andrew 'Bored full of holes'. He wrote books on health and diet, but became known for the humorous chapbooks attributed to him, such as the 'Tales of the Mad Men of Gotham'. Like Till Eulenspiegel, his irresponsibility led to his downfall. In 1549 he was imprisoned on a trumped-up charge of debt by an enemy he had satirised, and died in the Fleet prison the same year. The suite of rooms which Borde kept for the young Prince Edward is still pointed out in the Mint House. The house gets its name from the mint established by the Normans immediately after the Conquest; a 'minting chamber' with beams of enormous antiquity is at the back.

The Mint House has its own ghost, an Elizabethan woman who was horribly done to death there. She was the mistress of Thomas Dight, a London merchant, who lived at Pevensey in the 1580s. Dight came home unexpectedly and found his mistress in bed with a lover. He ordered his servants to cut out her tongue, and made her watch while her lover was roasted to death over a fire in the minting chamber – a scene as macabre as anything in a Webster tragedy. Dight's men threw the body into the harbour, and took his mistress to an unlit upper room, where she was starved to death.

Old Pevensey's justice was administered from the **Court House**, a small white building with a museum of local relics (open only in summer), up the road from the castle. If a condemned criminal was a freeman of Pevensey, he had the right to be drowned rather than hanged. Tied hand and foot, the prisoner was thrown from the parapet of the bridge into the harbour; if he took his time drowning, there was a pile of stones ready at hand for his fellow-townsmen to finish him off.

The **Parish Church**, a completely uniform thirteenth-century building, with the tower centrally placed on the north side, is dedicated to St Nicolas (spelt thus in the French way), the patron saint of sailors. The old town seal shows the saint stilling the waves. In the seventeenth century the chancel arch was walled across, and the chancel was used as a cattle byre and storehouse for smuggled brandy. Andrew Borde's brother, Richard, was vicar here in the early days of the Reformation. After announcing to his parishioners that he 'would rather be torn to pieces by wild horses than acknowledge King Harry as head in spiritual matters of the Church of England', he prudently fled overseas without waiting for the repercussions.

On the other side of the castle from Pevensey is **Westham**, with a pretty village street and its own parish church, which has one of the most ruggedly beautiful church towers in Sussex, built in the fourteenth century and patched, braced and mended down the years. In the south chapel is the original Norman altar stone, with five consecration crosses, restored to its original purpose; and in the same chapel is a memorial to John Thatcher who 'dyed without isshew' in 1649, leaving money to 'the Old Brethren' in the hope that Roman Catholicism would be once again the religion of England. A mile beyond Westham you are in the spreading suburbs of Eastbourne.

Pevensey is now cut off from the sea by the bungalow development of **Pevensey Bay**; but inland from the castle the Levels are still an empty expanse. The main landmark, due north, is the silver dome that marks the Royal Observatory at **Herstmonceux**. You can get there from Westham either by an incredibly circuitous route across Horse Eye Level; or by going back to Pevensey and taking the road north through **Wartling**. Wartling's medieval church is carved with the Pelham buckle (see p. 326), not on the tower as normally but on an outside stone of the south aisle.

The Royal Observatory, moved to Sussex from Greenwich in 1957 because of increasing atmospheric pollution and the glare of artificial light, must be the most idyllically placed scientific establishment in the country. At its heart is **Herstmonceux Castle**, in complete contrast to the observational buildings near by, yet ideally suited to its modern administrative task. The castle is so meticulously restored that it looks almost bogus; yet its battlements and turrets, following in brick the stone fortifications of the time, in fact date from the 1440s. It was built by Sir Roger de Fiennes, a veteran of Agincourt, to defend the Levels against possible French invasion. Large-scale building in brick was copied from Flanders, and Herstmonceux was one of the first extensive brick buildings in this country since Roman times.

After the castle had passed down the centuries from one family to another, the interior was largely dismantled in the 1770s to build Herstmonceux Place (up the road towards the village) In the last century guidebooks referred to its 'desolation and decay', but successive owners since 1911 revived its mellow glory. The fortunate Director has living quarters in one of the wings; the rest is used as offices and accommodation. In pre-scientific days a ghostly drummer nine feet tall was said to stride through the castle beating a spectral tattoo, but this has been explained away as a device used by smugglers to frighten off inquisitive locals. Though the castle itself cannot be visited, the beautiful gardens (complete with four-faced sundial) are open regularly in the summer. On the astronomical side, you can climb the silver-domed tower to see the Isaac Newton telescope, the largest telescope in Britain and the fifth largest in the world. Also on view is a replica of one of Newton's own telescopes, dwarfed to midget size by the modern instrument.

Outside the castle gates is Herstmonceux church, an attractively varied little building, with a fifteenth-century chapel at the west end, built of brick, like the castle. The low tower, built about 1180, is in the north-west corner, forming part of both nave and aisle. On the floor of the chancel (under a carpet) is a splendid brass showing Sir William Fiennes, father of Sir Roger, in full armour; and between the chancel and the north chapel is a noble canopied monument to two further members of the family, Lord Dacre, who died in 1533, and his son Sir Thomas Fiennes. The effigies, with their high cheekbones, bald domes and pudding basin haircuts, bear a strong family resemblance; however, Pevsner thinks that they may have been carved about 1480 for members of the Hoo family.

Herstmonceux village was the birthplace of the Sussex trug or garden basket over a hundred years ago; and the craft is still going strong.

Ninfield, five miles west of Herstmonceux, is a jumble of a village spreadeagled on a ridge. The little church is worth a glance inside for the magnificent blue-framed clock mechanism working away below the tower.

A couple of miles to the north is **Ashburnham Park**, where Capability Brown formed a chain of lakes to fill the low ground in front of **Ashburnham Place**. Brown's glorious park, with its plantation of great trees dropping steeply down to the water, still survives on the grand eighteenth-century scale, but the red-brick house is only a fragment of its former vastness. It now consists of a central two-storey section with single-storey wings, whereas before 1959 it was three storeys high throughout. A new block was added in 1967, and the house is now used as a Christian conference centre. Between the main house and the derelict stable block is Ashburnham church, medieval-looking (the tower is Perpendicular, and has the Pelham buckle by the doorway), but largely rebuilt by John Ashburnham in the seventeenth century. The Ashburnhams have their monuments in the chapel on the north side of the chancel. John himself lies against the north wall, carved in anachronistic armour, between the effigies of his two wives, with a frieze of sons and daughters below. A devoted Cavalier, he accompanied Charles I on his last journey to the scaffold, and was imprisoned by Cromwell in the Tower during the Protectorate. After the execution he got possession of the shirt, underclothes and watch that the king was wearing at the time, and the sheet that was thrown over the body. They used to be kept in the church as relics for those who wanted to touch them against scrofula, a glandular disease known as the 'king's evil'; as recently as 1859 a child suffering from the disease was wrapped in the sheet. The relics are now at Lewes.

The road that runs round the back of Ashburnham Park brings you to **Ashburnham Forge**, once powered by the Ashbourne stream which runs on through the park. The forge, together with Ashburnham Furnace near by, continued working until the first decades of the nineteenth century, the last survivor of the Sussex iron industry. Beside the cottage you can still see the race that fed the undershot wheel, and the base of the supports that held it. The cottage garden has lumps of iron slag to edge the paths. It seems incredible that this little hollow, miles from anywhere, was once a centre of industry; but so it was.

Penhurst, at the top of the hill, is a perfect little spot, like a Morland painting of gabled manor farmhouse, tiled church and great barn behind. The church still has its fifteenth-century oak screen.

Catsfield, south of the Battle road, is dominated by the tall spire of the Methodist church, which looks as though it has strayed across the Channel from North France. The parish church is tucked away down the road to Crowhurst, beside the manor house. Inside is an extraordinary encaustic tile memorial to Annie, Lady Brassey, showing a yacht against the setting sun. Lady Brassey died at sea in 1887; the trophies she collected on her voyages round the South Sea Islands are now in the Hastings Museum.

Crowhurst, a couple of miles towards Hastings, is a hamlet on a steep hillside. The church is a Victorian rebuilding, apart from its fifteenth-century tower with the Pelham buckle (see p. 326) on either side of the door. The giant yew tree in the churchyard is said to date back to the days when Harold held the manor. In a garden below the church are the ruins of the thirteenth-century manor house – one end of the hall, complete with window tracery, and a few other fragments.

CHAPTER SEVENTEEN

Eastbourne and the Downs

✿

Eastbourne, ten miles from Bexhill on the other side of Pevensey Bay, has avoided the twin traps that lie in wait for the seaside resort: brashness at one extreme, and timid gentility at the other. Admittedly it does not allow a single shop along the whole three miles of its landscaped sea-front; but it has a fine pier, with all the Victorian greenhouse effects that a good pier should have. Even the transistor radios are muted in the grassy somnolence of the gardens along Eastbourne's sweep of elegant Parades. Like Bexhill, Eastbourne was laid out as a speculation by a wealthy landowner; but it was laid out earlier, on a grander scale, and caught the high tide of nineteenth-century holiday making. The man responsible for Eastbourne was William Cavendish, later the seventh Duke of Devonshire, who developed it from about 1850 onwards. You can see his statue, robed, bewhiskered and slumped in an ornate throne, at the seaward end of Devonshire Place. Indeed, in the seafront area, you still feel as though you were visiting the Devonshires' private seaside estate: in the gardens west of the Wish Tower stands Spencer Compton, the eighth Duke, with his back to the sea; Devonshire Park is inland from the front; and the Devonshire Park Theatre, with its pair of handsome campaniles, looks across Compton Street to the Devonshire swimming baths.

Eastbourne is hemmed in to the west by the rampart of the Downs, with Beachy Head (the 'Beau Chef' or 'beautiful headland' of the Normans) as their culmination. But there is nothing to hinder its sprawl in other directions. To the north it has swallowed up Willingdon and Polegate, and to the east housing estates are proliferating towards Pevensey, and creeping seawards over the shingle of the Crumbles, within recent memory a wild stretch as lonely as Dungeness. The original East Bourne is a mile or so inland, along the main

Brighton road, and consists of a few streets of old houses, much bitten into by haphazard modern development, round the **Parish Church**. This is a big building, mainly of about 1200, on the site of a Saxon church. The flattened chancel arch is ornamented with a double row of late Norman dog-tooth moulding; the wooden screens have survived since the fourteenth century; and in the chancel are fine sedilia and an Easter sepulchre of about the same period. A curious feature is the step down into the chancel, instead of the usual step up, and the chancel itself is at a pronounced angle to the nave. Behind the church is the stone-built Old Parsonage, a sixteenth-century hall house, and across a lane is the Lambe Hotel, said to date back to the thirteenth century.

On the other side of the road from the church is the **Towner Art Gallery**, formerly the Manor House, a good sensible Georgian house built by Dr Henry Lushington, vicar of Eastbourne. At the beginning of the nineteenth century it was owned by Davies Gilbert, President of the Royal Society, friend of Thomas Telford, and a leading civil engineer. In the 1920s it was turned into the municipal art gallery, with emphasis on pictures of local interest, but also a good deal of modern work displayed, like the abstract statues in the formal gardens beside the house. Most fascinating are the watercolours of Eastbourne as it was about 1850, painted by a local girl, Louisa C. Paris, and annotated with the breathless comments of a Victorian miss. She draws cliff and beach, Sea Houses (the first resort, popular since 1780 when George III's children came there on holiday), and the new Eastbourne rising from the countryside, like Cornfield Terrace, a row of town houses waiting for neighbours literally in the middle of a corn field.

Eastbourne makes full use of the Napoleonic relics at either end of the sea front: the **Redoubt**, a squat redbrick fortification which still looks as substantial as any modern gun emplacement; and the **Wish Tower**, a martello tower made into a small museum. (The name comes from the Saxon word *wisc*, meaning a marshy place.) On the roof is a twenty-four-pounder gun, still pointing out to sea as a deterrent to Bonaparte. As the hotels went up along the front between these landmarks, the visitors flocked to Eastbourne, arriving at the station at the top of Terminus Road – very much a part of the Eastbourne scene, with its iron-framed clerestory on top. An improbable visitor, in 1905, was Claude Debussy, in search of peace and quiet after the breakup of his first marriage. He wrote to a friend: 'It's a little English seaside place, silly as these places sometimes are. I shall have to go because there are too many draughts and too much music.' The sea off Eastbourne is woven into his own greatest orchestral work, the glittering sparkle and surge of *La Mer*.

As a reminder of the cruelty rather than the kind face of the sea, the lifeboat museum near the Wish Tower has a collection of mementoes of the boats and their crews, with scale models beginning at the first lifeboat of them all, built on the Tyne in 1789.

In **Beachy Head** Eastbourne has the most spectacular chalk precipice in England, not excluding Dover's White Cliffs. The summer crowds who walk up the gentle grass slope, marked with the faint outlines of old anti-aircraft positions in the turf, to peer tremblingly over the edge get something more than a hackneyed clifftop view. At the highest point the sheer drop is over five hundred feet – a scale brought into focus by the lighthouse a few yards out from the base of the cliffs, a large enough structure anywhere else, but here dwarfed to the size of a toy. A mile away along the road to Birling Gap is the base of the old Belle Tout lighthouse now turned into a private house. It was built in 1834 by Mad Jack Fuller, of Brightling (see p. 270), and shows that his addiction to follies could give way to something far more practical.

Birling Gap is the first break in the cliffs past Beachy Head. Naturally enough, it was a landing-place for smugglers in the eighteenth and nineteenth centuries. According to Augustus Hare, it was once guarded by a gate and portcullis. From Birling Gap you can walk over the top of the Seven Sisters cliffs to Cuckmere Haven.

Eastdean, a mile to the north, is a vintage downland village of flint-walled houses neatly built round an oblong green. The church, in a hollow at the bottom, is a small aisleless building, with eleventh-century nave and thirteenth-century chancel, joined on askew. A new west end was added in 1962, with the organ high on an arch cleverly linking the old and the new. The low tower, said to be tenth-century, is hidden away on the north side and is invisible from the front of the church.

At the top of the steep hill beyond Eastdean is **Friston**, with a squat little church crouched beside the road. In part it may be pre-Conquest; it has magnificent roof timbering of about 1450, which gives it the effect of a large yeoman's hall. The new south door is in memory of Frank Bridge, the teacher of Benjamin Britten and one of the forgotten heroes of twentieth-century English music, who died in Eastbourne in 1941.

The byroad north across the downs from Friston brings you to **Jevington**, an old smugglers' village. The church, up a tree-shaded lane off the main street, has a Saxon tower probably built in the tenth century. Inside, on the north wall of the nave, is a wild and primitive Saxon sculpture – a small stone tablet carved with a stylised Christ, wearing a loincloth to symbolise the Resurrection and thrusting a tall cross into the throat of a beast squirming at his feet. Apart from the tower, the church is mainly Early English.

From Friston the main road plunges down to **Exceat Bridge** across the Cuckmere, with a bird's-eye view of the wide meanders of the river on its final mile to the sea. Like Birling Gap, **Cuckmere Haven** at the mouth of the river was much used by the smugglers (see Alfriston, p. 306). Why no port ever grew here is a mystery, as it would seem a perfect place – a shelving bay, protected by the cliffs of Seaford Head on one side and the Seven Sisters on the other. It is reached down a track, and is still lonely and remote, if you can forget the inevitable caravan site.

The gap in the downs made by the Cuckmere has a road on either side. The eastern road is much the prettier, though it lacks the spectacular viewpoint of High and Over (see p. 307). Past Exceat a lane by a stream brings you to **Westdean**, seemingly miles from anywhere, buried among trees deep in a downland combe. King Alfred is said to have had a palace there, and certainly he could hardly have chosen a more idyllic spot. It is a village of high flint walls and giant barns; the church (Norman but much altered) has a curious shingled cap to the tower, which gives the west wall, with its three windows arranged like eyes and nose, the look of a startled warrior in a pointed helmet with earflaps. Inside there are two modern memorial bronzes: a bust by Epstein, to Sir John Anderson the politician (1882–1958), who took the title Viscount Waverley of Westdean; and a head by Clare Sheridan above a plaque to Sir Oswald Birley, the artist (1880–1952).

Charleston Manor, where Birley lived, lies in a narrow valley north of Westdean. The garden, planted on the rich soil of the valley floor, is a remarkable one, long and narrow, and far more Continental than English with its parterres and terraces divided by low yew hedges. The house (seen by special arrangement) is a fascinating centrepiece. The oldest section, at the back, is Norman, traditionally said to have been built about 1080 for William the Conqueror's cupbearer; behind this there once stood a Norman chapel, built for the cup-bearer's mother and pulled down after her death to avoid the possibility of sacrilege. On to this Norman building later generations added a Tudor block and finally a Georgian front, so that within this one small house there are three distinct sections, unified by a fine collection of furniture, and the portraits and landscapes by Sir Oswald Birley that cover the walls. The huge barn in the garden, complete with stage at one end, is used by Lady Birley for an annual festival combining horticulture with gastronomy, music and modern ceramics. Behind the manor the round medieval dovecote, possibly Norman in date, still resounds to the burbling of a vast flock of white doves.

As far as Charleston the road runs by water meadows and reedbeds. At **Litlington** the valley narrows, hemmed in by spurs of the downs on either side, which gives the narrow village a rather cramped feeling. However, it is all very unspoiled, with a pretty little church, white weatherboarded below the spire.

You get to Wilmington past **Lullington** church, a tiny building in a sacred grove on the hillside. The church, which only holds about twenty people, is in fact the chancel of a much larger building, stumps of which appear here and there above ground. **Wilmington** is best known for its **Long Man** — a giant outline cut in the chalk, with a staff about 250 feet long in either hand. No one knows his date; he has traditionally been thought to be Bronze Age. He faces north, and can be seen from miles away across the flat plain of the upper Cuckmere. Apart from the Long Man, Wilmington has a trim village street, and the remains of a medieval priory, founded by King William's half-brother, Robert de Mortain, soon after the Conquest. The most obvious of the remains are the mullioned windows and corner turrets of the fourteenth century hall; and at one side is an elegantly vaulted thirteenth-century porch or gatehouse, carved with a grotesque face on the boss where the ribs of the vault meet overhead. The priory had decayed well before the Dissolution and become a farmhouse, so that early Tudor and medieval are inextricably jumbled together. Upstairs is an agricultural museum, crammed with every sort of bygone from a metal bottle for feeding lambs to a tripod for holding down recalcitrant oxen.

The parish church next door was begun about the same time as the priory for the two or three monks who lived there, and the villagers; the monks would have used the chancel and the parishioners the nave. There is a very fine Jacobean pulpit complete with sounding-board; and a small window worth hunting for behind the organ, depicting butterflies, moths and a bee. The church is overshadowed by an immense and ancient yew, its limbs held together by chains and supported by timber uprights, which may be as old as the priory itself,

The road along the west side of the Cuckmere (B 2108) crosses the A 27 a mile west of Wilmington, and runs through the valley's only sizeable village, **Alfriston**. Built at river level, it is the most substantial of all the downland villages, with timbered medieval inns and low brick and weatherboarded cottages, many of them now turned into tearooms and antique shops. It can be a bedlam of traffic; even the stone market cross, one of the last two in Sussex (the other is at Chichester), was smashed by a lorry beyond repair and now has a new shaft. Alfriston's chief beauty is not its old street, fine though it is, but the broad green behind the houses, stretching to the majestic fourteenth-century parish church. Like all churches built at the same time and in the same style, this one lacks the character of a building that has been added to and adapted down the centuries; it has the soullessness of strict logic. It is symmetrically cruciform, with nave and chancel the same length and low central tower. The broach spire has been recently reshingled, which gives the whole building a brand-new look. There are hardly any monuments inside; the only striking thing is the hideous reredos obtruding into the east window. Beside the church is the thatched and timbered **Clergy House**, a bare hall of about 1350, with a kingpost roof, where the vicar lived in medieval times. It was the first building acquired by the National Trust, who bought it in 1896 – for £10!

The Star Inn was built early in the fifteenth century, probably as a resthouse for pilgrims going to and from the shrine of St Richard at Chichester. On the front timbers are carvings of weird and wonderful medieval beasts, heraldically painted, including two snakes, and a basilisk being slain by St Michael. In the square is the Market Cross Inn, otherwise known as the Smugglers. At the beginning of the nineteenth century it was the home of Stanton Collins, leader of the Alfriston Gang, a highly successful group who knew every inch of the Downs and used Cuckmere Haven as their landing-point. They were a savage lot, like the Hawkhurst Gang over in Kent (see p. 278). One unfortunate revenue man, following a clifftop path marked out by lumps of chalk, fell over the edge, as the smugglers had deliberately moved some of the blocks to mislead him. He managed to cling to the top of the cliff and begged the smugglers to rescue him, but they stamped on his fingers and sent him hurtling to his death. Stanton Collins was finally arrested and transported, not for smuggling but for sheep stealing.

From the green at Alfriston you can walk across the Cuckmere by a footbridge and up a hillside path to Lullington Church. The walk back is the ideal way to appreciate Alfriston's harmony of church, village and water meadow.

South of Alfriston is a stretch of road called the **White Way**, the haunt of a well-vouched-for ghost which used to appear every seven years. Some time towards the end of the eighteenth century the young heir of the Chownes, a local family of landowners, was taking his dog for an evening walk along the White Way. He was set on by robbers, who knocked him down, killed him and buried him in a field near the road. The dog ran off, but came back and started whining by the grave, so the robbers killed it and buried it in the bank by the road. Seven years later to the day a couple walking along the road were accompanied by a mysterious white dog, which suddenly vanished into thin air – or rather, into chalk bank; and every seven years thereafter it made an appearance. Then, during a road-widening scheme, the skeleton of a young man was found by the road where the dog was seen to vanish. The bones were buried in Alfriston churchyard, and the hauntings ceased.

The road rises steeply to the aptly-named **High and Over**, hardly more than a gearchange or two to the driver, but a necessary place for a breather in the days of horsemen and stagecoaches. From High and Over, with its huge expanse of the downs all around and the glint of sea ahead, you drop down to the dull prosperity of **Seaford**, all golf courses, private schools and well-mannered housing estates, the quintessence of seaside gentility. Before the great storm of 1579 which changed the course of the Ouse, Seaford was at the mouth of the river and the port for Lewes, but after the storm the 'New Haven' superseded it. There are still traces of the old town in the streets round the church; this is basically medieval, much rebuilt in the last century, with a stepped tower that shows astonishing contrasts of stonework in its various layers. The modern esplanade has a high concrete sea wall: an obvious necessity, if you have ever tried to drive or walk along the front at Seaford during a high wind, with tons of water hurtling at you from the Channel. Beyond the martello tower at the end of the front the cliffs rise sharply to Seaford Head.

When the Saxons built **Bishopstone**, they sensibly placed it a good mile from the sea. It is still quite separate from Seaford, consisting of a large white-painted manor, a few houses and a noble church. This must be one of the few churches where the modern work is in fact Norman, as much of it, including the porch, was built before the Conquest, perhaps as early as the ninth century. The porch has a Saxon sundial over the door, inscribed with the name of the donor, Eadric. Inside there is some exceptionally fine arcading; and under the tower is a coffin lid decorated with crisp twelfth-century carving, including two doves drinking from a pitcher of water.

From Seaford you can either cross the Ouse to Newhaven (see p. 378), or follow the downs along the east bank of the Ouse. The Ouse is a more workaday river than the Cuckmere, but for that very reason its occasional surprises are all the more striking. The surprise on this road is **Tarring Neville**, a small square-towered church, with a sweep of mellow tiled roof, behind a group of large flintwalled barns basking in the sun. Across the river you can see the round tower of Piddinghoe church, and on the left the cranes of Newhaven docks.

Round a corner of the downs a cement works brings you back to earth. Its belching chimney covers all the ground and plants on the leeward side with white dust. **Beddingham** is a church without a village, but an impressive one, with a sturdy battlemented Perpendicular tower built in a pattern of flint and dressed stone.

Rising above Beddingham – and the most prominent landmark for miles around – is the rounded grass dome of **Mount**

Caburn, on the outlying bulge of downland that rises east of Lewes. About the third century BC, Celtic tribes built one of their strongholds there, surrounding it by the massive dyke and rampart that still form a great trough in the grassland. Caburn was hardly a town by modern standards – it is thought to have housed about seventy families – but it would have been the rallying point for defence for the villages round about, and the centre of organised crafts like cloth- and iron-making.

West Firle, a mile east of Beddingham, at the end of a cul-de-sac below the downs, is still very much the feudal English village. A gently curving street leads to the gates of **Firle Place**, and the church is full of the monuments of the Gage family. Firle Place was built by the Gages in Tudor times, possibly incorporating an older house on the site, and after four and a half centuries they are still there. The main front of the house, symmetrically classical, faces away from the village across an enormous park; the downland turf leads uninterrupted to the side of the building. Behind the eighteenth-century skin lies a Tudor courtyard house, with its great hall; a Tudor gable survives on the south front. This house was probably built by Sir John Gage, a tough soldier and un-compromising Catholic. Born in 1479, he fought in France and was appointed Comptroller of Calais; in 1542 he commanded the army that defeated James V of Scotland at Solway Moss. Henry VIII made him captain of the royal guard and Constable of the Tower of London. He still held this post in the reign of Mary, and presided at the execution of Lady Jane Grey. He died in 1556.

A portrait of Sir John in a long silver cloak dominates the white-painted staircase hall, a grand approach to the upper floor, which is part of the eighteenth-century rebuilding. Other portraits are of Lady Penelope Darcy and her three husbands. She had three suitors (one of them another Sir John Gage) and told them that if they were willing to wait she would marry them one after the other – which she did. Sir John, her second husband, died in 1633. Below the stairs a door leads into the great hall, still with its hammerbeam roof hidden by the eighteenth-century plasterwork. As it now stands it is a dull room, notable only for a huge Vandyck portrait of the Count of Nassau and his family, a pair of fine tapestries, and a portrait of General Gage, who was defeated by the Americans at Bunker Hill. If the eighteenth century sits uneasy in the great hall, the downstairs drawing-room is a perfect period piece. Gilt Ionic columns, portraits and furniture form a harmonious unity. The man responsible for Firle's reshaping was the first Viscount Gage, who set himself in a broken-pedimented frame at the end of the room; his wife, Benedicta Hall, looks down from the centre of the prettily ornate mirror over the fireplace. (His predecessor, Sir William Gage, has also been credited with the conversion.)

Upstairs the main feature is the long gallery, built by the first Viscount and stretching the length of the east front, above the wide entrance archway. The gallery is reached through an upstairs drawing-room, with a beautiful 'Holy Family' by Fra Bartolommeo over the mantelpiece. The anteroom beyond is an early-Victorian period piece; the fireplace wall is hung with a collection of blue-and-white porcelain plates, on a dark red ground. The gallery has a good sound collection of pictures, many of them from the collection made by the third Earl Cowper in the eighteenth century, and some elaborate pieces of furniture.

Firle church, with its massively buttressed thirteenth-century tower, is surprisingly wide and spacious for so small a village. It reached its final form only in the sixteenth century, when the Gage chapel was added on the north side of the chancel. By the door from the north aisle into the chapel are some very fine brasses; the chapel itself is dominated by the tomb of Sir John Gage and his wife Philippa, with every detail, from belt buckles to crowsfeet round the eyes, meticulously carved in alabaster.

Above Firle is **Firle Beacon**, at 713 feet the highest point on this stretch of the downs. To reach it is a good half hour's walk from the end of the road, but it is a walk well worth doing for its views southward of ridge beyond ridge of hills, with the glint of sea and the line of Newhaven breakwater in the distance. The width of the downs is hardly more than three miles as the crow flies, yet on a misty day they take on an illusion of immensity quite out of proportion to their actual size. The trackway runs past clusters of burial mounds – sunken in the middle and presumably plundered of their contents – to the Beacon, one of the South Coast warning beacons at the time of the Armada. From there it is another three miles' walk along the tops and down to Alfriston.

On the eastern side of Mount Caburn a narrow switchback road runs through Glynde, a quiet little village on a hill, generally ignored by those making for Glyndebourne a mile up the road. **Glynde Place** is a magnificent flint-built Elizabethan house. You get to it literally through the stables, passing under a blue cupola and then between massive gate piers surmounted by a pair of fearsome wyverns. These date from the mid eighteenth century, when the house belonged to Richard Trevor, Bishop of Durham. It was built in the 1560s for William Morley, on the site of a now-vanished medieval house. The original entrance was on the west side, facing the road; a Tudor arch leads under the west wing of the house into a peaceful quadrangle, where, by some acoustic trick of the surrounding walls, sounds fall unusually clear and sharp. The Morleys were mainly undistinguished, apart from Colonel Harbert Morley, a Parliamentarian and one of the judges at Charles I's trial. Fortunately for him, he refused to sign the death warrant, and so at the Restoration was able to buy his pardon from Charles II. The colonel's heir died young, and Glynde passed by marriage into the Trevor family. Bishop Richard Trevor inherited in 1743, after his cousin was killed in a duel.

The Bishop sensibly left the outside of the house unaltered, but thoroughly reconstructed the interior along classical eighteenth-century lines. His main innovation was to turn the whole place back to front, making the east side, facing across a sleepy expanse of parkland, into the main approach. The outcome is a kind of time-travelling, straight through an Elizabethan façade into a Georgian hall, with columns at either end, made of wood painted to look like marble. On either side of the front door are a pair of Alan Ramsay's coronation portraits of George III and Queen Charlotte. Ramsay churned out these portraits; there is another pair at Firle a couple of miles away. Much of the north wall is taken up by a large group portrait of the Trevor family, all most Puritanically dressed.

Upstairs, in the splendid Long Gallery, is a portrait of Bishop Trevor, a sleek prelate with a well-scrubbed countenance, who cut such a majestic figure in his canonicals that

George II called him 'the Beauty of Holiness'. Other Trevors hang round the walls, notably two brothers who both reached the summit of two very different careers in the first half of the seventeenth century, Sir Thomas Trevor, Chief Baron of the Exchequer, and Admiral Sir Sackville Trevor. Both portraits are by Cornelius Janssens. At one end of the gallery is an enormous silver centrepiece, with a statue of Victoria on top and plaques of politicians all around, given to Henry Brand (Lord Hampden), who was Speaker of the House of Commons in the 1860s. Much less obtrusive but far more interesting are the glass lacemakers' lamps collected by Mrs Brand, the present owner of the house. Filled with water, they magnified the light of a candle flickering behind, while the lacemakers strained their eyes over the intricacies of their craft.

Downstairs in the drawing-room is a sketch by Rubens for the ceiling of the Whitehall banqueting hall. It depicts the 'Apotheosis of James I', and shows a most reluctant monarch sprawled on an eagle's back, while brawny angels haul him towards whatever glory awaits him.

At the gates of Glynde Place is the parish church, built in 1763–5 on the site of the medieval church by Bishop Trevor. It is like a miniature version of St Paul's Covent Garden, in flint, with an open bellcote above the pediment. The architect was Sir Thomas Robinson, a follower of Wren and an enthusiast for Italian architecture. The interior is heavy with wooden columns and Victorian stained glass; unusually, the walls are covered in hessian with a faded arabesque design, which appears contemporary with the church.

Glyndebourne is now so much an international opera centre that it is hard to see it any longer as a prosperous country house with opera house attached. After nearly forty years, evening dress in mid afternoon and champagne and cold chicken by the lake have lost their novelty; but Glyndebourne still remains unique. The perfection of the setting has a lot to do with it – the clipped yews, the croquet lawn, the distant view of the downs beyond the lake, the cattle grazing on the other side of the ha-ha. The whole place is stamped with the personality of its founder, John Christie, schoolmaster, music-lover, and inheritor of the Glyndebourne estate. His marriage to an opera singer, Audrey Mildmay, confirmed him in his ambitions to bring opera to the English countryside,

and on May 28th 1934, Glyndebourne was launched on its
way by the cheerful intrigues of Mozart's *Marriage of Figaro*.
Christie's local interests in and around the estate included
hotels, building works and forestry, and it was this eminently
commercial base that enabled him to survive without over-
reaching himself. He set out the principles on which Glyndebourne should be run: 'One, we should aim at the sky, but
have our feet on the ground. Two, our work (being opera)
depends on having the necessary funds. It is our fault if we
cannot get the funds.' Spike Hughes, in his history of Glyndebourne, points out that the building of the opera house in the
lean years of the early 1930s saved many local labourers and
craftsmen from penury.

Ringmer, the gateway to Glyndebourne for motorists, is a
spacious village, with an enormous green, and a good deal of
modern building going on. The patron saint of Ringmer (if a
reptile can be a patron saint) is the tortoise who appears in the
centre of the elaborate village sign (on a triangle of land by
the road up to the church). This was Timothy, who belonged
to Mrs Rebecca Snooke, the aunt of Gilbert White of Selborne.
On his visits to Ringmer, White became fascinated by
Timothy's activities, and on his aunt's death in 1780 took the
tortoise back to Selborne with him. In *The Natural History of
Selborne* White observes the lethargic movements of Timothy
with his usual sharp-eyed amusement. 'It scrapes out the
ground with its forefeet, and throws it up over its back with
its hind; but the motion of its legs is ridiculously slow, little
exceeding the hour-hand of a clock; and suitable to the com-
posure of an animal said to be a whole month in performing
one feat of copulation.' Like all sensible tortoises, Timothy
disliked rain: 'though it has a shell that would secure it
against the wheel of a cart, yet does it discover as much solici-
tude about rain as a lady dressed in all her best attire, shuffling
away on the first sprinklings, and running its head up in a
corner.' Timothy's rain-proof carapace is now in the Natural
History Museum.

Ringmer church is basically fourteenth-century, with wide
side chapels of about 1500 which give a feeling of great
spaciousness and light. The chancel is slightly skewed on its
axis from the nave. The south chapel, known as the Springett
chapel, has a superb painted wall monument to Sir Harbert

Springett, who died in 1620. His son, Sir William Springett, is commemorated by a white marble bust. Sir William supported Parliament in the Civil War and was killed during the siege of Arundel in 1643, aged only twenty-three. His daughter Gulielma (with the additional name Posthuma, as she was born after his death) married William Penn, the founder of Pennsylvania. After heavy rain Sir Harbert Springett used to be driven to church over the atrocious local roads in a cart drawn by eight oxen. The notorious mud of the area before the days of field drainage and asphalt more than justified the derivation of Ringmer from Ryngmere, a place ringed by swamps and marshes.

East of Ringmer the A 273 runs along the northern edge of a flat plain, full of rich farms and crisscrossed by watercourses, with an angular grid of roads reminiscent of Romney Marsh or the Fens. **Laughton** is a scattered village; its church, half a mile south of the main road, has a long chancel built of flints and a lofty kingpost roof, and is dominated inside by a stone war memorial featuring a soldier and a sailor, with rifles carved down to the minutest details of bolt action and sights. The tower has the Pelham buckles (see p. 326), heavily weathered.

Beyond Laughton church the road zigzags down through **Ripe**, **Chalvington** and **Selmeston**, a trio of peacefully unmemorable villages. In the last century, when Selmeston was misleadingly pronounced Simson, its vicar was the Rev. W. D. Parish, who published his *Dictionary of the Sussex Dialect* in 1875. Apart from his dialect studies, he compiled collections of poetry for elementary classes, wrote an instruction book on the electric telegraph, and edited the Sussex Domesday Book. The *Dictionary* was a salvage operation. Even a century ago local dialects were dying out; so the vicar wandered among his parishioners, jotting down words, phrases and sentences. What could be more descriptive than 'Fluttergrub' for 'a man who takes a delight in working about in the dirt', 'Sussel' for 'disturbance; impertinent meddling', or 'Guess-sheep' for 'young ewes that have been with the ram and had no lambs'? Some of the usages he gives have been more tenacious than he expected. A gardener I knew about fifteen years ago still used the word 'terrify' in the old Sussex way. 'You can terrify that bellbine but you can't kill it' was his philosophy on getting rid of bindweed, based on half a century of unequal struggle.

Alciston, across the A 27 from Selmeston, once belonged to Battle Abbey, and is full of reminders of its monastic past – fishponds, a ruined dovecote, and a giant flint-built tithe barn which looms in front of the church, with its ancient roof timbers patched and repatched down the centuries, and sweeping red-tiled roof.

A mile along the main road is **Berwick**, an isolated farming hamlet, down a dead end like the neighbouring villages. From the outside its church is a simple twelfth-century building with broach spire; but inside it is a remarkable experiment in bringing the art of mural painting up to date. Commissioned by the go-ahead Bishop Bell of Chichester, Duncan Grant and Vanessa Bell decorated the upper surfaces of the walls with paintings including the Annunciation and Nativity (side walls), and Christ in Glory (chancel arch). The paintings, carried out in 1941–3, are not strictly murals, as they were painted on plasterboard and then fixed to the walls. Like Stanley Spencer's Cookham scenes, the Biblical stories are set in the countryside round about; thus for the Nativity Mount Caburn appears in the background, and two local shepherds were used as models. Bishop Bell and the rector of Berwick both appear on the Christ in Glory, beside the chancel arch. Nowadays the paintings look old-fashioned, yet as an overall scheme of decoration they make Berwick church well worth a visit.

The featureless landscape round the upper Cuckmere has recently been greatly enhanced by a new reservoir, best seen from the road north of Berwick station. Unlike so many similar schemes, this one has met with nothing but approval. Apart from supplying water to Eastbourne, it adds something of positive worth to the countryside, whether you look near by to **Arlington**, now a lakeside village, or in the distance to the downs, with a novel foreground of water. Arlington's church is Saxon and later, with an obviously Saxon window in the south wall and a few remains of medieval paintings on the walls. Seen across the lake, it now looks like an inland cousin to Bosham (see p. 430).

A couple of miles north of Arlington the Cuckmere was turned to good account by the Austin (Augustinian) canons

of **Michelham Priory** (owned by the Sussex Archaeological
Trust), who came here in the thirteenth century, taking over
the site of a moated Norman manor house. At first sight,
apart from the fourteenth-century gatehouse, Michelham is
not obviously medieval, as the later stonework of a Tudor
farmhouse masks what survives of the priory buildings. The
present building corresponds roughly to the south side of the
priory; to the north (marked out by stones set in the paths
and lawns of the immaculate garden) were the cloister, the
chapter house, and the long narrow church, of which nothing
at all remains. You go into the priory through the best of the
medieval survivals – a vaulted room which may have been the
visitors' parlour, now dominated by a lifesize figure of an
Austin canon, in black habit and wearing a broad leather belt.
The Tudor rooms are furnished with an impeccably presented
collection of Dutch paintings, Flemish tapestries and old
English furniture. Over the staircase is the upper half of the
tracery of the refectory's great west window; and at the top
of the stairs, above the vaulted parlour, is the Prior's Chamber,
presided over by the figure of a fork-bearded prior sitting at
his desk. In the gatehouse is a good group of brass rubbings,
and a reconstruction of a Sussex forge. On the first floor,
among the rubbings, a pre-D-Day map of the South Coast and
the Cherbourg Peninsula, scrawled on the wall, is preserved as
Michelham's most modern historical relic.

Hellingly, three miles upstream from Michelham, is a
pretty, loose-knit village, built between the Cuckmere and a
small tributary stream. The churchyard may well date back to
the eighth century, as it is in the form of a circular mound or
'ciric' typical of the early days of Saxon Christianity. Later
builders followed the circumference of this circle, so that even
the tilehung houses on the north side of the churchyard are
built round a curve. The church itself was built far later, about
1190, and has a good Early English chancel and north transept. The battlemented tower is a Victorian addition. Inside,
the church is dominated by a splendidly gilded organ on the
western gallery.

A couple of hundred yards down the road is the magnificently timbered **Horselunges Manor**, built about 1475 by the
Devenish family on a much older moated site. The timbers are
a mellow grey, as opposed to the usual startling contrast

between black wood and white infilling. The extraordinary name is probably a corruption of the names of two fourteenth-century owners of the house, Herst and Lyngyver. It was near Horselunges that in 1541 Lord Dacre of Herstmonceux murdered a gamekeeper while out on a poaching expedition; he was taken to the Tower and hanged at Tyburn after Henry VIII had turned down his plea for mercy. On the outskirts of Hellingly is a big comfortable pub, the Golden Martlet, with an aviary of exotic birds in the garden to give emphasis to its name.

In the last century, according to Augustus Hare, **Hailsham**'s rope factory had 'the privilege of supplying the cords used in prisons for executions'. Rope is still made there, though nowadays turned to less lethal purposes. Hailsham is a cheerful go-ahead place, with impressive plans for a completely car-free town centre, already partly achieved by a shopping precinct which is in scale and keeping with the Georgian buildings of the High Street. The fifteenth-century church has a sturdy pinnacled Perpendicular tower, built in chequers of flint and squared stone; the only trace of an older medieval building is an Early English capital set in a niche in the south chapel.

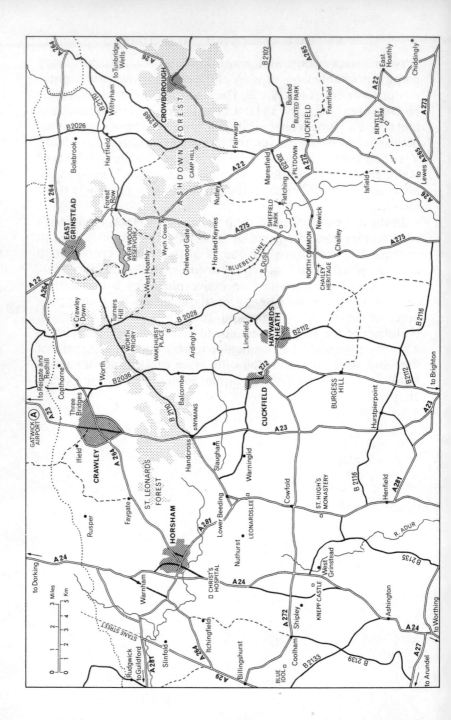

CHAPTER EIGHTEEN

Around Ashdown Forest

❧

Ashdown Forest, like Dungeness, is a world on its own. But whereas Dungeness is constantly altered and renewed by fresh additions of shingle washed round the coast, Ashdown Forest is immeasurably old – a tract of sandy heathland, where bracken, heather and scrub form an oasis of wildness amid the rich farmland that lies all around. A glance at a geological cross-section diagram through the Weald will show the reason for the Forest's uniqueness. It lies equidistant between the North and South Downs, and is made up of the lowest strata that lie beneath the great chalk dome which once covered Kent and Sussex. Millions of years of earth movements, erosion and weathering have worn away the crest of this dome, scouring the clays and greensands so that as you go inwards from the downs the soils get progressively older, with the sour sands of the Forest as the ancient core.

In shape it is a rough equilateral triangle, with the apex pointing downwards and the corners marked by Forest Row, Crowborough and Maresfield. It stretches for 14,000 acres, on nearly half of which the public is allowed to wander. On summer weekends it is crammed with picnickers, walkers and riders, who come here for the exhilaration of its tremendous views and wide expanse of sky. But you can get a better sense of the true solitude of the Forest on a sparkling winter's day, with the pine trees cut out against a blue background; while on a day of cold mist and sleet, when the views are hidden and all you can see are shrouded bushes by the road and the occasional startled sheep, it can seem hostile to your intrusion. Indeed, it is only modern town-dwelling man who has enjoyed the Forest as a place to relax in. Previous generations thought of it much as Cobbett did when he rode across it in 1822. He called it 'a heath, with here and there a few birch scrubs upon it, verily the most villainously ugly spot I ever saw in England.

This lasts you for five miles, getting, if possible, uglier and uglier all the way, till, at last, as if barren soil, nasty spewy gravel, heath and even that stunted, were not enough, you see some rising spots, which instead of trees, present you with black, ragged, hideous rocks.' Cobbett crossed it in January, so he may have been unfairly critical.

Like other high places, Ashdown Forest was used for track-ways by prehistoric man. The Romans drove the road from London to Lewes straight across it, using slag from the local iron bloomeries for the surface; stretches survive here and there. By Norman times the rights of the commoners living on the fringes of the Forest had become well established: the right among other things to graze cattle and pigs; to collect wood for fuel and bracken for roofing; to cut peat. Much of the story of the Forest (told most excellently by Garth Christian in his book *Ashdown Forest*) is concerned with the struggles of these stubborn Sussex men to maintain their rights. Their enemies might be kings or barons hunting deer in the Middle Ages, or landlords who wished to enclose and 'improve' the Forest in the eighteenth century. The commoners retaliated by poaching or illegally taking small bits of land for their own use; they were also great smugglers, even smuggling cannons to the enemies of England in the sixteenth century, as well as the usual brandy and lace in later years. These feuds and squabbles were not laid to rest until 1885, when the Board of Conservators of Ashdown Forest was set up, to resolve the conflicting claims and administer the Forest. (Though the conservators run the Forest, it is still owned by the De La Warr family.)

Nowadays the Conservators have all the usual environ-mental problems that arise where a large car-borne public is involved: first of all, what to do with the cars themselves; and secondly, how to make sure that the occupants do not set fire to the tinder-like gorse and scrub, obliterate the rare mosses and heathers, or scare off the badgers, fallow deer, curlews, and all the other creatures that survive in this delicately balanced wilderness. The Conservators make themselves plain enough by frequent small green notices telling you what is not allowed; however, gorse and withered bracken can be set alight by a cigarette end, and in a dry spring or summer brush fires are a recurrent menace.

Since the great trees were cut down for fuel to heat the ironmasters' forges, Ashdown has been a forest in name only. But there are still large woods here and there, like Five Hundred Acre Wood; and names like Hindleap Warren and King's Standing – the hunting post from which Edward II shot his game – perpetuate the chases of the past. The Forest's most famous sporting owner was John of Gaunt, Duke of Lancaster, who was granted it in 1372. For the next three hundred years it was known as Lancaster Great Park; and Garth Christian says that as recently as the last century the locals spoke about 'King John' as a living memory. But the sixteenth century saw the end of most of the large trees. The clumps of Scotch pines which are now prominent landmarks on every high point were planted in the last century, to give some relief from the monotony of which Cobbett complained.

Though the main coast road (the A 22) cuts across the eastern side of the Forest, the best quick impression of its wild spaciousness can be got from the B 2026 between Hartfield and Maresfield (incidentally following the Roman road for much of the way). The road climbs past the isolated Victorian church of **Fairwarp**, nothing much architecturally, but a curiously attractive place, with the hill rising steeply behind, and a backcloth of pine trees. The nearby hamlet of **Duddleswell** was formerly a haunt of smugglers and poachers. The summit plateau of the Forest begins at **Camp Hill** (650 ft.), near the red and white lattice aerials of the Diplomatic Wireless Service Station, where messages to and from embassies all over the world are transmitted and received.

Three miles to the north you leave the Forest again by **Chuck Hatch**, one of the many Gate and Hatch names that mark the perimeter, and date from the years when the Forest was a royal hunting park.

For over forty years Ashdown Forest has infiltrated the minds of children through A. A. Milne's Winnie-the-Pooh books, especially through E. H. Shepard's illustrations to them. Milne lived on the edge of the Forest near **Hartfield**; and all Pooh's adventures by sandy banks and streams, by gorse, thistles and snow, and above all by trees, have a firmly realistic setting, meticulously observed. Hartfield has no trace of the wilderness about it, but is thoroughly smart, to the extent of a painted-up Sussex cart outside the main pub. The village is built along a sharp dogleg; the church, with its magnificent landmark of a spire, is up an alley at the southern end. The lychgate originally led into the churchyard under a pair of Tudor half-timbered cottages, but only one is now standing, and a yew tree grows where its partner was.

Bolebrook, along the road to Edenbridge, was the home of the Dalyngrygge family, one of whom built Bodiam Castle (see p. 274). The towers of the Tudor gatehouse can be seen from the road.

Withyham, west of Hartfield, is hardly a village at all. In a way, it is an appendage of Knole (see p. 214), as the Sackvilles are buried in the church, the house and grounds of Buckhurst Park lie behind, and the pub is called the Dorset Arms. Buckhurst has been owned by the Sackvilles since about 1200 (the De La Warrs who live there are another branch of the family). From the stretch of grass in front of Withyham church you can see an English pastoral scene that cannot have changed since the eighteenth century, if not earlier: a pond directly below, gently undulating fields all around, and the spire of Hartfield glinting in the sun. The church is a hybrid. In 1663 it was struck by lightning, which 'came in at the steeple, melted the bells, and went up the chancel, where it tore the monuments of the Dorsets to pieces,' according to an eye-witness. It was soon rebuilt, spireless, and in a homely way, with dormer windows in the roof like those of a private house. The sundial over the porch is dated 1672, the year the re-building was completed.

All the old monuments in the Sackville Chapel were 'turned to lime and ashes' by the lightning; but what came afterwards is impressive enough. Below the coffered ceiling painted in blue and gold, and the rows of tattered banners, is a museum of two centuries of funerary carving, put there by a family who wanted nothing but the best and made sure that they got it. The centrepiece is the memorial to Thomas Sackville, son of the fifth Earl and Countess of Dorset, who died in France aged thirteen in 1675. Carved by the Danish sculptor Caius Gabriel Cibber, it shows the boy lying on a mat and holding a skull, while his parents kneel on either side. Cibber was paid £350 for the work, a vast sum in those days, and went on to become 'sculptor in ordinary' to William III. On the north wall of the chapel are three monuments by master sculptors

of their times: a composition of *putti*, urn and portrait of
the third Duke (died 1799), by Joseph Nollekens; two women
kneeling in grief for Arabella, his widow (died (1825), by Sir
Francis Chantrey; and a mourning mother figure, perhaps
Arabella, below a medallion of the fourth Duke, killed
accidentally in Ireland in 1815 (see p. 217), carved by John
Flaxman. Yet these grand monuments have no more real
dignity than the tablet which reads simply 'V. Sackville-West
C.H., poet', and nothing more.

On the aisle wall is a tablet to Sir David Maxwell Fyfe (died
1967), the Lord Chancellor, who lived in the village for the
last decade of his life.

When E. V. Lucas visited **Crowborough**, four miles south
of Withyham, in 1903, he found it plastered with posters de-
claring it to be 'Scotland in Sussex'. He goes on to say: 'Never
was a fine remote hill so bevilla'd. The east slope is all scaffold-
poles and heaps of bricks, new churches and chapels are
sprouting, and the many hoardings announce that Follies,
Pierrots, or conjurors are continually imminent.' Crowborough
is still growing, and growing fast. It spreads over Beacon Hill,
lapping against the edge of Ashdown Forest. Beacon House,
at its highest point (796 feet), is the highest inhabited spot in
Sussex. This house, built in 1838 and signed with the Abergavenny Arms (see p. 241) on its front, is one of the oldest in
the town, which shows how recent Crowborough is by Sussex
standards. At the heart of Crowborough is a triangular green,
with some buildings that look eighteenth-century on the south
side, and on the north a dark grey stone classical church,
built in 1744 and much enlarged in the 1880s. The modern
town centre is at Crowborough Cross, where two main roads
intersect and Edwardian gabled shops confront one another.
Conan Doyle lived at Crowborough for some time, as did
Richard Jefferies, the great observer of the Victorian countryside, towards the end of his life.

Maresfield, five miles south-west of Crowborough at the
southern corner of the Forest, is in dire need of a bypass, as it
stands where the A 22 makes a sharp bend and is joined by a
main east–west road. The most notable building is the tall
Georgian Chequers Inn, built on a bluff with the ground falling
away into the valley behind. Near it is a white-painted cast-
iron milestone, with the figure 41 and four bells in outline

surmounted by bows – one of the milestones on this road that refer punningly to the distance from Bow Bells. The church stands on the corner opposite. The Victorians sliced it right across the middle, leaving the medieval tower and west end, and adding a new chancel and transepts. It has a fine three-dimensional royal arms, carved and painted, and a Jacobean pulpit. Past the church on the Piltdown road are depressing acres of deserted Ministry of Defence hutments, formerly the headquarters of the Intelligence Corps, and now a blot on the landscape.

A mile east of Maresfield is **Buxted**, a featureless place: not surprisingly, in view of its history. For centuries Buxted had been the ordinary English village, with parish church, villagers' houses, and the great house of **Buxted Park**, all close together. Then in the 1830s the owner, Lord Liverpool, decided to shift the village outside the park, to give himself more privacy. The villagers refused to budge, so the noble earl refused in his turn to repair their cottages, until they became uninhabitable. The villagers finally moved out, and were transferred to new homes near the railway. This is the reason for the church's isolation, a short way down the park drive.

It is surprisingly large for a medieval parish church, but when it was built about 1250 it served an enormous area, covering Uckfield, Hadlow Down to the east, and Crowborough away to the north. It has an unusual dedication, to St Margaret the Queen, who was queen of Scotland in the eleventh century, and was, according to a local guide, 'the only saint who was canonised for the domestic virtues'. Three of her sons became kings of Scotland, and one of them, St David, inherited her sanctity. She is commemorated by marguerites carved on the Jacobean pulpit, and embossed on the magnificent moulded plaster ceiling of the chancel. Hop flowers decorate the sides of this ceiling, which is said to have been installed about 1600 by the rector of the day, in gratitude for a fine crop of hops. At the back of the church is an enormous chest for vestments, a good four feet high, reputedly thirteenth-century.

At the end of the churchyard a gate leads into the park. It is full of fallow deer and ancient trees – huge contorted oaks, and an avenue of vast limes, which runs at the foot of the hill, from the main road to the lake, and was the drive of the old house. This was pulled down in the early eighteenth century and the lake formed on its site; the present classical Buxted Park was completed in 1725. In 1931 it was bought by the architect Basil Ionides, who altered it considerably, mainly after a fire in 1940 had gutted it. He removed the top storey, reconstructed the interior, and made it a magpie's nest of bits from other houses that were being demolished or had been blitzed; thus the main staircase came from Old Burlington Street, and the front door from Clumber in Nottinghamshire. In recent years it has been run as a discreetly luxurious health home; but this closed down in 1971.

At the entrance to the park is the black-and-white half-timbered Hogge House, the home of Ralph Hogge, whose rebus (a hog and the date 1581) appears on the wall. Hogge is traditionally the first man to have cast guns in England, in 1543, according to an old rhyme which ran:

> Master Hogge and his man John,
> They did cast the first Can-non.

However, Ernest Straker, the expert on the iron industry, thinks it should be Huggett and not Hogge. In 1573 Hogge, describing himself as 'the quenes Maiesties gonnstone maker of yron', made a self-righteous complaint to the Queen about the malpractices of his competitors, stating that they were overcharging for shot, and illegally exporting guns overseas. The outcome was an immediate census of all the ironmasters, and a closing of the loopholes for illegal trade.

Maresfield is now practically joined to **Uckfield** by new housing estates. Uckfield's old town centre lies round the T-junction at the top of the High Street, which slopes steeply down to a level crossing (the cause of vast traffic hold-ups in summer). There are some good weatherboarded and tilehung buildings, and a large bow-windowed Georgian pub, the Maiden's Head. The rest of the High Street is an assortment of unmemorable twentieth-century shop design, except for the small cinema, which proclaims itself 'The Picture House, 1916', and is still showing films – surely a record among country-town cinemas. Uckfield church, long and low, with a grey-shingled spire, was built in 1839 on the site of a medieval building. Most of the churchyard is overshadowed by a gigantic and kingly cedar. Down the High Street and over the level crossing, Uckfield spreads south along the main road, and east along the A 272.

Uckfield's nearest neighbour in this direction is **Framfield**, which has a church similarly long and low, reached through an approach with good tilehung houses on either side. Built in 1288 and dedicated to Becket, this church has had more than its fair share of misfortunes: in 1509 it was severely damaged by fire, and in 1667 the tower collapsed and was not rebuilt for over two centuries. According to E. V. Lucas, in 1792 Framfield offered to field a cricket eleven from among its fifteen oldest inhabitants, whose combined ages added up to over a thousand years, but could find no suitably ancient opponents.

South of Uckfield the main road splits, one fork taking you in a zigzag way to Eastbourne, the other in an arc to Lewes and Brighton. The first place of any consequence on the East-bourne road is **East Hoathly**, at least twenty miles by road from West Hoathly. It is a compact village, and stands on what is probably the worst main-road bend in Sussex. The stocky church, up a side road, is mainly a rebuilding of 1855, but is a convincing piece of medievalism. The squat fifteenth-century tower is one of the so-called 'Pelham towers' found in the area; others are at Chiddingly and Laughton. They were built by the Pelham family, and have the Pelham family badge, a belt buckle, carved on them, usually on either side of the door. The badge was awarded to Sir John Pelham (who came from **Halland** near by) for his part in capturing King John of France at the Battle of Poitiers in 1356. There is a deep slit in the stone moulding on the right of the door, said to have been made by a bullet fired at a later Pelham, Sir Nicholas, in the seventeenth century. The would-be murderer was the Cavalier colonel Thomas Lunsford, who was fined £8,000 and outlawed. Lunsford had a wandering and adventurous life. During his exile he joined the French army, returned to England to fight for Charles I in the Civil War, emigrated to America, and died in Virginia in the 1650s. Like Sir Goddard Oxenbridge of Brede (see p. 290), the colonel left behind him a reputation for cannibalism.

Though not far from the main road, **Chiddingly**, three miles south-east of East Hoathly, seems utterly remote. The tall stone spire of its church looms up at you across the fields well before you get to the village, which is hardly more than a hamlet. The fifteenth-century spire, 130 feet high, was damaged by lightning in 1897 and is held together by an iron chain round its base. Inside the church there is a massive monument to Sir John Jefferay, Baron of the Exchequer under Queen Elizabeth. However, the reclining figures of Sir John and his wife are eclipsed by their daughter and son-in-law, who stand arrogantly large in niches on either side; the daughter's costume is a caricature of the Elizabethan farthingale. The drums on which they stand are said to be cheeses which they used as stepping-stones to walk from Chiddingly Place to church. At the top stand Father Time, and a grave-digger at work with his sleeves rolled up — a good near-contemporary illustration to *Hamlet*. The monument has lost hands and fingers, knocked off, the story goes, by infuriated locals who wrongly thought that the Jefferays were related to Judge Jeffreys of the Bloody Assize. Their Tudor mansion, Chiddingly Place, has come down in the world. Two sections of it survive, one a farmhouse, and the other used as a barn, with blocked-up mullion windows and straw poking out through the gaps.

Near Halland and **Terrible Down**, which looks as though it must have been given its name by Edward Lear, is the ideal antidote to a surfeit of villages or weekend traffic – the wild-fowl collection at **Bentley Farm** (open April–September, Wed. and weekends). Bentley is reached from a minor road linking the A 22 and the A 265, between big cylindrical flint gate piers. In the grounds about twenty-five acres have been dug with ponds, planted with trees and shrubs, and surrounded with fox-proof fences; and over a hundred varieties of wildfowl honk, hiss, squawk, swim and flap in as near-natural conditions as a reserve of this sort can provide. Flamingos stand philosophically on one leg; black swans with their brilliant red bills launch themselves silently upon the water; and the giant whoopers beat their wings, stretch out their necks, and utter their ear-splitting cries.

Isfield near by is a workaday farming village, stretching along a road above the Ouse. The railway station is closed and boarded up; but the tall flour mill is still functioning. The church, down a track and almost on the banks of the river, is worth visiting for the chapel and tombs of the Shurley family.

These begin with an inscription to John Shurley, who died in 1527 and was 'Chefe clerke of the kechen' to Henry VII and cofferer or treasurer to Henry VIII, and end a century later with the vast alabaster tomb of Sir John (died 1631), who lies impartially between his two wives, with nine children dutifully kneeling below. The chapel still has its sixteenth-century linenfold panelling and pews; the modern stained glass shows the Sussex Red cattle which are bred locally.

Going west along the A 272 from Uckfield, you come to the gorse, bracken and pines of **Piltdown Common**. Piltdown will always be remembered for the greatest archaeological hoax of all time; and the pub called the Piltdown Man still keeps its sign, with the famous skull on one side and a skin-clad stone-brandishing humanoid on the other. This skull, with its human braincase and apelike jaw, bewildered the archaeologists for forty years, from the time it was 'discovered' by Charles Dawson in 1912, until the fake was unmasked by modern scientific methods in 1953. Everyone believed in Piltdown Man because everyone wanted a 'missing link' between man and the apes. Besides, Dawson was a respectable lawyer. It is now known that the jaw was that of an orang-outang, and the braincase that of a medieval man whose bones had thickened by disease. Still, Piltdown Man was fun while he lasted.

Newick and Chailey are usually lumped together, though they are in fact two distinct and well separated places. **Newick** has expanded into a roughly oval shape along the main road and a minor one behind. It has a village green complete with long-handled pump, and a large new housing estate. The church, beside a farmyard a little way out of the village, is a simple building, with porch timbers about six hundred years old, and white doves flying in and out below the eaves. The Victorian chancel is elaborately tiled, painted and gilded.

Chailey is a much smaller place, built round a tiny green. The church has a strange pyramidal spire; though basically thirteenth-century it was much altered by the Victorians, which accounts for the angular jutting woodwork of the interior.

The modern centre of Chailey is not really a building or group of buildings, but an open area of land, the North Common. Nearly four hundred acres are now a local nature reserve, where wet and dry heathland and patches of rare sphagnum bog are preserved. This is not just an adult concern, as Garth Christian, whose book on Ashdown Forest has already been mentioned, had aroused the local children to an interest in and care for the land around them long before conservation had become fashionable.

Shooting up over the common is yet another tall spire, belonging to the chapel of the Chailey Heritage. The Heritage is one of the main centres in the country for rehabilitating handicapped children; as an inscription over one of the classroom doors says, with literal truth, 'We make men here'. It was founded in 1903 as an offshoot of a London home for boys with tuberculosis, called, in the patronising fashion of the time, 'The Guild of Brave Poor Things'. One of the founders, Dame Grace Kimmins, remained in charge for half a century and is commemorated by a tablet in the cloister. While TB no longer counts as a children's disease, the Heritage has expanded to deal with scourges like spina bifida and cerebral palsy, and looks after the victims of thalidomide. On the wall of the chapel is a rope from Scott's last expedition, placed there to symbolise the co-operation achieved at the Heritage.

Though **Fletching**, across the Ouse three miles to the east, was famous in the Middle Ages for making arrowheads, the name has nothing to do with the French word *flèche*, meaning arrow. It is another Saxon -*ingas* tribal name; fittingly, the church shows traces of Saxon work. Fletching does not sprawl: it has a beginning, a middle and an end. A large and prosperous-looking farm stands next to the church, and the smell of silage drifts lightly on the wind across the churchyard. The L-shaped village street has several good Georgian houses, and across the road from the church is a battlemented lodge and gateway to Sheffield Park.

Below the tall broach spire the church tower is Norman, with small rounded windows. Most of the building is Early English, completed about 1230; the arch between nave and tower may be Saxon, and is decorated with Norman chevron ornament. The unusually long chancel has lancets down the sides and an east window of strangely pointed Geometrical design. The church is connected with one of the great leaders of the Middle Ages, Simon de Montfort, who spent the night before the Battle of Lewes (see p. 375) in vigil there; after defeating Henry III he was virtually ruler of England until he was killed at Evesham the following year, in 1265. Another man as great in his way, Edward Gibbon, author of *The Decline and Fall of the Roman Empire*, is buried in the Sheffield mausoleum behind the north transept. He was a close friend of John Baker Holroyd, the first Earl of Sheffield, and spent the final months of his life at Sheffield Park. In the south transept is a unique brass showing not a human figure but a fashionable pair of fifteenth-century gloves. This commemorates a glover called Peter Denot, who is known to have taken part in Jack Cade's rising of 1450, but was pardoned. One of the new church bells, installed in 1949, was the gift of an insurance broker and is aptly inscribed 'I sing of heavenly assurance'.

When Gibbon stayed at **Sheffield Park**, the gardens that Capability Brown (or Repton, the authorities differ) had laid out can hardly have grown beyond the sapling stage. Now, after almost two hundred years, they are one of the glories of Sussex: trees and shrubs, lawns and glades around a series of four lakes, shaped like an inverted T, that lead down from John Baker Holroyd's Gothic Revival house. The house is privately occupied and cannot be visited, but it forms the pivot of the whole design, and its battlemented front and traceried chapel window make a perfect foil to the constantly changing vistas of trees and water. The National Trust bought the gardens in 1954 (open end of March to mid-November). At Sheffield Park the tree specialist can hunt for rarities like the coffin juniper which the Chinese grow (or grew in pre-Maoist days) to be sawn into planks for coffins; while the ordinary garden-lover can stand on one of the bridges between the lakes and marvel that the word 'tree' can mean such a profusion of column, sprawl, tight sphere, or shaggy irregularity.

Sheffield Park has no village; but there is an imposing Georgian pub, the Sheffield Arms, where even sandwiches are served up on a salver. It also has the southern terminus of the Bluebell Line, a five-mile stretch salvaged by enthusiasts from the old East Grinstead to Lewes railway, which potters gently through the countryside to **Horsted Keynes** (pronounced Kanes). The village is three miles north of Sheffield Park, off the A 265 and a good mile from Horsted Keynes station. The

'Keynes' in the name derives from a Norman baron called de Cahanges. There is a pretty village green, with a couple of good pubs. The Norman church, tucked away down a side road, has a tall shingled spire, round arches in the nave, and a pigmy Crusader's effigy, scaled down to fit a niche in the chancel.

Back on the main road is **Chelwood Gate**, where Harold Macmillan lives. In 1963 President Kennedy stayed with him here; a clump of pine trees and an inscribed stone slab commemorating the visit are on the west side of the main road, between Chelwood Gate and **Wych Cross**, where five roads meet at the heart of the Forest.

Forest Row, a couple of miles north, must be one of the few villages where the main pub – the tile-hung Chequers, once a coaching inn – is older than the parish church. The church is long and low, with a shingled spire, and was built in 1836. Opposite is the large village hall, built in 1892, which takes up most of the green; it is now the headquarters of the Conservators. A stone in the wall commemorates the visit of President Kennedy.

East of Forest Row are the ruins of the seventeenth-century **Brambletye House**; one of the corner towers, complete with roofcap, can be seen from the East Grinstead road.

Although **East Grinstead** is now a few miles away from Ashdown Forest, its name – the 'green steading' or clearing in the woodland – dates back to a time when the Forest was vastly more extensive than it is today. Like other commuting towns, it seems at first sight to consist of little more than an accumulation of new housing estates, especially if you approach it from the Surrey side. But its nucleus is a compact Sussex market town, with a High Street consisting largely of sixteenth-century half-timbered houses, and a large parish church towering up at its highest point. In fact, almost every building on the south side of the High Street has a Tudor look about it. One shop, which looks as though it is covered in strips of cork-bark between the timbers, has a strange collection of heads carved on the beams inside, including one that has been identified as Anne Boleyn's sister. On the corner at the eastern end of the High Street, set back a little from the road, are the grey stone walls and gables of **Sackville College**: not a college in the modern sense of the word, but a set of almshouses round an elegant quadrangle, founded by the Earl of Dorset in 1609. Over the turret at the back is the heraldic leopard of the Sackvilles, and until recently the men pensioners wore cassocks and the women capes and bonnets, embroidered with the Sackville arms.

Most eminent of the wardens who have run the college since its foundation was the Rev. John Mason Neale, who took it over in 1846 when it was at a low ebb and had improved it out of all recognition when he died twenty years later. Neale's tomb, in a small memorial garden in the churchyard, describes him as 'Liturgiologist, Ecclesiologist, Church Historian, author and translator of hymns.' The best known of his originals are *Good King Wenceslas* and *Jerusalem the Golden*, which he is said to have written looking down the valley to the spire of Bidborough church, ten miles away, lit up by the setting sun. Neale also appears inside the church, at the centre of the Oxford Movement centenary window in the north wall. He wears Byzantine vestments of green and gold, and is shown with John Keble and other leading figures in the movement for church reform.

The **Church** stands on an ancient site, but was rebuilt to James Wyatt's designs at the end of the eighteenth century, after the old tower collapsed in 1785, making the whole building unsafe. It is a great wide place, dedicated to St Swithun, whose connection with wet weather (and hence with ducks) is commemorated in the carving on the left-hand side of the high altar. Unusually, the rood screen is complete with a figure of Christ, as in a medieval church. Outside the porch are three plain graveslabs by the path in memory of the Protestants Thomas Dunngate, Anne Tree and John Forman, burnt at the stake in the High Street in 1556.

On the other side of the High Street, the Dorset Arms, a Georgian coaching inn, lends itself to some speculation by its inscription 'For Familes and Gentlemen'. Inside, if you reckon you come into either of these categories, you can find among other things a framed railway share of the East Grinstead Railway Company, valued at £25 and dated 1853.

In recent years East Grinstead has been most famous for the pioneer work in plastic surgery carried out at the Queen Victoria Hospital, inspired by Sir Archibald McIndoe, who worked there from the start of the Second World War until

his death in 1960. The hospital is about a mile north of the
High Street; the latest addition to the complex of buildings
is the McIndoe Burns Centre, built in the 1960s for research
into the treatment of severe burns. The hospital is still the
centre of the Guinea Pig Club, consisting of airmen who were
severely burned or facially injured in the war, most of whom
had been treated by McIndoe. There is a portrait of him in the
main vestibule below the clock tower.

South of the town is Saint Hill Manor, a dull stone eighteenth-
century house with some noble trees in the garden, proclaiming
itself the 'Hubbard College of Scientology'. You can go round
Saint Hill and look at rows of budding scientologists filling in
forms or listening to tape recorders, following in the steps of
Ron Hubbard, the American founder of the movement.
Warning notices like 'You may bump into Ron' keep them to
the straight and narrow. The house was owned by the Maharajah of Jaipur before the scientologists came there.

Beyond Saint Hill the road curves downhill to give wide
views over the **Weir Wood Reservoir**. With its wooded head-
lands, surrounding hills and rock outcrops, and flocks of
moorhen and mallard, it is the nearest approach to the Lake
District this part of England can provide. During the autumn
migrations the reservoir is visited by all sorts of wildfowl;
and curlews can sometimes be seen there.

South of the reservoir the road leads east to Wych Cross
(see p. 331). On the north side of the road is **Plaw Hatch
Hall**, a country club owned and run by trades unionists. The
gaunt stone house was built in 1874 by a banker called
Arbuthnot, and has a fine site looking north across the
reservoir to the hills beyond. In early summer the gardens are
appropriately ablaze with red rhododendrons. Inside the walls
are covered in socio-realist paintings; one vast canvas, showing
every manifestation of anti-establishment protest from John
Ball to CND, must be making Arbuthnot turn in his grave.
Arbuthnot's motto, 'Innocent and True', is carved in stone
above the front door: a good target for both bankers and
trades unionists to aim at.

West Hoathly, built on a ridge south-west of the reservoir,
was a centre for smugglers, who were especially fond of the
Cat Inn. The village church, with its squat tower and needle
spire, and the stone manor house face each other across the

street. Down the road is the fifteenth-century **Priest House**, a low half-timbered building with a roof of massive Horsham stone slabs. Before the Reformation this was the estate office for the monks of Lewes Priory, who owned the manor; it is now a small museum run by the Sussex Archaeological Society. The collection includes old furniture, and bygones such as mantraps, and shepherds' smocks treated with oil to keep out the rain. As recently as 1905 it was a ruin; it is now the perfect country cottage. West Hoathly church was begun soon after the Conquest. The north wall of the nave, built about 1090, survives from the original building, which was altered and enlarged throughout the Middle Ages, the tower being added about 1400. Inside are some iron graveslabs of the Infield family, who were ironmasters of Gravetye. By the door is a gigantic chest, said to be twelfth-century, hollowed from a single oak log; and on the south wall near by is a little brass to Anne Tree, one of the East Grinstead martyrs. Inscribed 'She was remembered in 1940. George Friend made this', it must surely be about the most recent portrait brass in the country.

In a combe north of West Hoathly is **Gravetye Manor**, an Elizabethan ironmaster's house, now a hotel. The road to Gravetye winds down through Forestry Commission conifer plantations, which cut off the house from the outside world. The stone house, gabled and mullioned, was built in 1598, but it was greatly extended by William Robinson, who lived there for over half a century, from 1884 to 1935. Robinson was a landscape gardener who pioneered the English natural garden style at the end of the nineteenth century (see Nymans, p. 342). Though there is a small formal garden at the back of the house, most of Robinson's plantings make use of the contours of the narrow valley, centring on a lake hidden behind tall trees and surrounded by reeds and bulrushes.

The tall spire and squat west towers of Chichester Cathedral, seen from the forecourt of the Bishop's Palace.

The Market Cross, Chichester. Octagonal in plan, it was built in 1501, with a space underneath for market traders.

CHAPTER NINETEEN

Crawley and Horsham

❧

I T is easy to feel depressed as you first enter a New Town, and contemplate the rows of monotonous houses, varied only by texture of wall and colour of roof, the shopping precincts with their concrete tubs of geraniums and plastic shopfronts, the regulation spindly churches and sprawling schools, the general impression of a thin urban gruel, sieved through the planner's mind and slopped down over a few thousand acres of country-side. As one of the original New Towns designated after the New Towns Act of 1946, **Crawley** is open to such criticism. Nevertheless, these towns are places where people can live and work without exhausting journeys to office or factory, and where housewives can shop and children can play without constant danger from traffic. A couple of hours spent wander-ing about Crawley will show how infinitely better it is than any unplanned alternative.

Crawley is really an amalgamation of the villages of Three Bridges and Ifield with the small market town of old Crawley. A quarter of a century ago the population was about 10,000, and by the 1980s it will probably have reached 100,000. In the process the old nuclei have been swamped but not com-pletely submerged. Crawley has been there probably since Saxon times. After centuries of a quiet life, it woke up briefly at the end of the eighteenth century when the Prince Regent and his friends used it as a convenient stopping place on their journeys to and from Brighton, faded again when the London–Brighton railway removed most of the through traffic, and has now presumably embarked on its ultimate phase of pros-perity. Before the New Town was started Crawley was hardly noticed; though at the turn of the century E. V. Lucas wrote of it: 'One would be hard put to it to think of a less desirable existence than that of dwelling on a dusty road and continually

A map for this chapter will be found on page 318.

seeing people hurrying either from Brighton to London or
from London to Brighton. Coaches, phaetons, motor cars,
bicycles, pass through Crawley so numerously as almost to
constitute one elongated vehicle.' The town centre is now
bypassed, so it may well be quieter today than it was in the
1900s.

Crawley's wide High Street runs due north–south. If you
turn your back on the vast bowling-alley building at the
northern end and look down the street, you can still get something of the illusion of a market town. On your right is the
George Hotel, a long low coaching inn, with Horsham stone
slabs on the roof and a 'gallows' inn sign across the road; and
on your left a row of old houses, among them the jutting
gables and timbering of the Ancient Prior's Restaurant,
thought to have been built originally for the parish priest.

The medieval church is down a small approach on this side
of the street, with the main shopping centre behind. The oldest
part of the church dates from about 1290, but much is nineteenth-century rebuilding. The best thing about it is the
fifteenth-century roof (contemporary with the tower), which
has the panels between the beams boarded over, and an
arcaded framework of strengthening timbers. An inscription
in medieval English on one of the beams warns of the vanity
of wealth. There is a nice Charles I pulpit, with an inscription
on the ledge which reads 'Be brief' (Acts XX, 9). The verse in
question runs: 'And there sat in the window a certain young
man named Eutychus, being fallen into a deep sleep: and as
Paul was long preaching, he sunk down with sleep, and fell
down from the third loft, and was taken up dead.' (Fortunately
Paul was able to resuscitate him.) Mark Lemon, the first
editor of *Punch*, is commemorated by one of the north aisle
windows. Lemon, who was a playwright as well as a journalist,
was co-founder of *Punch* in 1841 and edited it until his death
in 1870.

Immediately north of the church is the main shopping area,
centred on Queen's Square, a wide expanse of paving, with
curlicued bandstand, and clock tower. The tower is a constant
reminder of the London to Brighton run; when the mechanism
is in working order, models of veteran cars trundle below
the clock face, and a carillon plays the tune from the film
Genevieve. Along The Boulevard are the civic buildings – the

hulking GPO, the long low Town Hall, the tower block of the College of Further Education. Only a mile or so farther north, past the gleaming buildings of the factory estate, you are into Surrey and the roar of Gatwick Airport. The county boundary is still marked on the map as 'County Oak', though the tree was cut down in the last century. (At the time of writing a planning debate is going on as to whether Gatwick, the commuter town of Horley and the village of Charlwood should be taken from Surrey and included in the revised boundaries of West Sussex.)

Unlike **Three Bridges**, which is almost totally absorbed by Crawley's eastward spread, **Ifield** keeps some of its village character. It marks the western limit of the town. you can stand in the churchyard and look across miles of farmland. Church, pub and cottages lie down a cul-de-sac. The church (usually locked because of vandalism) is a typical thirteenth-century Sussex building, with a low tower surmounted by a shingle cap. Inside there are two fine tombs of about 1340, one on either side of the nave; the carved recumbent figures are thought to be Sir John de Ifield and his wife Lady Margaret.

From Ifield you can go by devious back roads to **Rusper,** a little village tucked away near the Surrey border. There used to be a nunnery at Rusper, and a prioress and four of the sisters are buried in the churchyard. The church has a medieval tower, but the rest of it was rebuilt in 1855 by the Broadwood family of piano manufacturers. Lucy Broadwood (1858–1929), who has a memorial tablet with a white profile medallion inside the church, was a key figure in the English folksong revival, led by Cecil Sharp. The fence on the north side of the churchyard is marked with Roman numerals, each number corresponding to a family responsible for the upkeep of that section of the fence. Rusper's forge has gone, but the two huge bellows can still be seen attached to the wall of the Star Inn, flanking the village pump.

South of Crawley the land is still heavily wooded, with St Leonard's, Tilgate and Worth Forests forming a fairly continuous belt. **Worth** village, south-east of Crawley off the B 2036, stands on the edge of the woodland, with suburbia to the north, and lakes and gnarled trees to the south. Its church is mainly Saxon, though it does not look it from a distance, as it has a Victorian tower and broach spire. Seen from close

to it is monumentally solid, with thick walls and little round-
arched windows high up, in pairs separated by dumpy pillars.
In the north wall is an enormously tall Saxon doorway, now
blocked up. Inside, the church is equally massive, with high
rounded chancel arch, and lower, narrower arches to the
transepts. This ponderousness is reflected in the heavy
balusters of the gallery, dated 1610. Pride in Saxon origins is
proclaimed on an inscription in the north chapel to Thomas
Whitfield (died 1631), who was 'discended from ye right
ancient and long before ye Norman Conquest generous
familye of Whitfeld'. And outside the south porch, the inscription to 'poor old John', the Victorian sexton, celebrates a
life spent

> Within the walls by Saxons reared of old,
> By the stone sculptured font of antique mould,
> Under the massive arches in the glow,
> Tinged by dyed sunbeams passing to and fro.

Worth Abbey, a nineteenth-century tycoon's home turned
into a Roman Catholic public school and monastery, is a
few miles away on the B 2110 to Turners Hill. From the road
you can see what was originally the stable block, a red-brick
quadrangle with battlemented brick gatehouse. The huge
grey stone house lies a little below, on a slope with magnificent
views away to the south. It owes its present form to Lord
Cowdray, who added greatly to Paddockhurst, as it then was,
after buying it in 1894. Cowdray made a fortune from civil
engineering works, including the Admiralty Harbour at
Dover and the Blackwall Tunnel under the Thames; he left
£6 million when he died in 1932. Paddockhurst was his weekend cottage – on which, when he was really working at it, he
spent £10,000 a month in improvements. The house is
plastered with the Cowdray crest (the unusual supporters are
a diver and a Mexican peasant, symbolising harbour engineering and oilfields in Mexico), and with its richly coffered and
painted ceilings and stained glass has a sumptuousness that
rivals its Tudor models. Around the room now used as the
monks' refectory is a moulded frieze done by Walter Crane
in 1896, showing the evolution of transport from Stone Age
man to the Age of Steam. Paddockhurst was bought by the
Benedictines in 1933 as an offshoot of Downside. The latest

addition, still under construction, is a round church that bears a close family resemblance to the Liverpool Catholic cathedral. Before Lord Cowdray bought Paddockhurst, it belonged to Robert Whitehead (1823–1905), a marine engineer who in the course of a much-travelled life was a friend of Garibaldi, and invented the torpedo.

Turners Hill has a big landmark of a late-Victorian church, which stands at the highest point for miles and catches every wind that blows. The village climbs the steep north face of the hill, with a crossroads pub and a bogus but nice group of half-timbered houses round a lawn, on the East Grinstead road.

Three miles south of Turners Hill, off the B 2028, is **Wakehurst Place**, the Tudor home of the Culpeper family whose ramifications spread through Kent and Sussex. The Culpepers got hold of Wakehurst in the fifteenth century, when two Culpeper brothers abducted two Wakehurst girls, who were carried off 'makyng grete and pittious lamentation and weping.' However, the *fait accompli* led to the respectability of marriage, and both couples settled down at Wakehurst. A descendant, Edward Culpeper, built the gabled stone house in 1590. Down the centuries, and especially since 1900, Wakehurst's owners have built up a magnificent collection of trees and shrubs, now owned by the National Trust and run as an offshoot of Kew Gardens (gardens open every afternoon except Christmas Day). As at Kew, the trees are labelled and often marked with the date of planting. To see the gardens properly, you must be prepared to walk at least a couple of miles, as they are on a vast scale, and include every kind of scenery from an enchanted lake studded with tiny islands to a long path below a rampart of dank and mossy rock.

Nowadays **Ardingly** is chiefly famous for the showground of the South of England Agricultural Society, which holds a three-day annual show in June. The modern village is next to the showground on the main road; old Ardingly, consisting of a church and a few houses, is on the twisting back road to Balcombe. (It is best approached from the Balcombe side, as you then become aware of its commanding position above the narrow valley formed by one of the headwaters of the Ouse.) The church, with its stocky fifteenth-century tower, is a mixture of the medieval and the Victorian. On the chancel floor are some exceptional brasses to the Tudor Culpepers, naively portrayed, one couple with ten sons and eight daughters. There is a delicately carved fifteenth-century screen, and at the other extreme of carpentry a tower staircase of rough-hewn logs cut across the diagonal to form wedge-shaped steps. In 1643 the men of Ardingly are said to have used the churchyard wall as a defensive position against Cromwell's dragoons, who had come to expel the Royalist rector.

Ardingly College, down another back road, is one of the Rev. Nathaniel Woodard's Sussex public schools (see Lancing and Hurstpierpoint, pp. 404 and 367). It is a large, red brick place, with a squat-towered chapel and huge east window as the central feature, and is set back behind lawns in a beautiful stretch of country.

Three miles south of Ardingly is **Lindfield**, a famous beauty spot and almost too done up for its own good; it is so popular that even in winter there are queues in the tea-rooms. Nevertheless, with its wide common, village pond and gently sinuous High Street leading uphill to the church, it is a beautiful place, and everybody's ideal of the English village. The houses are mainly brick and tile-hung; a few of them are pink-washed, more like Cornwall than Sussex. The grand Queen Anne and Georgian houses are at the top of the hill, near the church. Older and more fascinating is Old Place, down the lane behind the church. It is basically a small Tudor timber-framed house, with three gables, the central one leaning at a drunken angle. It owes its present great size to Charles Kempe, the Victorian stained-glass artist, who lived at Old Place and made it an accumulation of architectural bits and pieces. The original house is said to have been Queen Elizabeth's country cottage; similarly the pretty thatched cottage next door is said to have been Henry VIII's hunting lodge.

The church is mainly thirteenth- and fourteenth-century, almost as wide as it is long, and has an enormously tall spire – a necessary landmark when the country was still heavily wooded. Inside it is not particularly interesting. The roof of the north transept, originally reached from outside, was once used as a pigeon loft. In the nineteenth century the church was famous for its band, consisting of a flute, two clarinets, bassoon, violin and cello: six instrumentalists all made redundant when the organ was installed. Helena Hall's excellent parish guide prints several old churchyard inscriptions, now mostly illegible. An eighteenth-century one ran as follows:

> Long was my Pain, great was my Grief
> Surgeons I'd many, but no relief
> I trust through Christ to rise with the just
> My leg and thigh was buried fust.

Beside the churchyard is Church House, formerly the Tiger Inn. After the defeat of the Armada in 1588, the Tiger supplied so much strong ale to the triumphant bellringers that they broke all the ropes and cracked one of the bells. Now it is used for more sober church business.

At its southern end Lindfield links up with **Haywards Heath**, a commuting and shopping sprawl, with a mile or so of the A 272 as its centre. Its prosperity is due to the fact that both Lindfield and Cuckfield refused to have a railway running through them. So it was built across a stretch of heath running between the two; a church (said to be the centre of Sussex, if a county so long and narrow can have a centre) was built in the 1860s; and the houses proliferated.

Cuckfield (pronounced Cookfield) still keeps plenty of its small country town character. On the outskirts is a sign showing a cuckoo on a tree – a reference to one derivation of the town's name from the Saxon 'Cucufelda', a clearing full of cuckoos, Or it may mean 'land surrounded by a quickset hedge', less poetic but more probable. In Norman times it belonged to William de Warenne, son-in-law of William the Conqueror, who had a hunting lodge and chapel there. Cuckfield is built on the side of a hill, with a steep High Street running down to an attractively irregular group of old houses and shops, and the tall-spired church rising behind. This is a noble church on a noble site, which gives enormous views southwards over woodlands to the downs. The tower was built in stages in the thirteenth and fourteenth centuries, and the main structure was completed about 1366. The nave has a fifteenth-century wagon roof, painted in Victorian times with most medieval-looking roses and foliage. Under the tower is the old clock mechanism, dated 1667.

The White Hart near by is said to be thirteenth-century. On the other side of the road a footpath runs along the side of

Cuckfield Park, an Elizabethan house with a little Tudor gatehouse which can be seen through the trees. Ockenden Manor, now a hotel, is a seventeenth-century stone house built by the ironmaster William Burrell. Relics of old Cuckfield are kept in the public library (Queen's Hall) in the High Street.

Balcombe, three miles north of Cuckfield, is a largish village, with a few old houses at its compact centre, and an out-of-doors antique shop selling anything from a stone sphinx to a wrought-iron spiral staircase. The church, buried in holly trees and conifers, is a little way to the north. It was completely restored in the nineteenth century, apart from the medieval tower with its low broach spire. Near Balcombe are two of the highlights of the London–Brighton railway – a tunnel under the forest to the north, and a viaduct over the Ouse to the south.

The lane between Balcombe and Ardingly (see p. 339) is so pretty that it should be closed to all traffic except walkers and cyclists. Its curves and dips bring you to a scene like a Chinese painting – a small lake with an island in the centre and water-fowl everywhere, weeping willows, and the water cascading under the road to drive a vanished watermill.

North of Balcombe you are back in the forest. The best impression of these towering miles of trees can be got from the B 2110 to **Handcross**. Vast pollarded beeches have been left to shoot up to the limit of their growth, and in places the road is hemmed in by walls of self-sown rhododendrons.

Handcross itself is little more than a flyover across the Brighton road surrounded by houses; but near it are the superb National Trust gardens of **Nymans**. The centrepiece is a roughly circular walled garden, laid out in a wavering symmetry with the help of two of the pioneers of the gardening revival at the end of the nineteenth century, William Robinson (see Gravetye, p. 334) and Gertrude Jekyll. The rest of the garden is a series of outdoor 'rooms', like the heather garden, with heather shoulder high, and the sunk garden, with con-centric flower beds round a tall white Byzantine urn. Much of the great house was burnt down in 1947, and the empty shell of golden stone provides a hauntingly unreal backcloth to lawns and massed banks of rhododendrons.

To the south is **Slaugham** (pronounced Slaffem), only half a mile from the Brighton road, but amazingly remote. It has a heathland common, with a large pond surrounded by reeds and full of birds; a neat village centre with houses on either side of a dead-end; and a church that dates from Norman times. Its strange name has been derived from various Saxon words: *sloh* for a slough or marsh, *slogu* for iron dross or slag, and *slaga* for a slayer or hunter have all been suggested. The church was greatly restored about 1860, but still keeps its thirteenth-century tower. In the south chapel is a magnificent monument to Richard Covert, who died in 1579. Seventeen little stone figures all face the east, men and boys in front, women and girls behind. They have been spared the usual mutilations and knocks, and the carving is beautifully clear, down to the embroidery on the sleeves. The Coverts came from Slaugham Place, south of the church; the large lake in the grounds can be seen from the churchyard.

Warninglid is in the same quiet hinterland, a hamlet guarded by a village sign depicting a spear-brandishing Saxon, with the words 'Werna Gelad' inscribed mysteriously over his head. Down a lane is a very unrural inn called the Rifleman, a Chelsea or Brighton pub transferred to the country-side, and full of shakoes, Greenjacket uniforms, and engravings of riflemen in combat.

Hilaire Belloc cited **Lower Beeding**, a couple of miles west of Warninglid, as a typical example of a Sussex name that 'should give fools to think'. In *The Four Men* he wrote of 'the height called Lower Beeding, which means the lower place of prayer, and is set upon the very summit of a hill. Just as Upper Beeding is at the very lowest point in the whole County of Sussex, right down, down, down upon the distant marshes of Adur.' It has a solid grey Victorian church, and a solid yellow ochre eighteenth-century pub, the Plough. In late spring it is a Mecca for lovers of rhododendrons and azaleas, who come to see the marvellous **Leonardslee** gardens (open in May). Begun in 1887 by Sir Edmund Loder, after whom the *Loderi* rhododendron varieties are named, Leonardslee is an enthusiast's garden. It is formed in a deep valley, with a string of hammerponds along the bottom reflecting the plantings that rise on either side. The Victorian house stands on an open lawn above, from which you plunge into tunnel-like paths overshadowed by huge rhododendrons, their flowers white or pink-flushed, towards the sound of running water in the valley. Leonardslee, Nymans, Wakehurst and Sheffield Park form a quartet of superb gardens which must be hard to rival anywhere in the country.

Nuthurst, two miles farther west, consists of a few houses and a spindly church, worth a look for its brilliantly painted chancel and rood screen, a redecoration done in the 1940s. On the south wall is a tablet to Sir Nevile Henderson (died 1942), who came from Sedgwick Park near by. The inscription 'Blessed are the peacemakers' is an ironic epitaph for the man who, as ambassador to Germany at the time of Munich, supported the appeasement policy that made war inevitable.

You can get the best idea of **St Leonard's Forest**, east of Horsham, from the minor roads that cut across it. It gets its name from a chapel to the saint that once stood there. In the days when the trees were continuous and the gloom lay heavier, the forest was a great breeding-place for legends. St Leonard himself fought and finally conquered a dragon there; wherever the saint's blood fell on the ground, clusters of lily-of-the-valley sprang up. A later dragon was vouched for in 1614 by three locals from Faygate, on the edge of the forest. The *Harleian Miscellany* gives their account of the monster. It was 'reputed to be nine feete, or rather more, in length, and shaped almost in the forme of an axeltree of a cart, a quantitie of thicknesse in the middest, and somewhat smaller at both endes. The former part, which he shootes forth as a necke, is supposed to be an elle long; with a white ring, as it were, of scales about it.' As if that were not bad enough, the dragon could 'cast his venome about four rodde from him', and could kill at a distance; and wherever he walked he left 'a glutinous and slimie matter . . . which is very corrupt and offensive to the scent.'

Apart from the presence of dragons, the forest was famous for an absence of nightingales, after a sour-tempered hermit, like Becket at Otford (see p. 221), had banished them for disturbing his meditations.

Horsham is a town of contrasts, typified by the row of weatherboarded cottages, their gardens crammed with vegetables, directly opposite the busy station in the middle of the town. At the moment it is undergoing a drastic central redevelopment, which will integrate the ancient streets with underpasses, shopping precincts and car parks, bringing in the new without disrupting the old. Like Oxford, Horsham has a Carfax at its centre; and like Chichester it has a sensible arrangement of North, South, East and West Streets, so that you know where you are. The Carfax is a conglomeration of shops, pubs (the King's Head is dated 1401) and brewers' premises, with a bandstand and tall plane trees facing the battlemented town hall. Behind the town hall (about three hundred years old, and now virtually disused) is the Causeway, Horsham's architectural gem – a quiet cul-de-sac of old houses leading down to the church. At the top end is the gabled sixteenth-century Causeway House, now the town museum (open weekday afternoons except Monday). This big rambling house is ideal for the purpose; it specialises in local material from Horsham, or from Sussex in general, with wheelwright's and saddler's shops, a blacksmith's forge, and a Sussex farmhouse kitchen. Among the old prints, paintings and photographs is an extraordinary drawing of a hard-labour machine installed in Horsham Gaol – a long row of cubicles, each with a hand-operated crank connected to a vast wind vane which purposelessly beat the air. A parable on the futility of the penal system.

The Causeway ends at the church, and the town does too. Beyond are meadows where the Arun, still a small stream, flows by. The church has a massively buttressed tower begun in the twelfth century, crowned by a soaring, twisting spire. On the left as you face the entrance is the low cube of the 'Lollards' Tower', which is not a tower and is unlikely to have any connection with the Lollards, though it may have been used as a prison. Inside, the church is basically Early English, with a vast Perpendicular seven-light window filled with garish glass, and a strange Victorian annexe to the south aisle. There are medieval tombs on either side of the altar: on the left an altar tomb dated 1485, which has a lute-playing angel carved on the canopy frieze; and on the right the tough-looking effigy of Thomas de Braose (died 1395), minus his nose. The most famous local inhabitant of all is commemorated by a simple tablet under the tower, which reads 'Percy Bysshe Shelley. 1792–1822'.

Shelley came from Warnham, a small well-groomed village

two miles north-west of Horsham. A good many of the houses are roofed with slabs of Horsham stone, which give a feeling of antiquity, regardless of the age of the buildings they cover. The church, basically fourteenth-century, has a fine wall monument to Sir John Caryll (died 1613) and his 'sweetest and most religious wife' Lady Mary, and numerous Shelley memorials. The poet himself has no monument, though a case in the south aisle contains a copy of the entry of his baptism (on September 7th, 1792) from the parish register. His ashes are buried in Rome, and his heart is in his son's tomb in Bournemouth. He was born at **Field Place** outside the village, a largish country house, with a stuccoed and colonnaded front looking on to immaculate lawns (the gardens are occasionally open to the public). The lawns lead down to a small lake, where Shelley sailed paper boats as a boy.

Three miles west of Horsham, Stane Street (A 29) branches off from the A 281. A couple of miles west of the junction a side road leads to **Rudgwick**, running uphill to the sturdy church on the Surrey border. The oldest part is the squat west tower, built in the thirteenth century, with huge corner buttresses; the twelfth-century font is made of Sussex marble – a stone that preserves the shells of sea creatures fossilised and clearly discernible.

Back on Stane Street, for a mile or so south of the junction the road runs on top of a very obvious *agger* (raised causeway), several feet higher than the broad grass verge.

Slinfold is worth a detour down the back lanes. It has a gently curving village street, a good Victorian church with a choice of two stone-roofed lychgates, and a nicely varied collection of houses.

Itchingfield, still farther into the countryside to the south-east, is hardly a village at all. The church, down a cul-de-sac, is basically Norman, built about 1125; it has an astonishing 600-year-old belfry tower made entirely of vast beams held together by oak pegs. When Sir Gilbert Scott was restoring the interior in the 1860s, his workmen found a skull high up on one of the beams. It is said to have been the head of Sir Hector Maclean, executed for his part in the Old Pretender's rising of 1715. Maclean was a friend of the vicar of the time, who presumably put this macabre souvenir on the beam for safe keeping. In the churchyard is a pretty little brick-and-timber priest's house, put up in the fifteenth century as an overnight lodging for the priest who rode over from Sele Priory, at Upper Beeding (see p. 363), to collect the church dues.

From Itchingfield you can see the tall brick tower of **Christ's Hospital** a mile to the east. Another sign that you are near the school is the occasional boy in belted dark blue coat, white neckbands and yellow socks, wandering along the lanes. Christ's Hospital was moved from London to Horsham in 1902; E. V. Lucas, who saw it when it was brand new, called it 'a glaring red-brick settlement which the fastidiously urban ghost of Charles Lamb can now surely never visit'. To visit the school, ask at the Estate Office for a permit (any hour within reason), which entitles you to see the buildings in the gargantuan main quadrangle, designed by Sir Aston Webb. There are also guided tours every Wednesday afternoon in the summer term. The dining hall (at a rough pacing 150 feet long) has a vast painting by Verrio along most of one side. Painted between 1684 and 1690, it commemorates the founding of the Royal Mathematical School (an integral part of Christ's Hospital) by Charles II, who sits enthroned in the middle, gesturing expansively, with charity girls on the left and bluecoat boys on the right. Edward VI, who founded the original Christ's Hospital on the site of Greyfriars, Newgate, in 1553, has a modest little portrait on the opposite wall. The speech hall ('Big School') and chapel are huge and dull; the chapel walls are covered with large frescoes by Frank Brangwyn. In the quandrangle the boy king Edward VI surmounts a fountain, and four bluecoat boys, including Lamb and Coleridge, stand below.

The unique uniform is described in a school history as 'a modified survival of the ordinary dress of the Tudor period.' The yellow linings to the coats were perpetuated in the seventeenth century, following some medical myth of the time, 'to avoid vermin, by reason the white cottens is held to breed the same'.

Three great literary figures who were at the school at the end of the eighteenth century – Coleridge, Lamb and Leigh Hunt – all left reminiscences of their schooldays which are a similar mixture of pride and fascinated horror at memories of wretched food, floggings and solitary confinement. The first day of term the headmaster found Coleridge crying with homesickness, and bellowed at him 'Boy! the school is your father! Boy! the school is your mother! the school is your sister! the school is your first-cousin, and your second cousin, and all the rest of your relations! Let's have no more crying!'

Billingshurst, strung out along Stane Street, has been linked by etymologists with Billingsgate, where the Roman road entered London. Perhaps both were named after a Roman surveyor or official called Belinus. Less fancifully, it is more likely to be a Saxon *-ingas* or tribal name. The main street still has the general outline of a village, though not many of the old buildings are left. At its centre is a little sloping green leading up to the church, a sturdy building with a vastly disproportionate shingled spire. The best thing about it is the fine Tudor entrance porch below the tower, all brick and ancient timbers. Though the church stands on quite a high point, the view all around is blocked by featureless modern housing estates.

From Billingshurst the A 272 ambles eastwards towards Haywards Heath, in places hardly more than a country lane, in spite of its importance as a traffic artery. Near **Coolham** a sign points down a lane to 'Blue Idol', which sounds like an exotic country club, but is in fact a Quaker meeting-house and guesthouse, remote and peaceful. Originally an Elizabethan farmhouse, one end of the building was converted at the end of the seventeenth century into a meeting-house by removing the first-floor timbers; the result is a tall, galleried room, ideal for the purpose. William Penn used to walk here from Warminghurst (see p. 368) to worship, while his wife Gulielma and their children rode over in an ox-drawn coach. The strange name has been explained in various ways. The one generally accepted is that during the nineteenth century, when the building was no longer in use or 'idle' and was colour-washed in blue, it was known as the 'blue idle meeting-house' – hence Blue Idol. The whole place is completely self-effacing: no doubt deliberately so, in view of the hounding the Quakers had to face in their early days.

A mile south of the main road, reached down leafy lanes, is **Shipley**, the village where Hilaire Belloc lived from 1906 until his death in 1953. He lived in King's Land, a low rambling house on the outskirts of the village, and as a lover and praiser of windmills had his own mill at the end of his garden. Since his death Shipley Mill has been restored, and is now the only remaining working smock mill in West Sussex. (As a matter of terminology, a smock mill differs from a tower mill in having the top floors of wood, not of brick.) It was built as recently as 1879, the last of all the Sussex smock mills – and the biggest. On certain summer weekends, when the weather is right for milling, the great sweeps turn, sacks of wheat rise gently on the hoist to the top of the mill, and the grain drops through the shoots to the grindstones, then down the meal shoots to the bins below.

Across a field from the mill is Shipley church, a beautiful building, with a square central tower held together by iron cramps. It was built early in the twelfth century by the Knights Templars, and has fine Norman arches below the tower. Old pictures show it with a shingled pyramid cap on the tower, and minus the nineteenth-century north aisle, which destroyed its boxlike severity. In a niche in the chancel is a precious rarity, the Shipley reliquary, a thirteenth-century wooden casket decorated with Limoges enamel. On a background of dark and light blue the figures of Christ and saints stand out brilliantly in gold. The reliquary must have been a gift of the Templars, who owned a house in Limoges; the enamellers were craftsmen from Byzantium settled in France. Also in the chancel is a sumptuous monument to Sir Thomas Caryll and his wife, dated 1616. The composer John Ireland, as much a poet of Sussex as Belloc was, is buried in the churchyard. A tablet on the south wall of the church refers to his grave, 'marked by prehistoric sarsen stones to symbolise that antiquity the love of which inspired much of his music.'

West Grinstead, across the Worthing road (A 24), is seventeen miles from East Grinstead as the crow flies. Whereas East Grinstead is a sizeable town, West Grinstead is hardly even a village. The big house of West Grinstead Park has been demolished, except for the battlemented stables; A medieval moat and stewponds for fish survive in the centre of the park; and one of the fine old trees is still known as 'Pope's Oak' from the tradition that the poet wrote much of 'The Rape of the Lock' stretched out beneath its shade.

West Grinstead church is remote but well worth hunting out. It lies at the end of a back road, with a little bridge over the Adur just below, and is a rough-hewn place, roofed with Horsham slabs and with a broach spire that seems to rise straight from the roof. On the north wall is a patch of exposed Norman herringbone work, and round on the south side is a Norman door, shifted when the south aisle was added in the thirteenth century. The big wooden porch is fifteenth-century, and looks as though it has hardly been repaired since then. The monuments are of all shapes and sizes. In the south-west chapel are two tombs with good brasses, one to a lady who died in 1395, the other to Sir Hugh Halsham, an Agincourt veteran, and his wife charmingly named Lady Jocosa. The south aisle has three classical monuments in a variety of eighteenth-century styles: William and Elizabeth Powlett, carved by Rysbrack in Roman costume leaning on an urn; Sir Merrik Burrell, Governor of the Bank of England, portrayed in profile on a simple medallion; and Sir William Burrell, nephew of Sir Merrik, commemorated by an angular oddity by Flaxman. Sir William (died 1796) was an antiquarian who bequeathed his collection of Sussex documents to the British Museum. The old pews are marked with the names of the farms whose owners occupied them a century and a half ago, names as gnarled and worn as old oak trees – Freezers, Priors Bine, Sunt, Grinders, Hobshorts, Figland, Swallows Nest, White Soan, Thistleworth, and dozens more.

A fragment of the medieval **Knepp Castle**, stronghold of the Norman de Braose family, can be seen beside the Worthing road a mile south of the A 272 crossroads.

The cottages in the middle of **Cowfold**, three miles east along the A 272, sensibly turn their backs on the traffic and look in towards the medieval church. In the chancel is one of the most famous brasses in Sussex, to Thomas Nelond, Prior of Lewes in the 1420s. The tonsured figure is life-size, and the whole brass, with its elaborate canopy, is over ten feet long. The carpet above the brass is kept padlocked, but there is a rubbing hanging in the church.

Rising above the trees a mile south of Cowfold is the spire of one of the most astonishing places in the Weald: **St Hugh's Monastery**, the only charterhouse (Carthusian monastery) in the British Isles, where thirty or so monks of this contemplative order live cut off from the world behind high brick walls. It was founded in the 1870s, after persecution in France

Looking across the creek to Bosham's Saxon church.

The doll's-house symmetry of Uppark, high on the South Downs near the Hampshire border. It was built in the 1680s to the designs of William Talman.

The largest state room of Petworth House, decorated with limewood carvings by Grinling Gibbons. The portrait of Henry VIII is after Holbein.

drove the Carthusians to settle elsewhere. The vastness of its scale can only be guessed at from outside the huge and forbidding gatehouse. Once inside you cross an outer courtyard to the tall church; then through to the cloister, built on a scale that dwarfs any medieval foundation, and encloses three and a half acres of orchard. The monks' cells – small hermitages, each with its own garden and workshop – open off the cloister. The monks emerge only for services and main meals, and the occasional white-robed figure walking in the distance only enhances the solitude of the place. Though the buildings are Victorian brick rather than medieval stone, certain aspects, like the Prior's garden full of flowers and hidden below the towering walls of the church, have more of the real Middle Ages about them than the majority of piously tended monastic ruins. Most timeless of all is the small burial ground, where the monks are buried not in coffins but on wooden boards, with nameless wooden crosses above them. (Visits to St Hugh's by arrangement with the Prior.)

CHAPTER TWENTY

Below the South Downs

৵

FIVE miles from Billingshurst (see p. 348) down the dead straight line of Stane Street is **Pulborough,** which is divided into two distinct parts: the lower village, which straggles towards Storrington and has several pubs with gardens overlooking the Arun; and the upper, beyond a lethal crossroads, consisting of Georgian cottages round the church and a prosperous Queen Anne stone rectory across the road. The church stands at the top of the hill, and is a big commanding place, with two wide aisles and a clerestory, dating mainly from the early fifteenth century. The choir stalls have been removed from the chancel, which gives a great feeling of light to the interior. Apart from a fine brass to a fifteenth-century rector, Thomas Harlyng, in the north aisle, the only other monument worth looking at is a Victorian one, showing William Hammond dying at his ease in a wing chair, with wife and children in dutiful attendance.

Heading south along the A 29, it is easy to shoot past the tiny hamlet of **Hardham,** now bypassed; but it is worth stopping, as the whitewashed church has some of the finest medieval wall paintings in England – and some of the oldest, as they were done about 1100. Over the round chancel arch is the Lamb of God in glory; and on the walls are St George slaying the dragon and being broken on the wheel, the Magi, the Serpent tempting Adam and Eve, Eve milking an enormous cow in a homely Eden. A little to the south is **Hardham Priory,** now a farmhouse. Part of the cloister survives, turned into a flower garden.

Bury, three miles farther on, is a secluded village beside the Arun. The village street, hardly more than a lane, leads down to the tall-spired church, still with its fourteenth-century rood screen. The river is only a few yards away, and the remains of a jetty mark the old ferry across to Amberley.

Amberley is a dream village of thatched cottages draped with wisteria, dozing above the waters of the Arun. Even the name itself, said to mean 'fields yellow with buttercups', has a drowsy feel about it; you can say it with your mouth hardly open. Yet Amberley has not always been a place of somnolent rusticity. In the troubled times of the 1370s, when the French were harrying the South Coast, Bishop Rede of Chichester found it worth his while to guard the north side of the Arun gap with a square-towered castle, enlarging Amberley's old manor house with the great curtain wall that rises sheer from the river level. Though the manor (still inhabited) and the castle ruins cannot be visited, they can be seen well enough from the path down to the Wild Brooks, as the levels are poetically named, and over the churchyard wall; and the grouping of castle, church and village can be appreciated as a whole from the Arundel Pulborough road.

Amberley's history goes back to the early days of Saxon England, when lands there were granted to St Wilfrid by King Cedwalla about AD 680. There would certainly have been a Saxon church on the site; the present building and the manor house were probably begun about 1100 by Bishop Luffa, who built Chichester Cathedral. The nave has rounded Norman windows and a tall chancel arch, with multiple chevron ornament on the inner face. At the side of the arch are red ochre wall paintings of about 1200; a Calvary procession and a Crucifixion can be made out. There are also two consecration crosses on the nave walls.

The road below the downs leads east from Amberley along the southern side of **Parham Park.** Parham, the home of Mr and Mrs P. A. Tritton, is the westernmost, and the grandest, of the Elizabethan mansions built below the northern slopes of the downs. A rather dour building of grey-brown stone, it keeps the downs at a distance, set in a huge park where deer graze below the ancient oaks and horse chestnuts. The approach brings you in on the east side, and the visitors' entrance is across a courtyard and up a nineteenth-century staircase at the back, neither of which give any idea of the building as a whole. The best preliminary is to go round to the south side, in the direction of the church, where you can see the E-shaped Elizabethan front with its wide wings and narrow central porch, and the tall mullioned windows that light the Great

Hall. Overall, in fact, Parham is in the form of an H, as the wings project both north and south; the eastern wing is built on an earlier medieval house, which survives in the massive arches of the kitchen (now used as a tea-room).

In medieval times the estate belonged to the Abbey of Westminster, and at the Dissolution it came into the hands of the Palmer family. As a guarantee of good luck the foundation stone of the new Parham was laid by a child (Thomas Palmer, the grandson and heir aged two and a half) 'about tenne of the clock in the forenoone', on January 28th, 1577. However, young Thomas himself was not so lucky. He served with Drake and Hawkins, and died in 1605 of smallpox. Meanwhile Parham had been bought by Thomas Bysshop, a London barrister, whose family lived there for the next three centuries.

The Great Hall is the heart of Parham, and the first room you are shown. A splendid double cube, flooded with light from its lofty windows, it really looks the part. Medieval in shape and function, it is decorated in Renaissance style, with a moulded plaster ceiling, and oak screen carved in classical forms. A nineteenth-century owner of Parham, Robert Curzon, the Oriental traveller, filled the hall with suits of armour, which gave an uncanny effect described by a visitor. 'The only light came from a wood fire, so our end was all dim and ghostlike, for the fire flickered and the knights came to life and moved their helmets.' Nowadays all is clarity rather than ghostly dimness. Instead of armour, there are Elizabethan portraits round the walls – the Queen herself, her favourites Leicester and Essex, the young Edward VI, old Sir Thomas Bysshop, who bought Parham. The big equestrian portrait of Prince Henry, the eldest son of James I, who died young and left the throne for Charles I, was painted by Isaac Oliver, the miniaturist, who was usually content with an area an inch or two across. In one corner is the slender spiral of a narwhal's tusk, believed by the Elizabethans to be a unicorn's horn and a symbol of the rare and fabulous.

Parham is a treasurehouse of paintings and needlework, and the Great Parlour opening off the hall has both. The most arresting picture, over the fireplace, shows the man-of-war *Sovereign of the Seas*, launched at Chatham in 1637. Though the finest ship in the navy, she was not much use, as in all but the calmest seas her gunports were awash. A most unusual portrait of Charles I, by Mytens, shows him without his beard. There is also a portrait of the Spanish Infanta, unsuccessfully courted by Charles in 1623 (see Groombridge, p. 241). This red-lipped rouged dummy gives some point to James I's furious 'Take away this painted doll' when the engagement was broken off. Some of the chairs have their original seventeenth-century embroidery, hardly faded with the passage of time.

Next is the Saloon, an eighteenth-century Adam-style interior. Among the paintings are two views of London painted by William James, a pupil of Canaletto, which make the Thames into something approaching the Grand Canal.

Upstairs in the Great Chamber is a sumptuous four-poster bed, still with its sixteenth-century needlework coverings made traditionally for Mary Queen of Scots. (An alternative suggestion is the French queen Marie de Medicis; the M monogram would fit them both.) The Tudor-looking overmantel, showing Parham's south front, a knight, a jester and assorted animals, was in fact made by a twentieth-century plasterer, Esmond Burton, who had the true Tudor wildness about him. The Tapestry Room is name from its 'flame-stitch' wall coverings. Over one of the doors is a periwigged old man holding a little dog. This is Henry Bysshop, who hid from the Roundheads with his dog in his arms; during the search the loyal animal made no sound, and years later this picture was painted as a tribute. After the Restoration Bysshop was postmaster-general and introduced date-stamping for letters; some early examples are shown. Opposite old Bysshop is Sir Ralph Assheton and his wife. She ran off with a lover; Sir Ralph went after her and got her back, and on her return had himself painted with his foot placed on hers and his hand entwined in her hair to prevent any further straying. The Green Room has portraits of Sir Joseph Banks, the great botanist who sailed with Captain Cook, and his contemporaries. There are two pictures of Omiah, the first South Sea Islander to visit England, who came back with Banks and Cook and whose excellent table manners gave Georgian London a talking-point; and a Stubbs painting of a kangaroo, done from a skin but surprisingly full of bounce.

Finally the Long Gallery. This enormous room, stretching from end to end of the house at second-floor level, is as perfect in its own way as the great hall. The ceiling has recently been redecorated by Oliver Messel in a straggly foliage design, which is no improvement at all on its former unadorned state. The gallery is full of bits and pieces, from a Roman lead cistern to James II's ornate state saddle. A little bedroom off the gallery has a collection of naive Stuart needlework pictures, in contrast to the grandeur all around.

South of the house is Parham's small church, all that is left of the medieval village. The inside was remodelled in 1815–25, and a tower was added; the fireplace in the north transept shows an unusual addiction to comfort. The church still has its box pews, and there is a rare fourteenth-century lead font.

By contrast with Parham, **Storrington** outside its gates is a small town of little character. Its centre is a jumble of everything from traditional Sussex stone through Edwardian shop-fronts to horizontal concrete modern. The church lies behind, on a mound. Part of the original Norman building survives in the nave and north aisle. In earlier times the tower had a tall spire, but it was destroyed by lightning in 1731. The churchyard includes a piece of land called the Old Pillery Gardens – not, as you might think, a mis-spelling for Pillory, but called after the patent pink pills once dispensed by a Mr Dixon from his house near by.

The next place beyond Storrington is **Washington**, a village which hardly knows itself now that the Worthing traffic has been bypassed round the back of it. Seventy years ago E. V. Lucas wrote of it: 'There are few better spots in the country for a modest contented man to keep a horse.' At the top of the hill is the village church, much restored, with a sturdy battlemented tower; and at the bottom is the Frankland Arms, whose beer is good enough, though nothing like the brew Hilaire Belloc found there on his tramp through Sussex: 'nectar brewed in the waxing of the moon and of that barley which Brutus brought hither in the first founding of this land.' But then he was writing before the days of pressurised keg.

From Washington you look up to **Chanctonbury Ring**, the most famous landmark on the South Downs. The grove of beech trees on the summit looks as a sacred grove should; though it was not in fact planted until the mid eighteenth century. It is best to allow a good two hours for the walk to the top and back; and it is worth remembering that the steep parts of the chalk track can get extremely slippery after rain. From Chanctonbury you can see the whole of mid-Sussex spread out before you: the near-by villages of Ashington and Washington, Shipley Mill and St Hugh's Monastery in the middle distance, and far away the slopes of Leith Hill across the Surrey border. Southwards is a horizon of sea beyond Cissbury; and on a clear day you can see the bluff of Selsey Bill a good twenty miles away. Below the trees are the ditch and rampart of an Iron Age camp.

Chanctonbury's trees were planted by George Goring, who lived at **Wiston House**, a stone Elizabethan mansion in a park below the downs. Wiston is now run by the Foreign Office as a conference centre and is not open to the public; but you can still enjoy the beauty of the park and the house's faded stone façade on your way to the church. This has various memorials to the powerful de Braose family – heraldic glass to Lady Annys, a small wall tomb to the infant son of Sir John, Sir John's own brass on the floor of the south chapel. Dated 1426, it shows him in armour; the empty spaces on the brass are filled with little scrolls repeating the words 'Jesus', 'Mercy', like a Tibetan prayer wheel reciting the same words over and over. On the windowsill in the chapel is the shattered figure of Sir Thomas Shirley, who built Wiston about 1576. His son Sir Robert, one of the greatest of Elizabethan travellers, visited the Persian court, fought for the Persians against the Turks, and married a Circassian girl; their portraits by Vandyck are at Petworth (see p. 438). According to Fuller's *Worthies*, on his return Sir Robert 'much affected to appear in *forreign Vestes*; and, as if his *Clothes* were his limbs, accounted himself never ready till he had something of the Persian Habit about him.' With so much oriental influence around, it is not surprising that Wiston is claimed to be the first place where coffee was drunk in England, in the first decades of the seventeenth century.

The country round Chanctonbury inspired many of the works of the composer John Ireland. Towards the end of his life, in the 1950s, he bought Rock Mill below Chanctonbury, a converted tower mill now left high and dry on a spit of land above immense sand quarries. A plaque on the wall records that 'Dr John Ireland (1879–1962) lived his last and happiest years in this house.' He is buried a few miles away at Shipley (see p. 349).

The tiny church at **Buncton** is easy to miss: it lies across a miniature ravine by the back road from Chanctonbury to Ashington. You get to it by a path over a stream, and through a small wood carpeted in spring with bluebells, yellow dead-nettles and wild garlic – a magical approach. Buncton was the nearest that later generations could get to the unpronounceable Saxon 'Biohchandoune'. Hardly more than a stone barn surrounded by trees, it was built about 1150 and has a round Norman chancel arch and some rough carving, including the figure of a man lying down.

Steyning, Bramber and Upper Beeding have now more or less coalesced, sharing the nightmare thunder of heavy lorries rumbling up from Shoreham. **Steyning** (pronounced Stenning) is a pretty little town. The sloping High Street is filled with antique and handicraft shops, and has the clock tower of the Old Market House as its focal point. Steyning was an important place in Saxon times. It was a royal manor owned by Alfred the Great, had its own mint, and, in the days when the Adur was much wider than it is today, was a harbour town.

It also has its own saint, Cuthman, a favourite with Sussex designers of stained glass windows because of his estimable habit of trundling his old mother about in a handcart, a theme capable of endless interpretations. As a shepherd boy in the West Country, Cuthman would draw a circle on the grass with his staff, and command his sheep not to stray in the name of the Lord; and the magic circle was so powerful that the sheep stayed put. But on the death of his father Cuthman was forced to move, so he loaded his mother on to a cart and headed east. On one occasion the cord by which Cuthman pulled the cart broke while he was passing some haymakers. They roared with laughter, whereupon the saint, uttering the words 'Laugh men, weep heaven', called down a shower of rain that ruined their crop, and fell on the field in haymaking time for ever afterwards. The cart broke down irreparably at Steyning. Taking this as a sign, Cuthman built a hut for himself and his mother, and set up a small timbered church, the remote ancestor of the present splendid Norman building.

Though the solid sixteenth-century tower would look big

enough attached to a normal parish church, it is quite out of scale against the tall Norman nave, topped by a high roof above round-arched clerestory windows. The nave is of cathedral-like grandeur, with powerful arcading, and a chancel arch unusually high for a Norman church. This is the only survivor of the four arches that would have supported the central tower (it is not known if this was ever built). The present chancel was added in the eighteenth century, roughly where the Norman tower would have come. Too much Norman moulding can lead to visual indigestion; but all these stone spikes and zigzags are leavened by grotesque animal and human heads at the junctions of the arches, doodles in stone by craftsmen relaxing for a moment. At the east end of the south aisle is a Romanesque capital that looks as though it has strayed from Venice or Sicily. Perhaps the sculptor of these lions and tendrils had seen something similar on the Crusades. In the porch is a broken coffin lid taken from the Saxon burial ground; suggestions are that it came from the grave of Cuthman himself, or from that of King Ethelwulf, father of Alfred, who died in 857.

Church Street, which leads up from the High Street, is a harmonious undulation of timbered overhangs and Horsham stone roofs. The most substantial building is the grammar school, built in the fifteenth century as the home of a religious order and known as Brotherhood Hall. It has a good brick Tudor doorway. A plaque on the wall of a cottage up the street proclaims 'This is Sir Harry Gough's house, 1771'; it was put up there by the local M.P. after a tenant had refused to pay the rent. Chantry Green, where the road widens out, is a harmlessly peaceful spot today, yet it saw the burning of a Protestant martyr in Mary's reign. W. B. Yeats wrote some of his later poems in the big Queen Anne house facing the green.

High above **Bramber** towers a steep hill, with a fang of masonry at the summit. This is all that survives of the keep of the great Norman castle that once stood there, guarding the lower reaches of the Adur. The name derives from the Saxon 'Brymmburh', meaning a fortified hill; and a Saxon stronghold probably stood on the ground at the back of the castle. William the Conqueror gave the Rape of Bramber to William de Braose, and by 1090 the castle was complete, with an outer gateway somewhere on the line of the present main road, and an approach across a deep moat to the tall square keep. The castle survived the Middle Ages, but not the Civil War, when it was held first by the Royalists and then by the Parliamentarians, who finally dismantled it. The church on the slope below was built soon after the Conquest; it was a cruciform building, but lost its chancel and transepts in the Civil War. The Norman chancel arch survives; one capital has a very Chaucerian fox carrying off Chanticleer.

Until 1972, one of the sights of Bramber was Potter's Museum, in the main street. Walter Potter was a Victorian taxidermist, and master of the animal tableau. His 'Guinea-pigs' Cricket Match', 'Kittens' Wedding' and 'Death and Burial of Cock Robin', all using numerous stuffed animals and birds, formed a three-dimensional equivalent to his namesake Beatrix Potter's stories. The museum, rechristened 'The House of Pipes', has begun a new life as a display centre of tobacco jars, pipes, pamphlets and other items of 'smokiana'.

St Mary's, a few doors away, is one of the finest timber-framed houses in Sussex. It was built in the fifteenth century as a home for four monks, who were bridge wardens of the important bridge across the Adur and looked after the chapel that stood on it. Big though it is, what survives is only half of the original courtyard building. which was also a guest-house for pilgrims on their way to Chichester or Canterbury, and for other travellers who wanted a night's rest. An upstairs room, known as the King's Room, was very probably where Charles II stayed before escaping down to Shoreham and across to France (see p. 390). It is easy to imagine that tall swarthy figure, disguised as a groom, peering out of the window towards the bridge and slipping quietly across the river when the Roundhead patrols had passed. (The old bridge, far longer than the present one, began almost at the door of St Mary's.)

Before the Reform Bill, Bramber was a really rotten borough, returning two Members for less than a hundred inhabitants. One of its M.P.s was William Wilberforce, the anti-slavery campaigner. While driving through the village one day, he asked the postboy what it was called. 'Bramber,' said the boy. 'Bramber?' said Wilberforce. 'Why, that's the place I'm the Member for.'

In the Middle Ages **Upper Beeding** had Sele Priory to counterbalance Bramber's castle. Now it has nothing much except rows of nondescript houses and a grim Scottish Baronial mansion, straight from the wilds of Aberdeen.

Because it lies behind Brighton, the range of hills east of the Adur is better known and more visited than any stretch along the whole length of the downs. It is also more liable to encroachment: a glance at the map will show the tide of houses lapping up the contours towards the crest of the London road. But so far the steep northern slopes are as empty as they have been for centuries, and many of the little villages below consist of nothing more than an ancient church and a few cottages and farms.

Edburton, one of the smallest of them, is named after Edburga, grand-daughter of King Alfred, who is supposed to have built a church here in the tenth century. The present Early English building is large for a parish church. It has a Norman lead font, battered through having been taken outside and used as a horse trough in Cromwellian times.

Above **Poynings** looms the bulk of Dyke Hill, an Iron Age camp with the great gash of the **Devil's Dyke** forming a natural defence along the southern side. If you want the solitude of high places you will not find it up here, as there is a large hotel right on the summit. But it is a tremendous view-point, with the whole central Sussex plain lying below, and to the south the skyscrapers of Brighton and those inescapable landmarks the chimneys of Portslade power station. It was here that the Devil stood glaring at the churches of the Weald, and swore that he would drown them by cutting through the downs between sunset and sunrise, thus letting in the sea. Taking no notice of the pleadings of St Cuthman, he set to work, hacking out great lumps of chalk and hurling them all around him. Where they fell are the round hills that stud the lower slopes of the downs. At the last moment, when the Devil needed only a few more chops with his mattock for the sea to come pouring in, an old woman of Poynings lit a candle and looked out of her window to see what was going on. Inspired by St Cuthman, the candle gave out such a blaze that the cocks woke up and started to crow, the Devil fled with a howl of rage leaving the Dyke unfinished, and the Weald was safe for the next few thousand years. The Iron

Age works are naturally puny compared with those of the Devil (or the 'Poor Man', as he used to be called locally), but the rampart and ditch are still substantial in the south-west corner of the camp.

Poynings church is a big cruciform building, noble and austere inside and out, with a battlemented central tower. It was built under the will of Michael de Ponynnges, who died in 1369, and is Early Perpendicular in style. The pulpit, screen and other woodwork are Jacobean.

Newtimber Place (open Thurs. afternoons in summer) is remote from the rush of the Brighton road a few hundred yards away. There has been a house on the site since Saxon times, and at the back the building rises sheer from the moat on medieval foundations. The bulk of the house was built in 1681; it has an unusual classical front, made of squared flints with red-brick surrounds to the windows. Its main feature is the entrance hall, painted about 1750 with frescoes in the Etruscan style, with tapestries and chair coverings to match, showing improbable goddesses and charioteers in terracotta colours. Behind the stables is an octagonal dovecote, with hundreds of brick-built nests perfectly preserved, but no longer any doves to fill them. Newtimber belongs to descendants of the Buxton family, whose most famous member, Earl Buxton (1835–1934), was a great Liberal politician and friend of Gladstone.

The Earl's memorial tablet is in the little church down the road, a thirteenth-century building with an absurd little tower of 1839 tacked on the end. It is very much a Buxton memorial chapel. A gentle Epstein-like stone figure of a mother and child commemorates the Earl's daughter, who died in childbirth; a gilded St George is in memory of her brother, killed in the First World War; a St Francis window recalls a naturalist brother who died in 1911. Most recent (1955) is a tablet to the Earl's wife, the maker of Newtimber's beautiful garden.

The steep woodlands on **Newtimber Hill** are now owned by the National Trust.

Pyecombe has one of the smallest of all the downland churches. In the last century the village was renowned for its shepherd's crooks, known as 'Pyecombe hooks'. They were 'indispensable to every rightly-equipped shepherd', says Augustus Hare.

From the outside Clayton church, with its patched-up walls and shingled bellcote, looks nothing out of the ordinary. But inside it is exceptional, both for its pre-Conquest chancel arch, and for its medieval wall paintings, which have recently been cleaned and treated. Though the actual date of the paintings is disputed, at some time, possibly as early as 1080, the Saxon church was plastered and painted with an overall design centred on the Christ in Judgment, above the chancel arch. On the walls of the nave are processions of kings, clerics and laymen; and on the north wall can be seen the arcades of the New Jerusalem. Faded and mutilated though they are, the Clayton mosaics link this remote church with the great world of hieratic religious art that stretches across Europe to the mosaics of Ravenna and Santa Sophia.

From such sublimity you can step across the main road to the ridiculousness of the brick baronial entrance to the Clayton tunnel on the Brighton line. Between the corner towers is a small house, right over the mouth of the tunnel and rocked continually by the roar of trains passing underneath. The commuting townships of Hassocks and Burgess Hill were outlying farms of Clayton before the railway was built.

On the downs above Clayton, and reached down a side road, are two windmills that can be seen for miles around, called appropriately Jack and Jill. Jill is a post mill, complete with sails, built in 1821 and hauled here by oxen across the downs from Brighton about 1850. Jack has no sails, but is just the black painted tower of a smock mill. Sandwiched between the two is what must be the most windmill-dominated private house in the country, belonging to Mr Henry Longhurst, the writer on golf.

Ditchling Beacon is a landmark as famous as the Devil's Dyke, and a good deal higher (813 as opposed to 711 feet). However, it has no legends attached, and no restaurant for those who like refreshments to go with their views.

Plumpton is the last village in this direction before the main road to Lewes (A 275). It is now known mainly for its racecourse, which lies a couple of miles north of the old village, beside the railway. Leonard Mascall, a Tudor landowner with a botanical turn of mind, lived at Plumpton Place. He was a great cultivator of apples – a tradition carried on at the Plumpton agricultural college next door. You get to the church through an orchard; like Clayton, it has frescoes of about 1100, though not nearly so well preserved.

Ditchling, at the foot of the Beacon, is the most sizeable of these villages. In Saxon times 'Diccelingas' was the administrative centre of a vast Wealden royal estate, and there is still a good deal of pre-Conquest work in the nave of the church. This stands above the road near the village crossroads, and is a chunky building with central tower and pyramid spire. Inside there are four fine Early English arches below the tower, with foliated capitals on the arch into the chancel; and on either side of the elegant east window are the carved heads of a king and queen, possibly Henry III and Queen Eleanor. Across the road from the church is Wing's Place, a Tudor house with some intricate timbering and a fine arched brick doorway. There are plenty of smaller half-timbered houses, rubbing shoulders with Georgian symmetry in the High Street.

Since the turn of the century Ditchling has been a popular place for artists to live. A small art gallery keeps up the tradition by holding shows of paintings by local artists. Sir Frank Brangwyn lived there, as did Eric Gill, the sculptor and designer of lettering; and it may be due to Gill's influence that the modern tombstones in the churchyard have unusually stylish inscriptions. A secular commemoration that other places might well follow is a plaque to a well-loved local doctor on a wall in South Street.

Burgess Hill, a couple of miles north of Ditchling, is a complete contrast – an overgrown Victorian village, owing its existence to the railway. In spite of its lack of aesthetic appeal, it is embarking on an ambitious central redevelopment scheme, which puts many larger but less enterprising places to shame.

Hurstpierpoint, south-west of Burgess Hill, is an unpretentious place, with a good deal of Georgian building in the High Street. The tall church, built in the 1840s by Sir Charles Barry, looms over the surrounding houses. Inside there is some good pseudo-medieval arcading, and two genuinely medieval much-battered effigies of knights, reputedly members of the Norman de Pierpoint family. A mile north an immense grey flint building dwarfs the surrounding countryside – the chapel of Hurstpierpoint public school, founded, like the schools at Lancing and Ardingly, by the Rev. Nathaniel Woodard (see p. 404). Murray's *Hand-book* gives the annual fees at Hurst-pierpoint as 'from 25 guineas'.

The de Pierpoints' ancestral home was at **Danny**, below the smooth grass dome of Wolstonbury Hill. (Danny is still marked 'Wolstonbury College' on the one-inch O.S. map, as there was a boys' school there until recently.) About 1450 the de Pierpoints had to flee for their lives from Danny, after Simon de Pierpoint deliberately burned a number of his serfs to death, and his other retainers set fire to the house in retaliation. The site stood empty until George Goring built the present splendid Elizabethan house between about 1580 and 1595. The main front is of the classic E-shape, with tall mullioned windows lighting a great hall. Goring was a fervent Royalist and forfeited Danny at the end of the Civil War. At the beginning of the eighteenth century it passed to the Campion family, who added the symmetrical Queen Anne south façade and remodelled the interior; they put in a sweep-ing staircase (the original Tudor staircase is at the back), and altered the great hall by lowering the ceiling and building pilastered screens at either end.

Danny's moment of historical glory came at the end of the First World War, when the house was rented to Lloyd George, the Prime Minister. The terms for the armistice with Germany were drawn up in the great hall; a plaque on the wall near the fireplace gives the names of the War Cabinet, including Churchill. The house is now split into flats and run by the Mutual Households Association.

Lloyd George used to take his state papers up **Wolstonbury Hill** when he wanted to work in peace. No doubt he climbed the steps up the hill, which were cut, says an old parish guidebook, 'by the paupers when the workhouse was kept in the village. They were marched there under the charge of the parish beadle.' One can imagine this sad little procession of the elderly, the shiftless or the simple-minded, hacking at the chalk and flints under the self-righteous eye of local official-dom.

A couple of miles to the north, beside the A 23, are the grandstand and fences of the **Hickstead** show jumping course.

Henfield, four miles west of Hurstpierpoint, has more back alleys and is easier to get lost in than any other township I have come across. The name has nothing to do with the inhabitants' fondness for chickens: it comes from the Saxon 'Hamfelde', meaning 'settlement on the open land'. The church, which stands well away from the bustle of the High Street, dates back to a charter of AD 770. It was much restored in 1870, but still has its massive Perpendicular tower and thirteenth-century arcading. In the Parham Chantry is a wall tablet to Henry Bysshop, whose portrait is at Parham. Wood's Mill, an old watermill a mile south of the village towards Upper Beeding, is the starting-point for a nature trail through woodland and wetland (April–Sept., except for Mon. and Fri.).

Though **Ashurst** is only a couple of miles away across the Adur from Henfield, it is a good five miles by road, through Partridge Green. But it is worth the detour, as the small flint church, set among trees miles from anywhere, is one of the hidden gems of this area. The base of the tower seems to take up about half of the building, and the interior is a single space, with a roof that covers both nave and aisle. The church was built about 1200, by the Knights Templars; during the restoration of 1877 the tower was rebuilt, leaving the spire resting in mid-air on the beams – a tribute to the solidity of Sussex oak. In a case above the north door is a vamping horn, dated 1770; this is not a musical instrument but was used as a megaphone to keep the congregation more or less in tune (see also Charing, p. 189).

From **Ashington**, a bungaloid sprawl along the Worthing road, a lane leads to **Warminghurst**, just a remote church and a handful of houses. The village's most famous inhabitant was William Penn, who lived at Warminghurst Place and drafted the first constitution of Pennsylvania there. The hostility the Quakers had to meet is shown by an order for Penn's arrest made in January 1685, in which he was accused of being 'a factious and seditious person', given to holding 'unlawful Assemblyes and Conventicles' (see also Blue Idol, p. 348). The church is a modest building dating from about 1220, with a neat little tile-hung belfry, and a wooden chancel arch painted with a large royal arms of Queen Anne. The seating looks eighteenth-century: high pews, the front ones with drawers for the squire's prayer-books; and clerk's chair below the pulpit. There is a good Tudor brass to Edward Shelley, an ancestor of the poet, his wife, and a clutch of seven sons and three daughters.

Thakeham, only half a mile away across a field, though four miles by road, lies down a leafy lane, in an area given over to enormous glasshouses. It has plenty of pretty houses, and a big Early English church on a mound. The Perpendicular tower has a curious 'henhouse' roof on top instead of the usual pyramid cap.

At the heart of the network of lanes towards Pulborough is **West Chiltington**, a trim village built round a crossroads, with a sign proclaiming itself 'Best kept Village in West Sussex 1966–70.' The church is a rugged place, rough-rendered on the outside. Inside there is a Norman arcade with crudely carved capitals, and some faded medieval wall painting. The old stocks are kept by the churchyard gate.

CHAPTER TWENTY-ONE

Lewes and Brighton

❧

Lewes is one of the nodal points of East Sussex, straddling the main east-west road (A 27) between Eastbourne and Brighton, and the focus of a radiating fan of roads northwards towards Ashdown Forest and the Weald. Hemmed in by the downs and bathed in a brilliant light that springs from some interaction between the bare green hills and the nearby sea, it has the ability to make even the most cantankerous visitor feel cheerful. When Cobbett rode over from Uckfield in the winter of 1822 for a stormy meeting at Lewes County Hall, his ill-temper was soon charmed away. 'The town itself,' he wrote, 'is a model of solidity and neatness. The buildings all substantial to the very outskirts; the pavements good and complete; the shops nice and clean; the people well-dressed; and, though last not least, the girls remarkably pretty.' Lewes is still compact, hardly more than a mile in any direction, though Brighton is stretching out one long tentacle through Falmer to the west; and the general feeling of euphoria is lessened only by the roar of lorries thundering up the High Street, or slithering down Western Road with a screech of brakes.

Lewes was the natural place for a Norman stronghold, strategically placed near the mouth of the Ouse, between two spurs of the downs. The **Castle** is the best place for a first acquaintance with the town, as everything can be seen at a glance from the roof of the keep. Southwards the Ouse meanders towards Newhaven, with a glimpse of the sea in the gap between the downs. Due east are the steep slopes of Malling Hill, gouged with chalk pits; half way up stands the stone obelisk to the Lewes martyrs, a total of seventeen Protestants burnt between 1555 and 1557. West is a roof-scape, rising up the hill to the square tower of the prison; and

A map for this chapter will be found on pages 354-5

to the north is Offham Hill, where in 1264 Simon de Mont-fort defeated King Henry III.

Lewes was an important place in Saxon times. At the Conquest William gave it to his son-in-law, William de Warenne, who was married to William's daughter Gundrada (though this parentage is now doubted). De Warenne's castle is unique in being built on two artificial mounds – the mound on which the keep stands, and the hillock called Brack Mount a hundred yards to the east across the bowling green. Much of the surviving walling dates from his time; though the magnificent barbican, or outer gatehouse, was built in the early fourteenth century. The castle was never besieged but succumbed to natural causes and a desire for building material. Most of the buildings were pulled down in 1620, when the stone was sold at fourpence a load. An eighteenth-century owner turned the keep into a summerhouse (hence the Gothick windows); and it is now run by the Sussex Archaeological Trust, who keep some of their more cumbrous exhibits inside the walls.

The main street of Lewes runs up from the river, beginning as a gentle slope and rising more steeply to the western edge of the town. The buildings are mainly Georgian, dignified brick, plain or painted, flat or bow-fronted, with the occasional half-timbered survival, like the Bull House, dated 1450. Tom Paine, the radical and future author of *The Rights of Man*, lived at the Bull House as exciseman and tobacconist from 1768 to 1774. In the evenings he used to go down the road to the White Hart (a tall Georgian coaching inn, little altered) and debate on the burning republican topics of the day; according to E. V. Lucas he used to be a regular recipient of a copy of Homer, known as the 'Headstrong Book', sent round the next morning to the most obstinate debater.

South of the High Street run the steep little alleys which are among the delights of Lewes, some of them now closed to traffic: Keere Street, down which the Prince Regent is reputed to have driven a coach and four at full gallop (though as the gradient is about one in three I find it hard to see how he could have managed it); St Martin's Lane; and Church Twitten, which winds between high flint walls. (A 'twitten', according to the *Dictionary of the Sussex Dialect*, is 'a narrow path between two walls or hedges'; another local word, 'bostal' or 'borstal', used to be the name for the steep paths on the side of the downs, and is still found on the map, for example above Alciston. Hence the most famous Borstal, on the hills above Rochester, see p. 48.)

You can pick almost any of the buildings in the High Street and find something interesting about it. Thus on the wall of the pink-washed Castle Place is a plaque commemorating Dr Gideon A. Mantell, a nineteenth-century doctor and palaeontologist who discovered the first skeleton of an iguanodon in Tilgate Forest; below the red-brick Victorian mass of the town hall are the cellars in which the Lewes martyrs were imprisoned before being burnt in the market place (see Warbleton, p. 270); while the Georgian frontage of Shelleys Hotel hides an Elizabethan inn called the Vine. When the Shelleys owned the house Dr Johnson visited them and left his mark on their family history by lifting one of the little daughters into a cherry tree to get away from her chatter, walking away and forgetting all about her. Hours later she was rescued.

Lewes is a town of many churches, and the High Street has two of them. At the top, opposite Shelleys, is **St Anne's**, the oldest church in Lewes. It stood well outside the medieval town, which ended beyond the town wall in Westgate, and was originally known as 'St Mary Westoute'. It is a massively solid Norman building, with a tower built about 1150 and a late twelfth-century aisle, divided from the nave by stumpy columns. On the south side of the chancel a low window divided by a pillar looks into an anchoress's cell, where a thirteenth-century recluse lived and died in pious discomfort. The panels of the Jacobean octagonal pulpit are said by Pevsner to be carved with lions' heads, though they look to me like highly naturalistic baboons. This may account for the fact that the pulpit was thrown out of the church and only rediscovered in the last century, in a garden and whitewashed.

Directly behind St Anne's are the large new glass-panelled blocks of the East Sussex County Council's administrative buildings, opened in 1968. Over the main entrance is a long glass fibre abstract sculpture, already domesticated by house martins nesting in the interstices. The buildings have been sited tactfully below the brow of the hill; but they block the view of the downs from the churchyard.

The other High Street church is **St Michael's**, below the castle, a landmark with its twisting needle spire and round tower (the only other towers like it are at Southease and Piddinghoe, see pp. 377 and 378). The tower is thirteenth-century; the church much-altered fourteenth. The interior is on the gloomy side, except for the monument on the north wall, which shows Sir Nicholas Pelham, his wife and children, brilliantly picked out in black, crimson and gold. In 1545 Pelham defeated a French expeditionary force which had sailed on to Seaford (then the harbour at the mouth of the Ouse, see p. 308) after attacking Brighthelmstone. As the incription punningly says,

What time the French sought to have sack't Sea-Foord,
This Pelham did repel 'em back aboord.

On the same wall is an unreadable tablet to Dr Mantell, the iguanodon-discoverer. Tom Paine was married in this church in 1771.

With the parish church, **St John's**, in Southover High Street, we are back with William de Warenne and Gundrada. While Lewes castle expressed the strength of William's arm, the priory he founded at Southover expressed his piety, or possibly his conscience for the Saxons massacred at Hastings. At any rate, about 1077 he and Gundrada pulled down the little wooden Saxon church at Southover, built a stone church there and handed it over with a large tract of land to the monks from the abbey of Cluny, in Burgundy. This grew into the great Cluniac **Priory of St Pancras**, whose ruins can still be seen, surrounded by tennis courts and football fields, in the meadows behind Southover High Street. Though it had a church bigger than Chichester Cathedral and monastic buildings to scale, it was utterly destroyed at the Dissolution in 1537.

It was left to the railway age to bring the remains of William and Gundrada to light. In 1845 workmen on the Lewes-Brighton railway, which cut right across the priory, unearthed two lead coffins which had been buried near the high altar of the priory church, inscribed with the names William and Gundrada. The carved black marble slab from Gundrada's tomb, which had been taken to Isfield church at the Dissolution, was brought back to Lewes, and coffins, skeletons and slab now lie reunited in a side chapel of St John's church. The church itself once formed the *hospitium* or guesthouse at the gates of the priory; it was converted into the parish church when a bigger hospitium was built in the late thirteenth century. Externally it is notable for a most solid-looking brick tower, built in the early eighteenth century to replace one that had fallen down. The splendid nineteenth-century weathervane on top is in the form of a salmon-trout, 'reminding us', says the church guide regretfully, 'that the Ouse was once a salmon river.'

By the priory ruins (reached most easily through a lane under the railway west of the church) is a rugged bronze memorial, by the sculptor Enzo Plazzotta, commemorating the 700th anniversary of the Battle of Lewes – a helmet-like structure with a frieze illustrating the events of the battle round the top. It is put to good use by the local children, who run round it, climb up it, and shout through it.

Nearly opposite the church is **Anne of Cleves House**, a timber-framed house built about 1500, with the massive beams hidden externally by tilehanging. It is so called not because Henry VIII's 'Flanders Mare' actually lived there, but because she received the property of Lewes Priory as part-payment for granting Henry a divorce. It is now the folk museum of the Sussex Archaeological Society. Of unique interest is the collection of ironwork in one of the galleries, with its series of firebacks from the crudest sixteenth-century efforts to the ornate productions of the later ironmasters, like Richard Lenard, of Brede, who portrays himself grasping a hammer and surrounded by the tools and products of his craft (see also Bateman's, p. 273). In the kitchen is a black octagonal marble table top, medieval in date, from Malling House. A legend says that the knights who murdered Becket came to Malling after two days' hard riding from Canterbury, and wearily threw their arms and accoutrements on the table. As they were warming themselves by the fire they heard a loud crash: the table, sensitive to their sacrilegious act, had cast the murderous weapons to the ground. This must be one of the earliest of all poltergeist stories. Since then the table has relapsed into immobility.

Barbican House, the Society's other museum, on the north side of the High Street near the entrance to the castle, is a large town house which underwent continual alteration and improvement from the Middle Ages to the eighteenth century. The exhibits are much more those of a conventional museum, (though it is at present being completely reorganised) with rooms for the Stone and Bronze Ages, the Romans, the Anglo-Saxons. There is some superb Saxon jewellery including two gold crucifixes from Alfriston, and a good collection of Saxon and Roman coins. On the walls are a couple of pictures highly evocative of the town's past. One shows the 'Lewes avalanche' of December, 1836, when snow hurtled down from the hills on to the suburb of Cliffe, across the river, shattering and burying several cottages. The other shows the Lewes 'bonfire boys' parading through the streets in 1853, trundling barrels of blazing tar, jumping over fire-crackers, and waving banners with anti-Papist and anti-Russian slogans (the Crimean War was only months away). Lewes is still renowned for its November 5th celebrations, though blazing barrels no longer roll through the streets, and the onlookers no longer wear spectacles of wire netting to protect themselves from the giant rockets or 'rousers', which E. V. Lucas described at the turn of the century.

Cliffe, where the avalanche fell, is cut off from Lewes proper by the Ouse, with only a narrow bridge joining the two. The river is a muddy yellow, flowing by timber yards, with warehouses rising sheer from the water. In Cliffe High Street is John Harvey's brewery, founded in 1790, the last independent brewery left in East Sussex. Lewes has always been famous for its beer; and Harvey's, with its gleaming vats, rows of barrels and heady vapours, typifies not only brewing but the whole Lewes temper of individuality.

Immediately north of the town, the A 275 runs below the steep escarpment of **Offham Hill**, where the Battle of Lewes was fought. On the morning of May 13th, 1264, the armies of Henry and de Montfort met on the windswept summit of the downs; the previous night de Montfort had kept vigil in Fletching church (see p. 329), while the king and his generals had caroused in the castle and priory – one reason given by the moralists for the king's defeat. De Montfort's troops were drawn up in three divisions on three spurs of Mount Harry, facing towards Lewes; the corresponding royal divisions were led by Henry III, his son Prince Edward (later Edward I), and

his brother the King of the Romans. Shouting his challenge
'*Simon, je vous defye*', Henry led his troops up the slope to the
attack. The king's downfall was really caused by Prince
Edward's impetuosity. He broke the barons' left flank and
chased their troops for miles over the downs, whereupon de
Montfort brought up his reserves and routed the remaining
two royalist divisions. King Henry fled back to the priory.
The King of the Romans took refuge in a mill, and was
finally captured in the evening to cries of 'Come out, you bad
miller!' – which seems a remarkably polite command under
the circumstances. Prince Edward returned from his pursuit to
find the battle lost, and fled to the castle. Many of the king's
troops tried to escape across the Ouse to Pevensey, struggling
over the bridge, or picking their own way through the undrained marshland and the river, where many of them drowned.
For years afterwards the bodies of knights were found in the
mud, still seated on their horses with drawn swords in their
hands.

The Victorian church at **Offham** was built in 1859 after the
old church, at **Hamsey** across the fields, had become almost
deserted because of its inaccessibility. So Hamsey Old Church
was spared any touch of the restorer's hand, but has been
maintained just enough to prevent it from actually falling
down. You get to it from Offham, across a cut which isolates
it on a bend in the Ouse, through a farmyard and over a
derelict railway; and there it is, the typical church of a
thousand eighteenth-century engravings, with gravestones
cockeyed in the churchyard, yews growing close against the
sturdy stone tower, and the sweep of the downs behind.
Inside, it gives a feeling of even greater remoteness in time.
Birds flutter among the worm-eaten beams. In the Norman
nave ancient pews are pushed back against the wall, and the
chancel is almost bare, except for an unexpected and beautifully carved canopied tomb on the north side of the altar.

Barcombe, two miles north of Offham, is a loose group of
hamlets rather than a village, with a nucleus at Barcombe
Cross. The unpretentious church is almost as remote as the
one at Hamsey, in a pretty setting of farm buildings and large
pond. Barcombe has the distinction of possessing two boarded-
up railway stations.

Along the western bank of the Ouse the A 275 from Lewes

to Newhaven runs by a string of little villages – and mercifully bypasses all of them, as a French main road would do. First comes **Kingston,** with its village street petering out into a steep downland track; farm gates open directly into the street, and there is a small flint church an old pub called the Juggs Arms. Sussex University has a dons' enclave in Kingston. Next is **Iford,** memorable for the number of Continental-sized heaps of manure. The Norman church is unusual in having a central tower, where the chancel was, and a second chancel beyond; thus there are two chancel arches, both beautifully carved. **Rodmell** is a harmony of flint houses and walls, with a Norman church reached through the school playground. Two miles off the main road, in the heart of the downs, is **Telscombe,** buried away in a hollow like an Exmoor village – a few houses up and down the hollow, and a Norman flint church. If you go right to the top of the road, where it turns into a number of branching tracks, you can look over the crest of the downs to the bungaloid growth of Peacehaven and Saltdean near by; but Telscombe was bequeathed to Brighton Corporation and is now run by them, so is reasonably safe from being engulfed. It used to be a centre for training race horses.

Finally there are two villages with round-towered churches. **Southease** is just a hamlet, down a hill with a small green beyond the church. There was a church here in Saxon times (mentioned in a charter of 966); the present building is early twelfth-century. When the Normans came Southease was a flourishing village of farmers and fishermen, being assessed in Domesday Book, apart from farm produce, for 38,500 herrings and £4 for porpoises. Inside the church is a poor relation's chancel arch, made of wood, lath and plaster. On the walls are reproductions of medieval paintings, the originals now faded beyond recognition; and last but not least there is a most elegant chamber organ, all red and gold, made by Allen of Soho about 1790.

At **Piddinghoe** there is an unmistakable smell of the sea in the air. Boats of all shapes and sizes are drawn up on the mud-flats, and the Royal Oak is full of sea angling tackle. Piddinghoe (pronounced Piddnoo by old Sussex men) has its share of traditional sayings, some obvious, some obscure: for instance, 'Piddinghoe people shoe their magpies' (perhaps a reference to black and white oxen); 'Piddinghoe hangs out its ponds to dry'; and 'At Piddinghoe they dig for moonshine' (a clear reminder of smuggling days). The church stands on a bluff above the Ouse; the round tower has an awkward octagonal cap, unlike Southease and St Michael's, Lewes, which have conical ones. The theory that all three towers were built at the same time as watchtowers tends to be dismissed nowadays; nevertheless they would have formed a useful series of beacon towers to give warning of raiders off the Ouse. Piddinghoe church was drastically restored in the last century.

Augustus Hare, visiting **Newhaven** in the 1890s, found it 'an ugly, dirty, little town and smoky little port, with dangerous drinking water, and a long pier at the mouth of the Ouse, whence steamers cross to Dieppe in four and a half hours' (they still take the best part of four hours). Newhaven was originally called Meeching; but a great storm in 1579 diverted the mouth of the Ouse from its former outlet near Seaford, and a 'new haven' grew up at the new river mouth. If you are not sailing to Dieppe but just want to watch the boats go by, you can drive right down the west side of the Ouse to the breakwater below the coastguard station. There is a vestigial old town, with a steep High Street running up to the parish church perched on its hill. The white-painted Bridge Hotel, at the foot of the hill, is dated 1623. King Louis Philippe, deposed in the Revolution of 1848, stayed in the hotel after fleeing across the Channel, and booked in with Queen Marie Amelie as 'Mr and Mrs Smith'. The church is really in two parts: Norman sanctuary and apse; and Victorian west end, with timber supports painted red and gold. From the churchyard you can look inland to Lewes Castle, or across the Ouse to the dreary acres of Newhaven's eastward expansion. By the west wall of the churchyard is the famous gravestone to Thomas Tipper, a local brewer who died in 1785. His much-quoted epitaph details his virtues, and tells how

> The best old Stingo he both brewed and sold,
> Nor did one knavish act to get his gold.

Compared with the bustling modernity of Dover, Newhaven is very much a backwater among cross-Channel ports; you feel that the Newhaven boats should still be referred to as 'steam packets'. Their great advantage is that they land you at Dieppe – infinitely preferable to Calais or Boulogne.

West of Newhaven you are up and over a hill and into **Peacehaven**, that vast expanse of bungalows and small houses laid out on the grid pattern after the First World War, and held up to scorn in recent years as the ultimate in downland spoliation. Yet Peacehaven is no worse than the outlying suburbs of Brighton; what it lacks is any connection with the downs behind or the sea in front. In short, it is an intrusion and has no good reason to be there. On the clifftop is a memorial to George V, marking the Greenwich Meridian, which runs through Peacehaven, and listing the distances to all the outposts of Empire.

If the welcoming signs are to be believed, Brighton begins at **Saltdean**, similar to Peacehaven in its wanton engulfing of downland. But there is still **Rottingdean** to be seen before Brighton proper begins. Built in the only gap in the cliffs between Newhaven and Brighton, Rottingdean was naturally enough a smugglers' village. The old High Street runs inland from the shore – a street of pebble-walled houses, leading to a pretty green and village pond, with larger Georgian houses clustered round about. The artist Burne-Jones lived in a rambling house by the green for the last twenty years of his life (he died in 1898); while Kipling spent the years from 1897 to 1902 at the Elms, across the road, before moving to Bateman's inland (see p. 272). Lady Burne-Jones was Kipling's aunt; she virtually ran Rottingdean, and caused an uproar in 1900 by hanging an anti-war banner from her window after the relief of Mafeking. It was at Rottingdean that Kipling wrote many of his best-known works – *Kim*, the *Stalky* stories, the *Recessional*, and the poem *Sussex*, whose opening verse may have been quoted to death, but still sums up the magic of the downland:

> No tender-hearted garden crowns,
>   No bosomed woods adorn
> Our blunt, bow-headed, whale-backed Downs,
>   But gnarled and writhen thorn –
> Bare slopes where chasing shadows skim,
>   And, through the gaps revealed,
> Belt upon belt, the wooded, dim,
>   Blue goodness of the Weald.

The Grange, formerly owned by the artist Sir William

Nicholson, is now a museum, with a Kipling room of hand-written letters and other relics, a room of Sussex crafts, and a collection of toys.

The **Parish Church** nearby is a Saxon foundation, with pre-Conquest work surviving in the nave and centrally placed tower. The chancel was added about 1080, and the south aisle was enlarged and restored in Victorian times. Owing to the slope of the ground, three steps lead up from nave to tower, and a further three to the chancel. During the French raids of 1377 (see Hastings, p. 283) the villagers took refuge in the belfry. The French fired the church and burnt them alive, and the pink and grey colour of the stone is said to be due to the enormous heat. In the chancel and tower are seven windows designed by Burne-Jones and made by William Morris. The three-light east window, given in celebration of the marriage of Burne-Jones's daughter in the church, shows three angels and 'war in heaven' – not the happiest augury for a marriage.

A mile west of Rottingdean the vast brown frontage of **Roedean** girls' school, complete with central turrets and gate-house, frowns down on the road. Roedean has recently de-clared for equality of the sexes by appointing a headmaster.

This is by far the best side from which to approach **Brighton**, as you arrive right in the middle of it all, without the miles of housing that stretch along the roads to London and Lewes. From the hill that leads down to the front you can see the whole of Brighton foreshortened into the distance: the silver elegance of the piers picking their way out to sea, the long vista of hotels and houses, the skyscrapers of modern Brighton, the two columns of the Portslade power station beyond Hove, and high on the downs the black hulk of the racecourse grandstands. The whole scene is brilliantly lit by the sun danc-ing on the sea. Brighton is the ultimate touchstone by which all other seaside resorts have to be judged. What it has pre-eminently is a sense of style, the legacy of that spendthrift, dissolute, gouty, musical, changeable, loved and hated prince, who came to the fishing village of Brighthelmstone, liked what he saw, and built his fantasy palace there, away from the stuffiness of London and the whims of his mad old father.

The Prince Regent paid his first visit in 1783, but Brighton had been becoming known for thirty years previously. In 1750

Dr Richard Russell, a Lewes general practitioner, brought out a Latin treatise on the merits of sea water – for drinking, as well as for swimming in; and in 1752 the first English translation appeared. Three years later 'Brighthelmstone water' was being bottled and sold in London. Dr Russell prospered, bought property in Brighton, and gathered the nucleus of fashionable hypochondriacs needed to get a new resort off the ground. We know what he looked like from a portrait by Benjamin Wilson that hangs above the staircase in the **Art Gallery** and **Museum** (see also p. 383) – a colourless old man, in grey coat and grey wig, sunken-cheeked and shrewd-eyed. He died in 1759 and was buried at South Malling, a suburb of Lewes. On the other staircase in the same building is Sir Thomas Lawrence's coronation portrait of the Prince Regent, transmuted into George IV in 1821. Flamboyantly robed and glittering with decorations, he stands for the panache of Brighton, summed up by that extraordinary collection of buildings that has the Royal Pavilion as its centrepiece.

The **Royal Pavilion**, with its onion domes and minarets, its bizarre Orientalised interior, and its general air of sumptuously extravagant uselessness, passed through all the shades of public and private disapproval before its present acceptance as one of the glories of British architecture. To Cobbett it was a box covered in turnips and 'a considerable number of bulbs of the crown-imperial, the narcissus, the hyacinth, the tulip, the crocus, and others'; to Sydney Smith, the nineteenth-century wit, it looked as though the dome of St Paul's had come down to Brighton and pupped; to Queen Victoria (whose statue stands, looking far from amused, at the south end of Victoria Gardens) it was a prison. It was only saved from demolition by the inhabitants of the town themselves, who in 1850 got up a petition and raised the money to buy it from the Crown, spending the then-vast sum of £50,000 for what had become a virtual ruin. Over a century of restoration and handing back of the original contents has followed, and the Pavilion has now once again taken its rightful place as the hub of Brighton.

In its present form it is the culmination of three decades of building and alteration. The first Pavilion, built by Henry Holland and completed in 1787, was a simple classical design, with a central rotunda and wings on either side, which can still be traced under the exotic trappings of the later building. In the following years the Prince was bitten by the current mania for the mysterious East. From about 1802, beginning with the inside of the building, architects succeeded each other first with *chinoiserie* and then with Indian-based designs, until the great John Nash, architect of Regent's Park and Carlton House Terrace, produced between 1815 and 1822 the strange bird of paradise we see today.

The Pavilion is permanently open to the public, and is used for Brighton celebrations of all sorts. The entrance hall leads into a long corridor, with an exquisite wall decoration of blue birds and flowers on a pink ground. At the corridor's south end is the Banqueting Room, a riot of Chinese dragons and huge chandeliers, which pass beyond mere vulgarity into some special dimension of display. I remember a 'Regency breakfast' in this room, held as part of one Brighton Festival. Game pie and port, followed by kedgeree, at nine o'clock in the morning made a fairly indigestible substitute for bacon and eggs; but it all settled into place to the accompaniment of bawdy catches sung in the splendid Music Room – the kind of uninhibited social singing that George and his less reputable friends delighted in. Beyond the Banqueting Room is the kitchen, all gleaming copper pans and turning spits, with an iron hot-plate right along one end. In back of the corridor, between the Banqueting and Music Rooms, are two drawing-rooms separated by the round Saloon; this is the classical part of the Pavilion, with tall windows opening on to the lawns. These rooms are sober enough in comparison with the rest, but full of quiet beauty, like the Saloon's domed ceiling painted as a sky lightly covered in cloud. West of the Music Room, and still on the ground floor, are the King's Apartments – anteroom, library and bedroom, the bed set in a deep recess, with a hidden door to a private spiral staircase. This led to a bedroom above, reputedly occupied by one or other of the royal mistresses.

Several of the rooms upstairs have been furnished and decorated in Regency and later styles. Queen Victoria's Bedroom shows the *chinoiserie* influence persisting in coarsened form into the 1840s, in contrast to the delicate furniture and ornament in the Princess Charlotte bedroom, decorated in the style of 1815. One of the rooms contains a number of savage cartoons attacking George for his greed or his lechery, and above all for his unpopular marriage to Mrs Fitzherbert, whom he secretly married in 1785, when he was twenty-three. The cartoonists, for all their vitriolic portrayals, seem to have amused rather than annoyed him, as he used to keep a collection to show to visitors.

It was left to a twentieth-century artist, Rex Whistler, to express that sense of slightly malicious amusement with which we contemplate the foibles of Prinny. His allegorical painting 'HRH the Prince Regent Awakening the Spirit of Brighton' shows the swag-bellied prince, naked except for the Garter above his knee and the star of the order balanced on his backside, tiptoeing forward to unveil a drowsy-eyed and equally naked girl. This was Whistler's last work. Immediately after completing it he was killed in the D-Day landings of June 1944.

The Pavilion and the grassland of the Old Steine (pronounced Steen) were the centres round which all this activity revolved. The Pavilion's outbuildings have survived and been put to other uses: the stables, with their prominent glass dome on top, are now the Dome concert hall; and the vaulted riding school, known as the Corn Exchange, is a general-purpose open space for flower shows and other displays. The biggest of the exhibition rooms in the **Art Gallery** was built as an indoor tennis court. This gallery, also a museum, has some fine collections that would have appealed to the wide sympathies of the Prince Regent – old musical instruments, Greek coins, and a large group of Surrealist paintings.

While George enjoyed himself Brighton expanded. The old Brighthelmstone was in the area bounded by North Street, West Street and East Street; thus the Pavilion lay outside the original town. Some of it still remains, notably a few of the Lanes, narrow alleys between the streets, now filled with antique shops. Bartholomews, where the Town Hall stands, is named after a medieval chantry of St Bartholomew. The **Town Hall** is a tall white building of the 1830s, with huge double porticoes on two of the sides and a glazed central well that goes from ground to roof. The old **Parish Church** stands right outside the original town, a good pull up Dyke Road beyond the Victorian clock tower. Early pictures show it with open country beyond, but it has long been engulfed. Its chief treasure is a drum-shaped font of about 1170, beautifully carved with the Last Supper and scenes from the life of St Nicholas, to whom the church is dedicated. In the churchyard is a gravestone to Phoebe Hessel, who was born in 1713 and served in the infantry as a private. After a military career which included being bayoneted in the arm at Fontenoy in 1745, she retired to Brighton, where she died aged 108 in 1821.

From this small nucleus grew the squares and crescents, the colonnades and hotels. The first piece of Brighton planning was **Royal Crescent**, a discreet little row of houses half a mile east of the Old Steine, built in the late 1790s. From then on, Brighton houses were built to face the sea, instead of turning their backs on it as previously. Dwarfing all other developments on this side of the town was **Kemp Town**, laid out by Thomas Reid Kemp, one of the lords of the manor, in the 1820s. This colossal scheme, centred on **Lewes Crescent** and **Sussex Square**, is still virtually the eastern limit of Brighton. Behind the long stretch of the Marine Parade is much of Brighton's early nineteenth-century expansion, an east-west grid of streets a mile or so long. At the same time the town was spreading along the London and Lewes roads – an expansion for which **St Peter's Church**, the parish church since 1873, was built in the 1820s. Designed by Sir Charles Barry, St Peter's stands on a green at the junction of all the main roads serving Brighton from the north. Its pinnacled tower is the first recognisably Brighton landmark as you drive into the town from this direction. Strangely, it is orientated north and south, the 'east' window pointing north. It has recently been renovated; Barry's work has been painted white, and the later chancel left the natural stone colour in contrast. The ceiling bosses have been picked out in brilliant colours.

Between St Peter's and the station is a run-down area of nineteenth-century Brighton, with unexpected delights here and there, like the little houses round the green of Pelham Square, or the open-air street market of Kensington Gardens, traffic-free and with shops spilling their goods on to the pavement. In Ann Street is a monumental Victorian church, **St Bartholomew's**, built in the 1870s by Father Arthur Wagner, a wealthy High Churchman who built churches all over the poorer areas of Brighton. Pevsner says of it: 'As far as East Sussex is concerned it may well be the most moving of all churches.' It is certainly the most overwhelming, built entirely of brick and with a nave roof soaring up to the fantastic height of 135 feet – higher than Westminster Abbey. Like St Peter's it is orientated north and south, which means that the midday sun streams through the vast rose window, lightening the gloom of the tall brick arches along the nave. It was intended to have an apsidal north (altar) end, but the money ran out, and instead there is a blank brick wall, with a giant silver cross where the window should be. With its golden mosaics beside the altar, enormous baldacchino (altar canopy) and ornate silver sanctuary lamps, St Bartholomew's is as exotic in its way as the Royal Pavilion, and forms a weighty Byzantine counterpart to the Pavilion's mock-Indian frivolity.

From the station, Queens Road leads down to West Street and the front, passing modern Brighton on the way. Western Road is the main shopping centre, with the typical new-town precinct of Churchill Square on its southern side. In West Street is St Paul's church (built by Arthur Wagner's father), with a prominent octagonal belfry tower; and then you are on the front again, below the blatant modernity of the Top Rank entertainment centre's jazzy roofline.

Near by the two hotels that sum up Victorian holiday luxury stand side by side: the **Grand**, white-painted and black-balconied, built in the 1860s and by now matured into near-elegance; and the red-brick bulk of the **Metropole**, completed in 1890. They, like the other large hotels, are now used as much for conferences and exhibitions as for holiday visitors. The boxers, actresses and 'ladies of the Gaiety with their cavaliers' commented on by C. B. Cochran, have made way for a worthier though duller clientele.

Along the front towards Hove is the **West Pier**, which is at present under sentence of death if no buyer can be found for it. **Hove** itself begins with tremendous panache at the bow fronts and massive pilasters of **Brunswick Square**, built in the 1820s. Though it seems incredible nowadays, Hove was once a smuggling village. But any reminders of the past have long ago vanished under the relentless grid pattern of housing, with **Grand Avenue** as the main windswept thoroughfare up from the front. At the seaward end a green bronze statue of

Victoria, enthroned above panels symbolising Empire, Education, Science and Art, and Commerce, turns her back on the feeble modern blocks of flats and gazes out to sea. Set in the side lawns verging the avenue are 'dog toilets' – sawn-off lamp-posts surrounded by beds of cinders – where the Hove dogs primly relieve themselves.

Hove is the only place I know where the gasworks is built next door to the church, and in the main shopping street. Though the church has been completely remodelled externally, it still has Norman columns inside. Sir George Everest, the Surveyor-General of India after whom Mount Everest was named, is buried in the graveyard. Brooker Hall, the home of the Hove council offices in New Church Road, has a faint echo of the Royal Pavilion's orientalism standing in the fore-court. This is the **Jaipur Gateway**, made of ornately carved teak and crowned with a dome, which was built for the Colonial Exhibition of 1886. Between Brunswick Square and Grand Avenue, the plan of Brighton's Kemp Town is echoed in the hour-glass-shaped layout of **Palmeira Square** and **Adelaide Crescent**, with a landscaped garden between tall houses that look as though they have strayed from South Kensington. Hove makes its own contribution to marine gaiety in the long row of bathing chalets along the pedestrian esplanade, all newly painted blue-green, with the doors a brilliant spectrum of different colours.

At their western end, Brighton and Hove merge into the industrialised landscape of Shoreham Harbour (see p. 390).

For most people Brighton remains the front, and the strip of shingle that leads down to the sea. This was so in George's day, when Martha Gunn and Old Smoaker ruled over the bathing machines; and it is still true today, when holiday-makers (plus the hippies, who sleep rough much of the year and even spend hot afternoons in their sleeping-bags) are so tight-jammed that you can hardly get to the sea between them.

Though Brighton has two very fine piers, it has lost the father of them all, the splendid Chain Pier, which stood a little east of the **Palace Pier** from 1823 until it was destroyed by a storm in 1896. Built originally for the strictly utilitarian purpose of landing passengers at Brighton without getting their feet wet, and looking like a suspension bridge that came to an end abruptly in the middle of the sea, the Chain Pier became a fashionable place for a stroll, and was used for band concerts and firework displays. In 1843 Queen Victoria landed there after crossing from France in the royal yacht; a cheerful painting in the Royal Pavilion shows the yacht surrounded by an army of small boats and smothered in flags and bunting.

Another nineteenth-century enterprise still survives at this end of the front – **Volk's Electric Railway**, whose carriages, initialled VR with cunningly implied royal patronage, trundle backwards and forwards beside Madeira Drive. Magnus Volk was a great pioneer in the use of electricity, and his railway, opened in 1883, was the first electric railway in Britain. In 1896 he built an extension below the cliffs to Rottingdean. As the track was covered at high tide, he devised an extraordinary carriage on stilts, known as the 'Daddy-Longlegs', which could hold 150 people. This contraption wobbled along the coast until the turn of the century, when the Rottingdean line was abandoned.

Madeira Drive itself has a fine piece of Victorian elegance in the cast-iron arcade, painted blue and cream, which forms the backdrop for the end of the London to Brighton veteran car run. At the Drive's western end, opposite the roundabout where the Old Steine joins the front, is the most splendid cast-iron construction of all – the cathedral-like arcades of the **Brighton Aquarium**, where fish of every shape, colour and size goggle at you with a solemnity fitting to the place. The aquarium was opened in 1872, and from then on no visit, royal or otherwise, was considered complete without 'a tour of the tanks'. The aquarium's latest addition is a dolphinarium, where the dolphins leap, play football, and even sing in their buzzsaw-like voices.

At the eastern end of Madeira Drive, cranes, piledrivers and massive works out to sea show where Brighton is keeping up to date – as always – with a new **Marina**. This complex of inner and outer harbour, flats and hotels, is due for completion in 1978.

A mile or so inland are two very different museums worth hunting out. The **Booth Museum of British Birds** in Dyke Road is a real curiosity – an immense and well-lit hangar built in the last century to house the enormous collection assembled by E. T. Booth, a wealthy Brighton sportsman. At the door you are faced by the enormous punt-gun with which he wreaked havoc among the wildfowl; and the cases contain everything from golden eagles at an eyrie, reconstructed down to the last stone and twig, to bramblings in a landscape of snow and artificial icicles. More conventional is **Preston Manor**, beyond the arches of the great railway viaduct across the Preston Road. Once the manor house of a village right outside Brighton, it is now a museum with a fine collection of furniture from its final two centuries of private occupation. The low white classical house was built in 1738 on much older foundations: there are still traces of medieval work below ground level. House and contents were bequeathed to the town in 1933; strangely, it has far more of a lived-in feeling about it than many houses that are still occupied.

A little thirteenth-century church, the old parish church of Preston, adjoins the manor garden. It has traces of medieval wall paintings, one showing the murder of Becket, and carved heads on the choir stalls attributed to Grinling Gibbons.

A couple of miles along the London Road, on the northern outskirts of Brighton, the steep village street of **Patcham** keeps the old downland atmosphere. The hilltop church has a Norman chancel arch, with remains of medieval painting above; and behind the church a great barn marks the point where Brighton ends and the country begins.

Leaving Brighton along the Lewes Road, you come to the centres of higher education, first the glass box of the College of Technology, and at the very outskirts of the town **Sussex University** and the Brighton College of Education facing each other across the dual carriageway. Built in the beautifully undulating landscape of **Stanmer Park**, the university has such an idyllic setting that you wonder how anybody gets any work done. In its design Sir Basil Spence ingeniously combined the quadrangle principle of Oxford and Cambridge with the use of brick as a building material, and added a touch of his own by incorporating reflecting sheets of water here and there. A building of arresting originality is the circular Meeting House, an interdenominational chapel, with walls built of concrete blocks alternating with coloured glass. The Gardner Centre for the Arts, designed by Sean Kenny, takes the circular idea one stage further by tacking circular studios and music rooms round the periphery of a circular central auditorium. The university has the space to build out instead of up, and so the students have a cellular village to live in rather than tower blocks. The few farms that make up Stanmer village are at the end of the long drive to **Stanmer House,** a stone classical building now the university music school, which looks across wide lawns to a spiky nineteenth-century church.

Near by, unseen from the main road which brings you back to Lewes four miles away, is the village of **Falmer** – flint-built houses by a large muddy pond, a Victorian church with sheep grazing among the tombstones, and the open sweep of the downs behind.

CHAPTER TWENTY-TWO

From the Adur to the Arun

�֍

SINCE Roman times there has been a harbour at the mouth of the Arun, where the river gives access to the great hinterland north of the downs. The modern **Shoreham Harbour**, shaped like the letter T with an immensely elongated upper horizontal, runs for a good three miles, from the western end of Hove through Portslade and Southwick to the old town of Shoreham; it forms an inland lagoon protected from the sea by long spits of shingle. Shoreham is in fact the biggest commercial harbour between Southampton and Dover; and its wharves and derricks, stacks of timber and petrol storage tanks, not to mention the chimneys of the vast power station, strike a harshly industrial note on this holiday coast.

At **Shoreham** itself you come to the yachtsman's water, where crowds of sailing dinghies cram together at the riverside. The town keeps vestiges of its seagoing past, like the High Street pub with an enormous and gaudy ship's figurehead attached to the wall. In medieval times Shoreham was the busiest port on the South Coast, a centre for the export of wool from England and the import of wine from France. King John landed there with an army in 1199, and in 1346 Shoreham had to raise twenty-six ships – more than Bristol or Dover – to fight the French. Its most famous historical moment came in 1651, when Charles II, fleeing from England after the Battle of Worcester, escaped to France in the coalbrig *Surprise*. Her captain, Nicholas Tettersell, is said to have been paid £60 for his part in the escape. After the Restoration the *Surprise* was renamed *The Royal Escape* and enrolled in the English fleet (see also Bramber, p. 362).

Shoreham is famous for its two magnificent Norman churches, **St Mary de Haura** or 'New' Shoreham church, right

A map for this chapter will be found on pages 354-5.

in the town, and **St Nicholas**, 'Old' Shoreham church, half a
mile to the north near the river. They may have been built by
successive members of the de Braose family, the lords of the
Rape of Bramber (see Hastings, p. 282). With its noble tower,
centrally placed and square-cut, St Mary de Haura is a most
queenly building. (The name 'de Haura' means 'of the
harbour', as in the French Le Havre.) It was originally far
larger than it is now, with a nave that stretched to the ruined
wall in the churchyard beyond the west door. One bay of the
Norman nave still stands, but the most magnificent Norman
work is in the four arches below the tower. In the Transitional
period at the end of the twelfth century the Norman apsidal
east end was replaced by the present wide choir and aisles,
it has been suggested that the masons came on to Shoreham
from Canterbury, after they had finished the choir there in
1184. Unusually for a parish church, there is a triforium
gallery above the arcades; on the triforium arches are hook-
shaped corbels, of a type found mainly in France. An unlikely
celebrant of the beauty of St Mary's was that dogged atheist
Swinburne, who wrote of its

> Tower set square to the storms of air and change of
>   season that glooms and glows,
> Wall and roof of it tempest-proof, and equal ever to suns
>   and snows,
> Bright with riches of radiant niches and pillars smooth as
>   a straight stem grows.

And so on for several more wordy stanzas.

Roughly contemporary is the **Marlipins** building, now a local
museum, in the High Street – a small building full of character,
with a chequerboard stone front. Nairn suggests that it may
have been the de Braose customs office.

Old Shoreham church, **St Nicholas**, is much less dramatic
than St Mary's. Left stranded when the river silted up and the
port moved downstream, it still has its long narrow Saxon
nave; and later Norman and thirteenth-century work has not
destroyed the homely scale. The nave may date back to before
AD 900. As at New Shoreham, the tower and transepts are
Norman. The arches are carved in every variety of Norman
ornament: the church guide lists 'chevron with pellets; cable
with beads; billet, stud, lozenge and rose; wheel stud; limpet'.
There is also a grinning Cheshire cat over the arch into the

nave, and a bearded king (perhaps Stephen) and his queen on either side of the northern arch. The wooden screen across the chancel is late thirteenth-century and one of the oldest in the country.

From Shoreham two roads lead west along the coast – the A 259, which keeps close to the shoreline as far as Worthing, and thereafter runs a mile or so inland; and the more important A 27 to Arundel, which gives access to the villages of the South Downs. The A 27 traffic now crosses the Adur by a new bridge with a cloverleaf interchange beyond; and the old wooden tollbridge, which used to be one of the worst bottle-necks on the South Coast, has been relegated to the status of a footbridge.

South Lancing, half way between Shoreham and Worthing, is a haphazard seaside place, largely residential, with a good beach.

Worthing is recognisably of the same family as Brighton. While hardly a poor relation, it is altogether a quieter town, without the bounce but without the brazenness either. In place of the exuberant Prinny to set it on its course, Worthing had his delicate younger sister, Princess Amelia, who came there for her health in 1798. Until the bathing boom of the late eighteenth century, Worthing was a fishing hamlet, an offshoot of Broadwater up the road. By about 1820 it had a Steyne, like Brighton, and smart rows of houses like Warwick Street were springing up. The oldest parts of the town are concentrated in the streets round the pier: the bow windows of Liverpool Terrace and Montague Place, and the straight frontages of Montague Street, now turned into a most successful shopping precinct. Alas, the theatre in Ann Street, where Mrs Siddons acted Portia, and which Nairn called 'the most endearing of Worthing's old buildings', has been demolished to make way for a car park at present and a shopping centre in the future.

The spine of modern Worthing runs inland from the pier, up South Street and Chapel Road, to the neo-Georgian town hall topped by a feeble cupola. In the building next door is a first-rate local **Museum**, with cases illustrating the history of an area which has been inhabited since Palaeolithic times, and a special children's corner full of Victorian dolls, toys and games. A set of rooms is furnished and decorated in period styles, with dummies dressed in clothes from the museum's large costume collection. Upstairs is an art gallery which specialises in Sussex painters and puts on enterprising temporary exhibitions. Chapel Road is named from the big porticoed **Parish Church,** which was built in 1812 as a chapel-of-ease to Broadwater and became the parish church in 1892. Inside, with its white-painted galleries and flat ceiling, it is much more elegant than its ponderous outer appearance would suggest. When it was first built, the pews were sold freehold, together with the soil on which they stood – one way of making sure of a seat in church. In 1862 a pew cost between £37 and £70, according to size and position.

Sea-front Worthing can be bedevilled by piles of seaweed, yards wide and stinking as it rots in the sun. But if you are driven off the beach, there are good swimming-pools to choose from.

The most sparkling of Oscar Wilde's comedies, *The Importance of being Earnest*, may have taken some of its high spirits from the general good temper of Worthing. Wilde wrote it in three weeks while on holiday there in September, 1894, and named his hero John Worthing in appreciation.

Broadwater, the parent village of Worthing, has been largely obliterated by the needs of traffic; even its large green is isolated between torrents of cars. However, there are some old village houses left in Broadwater Street East, and the splendid low-towered Norman church still rises above the trees. Inside, below the tower, are two very fine late Norman arches carved with all manner of ornamentation, including a row of beakheads. Two of the best-known nineteenth-century writers on natural history, W. H. Hudson and Richard Jefferies, are buried in Broadwater cemetery south of the green. The name of the village derives from a wide tongue of the sea that once stretched inland below the downs.

Tarring (or West Tarring, to distinguish it from Tarring Neville near Newhaven) is another village that has been engulfed by Worthing. As it is lucky enough not to be on a main road, it has kept far more of its village character than Broadwater. The narrow High Street has plenty of pretty white-painted houses; but Tarring's showpiece is a row of fifteenth-century half-timbered cottages, run as a museum of local bygones by the Sussex Archaeological Trust. Near by is what remains of a palace of the Archbishops of Canterbury, a gabled medieval building now used as the village school. Though the Old Palace was built after Becket's time, there is a strong tradition that he stayed at Tarring. He is said to have planted the first fig tree grown in this country in his garden there; and Tarring is still a great place for figs. One garden (Bishops Garth) seems to grow nothing else. St Richard of Chichester lived at Tarring in the 1240s, and carried out a miraculous graft on a fig tree there.

Tarring has a massive church, with a tall spire rising above a battlemented tower. The nave was built in the thirteenth century at the same time as the Old Palace. In the chancel, it is worth upending the medieval misericord seats to look at the carvings of flowers and bearded heads on the under sides. The faded mosaics above the arcades were done in 1885 by Italian craftsmen brought over for the purpose; the result hardly seems worth the effort. Tarring still belongs to Canterbury and is, in ecclesiastical jargon, an 'archbishop's peculiar'.

Between Worthing and Littlehampton is a coastal strip that is a curious medley of half-smothered villages and exclusive seaside estates, guarded by barriers and notices telling you to keep out and not to park. The northern boundary is the A 259, lined with market gardens, huge glasshouses and ultra-modern laboratories where mushrooms and other plants are investigated and developed.

At **Ferring** there is a unique survival on this stretch of coast: about half a mile of road which runs with the sea untrammelled on one side and fields, open and unbuilt-on, on the other. How this has escaped the developers remains a mystery. Heading eastwards, you will not find another stretch of road remotely similar (downland roads excluded) until you are almost at Bexhill, a distance of over forty miles. Ferring can be a hard place to get to, as the level-crossing gates that give access to it close with the regularity of the jaws of a feeding crocodile. Its neat little Early English church, at the heart of a recognisable village centre, is full of tablets to the Henty and Olliver families, and has the bassoon and clarinet from the old church band in a glass case inside the door.

The most famous of the Ollivers is buried on **Highdown Hill**, a little way north of the main road. This was John Olliver, whose mill once stood on the hill and who died in 1793, aged eighty-four. When he was not actually grinding corn, his thoughts seem to have dwelt on the subject of death to a most un-millerish degree. He kept his coffin under his bed, and had his tomb made thirty years before his death. 'At his funeral,' says Murray's *Hand-book*, 'his coffin was carried round the field by persons dressed in white, and attended by a company of young women attired in white muslin, one of whom read a sermon over the grave.' The tomb is hidden away behind the gardens of **Highdown**, the prototype of all chalk gardens, made by Sir Frederick Stern and now run by the Worthing Corporation (open weekdays all the year). Where the hillside has been cut away the plants sprout happily from what appears to be a solid bed of chalk and flint rubble. Elsewhere sloping lawns look across Ferring to the sea.

East Preston, whose coastal extension is for some reason called Angmering-on-Sea, has a much-restored Early English church to which a remarkably thin tower (just over six feet wide internally) was added about 1500.

Angmering, half way between the two main roads, has managed to keep its separate identity. It is an unexpectedly hilly place, built round a small tree-shaded village green. The church stands high up on the northern side; virtually all that remains of the original building is the western tower of 1507, tacked on to the harsh stonework of a near-complete Victorian reconstruction. Inside the best thing is the Victorian font, carved with flowers and leaves of a Grinling Gibbons-like delicacy. Opposite the church is a nice little alley of stone cottages, several of them whitewashed; and up the hill on the other side of the green are some fine flint houses, including the Sussex Archaeological Trust's Pigeon House, which conceals the massive timbers of a medieval hall house behind its flint and brick exterior.

The nearest village to Littlehampton is **Rustington**, which has a good many old thatched cottages, and a fine medieval church dating mainly from about 1170, among the shopping centres and bungalows. Below the church tower at ground level is the sturdy eighteenth-century mechanism that works the clock. A few minutes' walk down Sea Lane is Knightscroft House, a large red-tiled Victorian building where the composer Sir Hubert Parry lived from 1879 until his death in 1918. He wrote his setting of Blake's *Jerusalem* there – an artistic link across the years with Blake's Felpham (see p. 423) a few miles down the coast.

Littlehampton is the least pretentious of all the South Coast resorts. Though it has no pier and no proper sea front, it makes up for these deficiencies by wide beaches, especially the expanse of dune and sand on the western side of the Arun, and the lively harbour, where speedboats zip about with Mediterranean panache. Littlehampton was an important port as far back as Saxon times, and in the Middle Ages was a landing-place for the Caen stone from Normandy used in churches and secular buildings all over Sussex.

In later centuries it pottered on quietly as a small port easily accessible from France, and at the end of the eighteenth century shared some of the prosperity brought by the bathing machine. In 1808 it was visited by Lord Byron; but it never acquired the elegant terraces of a Regency seaside resort. Most of the hotels and boarding houses, set back behind the enormous seafront green, are redbrick Victorian and Edwardian. A few old flint houses survive well inland, round the High Street and Church Street area; but even the parish church is modern – a brick rebuilding of the 1930s in a style well described by Nairn as 'eerie disembodied Gothic'. It is a simple building, full of light and surrounded by wooden galleries, to which all the monuments from the previous church have been banished. The tracery of a Decorated window was salvaged and built into the tower. There is a small museum in River Road, which has brooches and pottery from local Roman villas, and a good assemblage of old paintings and photographs of Littlehampton, best of which is a large oil painting showing Victorians walking along the gusty promenade beside the bumps and hollows of the green, not yet levelled out when the scene was painted.

The day cannot be far off when **Lyminster** links up with Littlehampton; but for the moment it is still a self-contained village, looking inland and across the watermeadows to the churches and towers of Arundel, rather than southwards to the sea. At the beginning of the tenth century the name appears in Alfred the Great's will as 'Lullyngminster', and by the early tenth century at the latest there was a Benedictine nunnery here. The church, long, tall and narrow, still keeps its Saxon form. Originally the nave was the parish church, and the chancel was set aside for the nuns. The north aisle was added about 1170, and the tower some thirty years later. A coffin slab behind the font is said to come from the grave of a local hero, a farmer's boy called Jim Pulk, who killed a dragon that was ravaging the countryside. This dragon lived in the Knucker Hole, a circular pool among the reeds a hundred yards or so down the track that runs north of the churchyard. The Anglo-Saxon word for sea-monster is 'nicor', and this legend may be the survival of some dim folk memory of a conflict between a local Beowulf and the Lyminster Grendel. The Knucker Hole still steams with a dragon-like breath in winter; though it was plumbed a few years ago and found to be about thirty feet deep, with no trace of even the smallest monster.

Arundel is everyone's idea of what an ancient town should be: a steep street of old buildings rising from a peaceful river, a huge church on the crest of the hill, the soaring towers of a castle against a backcloth of park and woodland. Even when you discover that the church (in fact the Roman Catholic cathedral) is a Gothic imitation of the 1870s, and that the castle's main buildings date from twenty years later, the medieval illusion is not really spoiled. Seen from a short distance away – upstream along the towpath, or from the byroad to South Stoke – Arundel blends the genuine and the sham harmoniously together. The heavy traffic, which will continue to shake the walls of Arundel until a bypass is built or the bridge at Littlehampton is strengthened, completes the picture of a town besieged.

Arundel first appears in history in 901, when it is mentioned in King Alfred's will. Until the eighteenth century, the name was usually spelt 'Arundell', which splits conveniently to mean 'the dell on the Arun'. But a much more fanciful and attractive suggestion derives it from 'hirondelle', the French for swallow, because it is the first place where summer reaches Sussex. Or, better still for so legendary a place, from a legendary horse, the swift steed Hirondelle, ridden by the giant Bevis of Southampton. Bevis was warder of the gatehouse of **Arundel Castle** (one of the castle's Norman towers is named after him). Every week he ate a whole ox, together with enormous quantities of bread and mustard, and drank two hogsheads of beer. When he felt his death was near, he climbed to the top of his tower and hurled his huge sword, called Mongley or Morglay, far away across the park. Bevis was buried where it fell. Mongley hangs on a wall in the castle armoury – an evident impostor, as it is a quite ungigantic medieval two-handed sword, much smaller than a Chinese execution sword that hangs near by.

The Saxons would certainly have had some kind of fortification at so strategic a spot. After the Conquest the combined Rapes of Arundel and Chichester were given to Roger de Montgomery, the most powerful of all the Norman barons, who began his stone castle soon after 1070. The inner gateway dates from his time; the square stone outer barbican was built by the Fitzalan family at the end of the thirteenth century. A little north of this entrance is the Norman keep, a circular building that fits neatly on the top of a steeply conical motte. About 1800 one of the Dukes of Norfolk introduced a colony of North American owls into the keep. The birds were named after various friends and acquaintances, sometimes without strict regard for biological accuracy, as happened when the butler announced: 'Please, your grace, Lord Thurlow's laid an egg.' This eminent bird died in 1859, aged over a hundred. The owls had gone by 1870. 'Their privacy,' says Murray, 'was destroyed by excursion trains.'

In 1135 the castle was given to Queen Adeliza, widow of Henry I, who three years later married William de Albini, created the fourth Earl of Arundel but first in his line. From the Albinis Arundel passed to the Fitzalans – who automatically became Earls of Arundel on possessing the castle – and then in the mid sixteenth century to Thomas Howard, fourth Duke of Norfolk. The Norfolks, Earls Marshal and senior peers of England, have lived there ever since, except for a brief interlude in the Civil War. In 1643 the castle was besieged by Sir William Waller's Roundheads, who bombarded it, captured it and occupied it until 1649. The damage was not fully repaired until the final restoration in the 1890s.

The great bogus baronial apartments that are open to the public have come in for consistent criticism; to Augustus Hare, for example, they were 'the climax of discomfort as well as of ugliness'. Personally, I like them; vast vulgarity in the right place never hurt anybody, and no one could call them mean-spirited. On the right as you go in there is a large chapel, all Purbeck marble columns and striped stone vaulting; and on the left is the enormous Barons' Hall, built with impossibly high hammerbeams, and hung with tapestries and portraits. Above the dais at the far end is an endearingly absurd Victorian historical composition showing Thomas, Earl of Surrey, pleading his case for clemency before Henry VII after Bosworth.

The long, low picture gallery, running the whole width of the castle, is lined with the procession of Norfolks and their forebears. Though he looks shrewd, the first Duke, known as the 'Jockey of Norfolk', backed the losing side in the last phase of the Wars of the Roses. According to Shakespeare, the night before Bosworth, when he was killed fighting beside Richard III, he found pinned to his tent a note which ran 'Jockey of Norfolk, be not too bold, For Dickon thy master is bought and sold'. Norfolk died in spite of the warning. His son, the Earl of Surrey shown in the Victorian painting, was taken back into favour by Henry VII and had the dukedom restored by Henry VIII; Henry's executed queens, Anne Boleyn and Katherine Howard, were both the second Duke's grand-daughters. The clean-shaven canny face of the third Duke is that of a man destined to survive – and survive he did, outliving both Henry VIII and his own son, the Earl of Surrey. Henry, Earl of Surrey, has the most magnificent portrait in the gallery; he stands in melancholy pose in a theatrical Renaissance setting of masks and cupids, wearing a sombre suit of dark brown and silver. Known as the 'sweetest poet' of his time, Surrey was executed in 1547, aged about thirty, on the charge of incorporating the arms of Edward the Confessor with his own. The real reason was probably that he wished to marry the king's daughter, Princess (later Queen) Mary. His son, Thomas Howard, the fourth Duke, who as already mentioned acquired Arundel by marriage, is shown as a long-faced dandy. Like his father he aimed too high, and was executed in 1572 for plotting to marry Mary Queen of Scots. In the gallery is a small round portrait of his son, the Blessed Philip Howard (thirteenth Earl of Arundel), beatified for remaining faithful to Roman Catholicism throughout Elizabeth's reign. He was a prisoner in the Tower for eleven years, and died there in 1595.

Obviously a capacity for survival was in the genes of the

Howards. But the fourteenth Earl, no doubt taking warning from the fate of his father, grandfather and great-grandfather, preferred fine art to politics and spent much of his time abroad. He was even out of the country when the castle was bombarded by Waller. A portrait of him in the Drawing-Room shows him in front of the 'Arundel Marbles', classical statues he collected on his travels in Italy. After the Restoration the dukedom was revived, and the Earls Marshal could get on with the peaceable business of organising coronations and other ceremonials.

Round the corner from the gallery is a suite of smaller rooms, of which far the most impressive is the Library, a wood-vaulted tunnel dating from the Regency phase of rebuilding, and lined with leather tomes behind gilded grilles. Mary Queen of Scots appears on an early portrait in the (comparatively) little Billiard Room, and several of her relics are preserved among the gorgeous ceremonial robes of the Norfolks in the Eastern Drawing-Room, including a rosary given to her suitor, the fourth Duke, and a crucifix she was holding as she waited for execution on the scaffold.

Medieval Arundels and more recent Norfolks lie buried in the Fitzalan Chapel, across the lawns west of the castle. The Catholic chapel in fact forms part of the Protestant parish church, from which it is separated by a glass screen; thus Catholic and Protestant services are held under the same roof. Chapel and church were built about 1380; at the Dissolution the chapel fell into decay, and the process of destruction was almost completed by the Roundheads, who stabled their horses among the tombs, while they bombarded the castle from the church tower. The chapel was restored in 1886 by the fifteenth Duke, who built the baronial parts of the castle; his bearded effigy, in green bronze, lies in the centre of the nave. The chief glory of the chapel is the Perpendicular seven-light east window, originally the east window of the parish church. On either side of the altar are Arundel tombs topped by immensely elaborate stone canopies. Near by lies the battered effigy of John, the seventh Earl. Called the 'English Achilles' for his prowess in battle, he was wounded and taken prisoner by the French in 1435, and died a few weeks later as the result of losing his leg. Below the armoured figure lies a *memento mori*, the effigy of a corpse reminding us that to this end must even heroes come.

To get into the parish church you have to go out of the castle and up the High Street. As the Fitzalan Chapel occupies the whole of the chancel, the interior of the church is very truncated. The stone-canopied pulpit is a rare pre-Reformation survival, thought to have been designed by Henry Yevele, the architect of the nave of Canterbury Cathedral. On the north wall are remains of medieval painting, including an angel in long robes that swirl like a Beardsley drawing.

In Arundel the parish church takes second place to the Catholic cathedral over the road. Built by the fifteenth Duke in the 1870s, this vast building was intended to be even vaster, with a spire soaring to 280 feet, which would have made it an overwhelming landmark. It is better seen at a distance than visited, as inside, despite its apsidal east end and forest of superimposed columns, it is not particularly interesting.

From this high point steep alleys of good Sussex pebble-walled cottages lead back to the town centre, and the mixture of small boats and mudflats that gives riverside Arundel its character.

Along the lower edge of Arundel Park a switchback lane runs past the picnic and beauty spot of Swanbourne Lake to **South Stoke**, at the end of a two-mile cul-de-sac. This tiny and peaceful place consists of a few farm buildings, an old rectory, and a small stone church with a Victorian witches'-hat spire perched on the narrow medieval tower. A foot-bridge leads over the Arun to North Stoke and the downs behind Amberley. The main road to Pulborough (see p. 352) skirts the opposite side of the park for two miles north of Arundel.

Heading back towards Shoreham, an even longer cul-de-sac wanders along the eastern side of the Arun for a good three miles before coming to rest among the thatched flint-walled cottages of **Burpham** (pronounced Burfam). The cruciform church has some remarkable bits and pieces inside, notably a vaulted stone roof to the early thirteenth-century chancel, and a late Norman arch in the south arcade, carved on the transept side with grotesque heads, one human and one ape-like, and fringed with savagely spiky chevron ornament.

Church, cottages and creeper-covered pub form as pretty a village centre as you could hope to find.

By comparison, **Poling** is hardly a village at all. It consists of a few houses down a cul-de-sac south of the A 27, and a small church almost swallowed up by farm buildings. The nave is Saxon, the south aisle of about 1200, and the chancel and tower were added at intervals of about a century. On the north wall is a plaque to Sir Harry Johnston (1858–1927), described as 'administrator, soldier, explorer, naturalist, author and painter'. An immensely able man, Johnston was largely responsible for the various treaties and annexations that added East Africa to the British Empire. He explored widely in East and West Africa, discovered the okapi, and exhibited at the Royal Academy.

Three miles along the road you come to a thoroughly rustic Clapham Common. **Clapham** village, half a mile to the north, off the A 280 to Findon, consists of a single narrow cul-de-sac. The church is in the depths of a wood up a stony track; at one side it overlooks an enormous farm. It is basically Early English, much restored by Sir Gilbert Scott in the 1870s, down to such details as Victorian saints painted in outline in the window splays. The chancel is full of Shelley memorials. On the floor is a brass of 1526 to John Shelley and his wife Elizabeth, who wears a robe decorated with the three whelk shells which formed the 'canting' or punning arms of the Shelleys; and on the north wall is the recessed tomb of their son Sir William, his wife and children, crudely carved one behind the other in line-ahead formation. The hamlet of **Patching** balances Clapham on the other side of the A 280; its church is likewise Early English, but in place of a pyramid cap has a tall spire, covered in green slates. There are eight tons of them, so I was told by a man tending the graveyard.

A mile to the north the main road makes a magnificent sweep through the cornfields along the valley floor. This stretch of road is known as the **Long Furlong**; it was constructed in 1818 by a member of the Shelley family, who tried unsuccessfully to start his own coach service between London and Worthing. The coaches may have failed, but the road is spectacular.

The northern suburbs of Worthing are spreading out towards **Findon**, but have not yet absorbed it. However, the

village has been cut off from the church by a dual carriageway. You get to it from the northbound lane, but if you over-
shoot the little turn you are liable to be carried helplessly
onwards in a surge of traffic. The church is built at the foot of
a steep wooded hill overlooking the pedimented classicism of
Findon Place. It is mainly thirteenth-century, with a wide roof
spanning the double nave, and a thirteenth-century oak
screen. Findon village, across the main road, is a pretty place
built on a network of lanes. One of them takes you past the
wide triangular green and up the hill to **Cissbury Ring**, the
Iron Age capital of this stretch of the downs. Cissbury is a
really grand hill fort, surrounded by a ditch and rampart that
still look defensible. The top is covered by plants of some small
variety of sorrel, which wave in reddish undulations when the
wind passes over them. At the western end Cissbury is gouged
into hollows – the remains of flint mines dug by Neolithic man
centuries before Cissbury became a fortress. Excavations in
the 1950s uncovered a 4,000-year-old tragedy in one of the
mines. The body of a girl was found lying where the roof had
caved in on her, still holding in her hand the charred remains
of the torch she had taken to light her through the galleries.

Back on the A 27 and continuing eastwards, the village and
church at **Sompting**, as at Findon, are sundered by a dual
carriageway. The village, south of the road, is remarkable for
its number of large glasshouses; the church to the north is
unique for its Saxon tower, built early in the eleventh century.
It has a spindly look, due partly to the narrow strips of stone
that run vertically up it. Each side terminates in a steep gable,
and the roof is formed of four diamond-shaped surfaces
meeting in a point – the 'Rhenish helm' shape found nowhere
else in Britain, though common in the German Rhineland.
In 1154 the church was given to the Knights Templars, who
pulled it down except for the tower and rebuilt it, leaving the
Saxon arch from the tower into the nave and keeping the
narrow shape of the original building. As unique as the tower
is the square Templars' chapel, now turned into the south
transept but originally entirely separate; the door through was
cut at a later date. Below the arch into the tower is a Saxon
carver's groping attempt at Ionic capitals; and other fragments
of Saxon carving are attached to the walls. One, a little figure
of an abbot with a book propped beside him, has all the

freshness of the Saxon world, breaking here at Sompting through the world-weary crust of later centuries and more knowing cultures.

North Lancing, a mile inland from South Lancing (see p. 392), still keeps a good deal of the genuine downland feeling in its curved street. The name may be among the most ancient of all Saxon village names, deriving from Wlencing, one of the sons of Aella who led the first Saxon invasion into Sussex in AD 477 (see p. 408). The old church is a comfortable building, typically Norman in plan with its central tower, but largely rebuilt about 1300. It has suffered more than the usual amount of damage from today's vandals: in 1969 an attempt was made to set it on fire, and the whole interior had to be replastered. East of Lancing much of the land towards the sea is taken up by the hangars and buzzing light aircraft of Shoreham airport.

The dominating landmark of the lower Adur is the bulk of **Lancing College Chapel,** standing guard over the valley. You get to it from the road north to Steyning (see p. 360), along the west side of the river. This great stone building is the testament of the Rev. Nathaniel Woodard, who founded Lancing (along with Ardingly and Hurstpierpoint, see pp. 340 and 367) in the middle of the last century. Murray's *Hand-book* gives the social stratifications: Lancing was 'for the education of the upper classes', Hurstpierpoint 'for sons of farmers', and Ardingly 'for sons of small traders'. The other school buildings of Lancing are typically Victorian educational, with flint walls, tall narrow gables, and slate roofs. Though the foundation stone was laid in 1868, the west end of the chapel is still incomplete, awaiting its rose window and flying buttresses. The bronze effigy of Woodard, the instigator of this blend of Victorian practicality and Gothic make-believe, lies in a chantry below the towering vault. The medieval cathedrals must have been like Lancing chapel when they were new. All the stone has a fresh look about it, and carved blocks lie here and there waiting to be placed in position.

The chapel's statistics are cathedral-like: the external height is 150 feet, on a par with Westminster Abbey, and the internal height to the nave roof is ninety feet. All the work was done by college craftsmen, using local materials and without any mechanical assistance. Behind the altar hang three enormous tapestries to scale with the building, each thirty-five feet high by ten wide, and among the largest in the world. They were designed in 1933 in an insipid medievalism, but they give a great splash of colour with their gilded figures and red backgrounds. Benjamin Britten's cantata *St Nicolas* was written for Lancing's centenary in 1948.

North of the college the road wanders past two small medieval churches. **Coombes** is tucked away behind a tall green silage tower and reached across a field. Outside it looks hardly more than a trim stone barn, pierced with Perpendicular windows; but, inside, the early Norman nave and chancel arch are covered with wall paintings, perhaps done as early as 1100. Among them is a fine Lion of St Mark above the arch; and painted inside the arch is an extraordinary figure – a man with a grotesquely elongated mouth, yelling as he strains to support the masonry that bears him down. **St Botolph's** (or Botolph's, omitting the 'St') is a narrow Saxon building, which expanded in the Middle Ages and has since shrunk back to its original size, as a blocked arcade in the north wall shows.

CHAPTER TWENTY-THREE

Chichester

✣

IT would be hard to imagine two places more different than the cathedral cities of Kent and Sussex. Where Canterbury tries to reconcile the needs of a grand administrative and tourist centre with shopping precincts, ring roads and the other trappings of modernity, **Chichester** remains very much the Georgian country town. Canterbury cathedral stands, lordly and aloof, at the centre of its close, cut off from the life of the city outside; whereas Chichester cathedral is a village church writ large, almost on the pavement and opposite the main hotel of the town, its cloisters used as a short cut, and the paths around it made into a display ground for the paintings of local artists. Bell Harry Tower demands attention, but Chichester spire steals upon your notice as you approach the city or wander through the streets. Canterbury takes a bit of getting used to; but you feel at home in Chichester within five minutes.

Chichester stands in a flat plain below the downs, ten miles west of Arundel (see p. 397). Its plan has the simplicity of the Roman town – a plain cross of four roads (North, South, East and West Streets), surrounded by a roughly circular wall, of which a good deal still survives. There may well have been a town of sorts here before the Roman conquest of AD 43; at any rate, the Roman name for Chichester, Noviomagus, seems to imply that it was a new successor to an older foundation. The local tribes (the Regnenses, or 'people of the kingdom') were among the first of the loyal supporters of Rome, and under their ruler Cogidubnus (see Fishbourne, p. 429) they made Chichester into one of the earliest of the thoroughly Romanised towns. The most striking relic of this period is built into the wall of the Council House in North Street, below the brick arcade – a battered dedication stone, dug up near by in 1723, from the Temple of Neptune and

Minerva. This temple was built by the shipwrights of Chichester, and the letters '. . . IDVBNI' (from 'Cogidubni') are still easily legible. The most recent Roman finds have been made during the current restoration of the cathedral, which seems to have been built partly if not completely on the site of a Roman public building. Chichester gets its present name from Cissa, one of the sons of Aella, the Saxon who invaded and conquered Sussex in AD 477 – 'Cissa's Ceaster', the camp or stronghold of Cissa.

Historically speaking, Chichester has always been a backwater, apart from a brief taste of violence in the Civil War. Even the local saint, St Richard, was not a martyr or a miracle-worker, but an ordinary well-loved thirteenth-century bishop. He would find his **Cathedral** far less altered than Becket would if he returned to Canterbury. The bulk of it is still very much the Norman building begun by Bishop Ralph de Luffa at the end of the eleventh century, and continued by Bishop Seffrid a hundred years later, after the great fire of 1187 had destroyed the wooden roof. Seffrid and his successors added the stone vaulting to the roof, and the external flying buttresses to take the additional outward thrust. They also built the bays of the retrochoir behind the high altar, in which the graceful pointed arches of the Transitional take the place of the dumpy rounded openings of Bishop Luffa's Romanesque, and livened up the austere columns of the nave arcades with shafts and stringcourses of black Purbeck marble. Apart from the side chapels and Decorated windows, the only major additions to the original cathedral were the detached campanile on the northern side, dating from about 1400, and the spire, built above the central tower during the fifteenth century. This extra weight was carried by the fire-weakened Norman stones for four hundred years; then, on February 21st 1861, while workmen who had been called in to shore up the tower were at lunch, spire and tower collapsed on to the cathedral floor. 'The beautiful airy spire,' a contemporary reporter wrote, 'sank gently below the cathedral roof, with no more noise, say observers, than that produced by the tilting of a cartload of stones in the road.' The damage was repaired with astonishing speed. Funds were raised, Sir Gilbert Scott was called in as architect, and between 1865 and 1867 the whole tower and spire were rebuilt.

Inside, the most startling novelty is John Piper's huge symbolic tapestry behind the high altar, installed in 1966. The design consists of seven tapestry strips separated by the buttresses of a sixteenth-century oak screen; the three central panels represent the Holy Trinity, and the outer pairs symbolise the four elements above and the evangelists below. They are in the tradition of art patronage established at Chichester by Bishop Bell, who was bishop from 1929 to 1958. Other modern works in the cathedral are the pulpit, an unobtrusive affair of concrete and cast aluminium dating from 1966; and the furnishings of the St Mary Magdalene chapel (closed for structural repairs), centring on a Graham Sutherland painting of Christ appearing to St Mary after the resurrection. (The painting is in temporary storage until the repairs to the cathedral are completed.) Bell is commemorated by a portrait plaque, and by the Bell-Arundel screen at the west end of the choir, a graceful stone arcade built by Bishop Arundel about 1475, taken down by the Victorians and restored in 1961.

An earlier patron of the arts, though a less disinterested one, was Bishop Sherburne, who in Henry VIII's time commissioned the enormous paintings on wood in the two transepts. The artist was Lambert Barnard, who does not seem to have been particularly competent. His portraits of kings and bishops look remarkably like Victorian bit-part actors dressed up as kings and bishops; no doubt they have been retouched down the years. The south transept painting shows Sherburne receiving a guarantee of the rights of the cathedral from the king. Sherburne's gilded tomb is in the south choir aisle, between the cathedral's greatest works of art – the two twelfth-century stone panels showing Christ arriving at the house of Martha and Mary, and the Raising of Lazarus. There is no feeling of joy or triumph over death on the faces of these hieratic figures, only intense concentration as Christ and the disciples arrive at the house, and intense weariness when the miracle is accomplished. The effect would surely not have been so overwhelming when the empty eye-sockets were filled with precious stones and the faces and draperies were painted.

It is surprising that these sculptures escaped the attention of Sir William Waller's Puritans, who captured Chichester after a brief siege in 1643. When the troops entered the cathedral, they 'ran up and down with their swords drawn, defacing the monuments of the dead, and hacking the seats and stalls'. St Richard's shrine, which stood on the dais behind the high altar, had already disappeared at the Reformation. Whether because of Roundhead zeal or for some other reason there are remarkably few ancient memorials in the cathedral. Best are the pair of Arundel tombs in the north aisle, to Maud, Countess of Arundel, about 1270, and Richard Fitzalan, Earl of Arundel, and his wife, carved a century later and lying with their right hands linked.

The strange conflict of emotion roused in a modern sensibility by these calm effigies is described in Philip Larkin's 'An Arundel Tomb'. Here are the first and last stanzas:

> Side by side, their faces blurred,
> The earl and countess lie in stone,
> Their proper habits vaguely shown
> As jointed armour, stiffened pleat,
> And that faint hint of the absurd –
> The little dogs under their feet . . .
>
> Time has transfigured them into
> Untruth. The stone fidelity
> They hardly meant has come to be
> Their final blazon, and to prove
> Our almost-instinct almost true:
> What will survive of us is love.

In the south-west corner, behind the font, a Flaxman relief shows the eighteenth-century poet William Collins, who was born and died in Chichester. He wrote a series of Odes, much approved of by Dr Johnson, which reacted against the fastidious classical style of Alexander Pope. His final insanity is referred to in the inscription.

Two great English musicians are commemorated in the north transept. Thomas Weelkes, composer of madrigals, was organist at the beginning of the seventeenth century. Fortunately he did not live to see the outrages of the Puritans, who 'brake down the organ in the cathedral, and dashed the pipes with their pole-axes, crying in scoff, "Harke how the organs goe!"' Below the tablet to Weelkes an inscription in the floor slabs marks the spot where the ashes of Gustav Holst are buried. The most striking of the post-Cromwellian memorials is the togaed figure of William Huskisson, M.P. for Chichester and later for Liverpool, in the north aisle. Huskisson was the first prominent rail fatality; at the grand opening of the Liverpool and Manchester Railway in 1830 he was knocked over by a train, and died from his injuries.

At the moment the cathedral is undergoing a vast programme of reconstruction, with all the inconveniences to the visitor that such works entail. The foundations have been underpinned with concrete down to bedrock, and for the restoration of the fabric stone is being imported from France, as similar to the original Caen stone as possible. Thus after almost nine centuries the imperfections of the Norman builders are at last being made good.

Adjoining the cathedral on the south side are the cloisters, not monastic cloisters at all, but a covered walkway round the old burial ground or 'paradise' outside the cathedral. From the cloisters a pretty alleyway, St Richard's Walk, runs down to Canon Lane, the residential heart of ecclesiastical Chichester. Canon Lane is given symmetry by a medieval gatehouse at either end, one leading to the Bishop's Palace and the other opening into South Street. The Palace, mainly flint with brick patchings here and there, is set back behind a wide lawn and forecourt; it evolved in a piecemeal way from the Middle Ages to the eighteenth century. Just before the South Street gateway the little houses of Vicars' Close lead the eye back to the spire of the cathedral. They were built in the fifteenth century as the homes of the 'vicars choral' responsible for the cathedral music. Vicars' Hall, at the northern end of the Close, is now turned to more secular purposes: the vaulted crypt is a coffee bar, and the massively beamed hall above a restaurant.

On the other side of South Street is Chichester's eighteenth-century theatre, transmuted into an antique market. The area behind, known as **The Pallants**, is the purest Georgian red-brick and is a microcosm of the larger city, with its four roads, meeting at a central point, called North, South, East and West Pallant. (The area should by rights be called the Pallant in the singular, as the name derives from *palantia*, meaning a district over which the Archbishop of Canterbury had, until

1552, jurisdiction or palatine rights.) Finest of all the fine houses here is **Pallant House**, now the headquarters of the Chichester R.D.C. The bewildered-looking stone birds on top of the gate piers look like dodos but are alleged to be ostriches, carved from written descriptions sent home by the wine merchant for whom Pallant House was built.

As splendid as Pallant House is the William and Mary house in West Street, built by John Edes and now used as the record offices of the West Sussex County Council. Behind, by way of contrast, is the wishy-washy pseudo-Georgian of County Hall. Best of this cluster of modern buildings is the West Sussex county library, opened in 1967, a glass and concrete drum of a place which looks exactly what it is – a highly efficient building for the swift retrieval and study of information.

On the corner of Tower Street and West Street is the **Church of St Peter the Great**, a bare Victorian building, with unusually graceful arcading and a splendidly bewhiskered collection of corbel heads. West Street ends just past the long grey-painted front of the Dolphin and Anchor Hotel, a coaching inn with cobbled central courtyard. A few yards away is the **City Cross**, the hub of Chichester, which survives unshaken amid the heaviest of traffic. The cross was given to the town by Bishop Story in 1501; it is an octagon, left open underneath for market traders, and surmounted by a crown of stone pinnacles and ribs rising to a central lantern.

The **Council House**, already mentioned, is the centrepiece of North Street. The main section, perched up on a brick arcade, was built in 1731; on top is a stone lion, 'in an attitude', says Chichester's excellent city guide, 'which is both uncomfortable and nonchalant.' This is the home of the city council, making, together with Pallant House and County Hall, a trio of official buildings, each in a different quadrant of the town. (The fourth quadrant is of course mainly given over to the authority of the Church.) The council chamber, lined with portraits of kings and city notabilities, is directly above the arcade. Behind are kept the regalia and other civic treasures, which you can see on request: the mayor's mace, the silver-gilt snuffbox which once belonged to 'Butcher' Cumberland, silver goblets, a model of a Battle of Britain pilot given by RAF Tangmere, the flag of Chartres, which is 'twinned' with Chichester. At the back of the Council House is a large assembly room, added by Wyatt in 1783, with tall mirrors that give it the illusion of being double its already considerable size.

Between the Council House and the market cross is **St Olave's**, one of Chichester's medieval churches, still serving an ecclesiastical purpose as an S.P.C.K. bookshop; and John Nash's hefty Doric portico, leading to a covered market where you can buy anything from groceries to antiques. The **Ship Hotel**, north of the Council House, is a magnificently tall red-brick Georgian house, built about 1790 for Admiral Sir George Murray, Commander-in-Chief at Portsmouth. Inside, a splendid iron-balustraded staircase soars up to the second storey, with an elaborate plaster ceiling overhead. Allied generals made the Ship their headquarters during the Second World War; and Sir George's traditions are maintained by having each hotel room named after a different ship of the Navy.

Directly behind the Ship is **Priory Park**, an open space which takes up a good third of the north-east quarter of the city. At one corner is the grassy mound where Chichester's medieval castle once stood; it was probably little more than a timber stockade, as there is no trace of stone fortifications. The park takes its name from the Greyfriars (Franciscans), who settled in Chichester about 1240. The choir of their church, flooded with light from the tall Decorated windows, is now an annexe of the Chichester museum, with cases tracing the whole history of the city, and exhibits telling the story of St Francis and his followers. The main **Museum** is near by, on the corner of East Row and Little London. Built in the eighteenth century as a corn store, it was converted with typical Chichester good sense instead of being torn down, as would have happened in so many less enlightened places. Strangest of all the local exhibits is the seventeenth-century 'municipal moon' – a vast circular lantern that was carried in front of the mayor on any official visits he had to make after dark. Near the entrance is a squat little statue of a blue-coat boy from Oliver Whitby's School (now incorporated with that other bluecoat school, Christ's Hospital at Horsham, see p. 347). This particular boy, so the story goes, was turned into a statue for falsely swearing that he was innocent of a theft of which he had been accused, and has remained an awful warning ever since. Upstairs are two rooms devoted to the history and uniforms of the Royal Sussex Regiment, full of redcoats, drums, portraits, and a diorama of the Battle of Quebec. Outside the museum a tall pillar of green stone, carved by John Skelton into the rough shape of a pair of hands, thrusts up from the cobbles of the pavement, a modern symbol of discovery perfectly at home in its eighteenth-century setting.

At the heart of this quadrant of the city is St Martin's Square, more a widened bend in the road than a formal layout, with grey-washed houses leading up to Priory Park. **St Mary's Hospital**, on the south side of the square, is the most extraordinary building in Chichester. It was built about 1290, and consisted originally of a hall (used as an infirmary) and chapel under a single enormous roof. Towards the end of the seventeenth century, eight small flats for old people were built in the infirmary section, and apart from modern mains services they have hardly been altered in the last three hundred years. Anyone planning for the needs of the elderly should take a look at St Mary's, which nicely gauges the requirements of the inmates – a communal central corridor, semi-privacy in the kitchens which look on to the corridor through wooden grilles, and complete privacy in the bedrooms and sitting rooms at the back. The chapel has fine Decorated piscina and sedilia, and a vintage group of grotesque miseri-cords.

A few hundred yards away, on the corner of East Street and East Walls, is the **Shippams Factory**, the modernised premises of the firm that has been making fish and meat paste in Chichester since 1750. You can look over the factory in working hours. It is unobtrusive, in spite of the large area of the city it takes up.

Modern Chichester has been put on the map by the **Festival Theatre**, which runs an outstanding series of different pro-ductions throughout the summer. The theatre is in Oaklands Park, north of the old city; it is a hexagonal building, built in the early 1960s on uncompromisingly functional lines. The open stage is surrounded by the audience on three sides, the upper seats are cantilevered externally to form a kind of entrance portico, and the whole paraphernalia of lights, acoustic reflectors and structural steel wires are displayed naked and unashamed above the auditorium. Sir John Clements, the director, has tried to make the season a 'festival of acting', putting on anything from Restoration comedy to Brecht and John Arden.

C.G.K.S.

CHAPTER TWENTY-FOUR

Around Chichester

꒰꒱

SOUTH of Chichester, the deep inlet of Chichester Channel isolates the Selsey peninsula. In E. V. Lucas's day you could take a tram from Chichester out to Selsey; but a whole fleet of trams could hardly carry today's holidaymakers. A pub sign at **Donnington**, where the main roads to Selsey and the Witterings divide, is painted with the red Selsey Tram as a reminder of that leisurely means of transport. Old Donnington is a little to the south; the church stands well back among the fields, and was largely rebuilt in 1939, after a disastrous fire.

Apuldram or Appledram near by derives its name from the Old English *apulder*, apple tree; this is still good orchard country. As at Donnington, the church lies by itself down a long path. Inside is a carved fifteenth-century oak screen in the south aisle; and the little organ, described in the church guide as 'of very sweet tone', was originally the Prince Consort's private organ at Windsor Castle, coming to this remote spot after some time in the church at Littlehampton. Near Apuldram is **Dell Quay**, a little yachting centre and the port of Chichester before the canal was built.

About a mile south of Apuldram the road passes a spot marked '**Manhood End**' on the Ordnance Survey map, but not in evidence on the ground. The name is a corruption of Mainwood, the vast forest which once stretched southwards from the downs to the sea, and came to be known simply as 'the Manhood'. This was an important area in English history, as it was on the coast near West Wittering that Aella landed with his Saxon followers in 477, and established the kingdom of the South Saxons that was to become Sussex. Two centuries later, in 665, St Wilfrid was wrecked on this coast, met with a hostile reception and was lucky to escape with his life. In 681 he returned south after being expelled from his northern bishopric. Perhaps the way had been paved for him by the monk Dicul (see Bosham, p. 431); at any rate, the elements were working for him. The Saxons were starving after three years without rain (it seems rather hard to believe while the rain lashes down on Selsey Bill), and were so desperate that many of them were drowning themselves in the sea. The Saxon king Ethelwald agreed to be baptised by Wilfrid; and as soon as this was done the heavens opened and the famine was at an end. Wilfrid was granted lands in 'Selesea' (the island of the sea-calf or seal), and built a monastery near Church Norton. He is also credited with teaching the people of Selsey how to fish, as an alternative to drought-ridden agriculture.

Birdham lies off the main road a mile beyond the serried ranks of masts in the Chichester Yacht Basin. The church-yard contains a gigantic conifer, gnarled and contorted like the most extravagant tree in a Japanese print. The yachting village of **West Itchenor** lies down a dead end on the way to West Wittering; the road ends with a row of cottages, a yacht club and a shingle foreshore. The little thirteenth-century church stands about half a mile up the hill from the harbour. Its most notable external feature is a great flint arch supporting the bell turret, added in the nineteenth century.

West Wittering village lies well back from the beach and the sea resort. The walls are mainly flint and rounded stones from the beach, typical of the whole of this stretch of coast. The church is a fine jumble, consisting of a twelfth-century core, with thirteenth-century chancel, and a tower with louvred belfry tacked on the north side. Inside there are many treasures. The tub-shaped font is probably Saxon; and there is a stone carved with a Saxon cross on each side on the wall in a glass case. This may have been the original gable cross of about AD 740, from the earliest days of Christianity here, thrown down when the Danes harried this coast about 1000, and then set up again with a new cross on the other side in the more settled times of Canute (1016–35). Built into the north wall of the chancel are a pair of magnificent tombs of the Ernley family, dating from between 1530 and 1550. The larger and earlier tomb has a mutilated relief of the Resurrec-tion at the back; the smaller has a carved Annunciation below, with three lily stems as the central motif. St Richard of Chichester may have a direct connection with West Wittering

through a coffin lid with a pastoral staff, at one time thought
to be from the grave of a 'boy bishop'. But Mr W. E. P. Done
(whose church guidebook is practically a history of the area
in its own right) thinks that it may have come from a reliquary
of St Richard, housing some part of the saint's body. Chichester
Cathedral had his head, St Paul's two ribs and Selborne a joint
of finger or toe.

West Wittering resort is a private estate, with the usual row
of seaside houses built behind the shingle bank. It has a
magnificent area of sand at low tide. **East Head** (on the east
of the entrance to Chichester harbour, though the westernmost point of the Selsey peninsula), now belongs to the
National Trust, who have done a lot of planting of marram
grass to stop these acres of dunes and saltings from being
washed away by the sea. There is also danger from sheer
weight of shoe leather, as on summer weekends East Head is
crowded with people sunning themselves. The strait between
East Head and Hayling Island is highly dangerous for
swimmers.

As a resort, **East Wittering** is larger than West Wittering, with caravans, bungalows and a holiday camp. It merges
into **Bracklesham**, which gives its name to the geologist's
'Bracklesham beds', rich in fossils which can still be found on
the shore. There is no road along Bracklesham Bay to Selsey,
though by wandering inland through hamlets like **Earnley**
(with a midget church on a triangular green) and **Almodington**
you can stay fairly close to the coast.

Sidlesham has a nucleus of picture-postcard thatched
houses, and a harbour a mile south of the village, on a creek
of Pagham Harbour. The Crab and Lobster Inn has a lobster
pot for an inn sign. Near by is the white-painted watermill
house; and there is a derelict quay, with a view across the silt
of Pagham Harbour to a skyline frieze of pine trees.

Of all the lonely spots on this coast **Church Norton**, at the
end of the road on the south side of Pagham Harbour, is
among the loneliest. An avenue of great trees ends abruptly
at a little chapel in a graveyard, with mudflats just over the
wall; on the right a path leads down beside a ditch and mound
covered in undergrowth to the seabird-haunted saltings of the
Pagham Harbour nature reserve. The chapel (St Wilfrid's)
was formerly the chancel of Selsey church. The rest of the

building was transported bodily two miles down the road in 1865 to a new site as the parish church of the growing village of Selsey. Old Selsey lies under the sea off Church Norton; there is a legend that the bells of Selsey Cathedral can still be heard pealing under the waters on stormy nights. On the north wall of the chapel is a quaint little Tudor monument to John Lewis and his wife, kneeling to face each other. He wears armoured gauntlets like enormous mittens; she might have been the model for Tenniel's Ugly Duchess.

Selsey consists of a busy main street, with roads left and right to seaside housing, running down to the foreshore. Vast sea walls have been built to absorb the pounding force of the sea, and there is no sea front to drive along. Selsey Bill itself is not obvious, but is marked by Bill House – a large holiday home with the coastguard lookout perched in its weird green-tiled tower. Though the raw materials of Selsey's transported church are so old, the Victorians managed to make it look very Victorian, with its enormous tiled roof and slit windows.

All around and behind Selsey lies rich farming land, with many large glasshouses, and huge fields of maize flourishing round Church Norton.

From Church Norton to Pagham is hardly more than a mile as the seagull flies; but it is a good ten miles by road, involving a detour almost back to Chichester, inland from Pagham Harbour. This is now a harbour only in name, though you can still see sailing dinghies nosing through its channels. But in the Middle Ages Pagham was prosperous; and certainly the big church implies a much larger population than the few houses that make up the place today. By the nineteenth century the harbour had become choked, and the land was reclaimed for agriculture in 1870; but in 1910 a great storm broke the retaining wall and turned the harbour into its present combination of wildlife sanctuary and yachting basin. You can get down to the harbour along the old metalled road which starts from the church. It is a breezy walk right along the harbour wall, with creeks towards the sea, and inland the wind shaking the tall grasses. The Sussex River Authority runs a complex system of sluices here to keep the land well drained. A notice warns the unwary of the dangers of being cut off by a fast-rising tide, even when large areas of the mud-flats are still uncovered by water; in this lonely spot there would be little chance of rescue. Pagham church is dedicated to St Thomas à Becket, and was probably built within a few decades of his murder in 1170. In the west wall is an unusual rose window, with glowing dark blue glass surrounding the royal arms; it commemorates the recovery of King George V in 1928 after a long illness at Craigweil House, two miles west of Bognor (the recovery that gained Bognor the title 'Regis').

Seaside Pagham consists of featureless acres of bungalows new and not-so-new – the western end of a continuous belt of housing from Pagham to Bognor, culminating in the gentility of the Aldwick Bay Estate, with its fantasies of bulging roof-tiles, sculpted thatch and bogus half-timbering (all roads strictly private).

Bognor Regis is a friendly jumble of a resort, making a virtue of the compactness of its seafront (only a mile and a half long), and with none of the urban grandeur of the terraces at places like Hove; Queen Victoria called it, rather patronisingly perhaps, her 'dear little Bognor'. Its biggest piece of development is Waterloo Square, where nineteenth-century seaside houses decked out with wrought-iron canopies rub shoulders with new houses and shops. A little farther west is the impressive white stucco of the Royal Norfolk Hotel, with newly gilded arms on the pediment. Bognor owes its beginnings as a resort to Sir Richard Hotham, a wealthy London hatter who bought up 1,600 acres in the area at the end of the eighteenth-century, intending to rival Bath with a resort called 'Hothampton'. Dome House, now a teachers' training college, was built in the hope that either George III or the Prince Regent would come there; but Hotham had to be content with Princess Charlotte, the youngest daughter of the king, who came to Bognor to regain her health. Though Hotham left at his death only £8,000 out of a vast fortune, Dome House and the green spaces of Hotham Park are no bad memorial. Like nearly all the South Coast resorts, Bognor developed from an inland village – in this case **South Bersted**, which still has a tall-spired medieval church, much Victorianised, and the occasional thatched cottage. Much of old Bognor lies under the sea. Throughout the nineteenth century storms washed away the coast, in the days before sea walls; and somewhere under the sands lie houses and a barracks used during the Napoleonic wars.

Next door to Bognor is **Felpham**, a village swallowed up in holiday housing. Felpham's chief claim to fame is the fact that William Blake lived there from 1800 to 1803; his white-walled thatched cottage in Blake's Road has a firm notice in the window 'Not on View'. Blake came down to Felpham to do some engraving for William Hayley (1745–1820), one of the prize bores of the period, who lived in a large house in the village. Before his stay at Felpham Blake wrote to Anna Flaxman, the sculptor's wife:

> Away to Sweet Felpham, for Heaven is there;
> The Ladder of Angels descends thro' the air;
> On the Turret its spiral does softly descend,
> Thro' the village then winds, at My Cot it does end.

(The turret was that of Hayley's house; Blake referred to him as 'the bless'd Hermit' elsewhere in the poem.) Though Hayley's patronising attitude eventually turned Blake's admiration to near-pathological hatred, at the beginning he was delighted with the change from the 'desart' of London and with Felpham's 'sweet air & the voices of winds, trees & birds, & the odours of the happy ground.' He even saw a fairy's funeral in his garden – 'a procession of creatures, of the size and colour of green and grey grasshoppers, bearing a body laid out on a rose-leaf, which they buried with songs, and then disappeared.'

Inside the rather dark church, up the road from Blake's cottage, is a tablet on the north wall of the chancel to Hayley, commemorating his liberality to artists.

Clymping (or Climping), four miles along the road to Littlehampton, is best known for its sandy beach, reached down a pretty country lane. The church is north of the main road, next door to the wire of Ford prison, which looks too like a concentration camp for comfort. An old saying refers to 'Bosham for antiquity, Boxgrove for beauty, and Clymping for perfection'; the main part of the church is a single unaltered Early English design, with lancet windows complete in nave, transepts and chancel. It was almost certainly built by John de Clymping, who was vicar of the church from 1220 until he became Bishop of Chichester in 1253. The tower, linked to the church by the south transept but virtually separate from it, is a fortress-like structure built about 1170; its main door is richly carved with Norman ornament. On the floor of the north transept is a thirteenth-century chest, reputedly for offerings to help Crusaders get to the Holy Land.

As its name suggests, **Ford** was originally a crossing-point of the Arun. Now it is taken up by the buildings of Ford airfield (a Battle of Britain centre) converted to prison use, and a Continental-looking campsite beside the river. The little church (usually locked) is isolated in the middle of a field. Mainly Saxon and Norman, it stands forlorn among the trees, while the paint of its white bellcote peels and the medieval murals inside fade slowly into indecipherability.

Yapton, a mile or so back towards Chichester, seems to be embedded in glasshouses. It is an open village, built round a rough rectangle, with a pub that rejoices in the gastronomically mixed name of the Shoulder of Mutton and Cucumber. The twelfth-century church has a squat tower that leans at an alarming angle, an ancient wood-framed porch, and crudely rustic carvings on the arcade capitals.

The modern sprawl of **Barnham** hardly looks like a fishing village, yet in the Middle Ages Barnham stood on a tidal creek, centring on the simple little Early English church which looks across the fields at the end of a side road. In more recent times the short-lived Arundel-Chichester canal ran just below the church; opened in 1820, it was made obsolete by the railway, and went out of use about 1880. **Walberton** is a cosily enclosed place; the dark church, down a side road, is on a Saxon site and still has a Saxon tub-shaped font. The north porch, built in the thirteenth century, is unusually large, with three trefoil-headed windows on each side.

Slindon, north of the A 29, has the great advantage of a dramatic site on the slope of the downs. The main street runs steeply up between typical downland houses; and the top of the hill is a miniature village square, complete with a perfect Tree of Idleness encircled by a bench. For all its Englishness, this corner of Slindon on a sunny afternoon gave me a sudden feeling of being whisked a couple of thousand miles to the East Mediterranean – but only for an instant. Slindon's church has a Victorian tower, but is basically twelfth-century. In the south chapel is a wooden effigy, unique in Sussex, believed to be of Sir Anthony St Leger, who died in 1539. The crisp carving of face and hair has lasted far better than many stone effigies of the same age. (There are wooden effigies of similar date in Goudhurst church, see p. 252.) On one of the arcade columns is a tablet to Stephen Langton, who as Archbishop of Canterbury at the time of Magna Carta in 1215 lent his tremendous authority to the barons in their struggle with King John, and died at Slindon in 1228. At the bottom of the hill a path by the village pond leads into the National Trust woodlands of the Slindon Estate – 3,500 acres of wood and farmland stretching over the downs to the hills above Bignor.

Eartham is a little flint-built village, which was the home of two early nineteenth-century celebrities, William Hayley (see Felpham, p. 423) and William Huskisson (see Chichester, p. 411). There is a tablet to Huskisson in the small Norman church, and a monument by Flaxman to Hayley's son, who died in 1800 aged twenty, 'having borne an agonising distemper with cheerful magnanimity', says the inscription signed by Hayley himself. On the capitals of the Norman chancel arch are comical carvings of a rabbit's head and a bearded face.

Half a mile to the north are **Eartham Woods**, where Stane Street can be followed right up to the downs behind Bignor. For much of the way the *agger* or mound of the road is perfectly preserved, sloping gently uphill with the beech trees pressing in on either side, until you come out on the open downland above Gumber Farm, and can look south to the narrow line of the sea glinting above the dark skyline of trees. As an additional bonus, the Forestry Commission have marked out a 'forest walk' through the woods.

On the top of **Halnaker** (pronounced Hannacker) **Hill**, above the A 285 a mile south of Eartham Woods, is Halnaker Mill, celebrated by Hilaire Belloc in one of his most famous poems. An eighteenth-century tower mill with white cap and sails, it is a tremendous landmark from the flat lands to the south.

Boxgrove, just off the main road, is a nice enough village in its own right; but it is completely eclipsed by the magnificent priory church, which looks across open country on the east side of the village street. **Boxgrove Priory** was founded within a few decades of the Conquest, about 1117, and what remains of the church is a superb compendium of architectural styles, culminating in the lucid precision of the Early English choir.

The church has a double dedication, to St Mary, and to St Blaise, the patron saint of the wool trade. Blaise was Bishop of Cappadocia in Asia Minor, about AD 300; during the persecutions under the emperor Diocletian he was tortured by being scraped with woolcombs, and was finally beheaded. The church looks impressive enough at first glance, but what is left gives a slightly unbalanced effect, as practically the whole of the nave has disappeared. This was the end built for the parishioners; the monastic half survives. Inside the church some idea of the original appearance can be got from the Norman transepts, though they have been split horizontally by sweeping wooden galleries added in the fifteenth century. Only the extreme eastern end of the nave is still standing; this was built a little later in the twelfth century, in the Transitional style incorporating the pointed arch. But all this earlier work is hardly more than a background to the astonishing choir, built about 1210. The arcade, with each pair of pointed arches coupled by a wide semicircle of stone, the vaulting, organised into double bays, and the tall lancet windows have a consistency and exactitude utterly different to the stocky Norman and Transitional work. The arcade piers show an almost experimental attitude to variety. At the west end they start with thin and thick octagonal stone; then, like an organist changing registration, comes a round pair in Purbeck marble, followed at the east end by pairs which combine a stone centre with marble outer shafts. The vaulting was painted in the sixteenth century with a design of stylised fruit and foliage, by Lambert Barnard (see Chichester, p. 409). All this is matched in miniature by the De La Warr chantry, in the southern arcade – a fanciful Tudor chapel, painted and gilded, supported on columns alive with human figures, birds, flowers and grotesques.

Outside, to the north of the church, are traces of the monastic buildings: fragments of the cloister and chapter house, and a substantial part of the guest house across an orchard of gnarled apple trees.

South of Boxgrove a group of villages have lost much of their farmland to the airfield of RAF Tangmere, though they make up for it by any number of enormous glasshouses. **Tangmere** itself consists largely of married quarters; it has an Early English church down a side turning, with a shingled belfry carried on a massive timber framework inside the nave. Oving's big cruciform church, with its set of Early English lancet windows virtually complete, looms up across the fields. Behind it is a mushroom-growing establishment. **Aldingbourne** is one of the largest and oldest parishes in England, first appearing in the records at the end of the seventh century, when a monastery was established there. The village sprawls round an enormous ploughed field; the church was greatly restored in the 1860s, though a Norman door and twelfth-century arcading survives. An ancient photograph in the porch shows a really pretty interior before restoration, all box pews, and beams painted with biblical texts.

This north-eastern section of the country round Chichester is dominated by Goodwood, the vast estate of the Dukes of Richmond. **Goodwood Park** runs right up to the crest of the downs, to the famous racecourse, which looks north towards Charlton (see p. 435) across a spacious amphitheatre of downland. Beside the racecourse is the rounded hill known as the **Trundle**, which the Iron Age inhabitants of West Sussex fortified and made their capital city; it is now topped by radio masts, and used as an enclosure for watching the races. **Goodwood House** (for visits, book in advance) lies well down below the ridge, where the steep rise levels out. Though large enough by any standards, as originally envisaged it would have been gargantuan. The central porticoed wing and the two side wings, flint-built and linked by green-domed towers, represent the first stages of an immense octagon designed by James Wyatt for the third Duke of Richmond at the end of the eighteenth century; but the money ran out before the scheme was even half completed. Goodwood is a most confusing house until you get the hang of it, largely because of the odd angles created by the abortive octagon. The key to its structure lies behind the main façade, in the old house which juts out at right angles to the rest, and is in fact the main block of a much earlier Jacobean house, adapted down the years and finally incorporated into Wyatt's sprawl.

This was the house that the first Duke bought as a hunting lodge in 1697. Born in 1672, he was the son of one of Charles II's favourite mistresses, Louise de Querouaille, who had the most adventurous career of any of them. She was sent over to England by Louis XIV to spy on the king, but

inevitably spying took second place to more personal con-
siderations, and Louise ended up as Duchess of Portsmouth.
A Kneller portrait of her at Goodwood shows one of the
typical plump, sultry beauties of the Restoration court. To
Charles she was 'my dearest dearest fubs', as he calls her in a
letter displayed in one of the rooms. ('Fub' or 'Fubs', says
the *Oxford Dictionary*, is 'a small chubby person, a term of
endearment'.) There are Lely portraits of another famous
mistress, Lady Castlemaine, and of Frances Stuart ('La Belle
Stuart'), who managed to ward off Charles's attentions; this
picture shows her in see-through negligée grasping the spear
of the goddess Minerva, and was used as the model for
Britannia on the British coinage. These are both in the reception room in the northern entrance tower. Beyond, in the
gilded splendour of the Ballroom, are the Vandycks which
form the showpieces of the Goodwood collection, notably the
enormous painting of Charles I, Henrietta Maria and their
children. Among the dozens of other pictures, collected mainly
by the third Duke, are two Canalettos of London, behind the
tall pink columns of the main entrance hall; and Stubbs race-
horse pictures in the Long Hall, which was constructed in the
Jacobean part of the house. From an older and more sinister
world comes the strange picture in the Blue Hall, known as
the 'Cenotaph of Lord Darnley'. In this naive but disturbing
painting Darnley, in armour, lies murdered on his bier, while
his relatives, including his son the infant James I, pray in Latin
for revenge on the assassins.

Apart from the portraits and other paintings, Goodwood
contains any amount of superb eighteenth-century furniture,
Gobelin tapestries, and Sèvres porcelain, and oddities like the
vast and hideous table centre in the Long Hall, given to the
fifth Duke by Peninsular War veterans after he had won them
the right to wear campaign medals. And for sheer professional-
ism the guided tours – which include a meal in the State Supper Room – are unmatched at any country house I have been
to. Goodwood has so far scorned safari parks and other outdoor attractions; yet earlier generations pointed the way, as
close behind the house an overgrown amphitheatre marks the
place where the second Duke kept his menagerie, and the stone
figure of a lion commemorates the chief exhibit.

Goodwood has adapted itself to the modern world by

diversifying into activities like running an airfield and a motor-racing circuit (now used for test purposes only).

Back again into Chichester and heading west towards Hampshire along the A 27, you come to **Fishbourne,** on the western outskirts of the city. This was the scene of the most astounding archaeological discovery made in this country in recent years – a vast Roman palace, first brought to light in 1960. A workman cutting trenches found some Roman tiles and reported his find; eight years of intensive excavation followed, and the result, laid out in a field north of the A 27, is a model of research and presentation. Under a stylish hangar of wood and glass the remains of a complete wing of the palace have been uncovered. This is enormous enough, but it represents only one quarter of the whole huge quadrangle which measured five hundred feet square and continues southwards under gardens, houses and the main road. The palace was built about AD 75 almost certainly for Cogidubnus a client king friendly to the Romans (see also p. 407), who spared no expense to make it an awe-inspiring sign of the advantages of Romanisation.

When it was built the waters of Chichester Channel came farther inland than they do today, and the southern colonnade probably looked across a terraced garden straight on to the sea. A stream ran along the eastern side, and still trickles down the ditch alongside the unexposed east wing. The main administrative wings were in fact the eastern and western, each of which had a porticoed grand entrance; the north (conserved) wing was residential, and continued in use when the rest of the palace had fallen into decay.

A visitor coming to the palace from Chichester in, say, AD 100 would have crossed the stream to the entrance portico, walked through the entrance hall to the formal garden, then along a broad path between formal hedges and up a flight of steps to an apsidal audience chamber. (The outlines of the main features in the east and west wings are marked in outline in the turf.) Even the plan of the garden hedges is known at Fishbourne, as the designers of the garden dug out trenches and filled them with fertile soil; the archaeologists found the trenches, and also some of the pipes which carried water to ornamental basins and fountains. The hedges are now planted with box, and the beds with roses and acanthus – all plants the

Romans are known to have used in their own gardens. The finest mosaic floor, a swirling composition of seahorses, scallop shells and urns around a boy riding on a dolphin, was laid in the mid second century. The owner at this time had obviously had enough of the English climate, as he put in the regulation hypocaust and flues for central heating. At the end of the third century the palace burnt down, perhaps accidentally or perhaps in one of the pirate raids on the coast which were becoming steadily more frequent. It became a quarry for other villas and probably for the fortifications of Chichester, and at some period in the Dark Ages its ruins were used as a cemetery. The mosaics show the scars of medieval ploughing, and of the twentieth-century excavator which brought the whole thing to light.

A couple of miles west is **Bosham** (pronounced Bozzum) deservedly one of the beauty spots of the Sussex coast. A Saxon church at its centre, a broad green stretching down to the harbour, harmonious groups of brick and flint houses, a riverscape crammed with boats: no wonder that at Bosham the artists seem to outnumber the ordinary sightseers. Bosham's greatest days were in the early eleventh century, in the decades before the Norman Conquest. Canute had a palace there, and it was at Bosham that he rebuked his courtiers when they asked him to hold back the tide (though Southampton also claims to be the site of this story). The great Earl Godwin, father of Harold, is said to have got possession of Bosham by a trick from the Archbishop of Canterbury. On meeting the Archbishop he mumbled the Latin words '*Da mihi Boseam*' (give me Bosham), which the unsuspecting prelate misheard as '*Da mihi basiam*' (give me the kiss of peace). The Archbishop kissed the Earl, who thereupon claimed Bosham and took possession of it. Harold set out from Bosham in 1064 on the visit to Normandy which led to his falling into the power of William the Bastard (later the Conqueror) and precipitated the Norman Conquest. Quay Meadow, the green from which Harold embarked, now belongs to the National Trust.

An early scene in the Bayeux Tapestry shows Harold, with Kitchener moustache, and hawk on wrist, riding to **Bosham Church** before his voyage. In this scene the main feature of the church is the splendid Saxon arch, which still stands at the

entrance to the chancel, and rises from Roman column bases
which may be from a basilica on the site. Roman tiles and
bricks are built into the walls. The crypt has connections with
the earliest days of Christianity in Sussex; it is associated with
Dicul, an Irish monk whom St Wilfrid found already established when he came on his missionary journey to Sussex in
681, and may be on the site of Dicul's monastery. At the foot
of the arch is a tombstone to a child believed to be Canute's
daughter, who died about 1020; nearly nine hundred years
later, in 1906, the children of Bosham placed the stone there.
About one-third of the chancel is Saxon work, as is the tower,
built about 1000 as a watch-tower and defence against the
Danes. It now has a sturdy shingle broach spire on top of it,
a landmark in every direction. If you walk round the outside
of the tower, you will be hard put to it to find a single right-
angle in the wall plan.

At low tide the road below the harbour wall is uncovered,
and can be followed right along. South of the inlet, the road
is uncovered at all states of the tide and gives a quiet riverscape
of estuary, church and waterside houses.

Bosham stands on the easternmost of the three large
peninsulas that jut into Chichester Harbour, stretching from
Chichester Channel to Emsworth Channel, where Sussex
merges into Hampshire across the swampy shallows. This is a
coast of deep-cut creeks and mudflats, where on a fine summer
afternoon the sailing dinghies cover the water like flocks of
sea birds, and where new marinas and moorings spring up
almost overnight.

Chidham, on the central peninsula, is a remote and scattered
village, the kind of place nobody goes to, because no road
runs through it. At **Prinsted**, a quietly idyllic cul-de-sac, two
lanes lined with pretty cottages converge to form a Y, which
leads down to a small harbour at the head of Thorney Channel.

There is only one road on **Thorney Island**. For most of its
length it goes across the runways and through the administrative buildings and living quarters of a large RAF station.
The island is separated from the mainland by the Great Deep,
and before the road was built in 1870 was reached by a
'wadeway', which was completely uncovered only at exceptionally low water, and where local inhabitants often drowned.
The road comes to a dead end at **West Thorney**, in a slipway

leading down to Thorney Channel. Perched up above the channel is St Nicholas' Church, a simple flint building, with tiled roof and stumpy spire.

Westbourne, a mile north of the A 27, is so nearly in Hampshire that it makes no difference: the River Ems, marking the county boundary, trickles by on the far side of the churchyard. The wide main street, opening by the church into a central space filled with a triangle of buildings, is a good village harmony of Georgian brickwork, thatched roofs and pink-washed walls. The battlemented church tower, with its tall, dark-shingled spire, is a landmark across the fields. The tower is late Perpendicular, built early in the sixteenth century. At the same time the arcades were rebuilt in flat-arched Perpendicular style, giving the whole interior an open, simple effect. A splendid avenue of tall yews, planted about 1545, leads to the north door of the church.

A few miles north is a circuit of small villages which are the quintessence of the West Sussex downs – the four Mardens, Compton and Stoughton.

West Marden consists of a single little street at right angles to the main road, and is a landscape-artist's delight of tiled and thatched roofs, and tree-covered slopes behind. **Compton** is a well-tended place, typically brick and flint. The church, right under the steep slope of Telegraph Hill, is mainly Victorian. On a perfect October day I had to stop for a herd of fallow deer stumbling across the road to Uppark (see p. 449) and Harting, north of Compton. On the other side of Telegraph Hill from Compton is the prehistoric long barrow called **Bevis's Thumb**, an unspectacular grassy mound right beside the road.

Up Marden is the remotest of all, but it is far from desolate. The minute Early English church is hidden behind farm buildings; the bare, peaceful interior is candle-lit, and has an odd triangular chancel arch, possibly Saxon stonework re-used. On the chancel floor is an ancient bell inscribed 'GOD IS MY HOPE 1620'. **North Marden** has a similar combination of farm and midget church. Here the church is even older, a simple apsidal Norman chapel, lit by small arched windows. The royal arms on the north wall are to scale, made of metal and less than a foot across. Outside, the window surrounds are carved with pencil-thin columns, like full-size Norman windows seen through the wrong end of a telescope. **East Marden** is the most cosily village-like of the four. At the centre is a small green, with rustic thatched well-house, rope and bucket. Above the well is a notice reading 'Rest and be Thankful But do not Wreck me', which has fortunately so far been heeded. There are beehives in the churchyard, and in the church is a prettily gilded chamber organ, which came originally from St James's Palace, and was reputedly played by Prince Albert.

Stoughton, two miles to the south, is a placid village, lying at ease in a wide valley. The church stands commandingly on a slope above; the low, massive slate-roofed tower was added in the fourteenth century above the south transept of a Saxon church. The most notable thing about the interior is the lofty Saxon chancel arch, roll-moulded above triple-shafted columns. Stoughton was the birthplace of the most demoniac of early nineteenth-century bowlers, George Brown, whose delivery was so fast that he needed two long-stops, the front one protected by straw padding. A ball bowled by Brown went right through a coat held out to stop it and killed a dog standing on the other side. And this was presumably underarm!

Funtington, on the B 2146 south of Stoughton, is a typical village of the Chichester plain, set in a flat and featureless countryside, with a wide main street and a number of good Georgian houses. **West Stoke** two miles to the east is by comparison hardly a village at all – just a white-painted Georgian manor house over the wall from a tiny medieval church. When I went there the seventeenth-century wall monument to Adrian Stoughton was being reconditioned by a professional restorer, one of a small band of experts who go from church to church counteracting the ravages of time, carelessness and vandalism. She was 'feeding' the slate slab at the back of the monument with linseed oil to rejuvenate its surface, mending and repainting the battered fingers and faces of the kneeling figures, and regilding the intricate capitals, making her colours a perfect match with the traces of original decoration that still remained.

West Stoke is the starting point for a walk up **Kingley Vale**, a steep combe rising to a downland ridge, now owned by the Nature Conservancy and run as a national nature reserve. Kingley Vale is famous for its yew woods, which grow thickly up the valley and fan out along the ridge. Most extraordinary, and sinister, are the gigantic trees towards the bottom of the valley, which form dark caves and tunnels, as the branches bend down to the ground, take root, and send out fresh reinforcements of banyan-like growth. It is not surprising that legends of Druid sacrifices grew up around these ancient woods, where few birds sing, and where even walkers rushing around with the Conservancy's nature trail guidebook are awed into temporary immobility. On the downs above are barrows said to be the tombs of warriors killed in battle against the Danes; and a stone which commemorates Sir Arthur Tansley, the first chairman of the Nature Conservancy. (To make the complete nature trail walk you should allow about two hours; however, the main yew groves are near the start of the trail.)

Two miles east are the Lavants. **Mid Lavant** is largely a roadside sprawl; but **East Lavant** is a prettily undulating village, with the River Lavant running beside the road. The small medieval church has a Norman west door, and a seventeenth-century brick tower stuck on the south side. **Singleton**, a few miles up the valley towards Midhurst, is even prettier, built compactly like a miniature town in a fold of the downs. The church has a big Saxon west tower and a nave which is probably Saxon as well. It is thought that it was originally built with a long room over the nave, lit by the window above the chancel arch and reached by the Saxon doorway half way up the tower. In the south aisle is a tablet to Thomas Johnson, huntsman of the Charlton Hunt, who died in 1744:

> Here IOHNSON lies – What Hunter can deny
> Old, honest TOM the Tribute of a Sigh
> Deaf is that Ear, which caught the op'ning Sound,
> Dumb is that Tongue, which chear'd the Hills around.
> Unpleasing Truth – Death hunts us from our Birth
> In view; and Men, like Foxes, take to Earth.

Outside Singleton is the **Weald and Downland Open Air Museum**, where on a gently sloping parkland site small houses saved from the demolisher are being reconstructed, and traditional country crafts revived in realistic, non-museum settings. Thus when the Bough Beech reservoir in Kent (see p. 224) was under construction, a Wealden timber-frame farmhouse was dismantled and re-erected at Singleton; the ancient timbers have been slotted into place, with modern renewals here and there where half a millennium of use and decay had worn them thin. At Singleton, as in a Thomas Hardy novel, you stroll through the woodland and suddenly come across a charcoal kiln (unlit, however, because of fire hazard) and charcoal burner's turf-covered hut; or a sawpit, with a half-sawn baulk of timber waiting for the sawyers to return to their task.

A mile back towards Chichester is **West Dean College,** a vast stone battlemented mansion mainly built in 1804 by James Wyatt. It holds adult residential courses in traditional country crafts, at all levels of proficiency; the subjects taught range from cookery to the craft of the armourer, and from drystone walling to the study of fairground art.

Heading into the downs from Singleton, you come to **Charlton** and **East Dean,** small flint-walled villages in the valley where the Lavant rises. East Dean's small cruciform church dates from about 1150. Like the Deans near Seaford (see pp. 303, 304) it claims a connection with an earlier church built by King Alfred.

To the south is the Trundle and the Goodwood racecourse (see p. 427), and to the east you can carry on to the Petworth road near **Up Waltham,** high on the downs – a couple of large farms, and a tiny apsidal Norman church in the middle of a field.

CHAPTER TWENTY-FIVE

The Western Approaches

❧

THE north-west corner of Sussex bordered by Hampshire
and Surrey, has something of the flavour of both these two
counties. On one side is the broad spaciousness of the downs,
opening out into the uplands that spread beyond Winchester
to Salisbury Plain; and on the other is the heavily wooded
cosiness of the hills and combes south of Haslemere. Between
woodland and downland is the broad valley of the Rother,
dawdling gently along until it meets the Arun near Pulborough,
and lined by little villages on roads that lead to nowhere, each
with its vintage medieval bridge. The vast parks of Cowdray
and Petworth give the final touch of romantic feudalism to a
stretch of countryside as unspoilt as any within fifty miles of
London.

Petworth is a main-road junction, and like Arundel is quite
unfitted to be one. E. V. Lucas quotes a joke to the effect that
a timber wagon once got into the warren of Petworth's narrow
streets and never succeeded in finding its way out again. The
only consolation for the frustrated motorist seventy years
later is that there is always something worth looking at, and he
may even be tempted to get out and walk around. Petworth
still has all the elements of feudalism about it – the old town,
the great house, and the high wall dividing the two, especially
noticeable if you come into Petworth from the north. But
Petworth House is not aloof. Its outbuildings open right on
to the street, and its upper windows overlook the town, which
must sometimes have given the townsmen the uncomfortable
feeling that the Percys or Egremonts knew everything that was
going on.

The town is compact and small-scale. At its centre is the
market place, with a stone town hall built by the third Earl
of Egremont at the end of the eighteenth century. Lombard

A map for this chapter will be found on pages 418-19.

Street, cobbled and virtually traffic-free, is the prettiest bit of the town, gently curved and gently sloping as old streets should be; while the finest individual buildings are in East Street, notably the stylish Georgian of Daintrey House and other town houses nearby.

The church is a most peculiar building. Its brick tower with shallow pyramid cap is quite a landmark as you approach the town from the south and east; but it used to be even more prominent, as it had a tall spire built by Sir Charles Barry, who drastically restored the church in 1827. The spire was condemned as unsafe in 1947 and demolished. Inside, virtually all that is left of the fourteenth-century church are the arches on the north side of the nave. It is a big, untidy place, with no kind of unity. At the back of the north aisle is a seated figure of the third Earl of Egremont, by Edward Hodges Baily, sculptor of the statue on top of Nelson's Column; and in the baptistery below the tower a communal monument to all the Percy family, in the form of a draped figure carrying a cross, put up by the Earl to his dead ancestors in 1837, the year of his own death.

The Percy connection with Petworth goes back to the twelfth century. The first Percy, William, came over with the Conqueror, married the daughter of the Saxon Earl of Northumberland, and founded the Northumberland dynasty. Petworth had been bequeathed by Henry I to his widow, Queen Adeliza, and she in turn gave it to her brother Joscelyn on his marriage to Lady Agnes, the Percy heiress; it must have made a welcome southern addition to the dour fastnesses in the north. Only the chapel survives of the Percys' medieval manor house, home of the eleven Earls of Northumberland from the end of the fourteenth century until the direct line died out in 1670. Shakespeare's Harry Hotspur was typical of this hard-living family, many of whom came to a violent end in battle, by execution or plain murder. But such things seem far away from the huge bland front of **Petworth House**, sprawling comfortably at the edge of magnificent parkland. The house was the first product of a new age at Petworth. The eleventh Earl was succeeded by his daughter, Elizabeth, who in 1682 married Charles Seymour, the sixth Duke of Somerset; and between 1688 and 1696 the Percy fortune was applied to the rebuilding of Petworth.

To see the house as a whole, you should go into the park and look back at it from down by the lake. This, the west front, is the true aspect of Petworth – a simple enough three-storeyed building, over a hundred yards long and only two rooms wide, looking more like a French château than an English country house (various architects, both French and English, have been suggested), with close-cropped turf stretching uninterrupted to the foot of the walls. Its restraint used to be taken for dullness, or worse; indeed Murray's 1893 *Handbook* likened it to 'a strip from an indifferent London terrace'. There is a complete and harmonious integration between house and park, well brought out by Turner in his Petworth paintings. House and much of the park belong to the National Trust, so Petworth is spared the desperate devices of stately home money-making. Lord Egremont still lives in part of it; the present peerage is a new creation dating from 1963.

The endless rooms opening one into the other make Petworth an ideal art gallery, which is largely its present function. (The best days to go there are on the first and third Tuesdays in the month, April–October, when three extra rooms are shown.) The paintings and sculpture are a complete guide to changing tastes in art from the time of Vandyck to that of Turner, and ideally need more than one visit, otherwise surfeit tends to set in. In the rather dark Oak Hall, where the tour of Petworth begins, you can see portraits of two of the less fortunate of the Percys hanging above the staircase: the kneeling figure of Thomas, the seventh Earl of Northumberland, a Catholic beheaded in 1572 for supporting Mary Queen of Scots; and Henry the ninth Earl, round-bearded and melancholy. Nick-named the 'Wizard Earl' for his interest in science and alchemy, he was suspected of involvement in the Gunpowder Plot and was imprisoned in the Tower for sixteen years. In 1621 he was released on payment of the enormous sum of £11,000. The staircase portrait shows him in 1602, before his imprisonment; a wonderfully subdued portrait by Vandyck in the Square Dining Room shows him weary and careworn, in the final decade of his life. This is pre-eminently the Vandyck room, with other notable portraits, best of all the pair on either side of the fireplace of Sir Robert Shirley in turban and Oriental draperies, and the dark Circassian wife who returned with him to England after his years of service at the Shah of Persia's court (see Wiston, p. 359).

At the centre of the west front is the wide, cool Marble Hall, overlooking the park. This room was the scene of one of Petworth's few forays into history, when in 1814 Egremont received the Prince Regent, the Tsar of Russia and other sovereigns of the anti-Napoleonic alliance. A painting in the North Gallery shows the rulers and their attendants entering from the park. South of the Marble Hall is the Beauty Room, so called because of the identical-looking vapid ladies of Queen Anne's court whose portraits hang round the walls; Anne herself is over the fireplace. The Grand Staircase opening off the Beauty Room is an unexpected piece of Baroque exuberance after so much staidness. Painted from top to bottom with murals by Louis Laguerre, it shows the triumph of the Duchess of Somerset and her family (after all, she had supplied the money for building Petworth), below a riot of Olympian gods and goddesses on the ceiling. South of the Beauty Room is the White and Gold Room, a fanciful mid-eighteenth-century interior, and beyond it the White Library. lined with the book collection started by the 'Wizard Earl'. This room contains one of the Petworth Turners, and a portrait of the Duke of Somerset, the builder of the house. He had such an overweening sense of his own importance and that of his family that he was known as the 'Proud Duke'. On one occasion, after a quarrel with George I, he threw his royal liveries into a dustcart and told his servants to deposit the 'rubbish' in front of St James's Palace.

One of Somerset's inspirations was to commission Grinling Gibbons to decorate the largest state room at Petworth. This room has its own splendid paintings, notably a formidable portrait of Henry VIII over the fireplace; but they are all driven into the shade by the virtuosity of the limewood carvings of fruit and flowers, dead game, trophies of war and musical instruments that cascade down the walls. With the Turner Room we are in the golden age of Petworth as a centre of art patronage, under the long and benevolent sway of the third Earl of Egremont, who from about 1770 until his death in 1837 set the existing collections in order and greatly added to them. The T-shaped North Gallery is his creation. Crammed with statues and lined with pictures, it is an amazing medley of the antique and the up-to-date, in terms of the taste of the day.

There are plenty of portraits of Lord Egremont at Petworth, beakily distinguished, like a kindly Duke of Wellington. He let the title die out by default, only marrying 'Mrs Wyndham' after six children had been born. Turner was the perfect choice to paint Petworth and its park. He delighted in the sunset slanting across the grass and outlining the trees and deer in a hazy glow, and in the calm reflections of the lake. More prosaically, he liked to fish there, and also got on extremely well with old Lord Egremont, an eccentric like himself, who told him 'I want a picture when you have time, but remember, none of your damned nonsense'. A less romantic view of Petworth, but equally delightful in its way, is W. F. Witherington's painting of a fête held in the park in the summer of 1835, with Lord Egremont doing the rounds in the foreground. A waspish account of the festivities is given by Charles Greville, who describes in his diary how 6,000 people were fed. 'Nothing could exceed the pleasure of that fine old fellow: he was in and out of the windows of his room twenty times, enjoying the sight of these poor wretches, all attired in their best, cramming themselves and their brats with as much as they could devour.'

From the gallery you go past the Percy chapel, redecorated by Somerset and oddly theatrical with its dark woodwork and its heraldic painting in the blocked thirteenth-century windows. Then out once more to the park and pleasure gardens, where the trees, and especially the magnificent Spanish chestnuts, have now reached their peak after two hundred years of growth.

The main road north from Petworth runs for miles beside the park; in fact there is no road to the west before the lane that leads to Lurgashall five miles to the north. The centre of **Lurgashall** is the broad green, rather than the houses that are scattered round it. The church, tucked away in a corner, is largely Norman and Early English, though hardly recognisable as such. West of the tower, where you would expect an aisle, is a wooden lean-to porch or narthex, which has been variously explained as a shelter for travellers coming to the service from a long distance, as a meeting place, and as a school. With the versatility of the Middle Ages, it was probably used for all three purposes. The huge chunky font, of Sussex marble, is dated 1661; as Nairn says, 'a formidable thing to be baptised in'. The shingle spire was replaced in 1969. **Northchapel**, at the top of a rise in the main road, has a good green, plenty of pubs and timbered houses, and a nineteenth-century church (usually kept locked) down a pretty alleyway.

A couple of miles to the west is the nearest approach to a mountain in these parts – **Blackdown**, over nine hundred feet high and shaggily coated in trees like one of the foothills of the Jura. The National Trust owns a large area of woodland on the southern slopes. Tennyson spent the last two decades of his life up here, in **Aldworth House**, which he built in 1869. The house (not on view) is unpretentious, the only unusual thing about it being the quantity of little stone carvings that decorate it; but the view from the garden terrace is breathtaking, across miles of rolling countryside towards the sea. The poet's bust gazes reflectively at the garden, where he wrote much of the *Idylls of the King* and his later poems.

East of the main road to Petworth, right on the Surrey border, enormous cedars by the roadside mark the entrance to **Shillinglee Park**, a handsome classical Georgian house gutted by fire during the Second World War. A driving range for golfers to practise has recently been opened in the grounds. **Plaistow**, a few miles away across the gently undulating countryside, has plenty of tilehung houses, and an odd little church which is a Victorian replacement of a timber-framed building of much the same dimensions.

Three miles south of Plaistow is **Kirdford**, a large open village. A tree-shaded street leads down to the powerful church, consisting of Norman nave, thirteenth-century north aisle, and fifteenth-century west tower and chancel. For centuries Kirdford was a centre of industry – glassmaking from 1300 to 1600 and ironworking from 1550 to 1650 – which may account for the prosperity of the church. The village sign incorporates diamonds of locally made glass. A painted sign entitled 'Degradation of Drunkenness' is set into the vicarage wall, the relic of some eighteenth- or early nineteenth-century temperance enthusiast. In spite of this constant reminder that drunkenness, among other things, 'is the shame of nature, the extinguisher of reason, the shipwreck of chastity, and the murderer of conscience', Kirdford's pubs continue to be patronised.

Wisborough Green, a couple of miles to the east on the A 272, is a perfect Sussex village, built round a smooth rectangle of grass surrounded by chestnut trees. There are nice half-timbered and tilehung houses, a good pub called the Three Crowns, and a pond covered with waterlilies below the church. This tall-spired building, standing a little to one side of the main village, is an architectural problem. Before the Early English chancel was added in the thirteenth century, it was a simple Norman rectangle. But why were the walls at the west end four and a half feet thick, and why were the north and south doors built thirteen feet high – tall enough to admit a mounted man? The suggestion has been made that it was originally a keep, later enlarged into a church; though Nairn thinks it was an Anglo-Saxon nave-tower, with vaulting over. In the thirteenth century the tower was built in the south-west corner, partly blocking a Norman window; its buttresses can be seen in the nave. On the right of the chancel arch is a mural painting in very good condition, showing St James of Compostella; and below are Christ and one of the thieves, crucified on the same crossbar. The rough-hewn stone altar may be pre-Norman, perhaps a pagan sacrificial stone. In the Middle Ages the church was a centre of pilgrimage, as it had numerous relics including the hair shirt, comb and bones of St James, and a crucifix incorporating a drop of the Virgin's milk set in crystal.

Half a mile west of Wisborough Green a narrow road branches off the A 272 to **Fittleworth**. In the middle of the woodlands here is **Brinkwells**, the thatched cottage where Edward Elgar lived for a few years from 1917, writing his cello concerto and other major works. He returned there for the last time in 1921, and heralded the end of his creative life in a letter to a friend: 'I feel like these woods – all aglow – a spark wd. start a flame – but no human spark comes.' Fittleworth is a pretty little place, built round a central tree-covered triangle. The church, by itself on a knoll, was well and truly filleted by the Victorians, who rebuilt everything between the Early English tower and chancel. Its Jubilee clock has a most musical chime.

Church, manor house and a handful of cottages make up **Stopham**, a few hundred yards off the A 283 towards Pulborough. The church has a wide low tower, a Norman south doorway so rough that it could well be Saxon, and a Norman chancel arch. Stopham bridge, across the Arun, has been called by Nairn 'easily the best of the medieval bridges in Sussex'. It is incredible to think that a bridge built in 1423 can still carry modern traffic; but even traffic lights do not save it, as when I last crossed it part of the sandstone parapet had been smashed away, and the stone was cracked all around.

South of Fittleworth you cross the Rother and come again to the villages below the South Downs. **Coates**, immediately above the river, consists of a few large stone farmhouses and a tiny Norman church, with a vast cedar in a corner of the churchyard. Behind Coates is magnificent wood and heath-land, with a spectacular stand of ancient oaks at the road junction near Coates Castle. Near by is the reedlined sweep of Burton millpond, with a millrace of ten steps cascading down on the opposite side of the road. Part of the woods are a nature reserve, marked by the butterfly sign of the Sussex Naturalists' Trust.

The downland villages proper begin at **West Burton**, an up-and-down, buried kind of place, on the other side of the A 29 from Bury (see p. 352). **Bignor**, a mile or so away, has one of the most famous Roman villas in the country (open Mar.–Oct., Tues.–Sun.), first discovered when a mosaic pavement was ploughed up in 1811, and a tourist draw ever since. A comparison with the modern hangars at Fishbourne and Lullingstone (see pp. 429 and 22) will show how presentation has altered since Bignor's thatched protecting huts were first built about 1814. The villa was built towards the end of the second century AD, on a site with splendid open views of the downs, and close to Stane Street; the first house was a modest timber-framed affair, and was not extended to the present enormous courtyard structure until early in the fourth century. As the administrative centre of an estate of about two thousand acres, Bignor was the home of an important agricultural magnate, who decorated his villa with some of the finest mosaics surviving in Britain. These display all the variety of the mosaicist's invention, from simple geometrical designs to Ganymede carried off by the eagle, a head of Venus flanked by pheasants and surrounded by a complex decorated frame, and a frieze of cupids in gladiatorial combat – a typically Roman combination of the whimsical and the sadistic. Best of all is the grave-faced head of Winter, wearing a hooded cloak of British type against the biting downland winds. The villa's end was not violent: it was abandoned probably in the fifth century, and mouldered gently into the ground.

Bignor itself is a pretty village, with one unbelievably picturesque timber-framed house fronting the road, and an Early English church with a tiled roof sweeping low over narrow aisles. Inside there is a Norman chancel arch. The next village, **Sutton**, is barely half a mile away; its undulating village street leads up to the medieval church, mainly four-teenth-century but with some Norman work surviving in the nave. In the south aisle is a painting by Claude Muncaster, showing Sutton and the hills on a fine summer day, from the high viewpoint of Barlavington Down. **Barlavington** has a perfect little Early English church, at the end of a steep-sided lane, with a large farm behind. Between the two lancets of the window is a shallow stone recess, which contains a modernish carving of the Annunciation, ingeniously contrived to fill the awkward rectangular space.

At **Duncton** you come out on the main Chichester road, which makes a sharp bend to avoid sending the traffic between the tall flint-and-stone chequered gate piers at the entrance to Seaford College. Duncton is a nice enough village, with a blatant Victorian church on the hillside above. It is worth going down the drive of St Michael's girls' school to glance at the overbearing classical front of Burton Park, now the main building of the school, and look into the small church beside it. The little building hardly seems to have been touched for centuries; the timber rood beam still shows traces of red paint, and on the wall are painted the royal arms of Charles I, dated 1636 – the only pre-1660 example I have seen in the two counties.

Graffham, three miles west of Duncton, has a sign stating simply that it is the best-kept village in West Sussex. This is hardly surprising, as its sinuous main street, lined with typical downland flint and brick houses, obviously has affection lavished on it. Beyond the Victorianised flint church the road fades away into a hill track; and above are the steep slopes of the downs, covered in trees rising wave on wave to the skyline.

Selham, a couple of miles to the north, is a leafy hamlet, with a pub called the Three Moles, and a tiny church looking

like a Welsh chapel, that is in fact Saxon. Inside is a surprise
for such an unimposing building – a capital of the chancel
arch carved with serpents devouring their own tails, the
Scandinavian symbol of eternity, miles from anywhere in the
English fields.

On the other side of the Rother and the A 272 is **Lodsworth**,
a largish village, whose main street jumbles up the old and the
new in a satisfactory way. So does the simple whitewashed
church at the edge of the village, which reconciles a Victorian
biblical oil painting with a broad new window made of brilliant
chunks of stained glass.

Tillington, back on the A 272, is very much outside the
walls of Petworth Park. Besides the houses on the main road,
there is a second peaceful village street running parallel at a
higher level. Tillington's landmark is the odd church tower
topped by stone pinnacles and a 'crown' that looks like the
bottom stage of the Eiffel Tower. It was built in 1810, and has
been attributed without much conviction to Turner.

Though **Midhurst** is also at the junction of two main roads,
it is not torn apart by traffic in the same way as Petworth. It
has a feeling of spaciousness, brought about partly by the
wide eighteenth-century layout of North Street, and still more
by the huge expanse of marshy land between the road and the
ruins of Cowdray, whose towered gatehouse forms the backcloth to this end of the town. North Street, with its shops,
Georgian façades and elegant, ochre-painted Angel Hotel, is
the real heart of Midhurst. The original town centre, round
the market square and church, is a backwater, though a very
attractive one. From North Street the oddly-named Knock-
hundred Row swings round into Red Lion Street, where
half-timbered and Georgian houses draw widely apart round
the Swan and the old timbered market house on their island
sites. In South Street the Spread Eagle, a huge old coaching
inn with a sign that claims the date of 1430, sums up the town
in its sprawling combination of two separate parts, brick and
half-timbered. Strangely enough, the only central building
that is worth hardly more than a glance is the church, mainly a
restoration of 1881. The lower part of the tower is twelfth- or
early thirteenth-century. The curfew is still rung from the
church at eight every evening, reputedly in memory of a
legendary commercial traveller, who was lost after dark in the

forest north of Midhurst, followed the sound of a bell to
safety, and as a thank-offering endowed a piece of land for the
bell to be rung in perpetuity.

For most visitors, the chief attraction of Midhurst is
Cowrday Park, a superb place for picnicking, watching polo,
or strolling about under the immense oak trees. The A 272
runs through the centre of the park; on the afternoon of a
polo match, when hundreds of cars are heading for home, you
can be held up here for a good half hour. In the south-west
corner of the park, behind the polo ground and looking on to
the cricket pitch, are the Cowdray ruins. They are best approached along the causeway from North Street, though you
can no longer walk straight up to the gatehouse but have to
make a detour to one side. The first great house at Midhurst
was the medieval castle of the de Bohuns, built on St Ann's
Hill behind the Market Square. About 1300 the de Bohuns left
their hilltop and moved to a level site by the river – a *coudrier*
or hazel coppice, from which the name Cowdray derived.
From the de Bohuns this medieval Cowdray passed by
marriage to Sir David Owen, natural son of Owen Glendower,
in the 1490s; and from then until his death in 1535 Sir David
set about building a grand courtyard house in the high Tudor
tradition. Owing to money difficulties, Owen had already sold
Cowdray to Sir William Fitzwilliam in 1529. A leading figure
at Henry VIII's court, Fitzwilliam was Lord Keeper of the
Privy Seal and Lord High Admiral, and was created the first
Earl of Southampton. He was largely responsible for the completion of Cowdray, and the finishing touches were added by
his half-brother Sir Anthony Browne, who elsewhere brought
down on himself the curse that his line would end by fire and
water (see Battle, p. 288). In 1554 Sir Anthony's son was made
the first Viscount Montague, and the Montagues succeeded
one another at Cowdray until in 1793 the young eighth
Viscount drowned while trying to shoot the Laufenburg Falls
on the Rhine. The same year Cowdray caught fire and was
reduced to the ruin we see today.

The most impressive of the remains is the tall gatehouse,
which still stands to its full height, flanked by the burnt-out
shell of much of the western range of buildings. The north and
south sides of the great quadrangle are now marked only by
foundations; but enough is left of the eastern side, where

Cowdray's state apartments were, to give an idea of the splendour that has vanished. The lofty stone mullions that lit the hall and parlour are blackened by smoke, and the roofs, floors, ceilings and panelling have gone. Fortunately drawings by Grimm, made shortly before the fire and reproduced in Torrens Trotter's *Cowdray, its Early History*, makes it easy to replace them in the mind's eye. You go in through a low porch, where the fan vaulting survives, decorated with the initials WS (for William Southampton), anchors (for the office of Lord High Admiral) and other devices. The hall beyond towered the full height of the building, up to an elaborate hammerbeam roof; it was known as Buck Hall, from eleven life-sized wooden figures of buck placed on brackets round the room. According to Murray's *Hand-book*, half-burnt fragments of the buck were still lying around the quadrangle at the end of the last century. Behind is the chapel, almost as large as the hall, with scraps of seventeenth-century plasterwork still clinging to the walls and the remains of a lofty altarpiece. It was here, early in the eighteenth century, that the fifth Viscount shot the family priest (the Montagues were Catholic) for beginning mass without him. After this crime he is said to have hidden away in a secret chamber, coming out at night to roam round the park, and inevitably being taken for a ghost. The odd hexagonal kitchen at the south-east corner was not harmed by the fire and has survived almost intact. Everything is still in place, from the great butcher's block by one of the Tudor chimneys to the iron hotplates, hardly changed since Edward VI came to Cowdray in 1552 and was 'marvelously, yea rather excessively, banketted'.

Easebourne links Midhurst with Cowdray Park. It has some superb half-timbered houses, and a much-restored parish church which was the priory church of a thirteenth-century Augustinian convent. Inside is a battered monument to the first Viscount Montague (died 1592), kneeling above his two wives; it stood originally in Midhurst church and may have been damaged by workmen during the move. Another suggestion is that Cromwell's soldiers were responsible.

West Lavington is Midhurst's southern suburb, a strung-out tree-filled place, with a Victorian church in a churchyard engulfed by enormous conifers. Beside the path is a large granite slab to Richard Cobden (1804–65), the Victorian politician and prophet of Free Trade, who lived near by at **Dunford House** (can be seen at weekends by prior arrangement). This pinkwashed building, buried away at the end of a long drive, is now run by the Y.M.C.A. as a conference centre. Cobden built the house round the small Sussex farmhouse where he was born; inside you can see an anteroom with a large bust of Cobden, and his own library, full of nineteenth-century copies of *Hansard*, signed photographs of Garibaldi, and vast tomes on the Great Exhibition of 1851, of which Cobden was a chief instigator. One of his daughters married the artist Walter R. Sickert, whose painting of Dunford is in an upstairs room. Another daughter, Jane, married Thomas Fisher Unwin, the publisher. She lived on until 1947, continuing her father's ideals and leading an association that ran Dunford as a centre for the discussion of political issues. His principles are stated bluntly on a sandstone obelisk on the hillside: 'Free Trade, Peace, Goodwill among Nations'.

Below the obelisk, at **Cocking Causeway**, the Greyhound Inn specialises in 'old English wines', ranging from white currant to wheat and raisin. They come from Hampshire, but are none the worse for that. **Cocking** village has a tiny pebble-dashed church below the downs; on the splay of a Norman window is a wall painting of a red-robed shepherd from a vanished Nativity scene. **Heyshott** near by was Cobden's village; it is a flat, spread-out place, not hemmed in by the downs but keeping them clearly in view. The village hall proclaims itself the 'Cobden Club Hall', and there is a tablet in the church commemorating Cobden, put up by Jane and her husband.

Roughly parallel to the A 272, and about three miles to the south, a narrow road along the foot of the downs twists and jinks through a string of villages built on the gentle slopes below the steep northern escarpment.

Bepton's church, on a mound looking across to the downs, has a massive Norman tower as wide as the main building. In the chancel is a niche of 'Easter sepulchre' type, with flames of stone rising from the triangular canopy; and below it in the floor a tombstone carved with a great sword, and an inscription in Norman French to Rado de la Hedol. He must have been a gigantic warrior, as the stone is seven feet long.

The simple Early English church at **Didling** has rough-hewn pews made in the fifteenth century, if not earlier, and is said to be haunted by the ghost of a singing choirboy. It nearly lost its ancient yew recently, as the axe marks that bite deeply into it bear witness. A few fangs of masonry high on the bank by the roadside mark where **Treyford**'s church once stood. At **Elsted** the little church, virtually in a farmyard, has a Saxon nave, a Norman chancel arch, and an Early English chancel; it was restored from dereliction as recently as 1951.

The westernmost and by far the finest of these villages is **South Harting**, in whose street Belloc left his travelling companions of *The Four Men* and turned back towards his home. An earlier and greater author lived in Harting: Anthony Trollope, whose paperknife, pen and letter scales are kept in a case in the church, along with local antiquities. Harting's long main street has more redbrick Georgian houses than most of the villages in the neighbourhood. The cruciform church, raised high on a mound above the road, is unusually large; its centrally placed tower is capped by a broach spire of brilliant green copper. Inside, it has a spectacular Elizabethan roof, a complex structure of squared beams and turned uprights, put in after the fourteenth-century church was gutted by fire in 1576; at the same time a strange supporting or 'crutch' arch was added below the chancel arch, giving the whole thing an unfocused look. The chief monument is in the south transept, a three-tiered seventeenth-century memorial to the Cowper family. The stone window frame had to be cut away to get the topmost kneeling figure into position. In the chancel old Sir Harry Fetherstonhaugh of Uppark is commemorated by a sentimental relief of a grieving woman and a drooping spaniel.

Uppark (National Trust) is a magnificent house in a magnificent position, on the crest of the downs at the top of a hill so steep that when the house was offered to the Duke of Wellington after the Napoleonic Wars, he declined the gift because of the constant replacement of horses that would be needed as the slope wore them out. Uppark stands foursquare like an enormous redbrick dolls' house, overlooking a huge sweep of hills and farmland. Apart from a couple of pylons in the middle distance, the view can hardly have changed since the house was built in the late 1680s. It was built for Lord

Grey of Werke, a somewhat dubious intriguer, who was one of the chief instigators of the Duke of Monmouth's rebellion of 1685, was a hopeless cavalry commander at the Battle of Sedgemoor and was taken prisoner. Luckier than Monmouth, he was let off with a heavy fine, and retired to the country to build his house in the latest Dutch style, to the designs of William Talman. Grey lived down his past so successfully that William III appointed him Lord Privy Seal and created him Earl of Tankerville. Apart from its modernity of appearance, Uppark was a technological novelty as well. The site was only made possible for building by a water pump invented by Lord Tankerville's grandfather, which brought water to the top of the hill from a low-lying spring.

Tankerville provided the external seventeenth-century setting, while a later owner, Sir Matthew Fetherstonhaugh, who bought Uppark in 1747, turned the interior into a treasurehouse of eighteenth-century taste, cramming it with rare carpets and furniture, and the paintings and objets d'art that the wealthy brought back by the boatload from the Grand Tour. He died in 1774, leaving the estate to his twenty-year-old son Sir Harry, who brought wilder times to Uppark. In 1780 he brought the beautiful Emma Hart, then only fifteen, down from London as his mistress. After a year or so he got rid of her, leaving her to future glories as wife of Sir William Hamilton and Nelson's mistress; in later life, when Emma had fallen on hard times, Sir Harry helped her out. For the next quarter of a century he was one of the Prince Regent's closest friends, racing and gambling with him, and keeping his grooms on call to trundle his incapacitated drinking companions on wheelbarrows down to Harting. When he finally fell out with the prince about 1810 he gave up his social life entirely, coming to life once more to brave the snobbery of West Sussex and marry his head dairymaid Mary Ann when he was over seventy. He died in 1846 aged ninety-two; and Mary Ann, succeeded by her sister Frances, kept Uppark as it had been in Sir Harry's time until 1895, when Frances died. Thus Sir Harry's reign, either in the flesh or from the grave, lasted for over 120 years. A witness of the final period of this immense span was H. G. Wells, whose mother was housekeeper at Uppark, and who spent his boyhood there kissing the maids and shooting airgun pellets at the pictures.

Visitors to the house make a circuit of the ground-floor rooms, beginning at the staircase hall. The paintings here set the scene for what is to follow – views of the house and downs by Tillemans, showing it as it was soon after it was built, and portraits of Sir Matthew and his wife, and the young Sir Harry. Two smaller rooms, one containing the Prince Regent's bed, lead on to the magnificent Red Drawing Room, with its Chippendale furniture and Grand Tour portraits by the Italian artist Pompeo Batoni. Then comes the double-cube Saloon, the centrepiece of the house, decorated in greyish-white and gold and designed to house pictures like the big portraits of George III and Queen Charlotte at either end. Next are two more small rooms: an Adam-style parlour; and the Stone Hall, the original entrance hall of the house, where Wells practised his marksmanship. Then comes the dining-room, whose endlessly reflecting mirrors look down on the long table where Emma danced for Sir Harry and his guests; and finally a lobby, which houses an enormous dolls' house made for Sarah Lethieullier, the future wife of Sir Matthew – a perfect Queen Anne microcosm of the world of Uppark.

Rogate, three miles north of Harting, up a hill on the far side of the Rother, is the last Sussex village on the A 272. It is built compactly round a crossroads; a good many of the houses are of the soft-coloured yellowy-brown stone so frequently found hereabouts. The church, with its low shingled belfry and spire, is not particularly interesting from the outside; but inside the arches show the change from Norman to Transitional, as though the masons were evolving their craft as they went along. Below the belfry is a massive medieval timber framework, hidden from outside by the later stone-work of the tower and moved bodily westward one bay when the church was enlarged in the nineteenth century. The sedilia have unusual cloth linings, elaborately embroidered. Deer no longer abound round Rogate, though the name is said to derive from the gate into the forest where the roe deer passed through.

Outside Rogate is the tiny Norman church of **Terwick**, known as the 'church in the field', impeccably restored and maintained. One suggestion for the building's remoteness is that it is on the site of an old burial ground, well away from any village for superstitious or hygienic reasons.

The astonishing thing about **Trotton** is that its medieval bridge over the Rother manages to take the continuous pounding of 1970s traffic; though a reprieve is in sight with the start of a relief road. There is no village to speak of, apart from a few cottages, the church and Trotton Place over the churchyard wall; but the church, built about 1300, is worth looking inside for two of the finest brasses in Sussex and the murals on the west wall. On the nave floor is the brass of Margaret de Camoys, who died about 1310. Said to be the oldest brass of a woman anywhere in the country, it shows her in tight-stretched wimple; the shields and lettering have been gouged from the brass by an earlier generation of mutilators. The other brass, far larger and more stylised, spreads across the top of the table tomb in the centre of the chancel. It shows later members of the Camoys family – Thomas, Lord Camoys, who commanded the left wing at Agincourt and died in 1419, and his second wife Elizabeth Mortimer, widow of Sir Henry Percy, 'Harry Hotspur' (see Petworth, p. 437). Thomas, in full armour, wears the Garter below his left knee and clasps his wife's right hand in his own. The murals, painted in the late fourteenth century, cover the whole of the west wall. In the middle Christ in judgment sits above Moses and the Tablets of the Law; on the right the Good Man stands fully clad surrounded by lively medallions of Good Deeds, such as giving drink to the stranger; and on the left is the Evil Man, naked among the Seven Deadly Sins, which include giving far too much drink to himself. The Restoration dramatist Thomas Otway, born at Trotton in 1651, is commemorated by a tablet on the south wall of the chancel. The taste of Charles II's court ran more to salacious comedy than to Otway's outmoded brand of heroic tragedy, and so he died in poverty in 1685. The story goes that he choked on a roll given to him when he was starving.

Between Trotton and Midhurst are four little villages on the Rother, each hardly more than half a mile apart as the crow flies, but far more as the river meanders or the road twists. **Chithurst**, though so near the main road, feels unbelievably remote, lost among the riverside undergrowth. The midget church, eleventh-century with a crude Saxon chancel arch (or very early Norman, according to Nairn), has hardly been touched since Domesday. It stands on an artificial-looking mound, a few yards away from a stone and timber manor house. At **Iping** the river widens out into a pond, with weir and derelict mill beside it; the church is dull Victorian, part-nered by a noble tiled roof which runs the whole length of the churchyard on the river side. **Stedham** is the biggest of the four villages, straggling from the common on the main road down to the Rother. The church, a little way above the river, is mainly nineteenth-century and replaces a Saxon church of about 1040. The base of the tower is said to date from this period, but it certainly does not look it. More memorable than the church is a vast yew tree, bound round with hawsers to stop it falling apart. **Woolbeding**'s church is more likely to be Saxon: it has the vertical stone strips of a Saxon exterior, jutting from the pebbledashed walls. (The road along the north side of the river is in places hardly more than a cart track, cut deeply into the ground and without passing places – what the French would call a '*voie ordinaire*'. Not for wide cars.)

Back to Midhurst again, and heading north along the main road to Haslemere (A 286), you come to **Fernhurst**, the only sizeable village in an area of woodland hamlets, and a com-fortable, unassuming kind of place. Half a mile to the south I.C.I. have taken over Verdley Place, a large Victorian man-sion, as the headquarters of their plant protection division. This has been responsible in the past quarter of a century for weedkillers like paraquat which have revolutionised horti-culture, though ecologists mistrust them. Surrounded by lawns shaved to a scientific precision of emerald uniformity, and by acres of glasshouses where anything from cucumber to chrysanthemums are grown, Verdley adds a flavour of unobtrusive commercialism to the lush countryside.

Along a lane two miles west of Fernhurst is **Shulbrede Priory**, like Michelham (see p. 316) an Augustinian priory founded about 1200, but much less of a showplace, and altogether on a smaller scale (can be visited by previous arrangement). The church, which stood on the north side of the cloister, has vanished; what remains is a vaulted parlour and buttery downstairs, and the prior's chamber upstairs. At the Dissolution the Priory became a farmhouse, and the chamber was decorated with Tudor murals. One of them shows animals heralding Christ's Nativity in words that correspond to their calls. The cock crows '*Christus natus est*' (Christ is born); the duck quacks '*Quando, quando*' (When?); the rook caws '*In hac nocte*' (Tonight); the ox bellows '*Ubi, ubi*' (Where?); and the sheep bleats '*in Bethlehem*'. A suitable country conceit for this idyllic spot.

North of Shulbrede the road shoots steeply up to **Linchmere**, a scattered farming village, green and open, which stands five hundred feet up at the edge of the Haslemere ridge. Its spindly little church is an odd building, with a narrow eleventh-century nave on the south side and a double north aisle, added in successive stages in the nineteenth and twentieth centuries. On the north wall is a bas-relief of the Seven Deadly Sins, said to be Italian work of about 1300, carved with white marble faces leering and smirking from monks' cowls and niches of grey volcanic rock. The little organ is decorated with seventeenth-century carved wooden cherubs, gilt and playing musical instruments. The village's most famous recent inhabitant was Richard Dimbleby, the television commentator, who is buried in the churchyard.

From Linchmere it is only a couple of miles to Liphook across the Hampshire border, on the London–Portsmouth road.

Opening Times of Houses and Gardens

❧

Alfriston Clergy House. Living-room all year during daylight

Allington Castle. All year, daily 2–4

Anne of Cleves House, Lewes. Feb–Nov, weekdays 10.30–1, 2–5.30. Easter–Sept, Suns 2–5.30

Arundel Castle. Mid Apr–mid June, Mon–Thurs 1–4.30. Mid June–end Sept, Mon–Fri 12–4.30. Also Suns in Aug, and Easter Mon

Aylesford, The Friars. All year, daily 9–dusk

Barbican House, Lewes. All year, weekdays only 10–1, 2–5.30. Easter–Sept, Suns 2–5.30

Bateman's, Burwash. Mar–Oct, Sat, Sun and Good Fri 2–6; Mon–Thurs 11–12.30, 2–6

Battle Abbey. All year, weekdays 10–1, 2–5; Sat 10 12.45. (Also Easter Sun, and Suns Aug–mid Sept)

Bedgebury Pinetum. All year, daily inc Suns and Bank Hols

Bentley Wildfowl Gardens. Apr–end Sept, Wed, Sat, Sun, 11–5.30. (Also Easter and Late Summer Bank Hols)

Black Charles, nr Sevenoaks. Apr–Sept, Wed 2–5

Bleak House, Broadstairs. Easter, May–Oct, daily at 2

Bodiam Castle. All year Apr–Sept, daily 10–7; Oct–Mar, weekdays 10–sunset

Boughton Monchelsea Place. Early Apr–early Oct, Sat, Sun and Bank Hols, also Wed in Aug, 2.15–6

Brickwall, Northiam. Late Apr–early July, Wed and Sat 2–4

Charleston Manor. Mid May–Sept, gardens Mon–Fri (also Sat and Sun when possible) 11–6. House by appointment Wed 2.15–6

Chartwell. Mar–Nov, Wed and Thurs 2–6; Sat, Sun and Bank Hol Mons 11–6

Chiddingstone Castle. Easter Sat–end Oct, daily (exc Mon) 2–5.30; Sat, Sun and Bank Hol Mons 11.30–5.30

Chilham Castle. Gardens only, May–Oct, Tues, Wed, Thurs, Sat and Sun 2–6. Falconry displays daily 3.30

Cobham Hall. Easter Hol weekend, Wed, Thurs and Sun late July–late Aug, and late Summer Bank Hol 2–6

Combe Bank, Sundridge. May–Sept, Sat 2–5

Firle Place. June–Sept, Wed and Thurs 2.15–5.30, Sun 3–6; also Easter, Spring and Late Summer Bank Hols 3–6

Glynde Place. Early May–end Sept, Thurs, Sat and Sun 2.15–5.30 (also Easter, Spring and Late Summer Bank Hols)

Godinton Park. June–Sept, Sun 2–5 (also Easter Hol weekend and Bank Hols)

Goodwood House. Early Apr–late Oct, Sun, and May–Oct 1st Wed in each month 2.30–5.30, by reservation only. Occasional Open Days

Great Dixter, Northiam. Good Fri–mid Oct, daily exc Mon (but open Bank Hol Mons) 2–5

Hever Castle. Easter Sun–mid Oct, Wed, Sun and Bank Hols 1–7 gardens, 2–7 castle

Ightham Mote. All year, Fri 2–5 (or dusk if earlier in winter)

Knole. Mar–Dec, Wed–Sat and Bank Hols 10–12, 2–5 (close 3.30 in winter)

Lamb House, Rye. Mar–Oct, Wed and Sat 2–6

Leonardslee Gardens. Early May–early June, Wed, Thurs, Sat, Sun 10–6 (also Spring Bank Hol Mon)

Lullingstone Castle. May–Sept, 1st Wed in month and Bank Hol Mons 2–6

Lympne Castle. July–Sept daily, Apr–Oct Wed and Sun (also Bank Hol weekends) 10.30–1, 2.30–6

Michelham Priory. May–late Oct, daily 11–1, 2–5.30 (also Easter Hol weekend)

Newtimber Place, Hassocks. May–Aug, Thurs 2–5

Nymans Gardens. Apr–Oct, Tues, Wed, Thurs, Sat, Sun 2–7 (also Bank Hol Mons)

Old Soar Manor. Apr–Sept, weekdays 9.30–7, Sun 2–7 (close 5.30 in Apr)

Owletts, Cobham. Apr–Oct, Wed and Sat 2–5

Owl House, Lamberhurst (gardens). All year, Mon, Wed, Fri and Bank Hol weekends 11–8, Sun 3–8

Parham. Easter Sun–end Sept, Sun, Wed, Thurs 2–5.30 (also Bank Hols)

Penshurst Place. Apr, Sat and Sun 2–6. May, Wed, Thurs, Sat, Sun 2–6. June, Tues, Wed, Thurs, Sat, Sun 2–6. Late June-early Sept, Tues, Wed, Thurs, Sat, Sun 1–6.'Bank Hols 11.30–6

Petworth House. Apr–Oct, Wed, Thurs, Sat and Bank Hol Mons 2–6. Connoisseurs' Day 1st and 3rd Tues in these months

Priest House, West Hoathly. Easter–Sept, weekdays (exc Fri) 10–6, Sun 2–5

Quebec House, Westerham. Mar–Oct, Tues, Wed and Sun 2–6. Bank Hol Mons 10–1, 2–6

Restoration House, Rochester. Apr–Sept, 1st Thurs in each month 10–5 (also Bank Hol Suns and Mons)

St John's Jerusalem. All year (gardens and chapel only), Wed 2-6

St Mary's, Bramber. Good Fri-mid Oct, Tues-Sun 2-6, Bank Hols 11-6

Scotney Castle Gardens. Apr-Oct, Wed-Sun 2-6 (also Bank Hols except Good Friday)

Sheffield Park Gardens. Apr-mid Nov: Apr, Wed, Sat and Sun, May-Sept daily 11-7 (also Bank Hol Mons); Oct-mid Nov, daily 11-5

Sissinghurst Castle. Good Fri-Oct 15, daily, Mon-Fri 12-6.30, Sat, Sun and Bank Hol Mons 10-6.30

Smallhythe Place, Tenterden. Mar-Oct, Mon, Wed, Thurs, Sat, Sun and Bank Hols 2 6 (or dusk)

Squerryes Court, Westerham. Mar-Oct, Wed, Sat, Sun and Bank Hols 2 6

Stoneacre, Otham. Seen by written application to tenant only

Uppark. Easter Sun-Sept, Wed, Thurs, Sun 2-6 (also Bank Hol Mons)

Wakehurst Place Gardens. All year, daily (exc Christmas Day): Easter-Sept, Mon-Fri 2-6, Sat, Sun and Bank Hols 10-7; Nov-Jan, 12-4; Feb and Oct, 1-5; March, 2-6

(Note. These opening times have been adapted from the 1972 edition of *Historic Houses, Castles and Gardens*, published by ABC Travel Guides, and should if possible be checked against the most up-to-date edition. The large number of gardens open to the public from time to time are listed in the National Gardens Scheme's annual booklet. Many museums are open daily, but here again, to avoid a wasted journey, it is worth checking with the ABC *Museums and Galleries* annual guide.)

The North Downs Way

✣

This walkers' route, 141 miles long, runs as far as possible along the crest of the North Downs from Farnham to Dover; thus the first forty or so miles are in Surrey. The route enters Kent near Chevening Park, crosses the Darent valley at Otford, and continues by field paths running above the Pilgrims' Way to Wrotham. Beyond Wrotham it follows the curve of the downs as they swing north-east above the Medway valley towards Rochester, and crosses the Medway by the footbridge beside the M2. It then continues along the southern slope of the downs above Wouldham and Boxley to Detling. From Detling to Hollingbourne the route is on the slopes above the Pilgrims' Way; and from Hollingbourne to Charing it follows the Way, which for several miles has hardly any made-up road coinciding with it. It drops down to the Stour at Wye, climbs the downs again near Hastingleigh, crosses Stone Street near Stowting, and goes by Etchinghill, Castle Hill and Sugarloaf Hill to the A260 on the northern outskirts of Folkestone. From here to Dover the route runs, via Creteway Down, along the top of the cliffs, with an alternative path when firing is taking place on the Lydden Spout ranges west of Dover. A 'Canterbury link' leaves the main track at Boughton Lees, between Charing and Wye, and runs above the western side of the Stour to Soakham Downs, Godmersham and Chilham, keeping along the same side of the river to Harbledown and Canterbury. On the far side of Canterbury it goes by Patrixbourne and Barham Downs, above the Dover Road, to Shepherdswell. Here it turns east through Waldershare Park, crosses the A256, and turns due south along the Roman Road to Dover.

The South Downs Way

❧

This route runs for about eighty miles, from the Hampshire border to Eastbourne; though considerably shorter than the North Downs Way, it coincides with the road system to a much smaller extent and for most of its length is along the ridge of the South Downs. Beginning near South Harting a few miles south of Petersfield, it runs roughly parallel with and above the minor road through Treyford and Bepton, and crosses the Chichester-Midhurst road (A286) south of Cocking. It continues along the steep escarpment above Heyshott and Graffham with fine woodlands to the south, drops down to the Petworth road (A285), and climbs to Stane Street and the hills above Bignor. The route crosses the Arun by Houghton and Amberley, and from Amberley runs above Parham and Storrington to cross the Worthing road (A24) near Washington. East of Washington it climbs to Chanctonbury Ring before dropping down again to the Adur valley, which it crosses by Steyning, Bramber and Upper Beeding. It follows the downs behind Brighton past the Devil's Dyke to Pyecombe, where it crosses the Brighton road (A23), continuing past the Clayton windmills to Ditchling Deacon. Above Plumpton it takes a zigzag course southward, crossing the Brighton-Lewes road (A27) and heading east again above Kingston. The route crosses the Ouse valley at Southease, and from there climbs to the north-facing scarp of the downs, which it follows past Firle Beacon to Alfriston. At Alfriston it crosses the Cuckmere valley, climbs to Windover Hill, above the Long Man of Wilmington, and runs by Jevington and Willingdon Hill to reach the western outskirts of Eastbourne. (An alternative route from Alfriston brings you to Eastbourne by way of the clifftop walk above the Seven Sisters and Beachy Head.)

The 'Strategic Plan for the South East'

✤

This important blueprint for the future of the whole metropolitan region, published by the Ministry of Housing and Local Government in 1970, makes prophecies and recommendations for as far ahead as the end of the century, and is likely to have considerable impact on an area of which Kent and Sussex form a large part. Appendix E of the report (beginning on p. 98) considers individual areas in detail. The relevant sections can be summarised as follows:

Planning Area 2:   Medway/North West Kent
'The Maidstone/Medway medium growth area . . . has potential for developing independently of London . . . There is scope for the development of deep-water port facilities in the Medway estuary; and the structure plan will need to ensure that the land adjacent to the deep water is safeguarded for development which requires such a location . . . The structure plan will need to make allowance for average growth rates of about 10,000 persons per year up to 1981 and for about 8,500-9,000 persons per year in the next decade, decreasing to about 6,000 persons per year in the last 10 years of the century.'

Planning area 3:   South West Kent
'The population in this part of Kent . . . is currently growing at about 1,600 persons per year. A continuation of growth at or slightly above this level to the end of the century would be appropriate.'

Planning area 4:   Uckfield
'This predominantly rural area is likely to be growing by less than 1,000 persons per year to 1981. There are no strong reasons for suggesting a different rate of growth during the rest of the century . . . There are likely to be pressures for housing arising from the expansion of employment opportunities in the Crawley/Gatwick area and possibly in South-west Kent.'

Planning area 6: Crawley/Burgess Hill
'This extensive area has been identified as having potential for substantial growth. The first factor, and the largest, is the expected continuation of employment growth at Crawley and expansion of Gatwick airport. The second factor is possible employment growth in the Brighton sub-region to the south. Development . . . near Burgess Hill might contribute towards relieving pressure in the Sussex Coast planning area . . . A number of issues . . . call for an early sub-regional appraisal, to indicate whether provision can be made for a total population of over 450,000 in this planning area by the end of the century.'

Planning area 19: North East Kent
'Unlike most parts of the region, this area at present has employment difficulties . . . Canterbury has however developed a momentum for growth which may, unless special care is taken, exert undesirable pressure on the historic city centre . . . An average population growth of 2,000 to 2,500 persons per year seems likely.'

Planning area 20: South East Kent
'The future of this area and particularly of Dover and Folkestone will remain uncertain until a decision on the Channel Tunnel is taken . . . Opportunities for expansion in the Ashford area should be provided for in the structure plan. Up to 1981 an average growth rate of just over 2,000 persons per year is suggested, followed by an increase to almost 4,000 per year in the 1980s and to over 5,000 per year for the remainder of the century.'

Planning area 21: Eastbourne/Hastings
'The structure plan will need to make provision for a moderate rate of growth of population in the area which could assist in achieving a better balance in the area's age structure . . . On the assumption that the Town Development Act Scheme at Hastings does go ahead, the average rate of growth is likely to be about 4,000 persons per year up to 1981. A similar or slightly higher rate for the rest of the century would be acceptable.'

Planning area 22: Sussex Coast
'The coastal resorts from Bognor Regis to Seaford are not likely to be able to expand to a significant extent after 1981 owing to the constraints imposed by the South Downs. However, pressures on Brighton . . . are likely to remain heavy and the structure plan will need to consider the possibility of linkages with the Burgess Hill/Haywards Heath area to the north.'

Planning area 23: South West Sussex
'This is a sensitive countryside area in which pressures may be exerted from several directions. To the west is South Hampshire, to the east Crawley and to the south-east the coastal towns . . . The structure plan will need to suggest how an average growth rate of about 1,500 persons per year may be accommodated without detriment to the character of Chichester and district.'

APPENDIX

Select Bibliography

❧

Books of historical interest

Cobbett, William. *Rural Rides*
Fiennes, Celia. *The Journeys of Celia Fiennes*
Furley, Robert. *A History of the Weald of Kent*, 3 vols., 1871
Handbook for Travellers in Sussex (Murray's Hand-book), 1893
Hare, Augustus. *Sussex*, 1894
Hasted, Edward. *The History and Topographical Survey of the County of Kent*, 12 vols., 1797
Hussey, Arthur. *Notes on the Churches in the Counties of Kent, Sussex and Surrey*, 1852
Igglesden, Charles. *Saunters Through Kent*, 30 vols., 1900–35
Jerrold, Walter. *Highways and Byways in Kent*, 1907
Lambarde, William. *A Perambulation of Kent: Conteining the Description, Hystorie, and Customes of That Shire*, written 1570, published 1576
Lucas, E. V. *Highways and Byways in Sussex*, 1912
Wyndham, Richard. *South-East England*, 1951

Major sources

Nairn, Ian, and Pevsner, Nikolaus. *Sussex* (The Buildings of England), 1965. (West Sussex by Nairn, East Sussex by Pevsner)
Newman, John. *North East and East Kent* (The Buildings of England), 1969
Newman, John. *West Kent and the Weald* (The Buildings of England), 1969
Victoria County History of Kent, 3 vols. to date
Victoria County History of Sussex, 6 vols. to date
Archaeologia Cantiana, annually since 1858
Sussex Archaeological Collections, annually since 1848

General

Armstrong, J. R. *A History of Sussex*, 1961
Betjeman, Sir John (ed.). *Collins Pocket Guide to English Parish Churches: The South*, 1968
Brabant, F. G. *Sussex* (Little Guide), 1917

Church, Richard. *Kent* (Robert Hale County Book), 1948
Church, Richard. *The Little Kingdom* (anthology of writings about Kent), 1964
Crouch, Marcus. *Kent*, 1966
Goodsall, Robert H. *A Kentish Patchwork*, 1966; *A Second Kentish Patchwork*, 1968; *A Third Kentish Patchwork*, 1970
Hammond, Reginald J. W. (ed.). *The Kent Coast*, 1968; *The East Sussex Coast*, 1967; *The West Sussex Coast*, 1966 (Ward Lock Red Guides)
Hughes, Pennethorne. *Kent* (Shell Guide), 1969
Jessup, Frank W. *A History of Kent*, 1958
Jessup, Frank W. *Kent History Illustrated*, 1966
Jessup, Ronald. *Kent* (Little Guide), 1950
Jessup, Ronald. *South East England* (prehistoric and Roman Kent and Sussex), 1970
Kaye-Smith, Sheila. *Weald of Kent and Sussex* (Robert Hale Regional Book), 1953
Margary, I. D. *Roman Ways in the Weald*, 1965
Mee, Arthur. *Kent* (The King's England), 1969
Mee, Arthur. *Sussex* (The King's England), 1964
Meynell, Esther. *Sussex* (Robert Hale County Book)
Oswald, Arthur. *Country Houses of Kent*, 1933
Parish, Rev. W. D., and Hall, Helena. *A Dictionary of the Sussex Dialect*, 1957
Willard, Barbara. *Sussex*, 1965
Wooldridge, S. W., and Goldring, Frederick. *The Weald* (New Naturalist series), 1953

Particular localities

Batcheller, W. *A New History of Dover*, 1828
Belloc, Hilaire. *The Four Men* (account of a walk from Robertsbridge to the Hampshire border), undated
Betjeman, Sir John, and Gray, J. S. *Victorian and Edwardian Brighton, from Old Photographs*, 1971
Brentnall, Margaret. *The Cinque Ports and Romney Marsh*, 1972
Christian, Garth. *Ashdown Forest*, 1967
Church, Richard. *Portrait of Canterbury*, 1953
Egerton, John Coker. *Sussex Folk and Sussex Ways* (Burwash in the nineteenth century), 1924
Gostling, William. *A Walk in and About the City of Canterbury*, 1796 ed.
Jennett, Sean. *The Pilgrims' Way*, 1971
Musgrave, Clifford, *Royal Pavilion*, 1959
Piper, John. *Romney Marsh* (King Penguin), 1950
Sackville-West, Victoria. *Knole and the Sackvilles*, 1922
Vine, P. A. L. *The Royal Military Canal*, 1972

Place-names

Mawer, A., and Stenton, F. M. *The Place-names of Sussex*, 2 vols.,
   1929
Wallenberg, J. K. *Kentish Place-names*, 1931

Ornithology

Harrison, James M. *The Birds of Kent*, 2 vols., 1953
Walpole-Bond, John. *A History of Sussex Birds*, 3 vols., 1938

Cricket

Arrowsmith, R. L. *A History of County Cricket: Kent*, 1971
Marshall, John. *Sussex Cricket: a History*, 1959

Miscellaneous

Dendy Marshal, C. F., revised by Kinder, F. W. *A History of the
   Southern Railway*, 1968
Stenton, Sir Frank, and others. *The Bayeux Tapestry*, 1957
Straker, Ernest. *Wealden Iron*, 1931

Index

❧